D0520623

REMADE
IN
AMERICA

Also by Jim Rohwer

ASIA RISING
Why America Will Prosper as Asia's Economies Boom

REMADE
IN
AMERICA

How Asia Will Change
Because America Boomed

JIM ROHWER

CROWN
BUSINESS
NEW YORK

Some passages of this book appeared in a different form in articles the author wrote for *Fortune* between 1997 and 2000. *Fortune*'s permission to reprint these passages is gratefully acknowledged.

Published by Crown Business, New York, New York. Member of the Crown Publishing Group.

Random House, Inc. New York, Toronto, London, Sydney, Auckland
www.randomhouse.com
www.jimrohwer.com

Crown Business and colophon are trademarks of Random House, Inc.

Printed in the United States of America

Library of Congress Cataloging-in-Publication Data

Rohwer, Jim.
   Remade in America : how Asia will change because America boomed / by Jim Rohwer.
      p.   cm.
   1. Asia—Economic conditions—1945–   2. Asia—Foreign economic relations—United States.   3. United States—Foreign economic relations—Asia.   I. Title.
   HC412.R64   2000
   330.95—dc21   00-031797

ISBN 0-8129-3251-X

10 9 8 7 6 5 4 3 2 1

First Edition

For Marty

CONTENTS

Prologue: Asia, Ants and Economics   ix

PART ONE
THE CHALLENGE

CHAPTER 1   The American Revolution   3

CHAPTER 2   The Rocks on the River Bed   24

CHAPTER 3   The Annihilation of Value   49

PART TWO
THE RESPONSE

CHAPTER 4   The Japanese Counter-Revolution   69

CHAPTER 5   The Convoy and the Snipers   82

CHAPTER 6   The Fall from Grace   106

CHAPTER 7   The Fight for the Future   130

CHAPTER 8   The Giant's Delicate Dance   145

CHAPTER 9   Structures, Cycles and Strengths   167

PART THREE
MAKING MARKETS

CHAPTER 10   Technology and the New Asia   203

CHAPTER 11   Asia Online   223

CHAPTER 12   What's the Asian for Milken?   256

CHAPTER 13 White Hunters 276

CHAPTER 14 The Anthill 309

PART FOUR
POLITICS AND SOCIETY

CHAPTER 15 Participation and Democracy 345

CHAPTER 16 Asia, America and Europe 368

Acknowledgments 385

Notes 387

Index 403

PROLOGUE:
ASIA, ANTS AND ECONOMICS

L ate in the summer of 1998, when it looked as though the whole world's financial system was being blown apart by the shock waves generated by Asia's financial crisis, I took a week off and went to a remote beach in Southeast Asia. For one thing, it made me tie my own hands so that I couldn't fool around with my investments at a time when nobody understood what was going on. Besides, sitting around financial centers listening to economists and analysts had told me next to nothing about why Asia had collapsed in the first place and about whether and how it was going to be rebuilt. Maybe getting away would give some perspective.

Something odder did. Late one afternoon, as I was sitting in a beach chair watching the sea, some young boys started playing a game that involved kicking a ball around. At one point it went astray and, chasing it, one of the boys ran by me and accidentally kicked a nearby anthill apart. Mass panic. Thousands of ants ran frantically and randomly all over the place with no apparent clue what they were doing. Some chased after the already gone intruder. Others, I supposed, were trying to protect the queen. After awhile the panic subsided a bit and the activity seemed more purposeful and systematic, directed at restoring order. This was familiar. It's what Asia itself had been looking like for the previous year.

Appearances, I later learned, were more than skin-deep. One quality of ant societies is that any individual ant is likely to communicate with any other individual to get a job done and, although the workers specialize by caste and their activities are subordinated to the needs of the whole society, they are democratically open to suggestions by anybody else in the colony. This works not just among ants at a certain level but between levels in the ants' special sort of hierarchy: orders do not just come down—though when they do they are obeyed—but information from the lower units also freely goes back up to influence the decision-makers. And the highest purpose of the colony is not to protect the interests of the clutch of individuals at the top who direct its activities but instead the welfare of the colony as a whole. It sounded like the way Asian companies worked—those in Korea and Japan as well as the family-run firms in the Chinese part of Asia—and also how most Asian societies worked. Moreover, when an ant colony is hit by an external shock only a small portion of the members, say a fifth, respond by trying violently to attack the intruders, with another third trying to engage them without violence, while half stoically accept the changed circumstances. So there were a few Mahathir-like ants, some more who tried to negotiate arrangements with the intruders, while most just got on with things. . . .

Hmm. This was starting to make sense—certainly a lot more sense than the completely unpersuasive torrent of macroeconomic and financial explanations (many of them my own) that were pouring out in papers, magazines, speeches and on the Internet to describe what had been going on in Asia since July 1997. In February 1998, at an annual world bigwigs' conference in Switzerland, someone asked a panel of investment-bank economists why none of them had had even a glimmer of foresight about what had been about to hit Asia the year before. The questioner was met with dead silence: they didn't even know why they didn't know. The usual economic and financial analysis could tell you a few things about how the surface was being rippled by deep currents but very little about the currents themselves. It seemed more profitable to think about what was going on in Asia as a process by which some extremely complicated and sophisticated societies and their institutions (economies, governments, companies) were rearranging and renewing themselves in response to a much bigger change than the sudden shift of a few score billions of dollars.

By the time I got up from my beach chair and wandered off in search of a cocktail, the anthill was returning to normal. This seemed right, too. Not for a moment had I bought the argument that the financial collapse of 1997–98 meant East Asia's miracle of 1965–95 had been a mirage and that its years of spectacular advance were over. In 1995 I had published a book called *Asia Rising,* a title that by the end of 1997 was causing much mirth, including an instant-book depiction of the financial crisis called *Asia Falling.* As far as I could see, by the time I was on my beach, Asia was still rising and would go on doing so for at least another generation. Strengths as deep and well-founded as those that had propelled East Asia to the fastest and broadest economic uplifting in history were not about to be blown away because some unimaginative bankers suddenly withdrew a lot of money they had lent without any care in the first place. So the anthill was being restored to normal. But not really to normal. When it was suddenly scattered to the winds, the ants' world was radically changed. Their success in rebuilding depended on how well they could combine what they had been good at before with what they faced that was new. This book is about how Asia is going to do it.

THE FORGE OF THE FUTURE

The kid who unintentionally kicked over Asia's anthill was America. This was not the act of a bully although, as the 1990s wore on and America's unprecedented combination of powers grew, a lot of non-Americans began thinking the exercise of its immense wealth and geopolitical authority must somehow be malicious. Instead, the United States was (temporarily) overmastering the world by being the first to divine and then to put to practical effect the technologies and the systems of financial and corporate organization that will shape economic and political life everywhere over the next 10 years. Leon Trotsky, a Russian revolutionary later exiled to Mexico by Stalin, understood some 70 years ago what was going on. "America," he said, "is the furnace in which the future is being forged."

That was an American destiny which a lot of people, including many Americans, thought was over and done with by the early 1980s. Its economy laid low by inflation and recession, its people's confidence in its government at an ebb, its companies performing poorly by most measures, the United States seemed in many ways to be fossilizing the past more than forging the future. Later in the 1980s, a lot of commentators were predicting that Japan's almost centrally planned economy, with its powerful smooth-bore export engine, pointed the way ahead for capitalism. Yet the trouble many Americans felt their country to be in during the 1980s—the job insecurity and unemployment, the corporate raids, the destruction of old industries, the "greed"—was in fact not trouble but what the Austrian economist Joseph Schumpeter called creative destruction. Several currents were converging to form a mighty flood of productive change. The growth of government was curbed though not reversed, and inflation was gradually subdued. Corporate sloth was made untenable, and rising entrepreneurs and industries more bankable, by the sidelining of banks themselves and by the proliferation of innovative financial instruments, especially junk bonds. Information began flowing more freely thanks among other things to satellite and cable television. And the ability of information to flow through channels whose importance virtually nobody foresaw 15 years ago—because nobody had heard of the Internet—was given a big boost by the breakup of AT&T and the price declines and burst of telecommunications innovations that followed.

By the middle of the 1990s, the wonderful impact of these changes on the United States was a well-worn story. America was in the midst of what would turn into the longest economic expansion in its history, productivity was rising, unemployment and inflation were both headed toward lows that had last been reached in the 1960s, and some of the fastest and most revolutionary technological changes in decades were transforming business and society and creating wealth on a scale never before seen in human history. In earlier days this would have been a marvel for the rest of the world to behold, but this time it was going to do a lot more than behold it. Much of what gave the changes their force in America itself—especially smoother and faster information flows—when combined with a lowering of barriers to the movement of capital and of well-educated people among countries meant that the standards of performance America was setting increasingly governed others as well. The implication of the "dollarization" of the world economy in the 1990s was that, if a country's risk-adjusted rate of return (broadly defined) did not meet the American standard, it could not attract the capital, technology and world-class talent it needed for its future growth. "You shape up or perish," was the pithy conclusion of one seasoned Asian statesman.

WAL-MART AND THE VILLAGE STORE

Globalization and technology together packed so powerful a punch that no place escaped their impact. But Asia was situated in a way that exposed it more than most to the full brunt of the changes. For one thing, East Asia's economies had soared for two generations in large part because, through extensive trade in goods and services, they had plugged themselves into the world economy much more than other developing regions had. So despite continuing restraints on capital flows in most of Asia, the region was unusually attuned to shifts in the global economic climate.

Second, as a Cantonese businesswoman told me in Hong Kong early in the financial crisis, "What these people [in Asia] don't realize is that, compared to America, this is just a series of villages." A few months later, sitting in a hotel room in Seoul watching the evening news, I was reminded of what she had said. By Asian standards, South Korea is an industrial powerhouse, with a bigger economy than all of Southeast Asia's. The TV news item was about the just-announced merger of Citicorp and Travelers in the United States. The item said the value of the merger was around $800 billion. I had heard earlier in the day that South Korea's entire gross domestic product (GDP) that year would be about $400 billion: two American firms had more in assets than the whole Korean economy could generate in income in a year. The European Union and even Japan had some powers to resist the imperatives of American-spawned globalization and technology. The rest of Asia did not.

At first Asia was oblivious to this, preening itself as it was on its undoubted economic accomplishments in the two generations—and especially in the decade—before the mid-1990s. But in the years, particularly the 1980s, when America was surreptitiously sorting itself out, Asia was getting itself into trouble. The trouble had deep roots. With a couple of exceptions—most notably Hong Kong—all of Asia followed a version of the development model Japan had pioneered with such spectacular success after 1945. Designed to promote fast industrialization and economic growth, the model relied on fierce domestic and export competition for manufacturing companies combined with a tight grip on financial transactions. This produced strong export-oriented manufacturing firms, an underdeveloped service sector, and a large surplus pool of savings available for a government to direct to the uses it thought best. Whatever the merits of this model in pulling a country up in the early stages of industrialization, it had inherent financial weaknesses. Because of the high savings and high barriers to the outflow of capital, there was plenty of money for investment inside the country, a fact reflected in Asia's persistently low interest rates.

The natural result of this was overinvestment in productive and unproductive projects of all kinds, a fault that was compounded by institutional weaknesses such as cozy ties between governments and business and opacities in corporate accounts and practices that made it hard to see what companies were using their money for (not that most lenders or investors cared anyway in those heady days). Beginning in the mid-1980s in most of Asia, the deep pool of domestic liquidity was deepened further by increased flows of foreign capital. This was lured by Asia's long-term promise and by misguided dollar-linked currency regimes that made Asian currencies seem relatively cheap and made foreign lenders think they were facing no currency risk at all on their Asian investments. One bad result of all this funny money, which hit Japan in the late 1980s and the rest of Asia by the mid-1990s, was inflation—not of consumer prices but of assets like stocks and real estate. A far worse effect was on the efficiency and productivity of big Asian companies. From the early 1980s up until the Asian crisis broke in 1997, Asian firms' return on equity (ROE)—probably the simplest and best measure of how a firm is using its capital—consistently drifted downward. In the worst case, that of South Korea, by the mid-1990s companies were using money so inefficiently that the cost of capital was higher than the returns generated by what it was invested in: almost every big firm in Korea was destroying value instead of creating it. Over the same period that corporate America's ROE was tripling, the ROE of corporate Asia was falling toward zero.

This could not go on, and the Asian financial collapse of 1997–98 put a stop to it. The crisis itself had many mysterious features (as financial meltdowns tend to) and these are discussed later on. In retrospect, though, the most striking thing about the Asian financial crisis is how brief it was. Unbeknown to anyone during the frightening turmoil of August and September 1998, when I was on my beach, the crisis was all but over only 15 months after it began. In the following couple of months, Asian currencies and stock markets stabilized and the convulsive economic contractions ended. In 1999, with currencies still stable, Asian stock markets soared and economies showed remarkable resilience.

The star was Korea, whose economy had shrunk by more than 6 percent in 1998 but then grew in 1999 by 11 percent. But all of Asia, even hapless Indonesia, enjoyed a significant recovery in 1999—Asian GDPs rose on average by 6 percent—and looked set for even more bracing growth in 2000. Some whiners say this is temporary and illusory, that Asia has not gone anywhere near far enough toward correcting the weaknesses that helped crash it in 1997–98, and that another debacle is probably around the corner. I say the swift rebound reflects Asia's immense strengths and potential, which is why it will prove to be solid. I also think a lot more change has already happened than many people believe, with much more on the way. And here is where the most interesting part of the story begins.

ASIA REMADE FROM ABOVE . . .

In response to the adversity of the 1990s, as in setting a course for development a few decades earlier, Japan took the lead for the rest of Asia; but whereas the earlier example Japan set had many merits, the latter-day one had none at all. The Japanese stock market peaked on the last day of 1989, eventually falling during the next decade by as much as 70 percent. Japan's economy grew during the 1990s by only 0.5 percent a year, a miserable performance by any standard but especially by Japan's own past record. Part of the problem was botched fiscal and monetary policies. But the root of Japan's failure during the 1990s was the obdurate refusal of the country's establishment—political, corporate and financial—to follow America's example of the 1980s and smash a system that had become too ossified to cope with a new world. For almost the whole of the 1990s, Japan did everything in its power to avoid cleaning up the banks' bad debts, liquidating bust assets, letting failed companies go under, and channeling finance to future winners instead of past losers. In other words, this once flexible and forward-looking economy and society clung rigidly to a dead past. Japan paid dearly for its nostalgia. Not only was economic growth practically non-existent and the new industries and firms that could provide for future growth stifled, but the government's repeated spending programs to prop up the old regime landed the Japanese people with the rich world's biggest-ever peacetime public debt just as the country became the fastest-aging society on earth.

Luckily for them, this course of action was foreclosed to other Asians by their economic puniness and relative poverty. Not that this stopped many of them from trying to resist. Malaysia imposed capital controls to keep foreign money flows from washing away the foundations of its politico-business economy. Many if not most Asian companies sought finance from whatever source they could to preserve methods and lines of business they had grown used to. A lot of companies simply stopped paying their debts, and because bankruptcy laws in most of Asia were primitive or non-existent, creditors could do nothing about it even if they wanted to. Yet change inexorably ate into the old order. Three countries—Thailand, Indonesia and South Korea—had to turn to the International Monetary Fund for help and were forced by the IMF to undertake various reforms of their economic structure.

Yet the IMF ran mostly a sideshow in the broader process of institutional reform in Asia. In Korea, for instance, a new president was elected in the midst of the crisis who was already hostile to the domination of the economy by big conglomerates, and he pushed for change even harder than the IMF would have obliged him to. In other places where the IMF never set foot, governments pursued reforms because they were convinced they were needed rather than because they were shoved down their throats. For example, China has for some time had a long-range program to revamp its creaky state-owned enterprises and the state-owned banks that have been milked to support them. Despite fears that the knock-on effects of other countries' problems would force China into a devaluation to protect its exports or into a freeze on its reform efforts, all that happened was a slowdown in some aspects of the overhaul, like housing reform; and by mid-1999 it was again full-speed ahead on the reform program, with a much higher gear promised as China looked set for imminent admission to the barrier-busting World Trade Organization in 2000. Or take Singapore, which had habitually kept both its financial and local corporate sectors on a tight leash (the multitudinous multinationals operating there had much more freedom of movement). By the mid-1990s, the island-republic's patriarch, Lee Kuan Yew, who is Asia's most acute observer of global currents and their likely effects on the region, had concluded that globalization was fast outmoding Singapore's strait-jacketed financial system, and plans were already in place to loosen it when the crisis broke. Rather than slowing this process down, the turmoil of 1997–99 caused Singapore's government to speed it up, adding embellishments like the hiring of foreign CEOs for local banks and companies and pushing state-owned firms as well as the banks to adopt international standards of practice and performance.

Throughout Asia, institutional reforms came in two phases. The first and more thorough involved a shake-up of banking systems. On this score nobody, not even Japan, had much choice by the end of the 1990s. Whether for policy reasons or otherwise, banks had been extravagantly imprudent in their lending, ignoring the notion of credit risk in favor of collateral or (worse still) relationships with the borrower in making their decisions. Once collapse or even a mere slowdown came (as in Japan's case), the quantity of bad loans piled up alarmingly as borrowers could not generate the cash flow to pay their debts, and the real estate that mostly secured the loans lost 90 percent of its value even assuming the banks had the way or will to foreclose on it. The share of bad loans in Asia's banking systems averaged a third or more of GDP, and in the worst case (Indonesia) more than twice that, compared with less than 5 percent during America's savings-and-loan fiasco of the late 1980s and early 1990s. The cleanup, which is still going on, required in essence the nationalization of most of Asia's bank assets and a deep restructuring of the sector. But it happened. Malaysia, which was so recalcitrant about reforming its economy in other ways, nonetheless carried out almost a textbook overhaul of its banks. Even Japan fell in line. In 1997, there were 21 major banks in Japan. By the spring of 2000, following a few bank failures and a series of planned mergers, there were eight.

Corporate restructuring did not keep pace with financial restructuring, but everywhere except Indonesia (where there was political chaos) and Malaysia (which had no desire to change) companies were noticeably altering the way they did business and the performance targets they set for themselves. Often this was voluntary, when firms saw the handwriting on the global wall, and sometimes involuntary as creditors, now equipped in places like Thailand with new bankruptcy laws, steeled themselves to do the un-Asian thing and push failures to the wall. Either way the result was the same. Companies started managing themselves in a more modern way. They relied less on connections, cleaned up their tangled and usually overextended operations, and began creating value instead of destroying it as returns on capital again rose above the cost of capital.

The upshot was that a new Asian economy started taking shape. This is a matter of degree, but the sources of growth shifted away from exports to the West and toward trade within Asia, from exports to domestic consumption, from old industries like machinery and shipbuilding to new ones like mobile phones, and from manufacturing to services. The institutional remake set in motion by the events of 1997–98 laid the groundwork for a new and more productive Asia. The currents of change sweeping ever faster around the globe made sure that this new Asia would be built.

. . . AND MORE SPECTACULARLY FROM BELOW

When the financial pressure eased off Asia in 1999, a lot of people started worrying that reform would ease off as well. There was some of that, of course—people tend to like what they had before unless they are forced to think otherwise—but there was more than strict financial necessity pushing Asia toward the future. In a reprise of America's experience in the 1980s and 1990s, as Asia enters the new century it is being transformed by technology, finance and the global market for corporate control. Technology will count the most.

The reason is the Internet. The stock-market hype of the Internet seemed to have reached its apogee worldwide late in the winter of 2000.

xviii PROLOGUE: ASIA, ANTS AND ECONOMICS

But the Internet as an economic and social force was not about to go away. Whether the Internet will turn out to rank alongside electricity as a radically transforming technology—as the joke goes, "if it weren't for electricity we'd still be watching television by candlelight"—or even will match the lesser inventions of cars or airplanes or antibiotics, can be hotly disputed, but that it will matter a lot cannot be: nothing that slashes most business transaction costs by as much as 90 percent is a flash in the pan.

Asia came late to the Internet. For one thing, hardware has been the technological long suit of modern Asia outside India, so understanding something so software-based did not come naturally. Then, too, the telecoms revolution—especially sharply lower rates—that did so much (albeit fortuitously) to prepare America for the Internet in the 1980s did not reach Asia until the mid-1990s. Yet once the telecoms pipelines were at last in place and Asia suddenly awoke to the Internet in 1998–99, it did so with a jolt. This is because, from two angles, the Internet has more to offer Asia than almost anywhere else.

It gives a boost first because of what East Asia has traditionally been good at: the dispersed manufacturing and assembly of components for internationally traded light-manufacturing goods, a business that Asia overwhelmingly dominates. No place stands to benefit more from the Internet's skill at organizing widely spread business activities, and cutting their costs, than this workshop of the world. But, second, the Internet will help Asia because of what it traditionally has been bad at: services in general and distribution in particular. If even America's already efficient wholesale and retail systems could spruce themselves up by going on-line, it is not hard to imagine the leap that their backward Asian counterparts are going to make, especially as these lines of business come to account for proportionally more of Asia's economic activity. One of the striking signs of how big an influence the Internet can have on Asia comes from India. Long the dunce of the Asian economic class, India saw its prospects begin to look up in the late 1990s. Part of the reason was that the elephantine-slow economic reforms and opening up begun in 1991 were at last showing results. The bigger and more surprising reason was the amazing growth of India's southern-based software industry, especially its exports, and the growing financial and personal links between India's south and Silicon Valley.

Finance, too, in Asia was breaking its old mold. Asia has not enjoyed any junk-bond-like breakthrough to a financial system that rewards winners lavishly and punishes losers ruthlessly but, considering where it started, it is well on its way. Asia commands the world's deepest single pool of household savings, about half the world's total—twice Asia's share of gross world product—and equal to some $14 trillion at the end of 1999. Thanks to grotesquely inefficient banks and near idiocies like Japan's low-paying postal savings system, these savings have been poorly rewarded and inefficiently deployed. That is not the whole story—Asia saves so much and so privately that informal savings, intermediated through extremely efficient devices like Chinese credit clubs, have briskly financed much of the continent's small-business development—but even the formal sector is fast improving. The banks' share of financial assets is shrinking, and those they still do control they are directing more in accordance with credit-risk analysis than fellow membership of golf clubs. It used to be that every company got the same interest rate, but spreads are widening depending on creditworthiness, and stock markets too have started differentiating among companies depending on their earnings—also, by past standards, an Asian novelty. With corporate-bond markets, venture capital, private equity and M&A activity on the rise, the old model of formal Asian finance is on the skids.

None too soon, since the whole point of free-flowing money is to lubricate the market for corporate control. This had always been lacking in Asia, partly because of family and other ties, but thanks to the disruptions of 1997–98 it cracked open, most significantly for foreigners. Some foreign companies in Asia had always built their own operations from the ground up, but because of the complexities of the operating environment, most of them strongly wished to get a foothold in Asia at least in part by acquiring a local firm. That was next to impossible before 1997–98, but then suddenly the lock was sprung. Foreign firms groused a lot about how little market-opening was happening, especially with regard to their ability to acquire local firms, but the complaints rang hollow. In finance especially, Western firms made deep inroads. The assets of GE Capital in Japan rose from some $1 billion in 1995 to almost 40 times that five years later. Japanese and Korean carmakers, hitherto among the world's most independent, fell wholesale into foreign arms, with Nissan, one of Japan's proudest, being run by the end of the 1990s by a Brazilian-born Frenchman working as the representative of Renault, by then the company's controlling French owner. Practically the whole of Asia's cement industry had been taken over by Europeans and Mexicans. And, thanks to WTO, China itself was about to open to foreign operations and even takeovers much more. The drawbridges were crashing down, not being ratcheted up.

What did all this mean for the anthill itself? Like the real one, the Asian version of cooperative corporate and social organization has always had great strengths notwithstanding the Western sermonizing about "crony capitalism" that followed the collapse of 1997. The environment has changed too much for traditional forms of organization to continue, but in adapting to their new surroundings Asian firms and societies will be preserving much of their heritage even while they jettison the parts that would hold them back. The biggest influence on this evolution will be the Internet. As I already mentioned, the economic impact of this on Asia will be strong, but the organizational impact is likely to be stronger still. The Internet replicates in an objective and transparent way the model of networking and information exchange that has been the hallmark of the Asian firm. As its use spreads, it cannot help but displace—though because of its similarities in a smooth way—much of the traditional governing apparatus of Asian companies, especially those of the Chinese diaspora. Several big shifts can be expected. One is the move from the founding generation of tycoons to their children, almost all of whom have been educated in America and are stamped with its business values. Second will come a move from old lines of business to new ones, and from diffuse ones to focused ones with a clear strategy. Third, politics will gradually give way to the market as the main source of business power. And the time-honored method for money-making, the trading of assets, will give way to managing businesses as the source of big rewards. The end result is likely to be an Asia Inc. in which matters like finance and technology are handled in an American way while people and their interactions will still be managed along Asian lines. It should be a powerful combination.

THE EAST IS BRIGHT

Just two years after some Jeremiahs said Asia was doomed to a long era of stagnation, the region's GDP was again expanding at twice the rich world's rate, a differential that will probably hold true for 2000 as well. My bet is that the changes outlined above will comprehensively work their way through Asia's system over the next decade. Unlike Europe or Japan in the 1990s, Asia (now including Japan) is characteristically embracing change instead of trying to repel it. With a couple of exceptions, Asia lacks the self-absorption and complacency that make it so hard for

Europeans to accept new things. One of my most vivid memories of the crisis years was a conversation with a Korean banker in which he said everybody in Korea knew that they weren't being disciplined by the IMF but by Americanization instead, and if America was that powerful they'd better learn from it. Even if Asia learns imperfectly and unevenly, it is intent on learning how the common future of mankind now being born in America is going to work and how Asia can profit from it. That will be enough to let Asia's underlying advantages—its hardworking people, its high savings, its strong families and societies and, most of all, its young populations everywhere but Japan—manifest themselves in fast economic growth over at least the next generation.

Politics or war could erect stumbling blocks to this happy prospect. Yet one of the most striking things about the severe economic and social dislocations of 1997–98 was that they fostered next to no instability anywhere in Asia except Indonesia. The possibility of war, especially involving China, Taiwan and America, cannot be dismissed, and such a war would be a severe blow not just to regional stability but to modernization throughout East Asia. But even here some perspective is needed. Between the late 1950s and the mid-1970s scores of millions of Chinese were killed, and hundreds of millions had their lives disrupted, by a series of Maoist follies. A mere quarter-century after the end of the Cultural Revolution, the Chinese people are enjoying the greatest prosperity in their long history. On any reasonably long-term view—say 10 or 20 years—it has never paid to be a pessimist about modern Asia. Especially not now.

PART ONE

THE
CHALLENGE

1

The American Revolution

You shape up or perish—
—*Lee Kuan Yew*

M ost people would say that Asia's financial crisis began in Thailand on July 2, 1997, when the Thai government devalued the baht. It actually began in America 20-odd years before, when the United States started to remake itself for a new era. It is this American-forged new era that has set the rules for how the world economy now works, that led Asia to its 1997–98 financial crisis, and that will now do more than anything else to reshape Asia during the first decade of the twenty-first century.

The real role of America in Asia's troubles and in its evolving reconstruction has usually been misunderstood. Some see America as largely beside the point, except when it comes to the narrow question of the policy-making powers of the U.S. Treasury Department and its influence over the International Monetary Fund (IMF). This camp thinks Asia's crash was largely home-grown, the product of overinvestment, poor banking supervision, corporate and government opacity and the interaction of those latter two through cronyism. The main foreign involvement, on this view, was overseas bank lending that turned out to be unserviceable—and currencies that turned out to be insupportable—because the debtors borrowed short term but used the money for speculation or long-term investments that couldn't generate enough hard cash to repay the loans when they fell due.

The trouble with this view is that, although all these elements contributed to Asia's violent collapse, they had been present for a good 15 years beforehand without doing any apparent damage to one of the greatest bursts of economic growth in history. This set of explanations, in other words, is too shallow. A small but telling example came in the Philippines. In the years leading up to the crisis, all overseas borrowing by Philippine companies was scrutinized by the country's central bank under IMF supervision. The bank was careful to make sure that there would be sufficient foreign-exchange earnings in any one year to cover whatever overseas loans fell due that year. If term mismatches on overseas borrowings were so important in causing the Asian crash, why did the Philippine peso fall just as much as the currencies of most of its neighbors? There was something deeper going on.

A different idea is advanced by many Asians—notably Mahathir Mohamad, the Malaysian prime minister—who find something much more sinister at work, cooked up by the United States. They tend to argue that what went wrong in Asia was the consequence almost entirely of a sudden surge of foreign capital out of the region. This outflow, say the more paranoid, was abetted by financial-market speculators who are often out to lay low the countries whose assets they buy and sell, and who have been given the means to do this by an unregulated international financial system designed to serve America's hidden agenda to "recolonize" Asia on behalf of the world's "ethnic Europeans," as Mahathir put it in 1999. There is some truth in the idea that uncontrolled surges of hot money in 1997–98 wreaked a lot more damage than Asia's economies deserved, and that America had something to do with it. But it is not what the conspiracy theorists think.

What both explanations miss is the strength and impartiality of the forces America has unleashed. To the extent it can the United States will, as great powers do, try to turn these forces to its advantage. But the revolution that began in America in the 1970s has not been directed by the United States to serve its conscious purposes. Indeed, America went through its own agonies in the 1980s as the relentless thrust to efficiency took shape there. The standards of corporate, financial and economic performance now set by America are really objective standards that happen to have been established first in America; but they are imposed mostly by technological innovation and are spread by globalization.

Resistance to the power of technology and globalization already exists and will no doubt deepen—including in the United States once its stock markets and economy at last falter, and other countries get the hang of competing in the information age and inevitably start closing the performance gap with America that opened in the 1990s. But, especially with the breathtaking rise of the Internet and its ability to spread information both universally and instantaneously (a phenomenon whose importance Asians started realizing only in 1999), it is likely that governments everywhere will be largely powerless to slow down globalization or lessen its pressures. The proper epigram for the era that Asia began getting to grips with in 1997–98 is the one with which this chapter opened, coined by another, and farther-seeing, Southeast Asian leader, Singapore's senior minister Lee Kuan Yew. America learned the harsh lessons of modern global competition first, which is why Asia's story begins there.

THE GREAT INFLATION

In 1970, around the time when the first Internet entrepreneurs were born, few people had any inkling of the depth and breadth of the changes that would transform America over the next generation. In fact, the notion that the American economy was going to need fundamental change would have seemed far-fetched.

In America, as in most of the rich world, the quarter-century or so following the end of the second world war had been the most bountiful years in human history. Between 1950 and 1973 the American economy grew by 3.7 percent a year—almost twice as fast as in the next 25 years—and in real terms was close to three times bigger at the end of the 1950–73 golden age than it had been at the beginning. The average American's real income went up by 2.2 percent a year, an astonishing 50 percent faster than over the long haul of 1870 to 1995 (meaning the figure for 1950–73 was even farther ahead of America's long-run performance than it seems). Inflation in 1950–73 grew by an unalarming 3.1 percent a year, a lower rate of price rises than even Japan enjoyed in the same years. By the end of the 1960s, egged on by the vast bulge of baby-boomers who were then in their most arrogant and riotous university-attending years, fashionable commentators were speculating about what the United States should do now that the economic problem of scarcity had been solved.

In 1973 the golden age ended. It had, in fact, been tarnished for many years, first as President Lyndon Johnson in the 1960s decided (interestingly in tune with his student tormentors) that, since scarcity was a thing of the past, both the Vietnam war and the Great Society were simultaneously affordable and the government could start running up debt with impunity; and then by President Richard Nixon's decision in 1971 to end the 1945 Bretton Woods agreement on fixed currency exchange rates that had given the post-World War II international financial system such reassuring stability. But the end came in October 1973, when the Organization of Petroleum Exporting Countries (OPEC) more or less overnight quadrupled the price of a barrel of oil.

By the end of the decade, after a second OPEC price shock, the price of oil was as much as ten times what it had been in September 1973, and the United States had suffered an unparalleled post-Depression collapse in both economic and business performance and self-confidence. The economy itself had bumped along through two recessions in the 1970s. The stock market, not a bad indicator of the state of corporate America's health, performed dismally. By early 1980 the Dow Jones Industrial Average stood at around 750, no higher than it had been in 1963; in real terms, the stock market's fall between 1969 and 1980 took longer but was almost as big as the one in 1929–32.

But the central theme of America's apparent breakdown in the 1970s was the rise of inflation—what later came to be known a little ostentatiously as the Great Inflation. Fueled partly by (modestly) rising government deficits and the endless vacillations of a weak president, Jimmy Carter, but mostly by the loose money policy of the Federal Reserve, consumer price inflation rose from just under 5 percent in 1976 to an annual peak of more than 13 percent in 1979 (at times during 1980 it hit annualized rates of 16 percent and more). Interest rates for the best corporate borrowers approached 20 percent. Not since the nineteenth century had America had to cope with price rises and interest rates like this. It was not coping well, as a sense of disquiet and then near-panic set in about the apparently inevitable drift of the country into uncontrollable inflation.

Against this background, and in many ways in response to it, America's immensely flexible society and economy began changing more deeply than they had in the supposedly revolutionary 1960s. Until well into the 1990s, this process of change was routinely denounced by most of the country's misnamed "opinion leaders" as everything from the triumph of greed-based immorality to the beginning of America's long-term historical decline. It was really the beginning of a revival that, by the turn of the century, had made the United States more powerful in more dimensions than it had been even at its presumed zenith in the 1950s, and had redefined the terms on which the whole world would have to compete.

THREE CHANGES AND FIVE HEROES

The changes in America had three main thrusts. The first, at the national policy-making level, was to redefine what a government was supposed to do and how much of people's money it was supposed to redistribute, and how the supply of money should be regulated: this was macroeconomics, broadly defined. Second came the two most influential new tools of technology, the ones that have contributed most to the creation of an "Information Standard" for judging economic and political performance globally. The developments that allowed this were the democratization of information through satellite television, and the building of increasingly cheap and capacious telecommunications links that, a decade later, put America far ahead of its competitors when the networked computing age came into its own. Third, and most pivotal, was the unclogging of the channels of finance so that savings could flow freely and in high volume to the people who could use the money best. This allowed small companies to get started and eventually take on (and often slay) big ones. It sluiced out poor financial returns in the economy as a whole and created the devices for ousting underperforming company managements as well. The interaction of these changes over a period of 20 years created the world's most efficient economic machine.

The following list will sound as arbitrary as such lists always do, but I think five men can be credited with doing the most to push forward these changes: Ronald Reagan and Paul Volcker for the macroeconomic framework; Ted Turner for imposing a global information standard through CNN; Harold Greene, the federal judge who oversaw the breakup of AT&T; and Michael Milken, who perfected the financial instruments that made the American business jungle as ruthlessly Darwinian—and hence wealth-creating—as it now is. If it seems odd not to include (to take the most prominent examples) Andy Grove and Bill Gates, recall that vital though chips and software have been it is information and networks, coupled with a dwindling scope for government meddling and almost frictionless flows of capital, that gave America its biggest lead over the rest of the world as the twentieth century drew to a close.

THE CAPTAINS: REAGAN AND VOLCKER

The contributions of Volcker and Reagan are well-known. Paul Volcker became chairman of the Federal Reserve Board (the Fed) in the summer of 1979, at the most feverish stage of the Great Inflation and barely a year before Reagan was first elected president. For more than a decade the Fed had been dominated by members who, as one of them later put it, "philosophically didn't believe in the importance of controlling the money supply." Arthur Burns, the Fed's chairman in the early 1970s, didn't go quite that far but he may as well have: "Well," he told the chairman of the president's Council of Economic Advisers, "I think that the rate of growth of the money supply is important, but I don't know if it should be 3 percent or 12 percent." As inflation swelled during the 1970s, the Fed concentrated its attention on keeping short-term interest rates stable, and at a fairly low level. The money supply was allowed to grow largely at whatever rate it would. In an environment of accelerating price rises that rate was fast: before Volcker took over, money-supply growth was running at more than 10 percent a year.

Volcker was openly skeptical of the purist claims for monetarism put forward most eloquently by Milton Friedman, a Nobel prize-winning economist; but, because Volcker realized that inflation-fighting was by then America's greatest imperative, in practice he turned to the recommended tools of monetarism. As soon as he became chairman, the Federal Open Market Committee (the bank's policy-making body) set a target of 1.5 percent to 4.5 percent annual growth in money supply. It was now going to be interest rates that gyrated, not money-supply growth. And interest rates, which until then had been both steady and negative in real terms—lower than consumer-price rises—suddenly became volatile and very high: the key short-term rate, the Federal Funds Rate, averaged more than 11 percent in 1979, more than 13 percent in 1980 and more than 16 percent in 1981. There were sharp recessions in 1980 and 1982, and during the second dip unemployment went into double digits for the first time since the 1930s. But by 1982 serious inflation had been slain—consumer prices rose 3 percent that year—never to return that century; and with prices stable, a big part of the framework was in place for a good 15 years' worth of innovation, growth and stock-market exuberance.

The rest of the policy framework was built by Ronald Reagan. Part of what he did was never to flinch as Volcker carried out his inflation-crushing campaign (though, to be fair, neither had Jimmy Carter in 1979–80), even when its greatest damage to economic growth came in an election year. Reagan also did his bit to whittle down inflationary expectations, and to curb the power of labor unions to exact productivity-sapping wage deals, by firing all of the country's air-traffic controllers when they went on strike six months into his first presidential term. His attitude stood in sharp contrast to that of Jimmy Carter in 1977, who after pressing in labor-management negotiations for wage restraint meekly let pass a staggering 37 percent wage hike won by the mine workers' union after a strike against coal-mine owners. It was an early message from Reagan that market forces rather than politics would now have the upper hand.

Reagan cleared the field for competitive forces to work their will in the American economy in two other ways as well. One was to promote a program of deregulation that had been begun by Carter with airlines and trucking and was extended under Reagan to telecommunications, television and other previously government-bossed industries.

The other was to straitjacket the government's tax-raising powers. Through sharp cuts in the top marginal rate of income tax, Reagan made it progressively harder for the government to raise the revenues it needed to keep growing its spending. For more than a decade this had the effect of raising America's budget deficit and national debt, because spending was not constrained in line with revenues. But by the mid-1990s the government's practical inability to expand had so tied the hands of the next generation of politicians—raising tax rates had become electoral poison—that, thanks to flat real levels of spending and tax revenues rising because of the economic boom, the government budget swung into surplus. By the last year of the century, there were extravagant projections that government debt, which some respectable people in the late 1980s had said would grow inexorably, would in fact be extinguished by 2015. If so, the American government was heading toward the least influential position it had had in American life for a century.

The Information Providers: Turner and Greene

Walter Wriston, who ran Citibank from 1967 to 1974 and did more than almost anyone to change commercial banking through the intensive application of high technology, has said that the world now runs on an "Information Standard that is far quicker and more draconian than the old gold standard." Under this new standard, "governments responsible for [bad] policies" are quickly punished, and thus "naturally want to isolate themselves from the consequences of their own actions and cry for regulation." But isolation is less and less of an option, Wriston claims, as the sovereignty of the nation-state is sapped by the ever freer flow of information and of capital.

One of the two great sovereignty-sapping innovations of the past generation was 24-hour satellite television news. The first of these channels was Cable News Network (CNN), set up in 1980 by a Georgia media entrepreneur named Ted Turner, the head of Turner Broadcasting Systems. At the time American television news was dominated by three well-established broadcast networks with heavy overheads and famous on-screen personalities reporting and reading the news; there was no global service at all. Turner rejected all the premises on which broadcast news then rested: CNN was run as a (relatively) low-cost start-up, it was distributed through subscription cable networks instead of free over the air, and it quickly went global, being offered in Japan and Australia as early as 1982 and with a whole international division in operation by 1985.

Turner's ambitions were immodest: in 1990 he told a group of CNN interns, "We're gonna take the news and put it on the satellite, and then we're gonna beam it down into Russia, and we're gonna bring world peace, and we're all gonna get rich in the process." However extravagant, the ambitions (save for the world peace part) were met. What really distinguished CNN was its ability through global and continuous coverage of events as they were going on to sideline the commentators, analysts and news anchors who until then had filtered them for the consumers of news; it also began to shove aside mere diplomats as bearers of tidings and leaders of countries as powerful opinion-formers.

By the time of the Gulf War in 1991, where CNN's constant eyewitness coverage gave the network the worldwide breakthrough to more than a billion viewers that it had long coveted, CNN was often able to offer a clearer and quicker glimpse of unfolding events than even governments' internal communication channels were able to provide. President Bush's press secretary said that to convey to America's allies its response to various Iraqi diplomatic feints, the "quickest and most effective way was CNN, because all countries in the world had it and were watching it on a real-time basis."

CNN now has many competitors, and the effect of what it started has been deep and pervasive. Lawrence Eagleburger, a thoughtful former American Secretary of State, said in 1997 that "particularly because of CNN, the speed with which these things [foreign-policy crises] are reported sort of demands an answer from the government, from policymakers, almost instantaneously and that's not always good. But whether it's good, bad or indifferent, we're stuck with it." And it is not just America's government that is stuck: from the fall of the Soviet Union to the 1999 war in Kosovo, thanks to satellite TV a lot of information about what is happening inside a country in turmoil has come to its people from the outside without any official varnish.

A second strand to the information standard is even more important, at least in economic and financial terms. This is the increasingly powerful ability of computers linked in networks to disseminate huge amounts of information and aggregate and bring to bear millions of individual judgments about what is happening in markets of all kinds. In financial markets this has created, in Wriston's words, "a giant voting machine, casting its ballots against bad economic policies and in favor of good ones." But much more is involved than quick (and often overshooting) international capital flows. With the unexpected rise of the Internet, computer networking has become one of the biggest sources of competitive advantage. The source of the advantage is not the computers themselves but the sophistication and cheapness of the telecommunications system that ties them together. Thanks to the breakup of AT&T in the 1980s, the United States got at least a decade's-worth head start on anybody else at modernizing its telecoms system. And the most significant figure in the breakup of AT&T was a federal judge named Harold Greene.

It now seems hard to believe, but 30 years ago America's phone system (like ever other country's) was a government-regulated monopoly—a "natural monopoly," it was then thought. It provided a narrow range of services in a paternalistic way: most people couldn't even buy their own phones, they had to rent them from AT&T's equipment subsidiary, Western Electric. Any services out of the ordinary tended to be inconvenient and costly. In 1968 making a one-minute call from America's east coast to London involved booking the call hours in advance and cost the equivalent of $28.65 in 1998 dollars. (Thirty years later the same call—but now instantaneous and self-dialed—would have cost 12 cents at the cheapest transatlantic rate.) For the average American such cost and bother mattered little, but for American business it mattered a lot. Regulators kept business and long-distance rates for phone service artificially high as a way of keeping residential rates low. Moreover, technology was creating cheaper and more flexible alternatives to AT&T's massive systems. In 1969 the Federal Communications Commission gave permission to a start-up company called MCI to set up a long-distance microwave link between Chicago and St Louis.

The next year William McGowan, an aggressive business consultant and entrepreneur, took over MCI and began driving it toward much wider long-distance competition with AT&T; many other long-distance upstarts joined in, but all were stymied by AT&T's foot-dragging over giving them access to its local networks—and without that, running a competing long-distance service was impossible. In 1974 the Justice Department filed an antitrust suit against AT&T asking for the breakup of the company.

The suit, whose politically explosive implications for home phone service made the government less than eager to pursue it vigorously, got nowhere until 1978, when the judge who had been in charge of it fell terminally ill and it was reassigned to the newly arrived Judge Greene. Greene immediately cracked the whip over the parties, ordering an exceptionally speedy program of pre-trial evidence-gathering. Greene ordered the trial itself to start in January 1981; and the Reagan administration's new antitrust chief, William Baxter, a former Stanford professor, pushed hard for AT&T's breakup. Early in 1982, AT&T threw in the towel, settling the case pretty much on Baxter's terms: there would be free competition in the long-distance and equipment markets, which AT&T itself would continue to participate in; but it had to divest itself of the companies providing local service, which would continue to be government-regulated.

In the mid-1980s I twice interviewed Judge Greene, who died early in 2000. It seemed hard to detect in the kindly and avuncular figure sitting behind his government-issue desk in a Washington courthouse one of the great revolutionaries of the information age. But he was. As two telecoms scholars pointed out in 1988, "the outcome would have changed completely if [the original judge] had lived and retained jurisdiction of the case. In light of what happened later, the case would almost surely have ended in a negotiated settlement. [It] would have been one that was really negotiated, a mutually acceptable compromise, rather than what actually happened—AT&T's acceptance of Justice's terms. . . . [T]he Bell System—somewhat curtailed in size and activity—probably would still exist today." Nor did Greene's role end with the settlement. For the next decade, during which he was known in the industry as "Czar Harold," he almost single-handedly supervised the execution of the settlement agreement, changing it as he saw fit to match the changes in technology and the telecoms markets.

By the mid-1990s technology had advanced far enough, and markets (e.g., cable TV and local telephone lines) had commingled deeply enough, that everything in the telecoms business could be opened to fierce competition. Governments everywhere had woken up to this fact by then. But America's 10 to 15 year lead in blazing the trail for this new telecoms world told heavily in all sorts of ways. For one thing, the United States was well advanced in putting in place much of the infrastructure of the coming age: in 1997 it had four times as much installed fiber-optic cable as Europe and Japan put together. Asia was even farther behind. Intel, the Silicon Valley chipmaker, said in 1999 that it had more bandwidth available in its private communications system than existed in all of South Korea. America was also busy developing the technology of the future. Between 1980 and 1988 the American share of communications equipment patents granted by the U.S. Patent Office fell from 60 percent to 50 percent, but then rose slightly and has not declined since.

The American market was more competitive than others: New carriers in America had almost half the market for national long-distance traffic in 1997, more than twice the average share in the rest of the rich world. Pricing, too, reflected a competitive atmosphere: By 1998, the lowest long-distance rate in America was the same as the average peak rate for a local call in Europe, whereas six years before the ratio had been three and a half to one. Probably most important of all for the immediate future, America's advanced technology, market and pricing positions had put it far ahead of anywhere else in development of the Internet. In mid-1998 America had more than 90 percent of all the Internet hosts in the world, more than two-thirds of the web servers and of the secure web servers for e-commerce, and already a quarter of the U.S. population with access to the Internet. Being first in freeing telecoms had given America a huge head start.

MILKEN'S MAELSTROM

Michael Milken likes to say that junk bonds have existed at least since Alexander Hamilton, as America's first Treasury Secretary, issued $80 million-worth of high-yield securities in 1790 to pay off the new country's debts from the Revolutionary War and its aftermath. But it was Milken, as head of junk-bond trading for a now defunct investment bank called Drexel Burnham Lambert, who took a hitherto modest though long-standing tool of American corporate finance, perfected it and widened its use in the 1970s and 1980s to the point where it may now be the most famous and influential instrument in the corporate debt market.

And the most controversial. Apart from anything else, it is still hotly debated whether it was fair for Milken to be imprisoned in 1991–93 on the basis of his guilty plea to six arcane fraud and securities charges in connection with junk-bond deals in the 1980s. Given the establishment enemies Milken made, the politically charged nature of the junk-bond phenomenon by the late 1980s, and the personal ambitions of some of those who went after Milken (his chief pursuer as a government prosecutor in the late 1980s was Rudolph Giuliani, soon afterward elected mayor of New York City), it is hard not to feel more sympathy for the fox than for the hounds. But whatever you think about that, nobody has much doubt about this: Milken's junk-bond drive did more than any other single thing after 1970 to shake up American financial and corporate life, and to lay the groundwork for the competitive change-favoring business system that Asia is now trying to cope with.

Junk bonds are not rocket science: they are a snazzy name for corporate debt that pays a relatively high yield because it is issued by companies whose credit rating is not of the best. And that is most companies. In 1990 only 800 American companies had issued "investment-grade" bonds (meaning, in those days, debt considered safe enough for insurance companies, pension funds and other government-regulated investors to put their money into); of the 23,000 American companies that then had sales above $35 million a year, only 5 percent would have qualified for investment-grade credit ratings. Debt issued by the other 95 percent would have been classified as junk.

The junk-bond market in America exploded between 1970, when there were $7 billion-worth outstanding, and 1990, when the figure was $210 billion. Two developments in the 1970s opened the way to this takeoff. The first, which Milken himself thinks is the more important, was the collapse of American financial markets in 1974–75. As Milken explained it to me in 1998:

> What I would say to you is the fulcrum, the '73–'75 period, forever redid the financial system of the United States. In '74, recall, you stepped into a panic. If you go back to the research reports, you will find people predicting the demise of all major money-center banks, the airline industry, industry after industry; credit-rating people of the day were predicting 70 percent of the major companies in America might fail. The concentrated system of economic power had to save itself and therefore it couldn't think about its customers: the money-center banks for starters, insurance companies whose portfolios were under unbelievable pressure due to interest rates doubling and the failure of growth-stock investing. So Morgan Bank lost its cachet as the manager of your pension fund, as an industrial business your bank has forsaken you, your other traditional financial institutions have forsaken you, the value of your pension fund has dropped, requiring you to make more potential contributions.
>
> In the next two years, not only did the companies not go bankrupt, but people that bought "non-investment grade" debt made 100 percent on their money. And companies that had their bank funds cut off found a way to survive. They were never going to rely on a bank again for their financial strength, or growth, or survival. They weren't going to rely on short-term interest rates either, which doubled. So it was the breaking of a few financial institutions that controlled access to credit: the public marketplace replaced the private marketplace as a source of capital. Financial technology provided the freedom from dependence of a company on any financial institution, and that's what occurred in this country in '73–'75.

Yet if it was the 1974–75 panic that opened the door to junk bonds, it was the Great Inflation that began pushing them through in a rush. For investors, high inflation made it crucial to find high yields; the stock market was going nowhere, and thanks to their relatively low default rates from 1974 onward junk bonds no longer seemed so scary in relation to the returns they could offer. For companies seeking finance, issuing stock made no sense at all—for many companies shares were trading at less than the firm's book value (i.e., it would theoretically have made more sense just to stop doing business and sell the assets)—and short-term credit from banks and elsewhere was prohibitively expensive. Between 1979 and 1980 the face value of junk bonds outstanding rose by 50 percent, and for the next decade it rose by an average of almost 30 percent a year.

The growth of junk bonds was merely one aspect to a remaking and deregulation of American finance that brought such innovations as credit cards, brokerage accounts with check-writing privileges, cash-management accounts, money-market funds and the eventual triumph of mutual funds. One way or another, all these involved taking business away from traditional banks and brokerages and widely fanning it out through decentralized capital markets. That is what junk bonds were about too: although, as Milken's words above suggest, with far deeper consequences for American capitalism.

The reason is that, before junk bonds, it was hard for outsiders to raise the money they needed either to start a business (especially in a new industry) or to take over a business that was being badly managed. The lending practices of commercial banks had never been geared to assessing the potential of new businesses (and the venture-capital and intitial-public-offering culture that became so familiar in the 1980s and 1990s was still in its infancy). And the comfortable and cordial ties between banks, investment banks and blue-chip companies usually precluded such banks as a source of finance for a takeover.

Junk bonds changed all that. Milken's client list included a who's who of owners of start-up businesses, or acquirers of troubled ones, which were derided at the time but later became giants: Bill McGowan of MCI, Ted Turner, Craig McCaw of McCaw Cellular, Sumner Redstone of Viacom, John Malone of TCI and Rupert Murdoch of Fox Television. By the mid-1980s, however, junk bonds were being used to finance not just up-and-coming firms but also raids by outsiders on existing firms, many of them large and well-connected. Buyouts and takeovers (or attempted ones) that Milken helped with include Metromedia, Union Carbide, Revlon, Beatrice, ITT, TWA, Gulf Oil and Unocal. Politicians mostly kept quiet about junk financing of start-ups; but almost everyone got heated about hostile takeovers.

Milken rejects the distinction:

> It was not the battle for control, it was the access to capital. I can give you the example of a little start-up steel company, where the pressure not to lend money—by banks and large financial institutions, by industry associations, steelworkers in the steel industry—was really behind the scenes, attempting to stop the provision of capital to new companies like this little company that could make steel substantially cheaper and better. I received a visitor from Washington who informed me that it would not be good for my health if this company was given money to build its factory, it wasn't in Bethlehem Steel's interest that this company get capital.

Whatever the case, the corporate establishment did swing into action by the early 1980s to fight the threat posed by junk bonds. The Business Roundtable, founded in 1972 with a membership consisting of the CEOs of the 200 largest American companies, began lobbying Congress to restrict leveraged (debt-financed) takeovers. As a reminder of how quickly things can change, and to correct the impression of anyone prone to believe that American firms would never have followed the Japanese habit of ignoring their owners, the Roundtable was led in the 1980s by Andrew Sigler, a CEO who was fond of saying that "the overriding concern of American corporations should be the public interest, and that shareholder rights were secondary." The anti-junk campaign was much aided by the fact that, as in every bull market, plenty of abuses cropped up and a lot of laws were broken. In this atmosphere, the lobbying and generally high level of public denunciation worked. Congress held endless hearings and considered many laws to restrict junk, and the SEC and the Justice Department conducted several investigations. By the late 1980s savings and loan institutions had been ordered to get rid of their junk-bond portfolios, Drexel was out of business and Milken had been indicted.

But also by then the American corporate landscape had been transformed. By one calculation, companies that issued junk bonds "created jobs four times faster than the economy as a whole, experienced one-third greater growth in productivity, 50 percent faster growth in sales, and about three times faster growth in capital spending." This was not purely a small-firm phenomenon—during the 1980s more than a third of the Fortune 500 companies were merged, acquired or taken private—but it was the boost that junk gave to the creation of upstart firms that mattered most. One reason is that this is where the industries of the future were created. Another is that upstart or mid-size firms are the ones that create jobs in America—55 million of them since 1970—compared to a shrinkage of 3 million in Fortune 500 employment over the same period.

Milken for one thinks that the lessons from America are perfectly transferable to Asia:

> If political interference happened in this country, we can only assume in Asian countries, where there's enormous overlap between people on the boards of industrial companies and boards of financial institutions, that with concentrated economic power in the hands of a few institutions, it inhibits the growth of young companies and their ability to create jobs.

Yet is Asia likely to change this?

DOLLARIZATION

What has been created in America over the past quarter-century by these intertwined revolutions is a powerful system for promoting rapid technological, economic and social change while undercutting the ability of any government to assert much control over the process. It is fairly easy to see how this has happened in America itself. The next question is what resistance the rest of the world can offer, to the extent it wants to.

Markets buttressed by information flows have largely tied the hands of the American government when it comes to exercising discretion over monetary and especially fiscal policy. Any hint that a proposed line of action might seriously raise the risk of inflation is punished by a falling bond market. When he took office in 1993, President Clinton is famously said to have exploded in exasperation when told the market wouldn't allow certain aspects of the program he wanted: "You mean the success of my program and my re-election hinges on the Federal Reserve and a bunch of fucking bond traders?" In the American system presidents have always been pushed to the political center, but the push has recently gained force. By 2000, on the biggest matters of economic policy there was so little room for maneuver that it hardly mattered who was elected.

Moreover, the limits on government's ability to spend seem sure to become tighter as the spread of the Internet inevitably makes it easier for people to avoid paying income and capital gains taxes. This will apply everywhere but probably nowhere faster than in America.

The framework of limited government built by Volcker and Reagan was also made substantially sturdier during the 1990s by the rising power of the markets as repositories of household wealth. In the mid-1990s the assets of American mutual funds became bigger for the first time than the assets of the banking system; by the late 1990s almost half of Americans personally owned shares. The pressure on companies to perform and especially to cater to shareholder value—and on the government to create a policy environment in which they can do so—now has a populist as well as a corporate dimension. If junk bonds created a playing field on which CEOs had to do well in terms of earnings or face elimination, the triumph of mutual funds in the 1990s made sure that the speed with which performance was judged became even greater than it had been. The pressure became merciless, but it worked. The single best measure of how well a company is using its shareholders' money is return on equity (ROE, a set of initials that will haunt the rest of this book). ROE in America declined from a long-term historical rate of about 15 percent to half that in the late 1970s; in the 1990s it rose from 12 percent to more than 25 percent, twice the figure for Europe and maybe ten times bigger than Japan in the same period.

This state of affairs was far from being universally welcomed. In Europe and Asia alike—though in very different ways on the two continents—governments had grown used to exercising controls over social and economic development that were inconsistent with the freewheeling standards of America's new techno-economy. Many Europeans and Asians reflect that there must be some way for them to enjoy the fruits of freer capital flows and America-born technological innovation without losing complete control of the organization of their own societies.

At the margin that is undoubtedly true. Later parts of this book will describe how China, India and (in a much more clever way) Taiwan were able to insulate themselves from the worst devastations of the Asian financial crisis through capital controls, and how Singapore intends to internationalize itself while maintaining its traditionally strict social order. But at the core of economic competitiveness everyone around the world is being held to the same standard—one that information may create but that the dollar enforces.

"Dollarization" is a coinage (sorry) of Toby Brown, an American based in Hong Kong. Brown heads General Oriental Investments, the Asian arm of the worldwide investment empire founded by an Anglo-French financier and sometime American corporate raider, Sir James Goldsmith, who died in 1997. The term usually has a technical meaning: the substitution of the greenback for another country's own currency as legal tender there. Brown means something else by it: the role of the American currency in transmitting globally the standards of corporate, technological and economic performance that have been set in the reinvigorated America of the late 1990s.

The world has had a long line of currency regimes, harking back to the strong gold-plus-sterling standard of the late-nineteenth and early-twentieth centuries. This was followed by the post-1945 Bretton Woods era of fixed exchange rates and capital controls, and the floating/managed regime of 1971–1995. After a ten-year period of weakness, the dollar began to strengthen in 1995 against almost every currency, in particular the yen; contrary to expectations, it also rose against the euro when the new common European unit was introduced at the beginning of 1999. It is possible that, because of the relative strength of the United States economy, a dollar-based global currency regime—counterbalanced to some extent only by the euro—is coming into existence. If so, it will considerably undermine the ability of smaller countries (meaning anyplace smaller than Europe) to evade the standards of corporate and economic performance set by America.

The reasons can be found in an analogy Brown draws. Traditionally, he says, a country's central bank and its currency have performed a role for the national economy similar to that of a commercial bank at a micro level: they have served as the intermediary for the country's economic potential and its sources of finance, domestic and foreign. But because global information flows have become instantaneous, the rush of capital across borders is dictated not by local conditions but instead by global trends and the standards set by the world's most efficient economy. Brown says this means the governments of smaller countries are in effect being disintermediated. They are no longer the ones that control the interaction of their economies with the outside world. The dollar does this instead. One piece of evidence: the inability, even before the financial crisis, of Asian countries to issue international debt in their own currencies beyond five or seven years. This in essence robs them of the power to run an independent monetary policy.

Of course, such countries can sell long-term debt that is dollar-denominated. But what this means—and what the Asian crisis has shown—is that nobody can now raise money on global capital markets without meeting the world standard set by U.S. dollar returns. This in turn implies that all those wonderful profit-making imperfections and opacities behind which fortunes were built in non-American markets are being driven out of existence, to be replaced by more American-like standards of corporate behavior and performance. The only two possible sources of resistance to the American efficiency juggernaut are, first, the trivial one of the odd country choosing to take less economic growth in exchange for preserving more of its sovereignty (Malaysia? Russia?); and, second, the significant one of Euroland, whose wealth and size will allow it to preserve some (though by no means all) of the inefficiencies and social subsidies that its welfare-state mentality has accustomed it to and that nobody else on earth will be able to protect.

However much American power waxed during the 1990s, two misconceptions grew along with it. One is that the American economy has become invincible, that some ill-defined "new economy" has succeeded in repealing the laws of economic gravity and the pesky vagaries of the business cycle. In the mid-1980s an absurd notion took hold, peddled in countless books and articles, that Japanese capitalism had unequivocally proven its superiority to the American version and that the United States had better start imitating Japan if it was to have any hope of remaining a global economic player. By the mid-1990s a mirror had been held up to conventional wisdom to show the reverse: that America's boom would be endless and the lead it had opened over the rest of the world in technology and economic performance would widen forever.

Things don't work like that. Complications and weaknesses as yet unforeseen will eventually humble the American economy again (remember how rosy the future looked in 1970). And the nature of the tremendous technological burst in finance, the media and the Internet which pushed America ahead of the pack in the 1990s will be mastered by others, many of whom will be more accomplished than the United States at thriving in the next phase of the new industries' development—i.e., when satisfying consumers' wants cheaply will matter more than technological leadership. It is a fair bet that by 2005, midway through the decade whose Asian outlines this book will try to sketch, deep thought will be going into attempts to explain the causes of the by then recent American crisis (see cartoon).

Second, there is a temptation to assume glibly that, because it is America's strength which cracked open the fault lines in Asia, Asians will come out of their trial looking like Americans. This lazy syllogism overlooks some important things. One is that Asia's own strengths, as displayed during the two decades of fast economic growth before the crash, are not negligible; a lot was being done right and will not be thrown out

Illustrated Prophecies

CAUSES *of the* AMERICAN CRISIS

- Open Markets
- Rule of Laws
- Private Enterprise
- Free Press
- Democratic Ideals

DOW JONES INDUSTRIAL AVERAGE
12000
6000

MINISTER
of
FINANCE
VIETNAM

INTERNATIONAL MONETARY FUND

2000 Washington

After Wall Street's Crash of 2000, delegates at the World Bank-IMF meetings got doses of crisis analysis blaming "Western values."

Source: ASIAWEEK, June 4, 1999

just because some correction is needed. The overseas Chinese business network, for instance, was for the most part perfectly capable of making sophisticated assessments of credit risk without the use of spreadsheets; it will continue to be. Another point to bear in mind is that businesses and economies are every bit as much social organisms as they are machines for creating wealth. Objective norms have to be met, but they will be met within the context of widely differing cultures that are not about to be obliterated overnight by technology or the demands of shareholder value.

In analyzing what happened in Asia in the late 1990s Amartya Sen, a Nobel prize-winning economist, wrote, "We may have to look for new departures, but we also have reason to protect and build on the richness and creativity on which the region's accomplishments have been based. In an important sense, the new has to emerge from the old." American business and technological standards are being transplanted to Asian soil but, for both western and Asian companies, understanding just how the global seed will sprout in the native soil is where the big opportunities of the next decade will be found.

The Rocks on the River Bed

Massive and rapid growth is a wonderful buffer.
Like a river in flood, it hides the rocks on the river bed—
—*Mahathir Mohamad, 1997*

By 1996 the traffic in Bangkok was so bad that you were lucky to make it to three appointments a day before heading for the airport. The scene was not much different elsewhere in East Asia: it was hard to tell whether the Mercedes cars on the road or the construction cranes on the horizon were more crowded. In fact, neither was the most crowded—that distinction belonged to bank accounts. There was far too much money sloshing around Asia, and a year or so later it began drowning the place.

How this happened had, by mid-1999, been the subject of at least a dozen books. A website on the Asian crisis set up in 1997 by a New York University professor named Nouriel Roubini had, again by mid-1999, grown to the size of 50 or so broad subject categories, the most basic of which ("Basic readings and references on the causes of the Asian crisis") alone contained more than 80 items (www.stern.nyu.edu/~nroubini /asia/asiahomepage.html). The compulsion to try to explain what had gone wrong is understandable. For one thing, Asia's collapse had been as little foreseen in the decade before it happened as America's crisis in the late 1970s had been. This may be an unscientific sample, but it is telling: I spent my entire work life in the two years before the Asian storm broke living and traveling in Asia, reading reports and articles on Asia by economists, strategists and experts, and talking to hundreds of people about

Asia, most of them thoughtful and well-connected. Amid this avalanche of well-informed opinion, I recall hearing one and only one accurate prediction of what was to come—from a New York investment banker and hedge-fund adviser who, to much scoffing, told a group of bankers in early 1996 that Thailand was going to go the way Mexico did.

A second cause for perplexity is that the Asian economic miracle was no mirage. During the last burst of growth before the crash, the average annual growth of output per person in four Southeast Asian countries over the years 1991–96 was about 5.4 percent, almost four and a half times higher than the American figure for those years. Such achievements were not a flash in the pan, reminiscent (in one notoriously glib and completely inaccurate formulation) of the specious spurt of growth the Soviet Union enjoyed in the late 1950s thanks to its single-minded investment in heavy industry. East Asia's remarkable performance up to 1997 stretched back for two generations: between 1960 and 1985 real incomes rose fourfold in Japan, and four economies—those of South Korea, Taiwan, Hong Kong and Singapore—octupled in size. And growth benefited the poor every bit as much as it did the well-off—in terms of positive impact on their lives even more so. There is no parallel in history for such a speedy and massive uplifting of incomes. Moreover, what Asia accomplished in 1955–95 was well-grounded—in such basics as high rates of savings, small governments that spent little, openness to the outside world and ideal demographics—and, as this book will argue, the continent's ability to rise to rich-world levels remains unimpaired today. So how could the huge derailment of 1997–98 have happened? This is not an academic question. Asia must absorb the lessons of why it stumbled if it is to recover and fulfill its ambitions and potential.

Those lessons are varied but, although the volume and firepower of analytical artillery trained on them over the past couple of years may make it seem like they must be impossibly complex, they are not that hard to describe:

> ▶ Thanks to the region's extraordinarily high savings rates, local capital was plentiful and therefore cheap; and it was funneled in the formal economy mostly through domestic banks whose ability (or even desire) to judge the credit risks of their lending was low to nonexistent. Although much of the borrowed money went into productive investments much also went into speculative property and

stock-market ventures, or at least into uses for which the borrowers had to give no account to their creditors.

▶ Almost all of Asia (excluding to some degree only Hong Kong and Singapore) was rife with institutional weaknesses, ranging from companies unbeholden to minority shareholders, to poor banking supervision and regulation, to intricate entanglements between government and business, to the absence of such elementary cleansing mechanisms as bankruptcy laws.

▶ Asia's open and intense relations with the outside world—vital though they were for increasing the efficiency and productivity of its economies—also increased the mindless liquidity coursing through the region's financial channels and exposed it to a sudden and disastrous reversal of confidence. The risks rose sharply with an unexpected collapse in Asia's export growth in 1996–97.

The result of all this—as Chapter 3 will explain—was that Asia found itself in the same pickle America did at the end of the 1970s, albeit for completely different reasons (in America the cause was inflation, in Asia it was cheap capital): companies that weren't creating much value for the amount of money that had been sunk into them. It was a position even less sustainable for relatively small Asia in an increasingly globalized world than it had been for mighty America 20 years before. For this unenviable position Asians have first to thank the Japanese model that they had come to admire so much.

THE JAPANESE FISH-TRAP

The most perceptive and succinct sketch of the modern Asian economic system comes from Andrew Sheng, an American-educated Malaysian who worked in his own country's central bank before going to Hong Kong and becoming head of the Securities and Futures Commission, the territory's financial-markets watchdog. Excepting only free-wheeling Hong Kong and (until recently) sequestered India, Asia has followed a policy template designed in Japan to produce fast industrial modernization through fierce domestic and export competition for manufacturing companies combined with a tight grip on financial transactions both domestic and international. The result: a dangerous imbalance, with strong export-oriented manufacturing firms, an underdeveloped service sector, and a large surplus pool of savings available for a government to direct to the uses it thinks best. Put crudely, on the home front the model produces a two-tier economy with highly efficient manufacturers, many honed to world standards by global competition, but dismally inefficient service firms; and, in terms of the country's relations with the outside world, relatively free trade in goods but high barriers to outflows of equity capital.

Sheng says the Japanese model works well at quickly propelling a backward country toward operationally efficient industrialization—though, as Singapore's Lee Kuan Yew puts it, "That was the easy part. That was the part when you moved from agriculture into assembly-line production and so on. Nothing can go wrong there; that's textbook stuff." The troubles come only later, when a country needs to move into more sophisticated and higher-value-added businesses.

The problem is not in the manufacturing economy: because of its export orientation, the country is capable of picking up technology and business practices that are up to global standards. But—because of constraints on the flow of capital—money and credit in the formal economy do not always go toward financing new businesses with the highest potential returns. It is important to remember the phrase "formal economy," i.e., businesses that are financed by banks, show up in official statistics and tend to be listed on stock exchanges. In much of Asia, though not Japan, a lot of small-business growth—especially among ethnic Chinese firms—is financed not by banks but through private capital markets that charge high real rates of interest and impose ruthless not to say violent mechanisms for the enforcement of obligations.

The inefficiencies of capital allocation in the formal economy are twofold. First, liquidity is abundant and money is therefore cheap—and it is duly wasted. Until the 1990s most of Asia's financial systems were virtually closed to the outside world, and even though all were then opened up to some extent, relatively high barriers to capital mobility remained in place up to the year 2000. Japan's system, says Sheng, was like a fish-trap: capital from abroad could swim in and join the already large mass of domestic savings, but very little money of either sort swam back out to be invested in other countries' stock markets. One sign of this process at work was the inexorable rise of Asia's foreign-exchange reserves, which by the mid-1990s had grown to account for almost half of the world's total—or about twice Asia's share of gross world product.

The combination of high savings rates and closed finances also meant that, for the 10 or 20 years before 1996, real interest rates in every country in East and Southeast Asia were far below economic growth rates; in America, by contrast, real interest rates on average were 0.2 percentage points higher than GDP growth in 1970–96. The result of cheap money in Asia was over-investment of all kinds, most perniciously in asset markets like real estate and stock markets. Consumer price inflation remained low in most of Asia, but from the 1980s into the 1990s asset bubbles swelled enormously throughout the region. At their peaks, the price/earnings ratio for Asian stock markets ranged from the 40s to the 70s for every market save Japan, which reached the 120s (American stocks were at their most highly valued ever when they hit the low 30s in 1999).

Sheng points to a second inefficiency that, in his view, is even more damaging than the simple underpricing and waste of capital. A financial system, he says, is not there merely to allocate resources but also to spread and manage risk. The problem with the Japanese model is that it prevents or at least impedes risk-spreading across borders; all the risks are concentrated in the domestic economy alone, an all-eggs-in-one-basket approach which insures that when something does go wrong it will go wrong in a big way. True, for most of the 1980s and 1990s Japan exported large amounts of capital. But the overwhelming chunk of this was in the form of foreign direct investment (real estate in America, factories in Southeast Asia and China), bank loans and purchases of U.S. Treasury bonds by the Japanese government and big insurance companies. Very little private money flowed abroad for investment in stock markets, meaning that the risk-spreading benefits of a diversified equity portfolio were unavailable when the downturn came. In other words Sheng's compatriot, Malaysia's Prime Minister Mahathir, stood logic on its head with his repeated denunciations in 1997–99 of speculators and unimpeded flows of portfolio capital: these reduce the risk for an economy, not deepen it. And by the mid-1990s Asia badly needed some risk-reduction.

BANKING ON A WING AND A PRAYER

The pressures building in Asia as the mid-1990s approached were out of the ordinary for an impending financial crisis. The usual problems, familiar from Latin America's debt crisis in the 1980s and Mexico's in

1995, are inflation and government budget deficits. But throughout the 1990s every Southeast Asian country save the Philippines ran budget surpluses (and the deficit in the Philippines was only 0.3 percent of GDP). Inflation was mostly low (Indonesia's 8 percent to 10 percent was the highest) and everywhere steady. As Simon Ogus, then SBC Warburg Dillon Read's chief economist in Hong Kong, said in 1998, by contrast with Latin America "Asia's problems are ones of debt deflation, excessive private-sector leverage and weak financial systems." The specific trouble was the accumulation of corporate debt provided by banks both domestic and foreign.

Banks overwhelmingly, and unhealthily, dominate finance in Asia. In Hong Kong, for instance, just before the crisis domestic bank credit amounted to 120 percent of GDP whereas corporate bonds equaled a mere 15 percent of GDP. Even where substantial corporate-bond markets exist—notably Japan and South Korea—banks are still significantly bigger providers of capital. Among rich countries, only Germany has banks that are as dominant as those in Asia; German bank credit in 1997 was equal to about 100 percent of GDP, compared to a bond-market size of about half that. In America bank credit added up to only 60 percent of GDP, with the bond market almost as big.

This is unhealthy for several reasons. First, by global standards Asia's banks are generally small, inefficient and incompetent. As Philippe Delhaise, then the head of Thomson BankWatch Asia, put it in 1998, Asia's "financial sectors did grow, but they never matured." Because of the closed capital system and obstacles erected everywhere in Asia to the penetration of multinational banks from the West, Asian banks performed in ways that would long ago have driven them out of business in America.

Take an example everyone can relate to. Japanese banks are comically bad in operational terms, as any consumer who travels internationally can testify. It is, for example, easier to get cash out of an ATM in China's major cities than it is in Japan's. Few of the Japanese ATMs are linked to international networks that give foreigners visiting Japan access to their home bank accounts. Japanese banks installed ATMs late and reluctantly. At first they were open only during regular banking hours. Then, when the hours were extended, you had to pay the ATMs overtime (in the shape of a surcharge) for working late. Even now, few are open round the clock. It is no wonder that only one homegrown Asian bank—Hong Kong's HSBC—has attained global stature; and technically even it is no longer Asian, having been forced by the Bank of England to move its group headquarters to London when it took over Midland Bank in 1994.

Otherwise Asian banks tend to be astonishingly small and parochial. In early 1999 the Philippines had 53 commercial banks, whose total assets were nonetheless smaller than those of one Singapore bank, DBS Bank. Yet you would have to add up all the banking assets of Singapore and Malaysia together to get to Hong Kong's size. China's commercial banking system had assets in 1998 that were about equal to the size of the country's GDP but, according to Delhaise, were still no bigger than the combined assets of the world's two biggest banks. Even Japan's asset-laden monster banks have puny revenues. David Atkinson, Goldman Sachs's banking analyst in Tokyo, calculated in late 1998 that Japan's biggest bank, Tokyo-Mitsubishi, had twice the assets (loans) of Citibank and the same capital but—at $7.2 billion—only one-third of Citibank's revenues, making Tokyo-Mitsubishi not only vastly less profitable than Citibank but also by the revenue measure only the world's 15th biggest bank. He went on to reckon that if Japanese banks wanted to compete on a world-class level, the country should have no more than two to four commercial banks, down from the 19 it then had.

The size of a bank's revenue stream matters in many ways, but the most important is that it furnishes the wherewithal for the enormous investments in computer and other technologies which, ever since Citibank pioneered their use in the 1970s, have become the single biggest source of competitive advantage for a modern bank. This matters not just for the provision of services but also for a bank's ability to manage its risks properly. Asian banks are almost hopelessly small and far behind in this. Certainly, their financial performance reflects dismal levels of profitability. In South Korea, for instance, in 1996 (a year before the Asian crisis broke) the banking system as a whole had negative capital thanks to bad loans and poor investment decisions on the stock market; in effect, this means that the banks were already bankrupt. Japanese banks were not much better off. Overall, in June 1997, one month before the crash, Moody's ranked Southeast Asian banks' financial strength thus: Singapore B, Malaysia C–C+, Philippines D+, Thailand D–D+, Indonesia D. In ratings-speak, all except Singapore were flashing various shades of red.

A second drawback to Asia's heavy reliance on bank financing is that it puts great power into the hands of politicians and bureaucrats to direct credit, sometimes corruptly to their chums and sometimes merely misguidedly through "policy loans" that advance a government's agenda, though usually with no consideration of profitability or even rationality. The "policy" component of lending has been high almost everywhere in Asia. This has been most obvious in the case of Indian and Chinese state-owned banks, but it has happened as well in Japan, South Korea, Taiwan and everywhere in Southeast Asia. Once a certain level of industrial efficiency and sophistication is reached, such "nation-building" exercises can quickly become—as Asia learned in the 1990s—wealth-destroying ones instead.

Lastly, banks are much poorer than securities (stock and bond) markets at assessing and pricing risk. In fact, partly because of their technological and managerial backwardness and partly because no lending officer has ever been promoted for defying orthodoxy (to the contrary, in Taiwan loan officers were personally liable for loans they made that weren't repaid), Asian banks outside Hong Kong and Singapore have rarely bothered with assessing risk. Loans were seldom made, as they often are in the West, on the basis of a business's expected cash-flow. Instead, collateral in the form of real estate or shares was the basis for granting a loan. One natural result was to help inflate the bubbles for these assets. Another was to reward the well-connected and well-established and make credit for the rebellious and the upcoming (and probably more profitable) harder to get, though this blow was softened by vigorous informal sources of finance.

Against this banking background, and with economies booming and optimism unbridled, it is no surprise that Asia suffered an explosion of credit in the 1980s and 1990s. Throughout the 1980s in Japan, bank credit grew at twice the pace of nominal (i.e., pre-inflation) GDP growth; in America, by contrast, since 1960 bank credit has grown in line with GDP and the money supply has actually fallen slightly as a share of GDP. In the rest of Asia in the 1990s bank credit grew by 10 percent to 20 percent a year, as in Japan also about twice the pace of nominal GDP growth. By 1996 the ratio of total debt to GDP (this includes foreign borrowings of non-bank private firms) was above 200 percent in most of Southeast Asia and 300 percent in Japan, and it continued rising into 1997; in most other emerging economies the figure was 50 percent to 100 percent. In corporate Korea debt reached fantastic levels, with conglomerates building up debt-to-equity ratios of 400 percent to 500 percent, in the case of the biggest *chaebol* (as the conglomerates are called), and as much as 2,000 percent in the case of some smaller fry. By comparison, American investors start twitching if American firms' debt-to-equity ratios go much above 70 percent.

A common rationalization among foreign investors as this debt was building up was that, unlike in Latin America, Asia was borrowing for investment in things that would produce a stream of income to repay the loans rather than for frivolous consumption. That was technically true. One problem, however, was that because of the primitive state of credit analysis in Asia nobody knew whether the projects would generate the revenues needed to repay the loans. The bigger problem was that so much of the borrowed money went for real estate or share purchases. By the end of 1997 bank lending for real estate ran from 20 percent to 50 percent of the outstanding loan books throughout Southeast Asia. The volume of property development was staggering. By 1997 the capacity of office space in Bangkok and Jakarta had incredibly grown five- to eight-fold since 1990—and almost all the increase had been financed by loans. Loans on margin for share purchases were 10 percent to 15 percent. It was well-known in Malaysia that a lot of "corporate" loans were being made so that controlling shareholders in companies could use the money for personal stock-market speculation.

Asia's excessive expansion of domestic credit and all that went along with it ensured that, even without the region's chronic institutional weaknesses and its external financing problems, there would have been trouble. But those other flaws were present too, and they made the trouble severe and concentrated when it came.

WEAK INSTITUTIONS

In my earlier book about Asia, published in 1995, I said this:

> While Asia has a good deal to teach the West about society, it has a lot to learn about the institutions of a modern political and economic system. Asia's worst weakness—and the only flaw that could grievously wound it— is its failure to move beyond the informal and the personal in its ways of doing business, of governing and of handling relations between states.
>
> That Asia, in the early stage of its development, was free of institutional constraints helped it grow fast. Yet at some point—usually around the time economic growth slows down—a more transparent and rule-based system becomes a necessity. The public aspect, whether in the physical shape of a

road or railway or the institutional shape of a set of company accounts that can be read by potential investors from New York as well as Bangkok, claims more attention. It is, for example, starting to become clear that if Asia is ever to produce countries with a global reach, they will have to find some way of institutionalizing management and financial controls that are now made on a mostly personal basis.

The idea wasn't bad, but what I did not imagine five years ago is how deep the institutional weaknesses were or how swiftly and comprehensively they could bring Asia to a crisis. I thought Asian institutions could and would modernize at a stately and controlled pace. That is not the way it happened.

You can begin almost anywhere with a list of the institutional defects that helped bring Asia to the brink. But in thinking about such a list it is important to keep a few things in mind. One is that the weaknesses were there, and usually worse, in the decades before Asia crashed but they nonetheless did not stop it from two generations'-worth of spectacular economic success. Another is that these weaknesses tend to be a matter of degree; being human creations, all societies—even the richest and most law-abiding—have their own versions of such failings. It is just that they are rarer and less widespread in the richer places. Lastly, what I am calling weaknesses are in many cases natural outgrowths of particular histories and cultures, have good sides as well as bad, and although they will evolve as Asia modernizes they are therefore unlikely to disappear. They nonetheless are still weaknesses because, when combined with the cocktail of loose credit, fast money from abroad and shrinking returns on capital, they added an element that made the concoction that much more devastating.

Among Asia's institutional failings, five stand out as the biggest contributors to the region's collapse. They are (in roughly the order of their importance in bringing about Asia's crisis): poor bank regulation and supervision; lack of trained people both in government and outside who understand the control mechanisms of a modern society; poor corporate governance; lack of enforceable bankruptcy and other commercial laws; and cronyism and corruption, which is not the biggest institutional weakness but has the most complicated explanations and effects and is therefore the subject of the next section.

1. *Bank supervision.* Apart from Singapore and Hong Kong—the former because of its relentless drive to earn the respect of international

money-men and the latter because of its British colonial administration—no Asian country before the crisis had remotely adequate supervisors and regulators for the only formal financial institution that counted for much. It was rare for a central bank or finance ministry to have even elementary information about the state of health of its all too numerous commercial banks, let alone of non-bank finance companies. Banks were seldom forced by regulators to make provisions (i.e., set aside money) for loans likely to go bad, to disclose liabilities off their balance sheets such as contingent guarantees or derivatives obligations, or not to lend large amounts to their own main shareholders (a lot of Southeast Asian industrial tycoons set up banks for precisely that purpose). In many cases, Japan being the most prominent, the regulator—then in Japan the Ministry of Finance, a role that has since been taken away from it—actually encouraged imprudent banking practices to fulfill the government's own policy agenda.

2. *Little expertise.* The then head of research at a western investment bank in Thailand guessed in 1998 that Thailand had 400,000 corporations but only 1,000 qualified accountants. It is easy to guess how good the accounts of even a well-intentioned Thai company are when the average outside auditor has an average of slightly over half a workday a year to peruse them. India, proud of its British-based rule of law, in 1997 had a backlog of 40 million commercial cases according to the country's law minister, which suggests that—assuming justice deferred is justice denied, as it would be in India for about 350 years while that backlog was cleared—the "rule of law" does not mean much more in practice there than it does in China or Indonesia.

For all its impressive economic performance, Asia is plagued as it moves upscale by a lack of people educated well enough to do the supervisory work for a modern economy. This lack afflicts both companies and governments, but governments probably more. Table 2.1 gives an interesting snapshot of what 500 expatriate businessmen in 1999 thought of the competence of the main government institutions in the Asian countries where they worked, with their rankings of America by comparison. On this score, Asia as a whole is not looking good.

3. *The way companies run.* It is a rare Asian company where minority shareholders have any rights at all. Not only are accounts inadequately audited; unless stock-market regulators intervene, the books are often deliberately cooked to deceive both tax collectors and other shareholders. The most vivid example of how this works in practice is a

Table 2.1
Rating Key National Institutions in Asia

	Police and Judiciary		Central Bank/ Monetary Authority		Legislature/ Parliament		Stock Market Regulatory Authority		Average	
	1999	1998	1999	1998	1999	1998	1999	1998	1999	1998
China	8.00	7.63	6.67	5.38	7.89	8.75	6.78	7.25	7.30	7.25
Hong Kong	3.33	3.11	2.93	2.68	5.83	5.47	4.20	4.16	3.94	3.86
Indonesia	9.73	9.00	7.18	6.73	8.45	9.00	6.82	7.73	8.13	8.11
Japan	3.38	4.27	5.00	5.60	6.75	6.87	5.38	6.60	5.32	5.83
Malaysia	7.29	6.86	6.57	4.86	7.71	4.57	7.14	6.57	6.43	5.71
Philippines	7.43	8.22	3.86	5.33	6.86	7.44	5.71	5.89	6.41	6.72
Singapore	3.55	2.87	2.18	1.87	5.00	4.20	3.91	3.07	3.37	3.00
South Korea	7.40	6.40	7.10	8.13	8.20	7.73	7.10	7.47	7.44	7.43
Taiwan	6.31	6.00	3.92	4.00	5.85	7.00	5.81	6.50	5.55	5.88
Thailand	7.57	8.50	6.14	8.13	7.43	8.00	5.43	8.13	7.31	8.19
USA	2.66	3.00	1.16	1.47	3.50	3.94	1.50	1.62	2.46	2.51
Vietnam	8.75	7.50	8.25	8.00	8.25	7.00	9.00	10.00	8.11	8.13

Grades are scaled from zero (the best grade possible) to 10 (the worst).
Source: Political and Economic Risk Consultancy

personal one. For a brief time in 1996–97, I was trying to convert a Thai-owned Hong Kong-based monthly magazine into a weekly business and finance publication. The Thai owner, Sondhi Limthongkul, owned scores if not hundreds of companies set up to satisfy his grandiose but never well-executed corporate vision of an Asian media empire. The one I was involved with, called *Asia Inc.,* had an equity capital of $HK1 ($0.12) even though its revenues approached $3 million a year and it never turned a profit. In other words, the whole thing was run on bank and other loans with no conception of or interest in shareholder return (even though the group was listed on the Bangkok Stock Exchange). In pre-crisis Asia, this story was unremarkable. This will be explained in more detail in Part Two of this book.

    4. *Lack of bankruptcy and other commercial laws.* If Asia—excepting, as usual, Singapore and Hong Kong and in this case Japan as well—is plagued in general by a weak rule of law, a particular legal gap has caused disproportionate damage to the ability of the region's business systems to cleanse themselves. It has never been easy in most of Asia to enforce commercial contracts in court, which is why when disputes arise everyone—including foreigners—tries to hammer out a deal through negotiations

rather than lawsuits. Worst of all, in the conditions Asia increasingly found itself in as the 1990s moved on, much of the region had no bankruptcy laws.

Even where bankruptcy laws were on the books, as in Japan, there was strong cultural resistance to using them. In many cases creditors themselves wanted to avoid this unpleasant subject; this was especially true of banks, which were weak anyway and had little interest in doing something that would force them to recognize the bad loans on their books. Yet, remarkably, in many countries the laws simply did not exist (Thailand) or were so archaic that they were unusable (Indonesia, whose "law" had been written in the sketchiest of terms in 1904 by its Dutch colonial masters and had never been updated). Indonesia finally passed a bankruptcy law in 1998 and Thailand in 1999. But I got a vivid impression of how little this was to mean in practice when, in September 1998, I visited the Jakarta law offices of Hotman Paris Hutapea.

Hotman was one of only 30–50 Indonesian lawyers qualified to act in bankruptcy cases (out of 20,000 Indonesian lawyers in all, of whom Jakarta—where the country's best were naturally to be found—had 1,000, about as many as you can find on a dozen floors of any number of buildings in Manhattan). In a blue-jean jacket with brown suede elbow patches, a blue cowboy shirt with heavy red trim, and lots of jewelry, Hotman looked the part of a bankruptcy specialist. He expected to get a lot of business from the new law, and in fact over the next year, acting in different cases on behalf of both creditors and debtors, proved himself the country's leading bankruptcy litigator. He felt the business could be "massive," since under the new law any unsecured creditor, no matter how small, was able to file a claim that could bring down a very big company, and personal guarantors could also be bankrupted through this process (Hotman reckoned that about two-thirds of all Indonesian loans were personally guaranteed by directors or major shareholders).

This would put immense pressure on the 17 judges who manned the new bankruptcy court—or, more likely, subject these woefully underpaid civil servants to immense temptations from debtors who wanted to move on. The only training in bankruptcy law for the 17 judges came during several weeks of tutoring while the court was being set up. Whether or not they had doubts about the whole matter, Indonesia's Supreme Court certainly did: on technical grounds it threw out the first two cases that reached it, one of them brought by American Express. Even as 2000 rolled around both Indonesia's law and Thailand's were barely functioning as courts and litigants alike still had so little experience with them and remained instinctively hostile to their use. It was not the most propitious legal setting for fixing a financial breakdown in which 50 percent to 70 percent of bank loans became delinquent and the assets which had been used as collateral for them (mainly real estate) could not be seized and sold to help lower prices and clear the market.

THE CRONIES AND THEIR LOOT

Cronyism is a pretty elastic term, and it is far from being unknown in the West as well as Asia. David Herbert Donald's biography of Abraham Lincoln describes the way in which probably the greatest American leader ever, when he was a postmaster in Illinois in the 1830s, abused his office to frank letters for his friends so they would not have to pay postage. On a far grander scale—bigger, relatively, even than Asia's meltdown of 1997–98—America's railway-finance scandal of 1873–74, involving Congress as well as banks and foreign investors, caused huge capital flight from the United States and a five-year recession that, until eclipsed in the 1930s, was known as the Great Depression. And, to prove that the passage of centuries is no barrier to roguery, Charles Keating, notorious for his involvement during the 1980s in America's savings and loan (S&L) scandal, made campaign donations to nine Senators and several Representatives, and offered good jobs to government regulators and auditors of Lincoln Savings and Loan, one of the firms he controlled during the scandal. Even Alan Greenspan, then just a respected private economist with good government contacts but later practically canonized as Chairman of the Federal Reserve, was paid $40,000 by Keating to write two letters and testify to California bank regulators on his behalf. Greenspan wrote among other things that the soon-to-be-found-fraudulent management of Keating's S&Ls was "seasoned and expert . . . [with] a long and continuous track record of outstanding success in making sound and profitable direct investments." If this was not cronyism, it is hard to know what the word means.

Even so, in much of Asia—including otherwise rich-world Japan—the connections between politicians and businessmen are, by modern rich-world standards, unusually close and prone to abuse. While pure rapacity is often the overriding theme, as it was in the Philippines under President Marcos and in Indonesia in President Suharto's later years, in many cases these connections rise to the level of national policy. This was so in South Korea, where the huge conglomerates and successive governments scratched each other's backs in pursuit of a Japan-like export-oriented industrial policy, and in Taiwan, where the ruling Kuomintang (Nationalist Party) controlled a large corporate empire that both fed it cash and gave scope for generous patronage. But cronyism-as-policy reached its most highly developed state in Malaysia during the prime ministership of Mahathir Mohamad, who took office in 1981 and was still there almost 20 years later.

Following devastating race riots in 1969, Malaysia in 1971 brought in a stern affirmative-action plan called the New Economic Policy that was designed drastically to increase the share of the economy controlled by the ethnic Malay majority, which had always been commercially outclassed by the ethnic Chinese (and to some degree by the Indian) minorities. After becoming prime minister, Mahathir executed the policy in part by picking favored Malay businessmen to receive government contracts and concessions and other public largesse. This not only produced, through part ownership and donations alike, a handsome stream of income for the ruling United Malays National Organization, Mahathir's political party, it also created a powerful and apparently successful class of Malay businessmen who could spearhead the drive to increase the weight of Malays in the country's commercial life. Far from recoiling from this way of doing business after the financial crisis hit Malaysia in 1997–98, Mahathir pushed it further. Government-run firms—especially Petronas, the cash-rich national oil company—invested in favored Malay-owned companies that needed help; and in mid-1999 the government tried to knock heads together to force the country's 21 commercial banks and 37 other financial institutions to merge into six large groups, a plan that was later watered down (but not abolished), among other things because of protests by influential Chinese that the thing was designed to better the position of Malay bank proprietors at the expense of the Chinese. In any event, the whole Malaysian set-up is hardly an ideal method for the efficient allocation of either resources or risk.

Cronyism is a natural handmaiden to corruption, but corruption runs much deeper and more widely. Singapore is the only place in Asia where surveys of businessmen and experts suggest that corruption is as minor a factor as it is in the rich countries of the West. Everywhere else, though to the least extent in Hong Kong, it has a significant impact—including Japan and South Korea, where corrupt ties between politicians (and occasionally bureaucrats) and certain industries, notably construction, lead to huge exchanges of money and favors. In the less developed countries illegal transactions are woven almost inextricably into the economic and social fabric. A recent book on Thailand called *Guns, Girls, Gambling, Ganja* (you can imagine the industries it covers) guesses that the illegal economy there in 1993–95 may have amounted to as much as 20 percent of the country's official GDP—led by unlicensed gambling, with prostitution a distant second (yes, despite appearances it is illegal in Thailand). Guesses for Taiwan run upwards even of that 20 percent figure.

A respectable argument can be made that, for a poor country on the rise which lacks the institutions that make a fairly clean market economy workable, a certain amount of corruption can act as a market-friendly lubricant that at least allows the wheels of commerce to turn. But expert studies are piling up that show tight correlations between corruption and weak banks, poor bank supervision, curtailed investment both domestic and foreign, low quality of infrastructure and below-potential GDP growth. None of this proves that these bad things can be traced exclusively or even mostly to corruption, but the coincidence is strong. And then, perhaps more persuasively, there is the example of Singapore.

When Lee Kuan Yew became Singapore's prime minister in 1959, the place was practically as poor as its neighbors and certainly as prone to corruption—a propensity sharpened by the efforts of a strong communist movement, led by ethnic Chinese, to subvert the elected government. Lee immediately set about simultaneously thwarting the communists and making sure, through devices like the approval in 1960 of strong anti-corruption laws and an independent Corrupt Practices Investigation Bureau (then without precedent in Asia), that corruption would be stamped out before it could take root. A significant element in the policy—and one that is unique in Asia if not the world—is that as soon as the government could afford the cost it started paying politicians and civil servants extremely well, as much as they could make for comparable work in a private company. In Singapore there has never been any of the hypocritical balderdash so prominent in, e.g., the United States about the nobility and sacrifice of "public service," an attitude that leads in rich democracies like America and Japan to the corruption of money-politics and the prominence of multi-millionaires in legislatures and parliaments, and in poor countries to irresistible temptations for civil servants to take bribes (a point graphically brought home to me on a visit to Jakarta in 1998, when I was told that the policeman we passed directing traffic in the stifling heat was paid less each day than the cost of a bottle of local mineral water). By mid-2000 Singapore's prime minister, presiding over a city-state of fewer than 4 million people, had a salary of $1.2 million, six times that of the President of the United States.

It is hard to believe there was no connection between Singapore's aggressive anti-corruption stance and its startlingly superior economic performance in the next 40 years compared with that of Malaysia (with which Singapore was briefly federated during the early 1960s, and which has never cared to copy its neighbor's anti-corruption vigor). Lee himself is sure that Singapore's attractiveness to multinational investors has much to do with the fact that "you have to get the system right to use manpower to advantage. You must have a clean system, with trust and confidence."

When I asked Lee in 1992 whether China could imitate Singapore in ridding itself of corruption, he said:

> It's difficult. They should have started their anti-corruption drive much earlier, before it seeped through the system. Now it's too deep-seated to eradicate completely.
>
> We inherited the British system where the rulers are subject to the rules, and so if I tried to stop an investigation I stand a very serious risk of the morale of the whole unit collapsing. Word will get around, the whole establishment will get to know of it.
>
> Fortunately for us, we took over before the system got corrupted. This was one of the reasons we were forced to take over as early as we did. We knew the communists were so powerful that the moment we got in we would probably be eaten up. We didn't have the strength to resist that. But we were forced in 1959 to take over because if we had allowed the other [corruptly mayor-run] government to carry on, they would have so eaten into the system that by the time we took over it would be no longer sharp. So we had to take over.

Seven years later, Lee had this to say about China:

> The redeeming factor is that the top people at the center are clean. Jiang Zemin, Zhu Rongji, Li Peng haven't accumulated wealth. They don't need the

wealth. As long as the center is wholesome, they can cope with disaffection at lower-level corruption. But if the center goes bad, then the risk of disorder is very real. But if for now the key players command respect for their integrity. That's their saving grace. They haven't descended into the mire that KMT leaders sank into before they fled the mainland in 1949.

So, as Lee concluded in 1992:

[In China] the actual siphoning of state budgets has not happened. So if Taiwan could clean up the system, and they were very corrupt in the 1950s and 1960s, so can China. But of course that means that instead of you pouring one dollar in and one dollar reaches the ground, maybe 70 or 75 cents reaches the ground and 25–30 cents is siphoned off along the route. It's a waste, but still.

THE WORLD'S COFFERS

The third strand in the rope that eventually hung Asia—after excessive growth in domestic credit and the region's weak institutions—was the way foreign capital came into the region. The danger with this subject is that xenophobes and protectionists always find it a useful instrument for attacking the idea that economies highly open to the outside world are better off than those that insulate themselves. In fact, Asia has benefited immensely from its relative openness to globalization, and if that seems dubious just look at how East Asia's tiger economies outperformed Africa and India in the years after 1995. The tigers—South Korea, Taiwan, Hong Kong and Singapore—grew their incomes from about 15 percent to about 70 percent of western levels while incomes in Africa and India were declining relative to those in the West; and the tigers' share of world exports went up five times while those of protectionist Africa and India fell. Even so, from 1989 onwards East Asia's financial intercourse with the rest of the world could be described as the moneyman's version of unsafe sex: thrilling, risky, addictive and possibly life-threatening.

As investors everywhere gradually became aware of the basic soundness of East Asia's economies, foreign money started pouring into the region. Between 1990 and the onset of the financial crisis in mid-1997 net private capital inflows to Asia amounted to $420 billion. In 1989–92 foreign capital flows to the four countries that were later worst hit by the crisis equaled 1.8 percent of their GDP; in 1993–96 the figure was 6.4 percent, with Thailand receiving the equivalent of 13 percent of its GDP in foreign capital flows in 1995.

If this bounty had been showered on Asia because of a cool calculation of its long-term prospects, that might have been one thing; but it was almost never because of that. One reason is that, in global terms, Asian financial markets outside Japan are minuscule. Chris Wood, the Asian strategist for ABN Amro, a big Dutch bank, in January 1999 concocted his "Jack & Bill" index, named for the heads of America's two biggest companies, comparing the combined market capitalization of every company on every Asian stock market outside Japan with the combined market capitalization of General Electric and Microsoft. The week the index was started, the whole of Asia was only 1.7 times bigger than these two American companies. Distant fund managers' decisions simply are not, on average, made with the same care for the minnows of Asia as for the whales of the West; conversely, even minor shifts in the allocation of money by Western fund managers can have huge consequences in Asia on the way up but even more so on the way down. However, the most important reason foreign money cascaded in during the early 1990s was that international markets grossly underestimated the risks of Asian investments. This miscalculation was abetted by several interlocking elements of financial policy in Asia, which also made it inevitable that, when the crunch came, foreign money would zoom out even faster than it had arrived.

The first piece of the puzzle is the way many East Asian countries managed their exchange rates in 1985–97. In 1985 the world's rich countries agreed in the Plaza Accord (named after the hotel in New York where the deal was struck) to drive down the value of the dollar against the yen and the Deutschemark. Around this time, the currencies of most Asian countries excluding Japan were tied to the dollar in a semi-fixed way.

In Hong Kong's case alone the link was rigid, a variety of the "currency board" exchange-rate system invented by Britain in the mid-nineteenth century for use in some of its imperial possessions. The basic idea of a currency board is to deprive a government of any control at all over money supply. The board is not a central bank but an automaton that takes in or releases supplies of domestic currency entirely at the behest of market demand for it. All adjustments in the economy are made through the automatic effect this has on money supply, interest rates and asset prices, none of it through movements in the exchange rate. The mechanism by which this works is that for every 7.8 Hong Kong dollar banknotes that are issued to the public one U.S. dollar has to deposited with the currency board (called the Hong Kong Monetary Authority). Reserves are thus always large enough to buy up every Hong Kong dollar banknote in circulation, so there is never any doubt that the exchange rate can be preserved provided that interest rates, property prices and so on are allowed to take the strain of adjustment. In practice this means that Hong Kong's short-term interest rates must slavishly track those of the reserve currency—i.e., Alan Greenspan sets Hong Kong's monetary policy whenever he sets America's.

Elsewhere in Asia—excepting Japan, Australia and New Zealand, whose currencies have long floated freely against other currencies—from the mid-1980s to July 1997 countries ran semi-fixed rates of exchange against the dollar. This meant that a rate was targeted, and central banks intervened in the currency markets to support it, but the rate could move as circumstances seemed to demand. Often the rates were remarkably steady—the Thai baht spent years at almost exactly 25 to the dollar—but even when there was movement (the Singapore dollar consistently rose, the Indonesian rupiah consistently fell) it occurred at a steady and predictable pace. Moreover, unlike in Hong Kong, the central banks elsewhere in Asia had a free hand to run an independent monetary policy, moving domestic money supply and interest rates to try and meet local economic conditions as well as keep the exchange rate where they wanted it. (A mistake in itself, see Chapter 6.)

This system had several important consequences. The biggest was that, as investors both domestic and foreign gained confidence in the predictability of Asian currencies against the dollar, they began to think there was little or no currency risk in holding locally-denominated assets. They also thought there was little interest-rate risk, since sharp movements to raise rates to protect the currencies seemed unlikely, and not much credit risk since exports and economies looked like they were going to boom forever. The apparent absence of credit risk was reinforced by the impression all investors had that no Asian government would allow the shareholders in Asian banks or big companies to suffer much even if something did go wrong. The existence of this "moral hazard," as it is called, made everyone bolder with their investment choices than they might otherwise have been. Lastly, the temptation to borrow from abroad thanks to this pleasant state of affairs was made all the more irresistible by the availability of the "carry trade." If you could borrow, say, yen at 2 percent interest and deposit it in a Thai bank at 7 percent or corporate bond at 10 percent, it was a lot of return for no work and (so it seemed) negligible risk.

Asia's magnetic attraction for foreign funds began to exert itself more strongly as, willy-nilly, much of Southeast Asia began liberalizing its financial systems and opening its capital accounts in the late 1980s and early 1990s. Under the guidance of some gung-ho free marketeers— known as the "Berkeley mafia" in recognition of where they had earned their economics PhDs—Indonesia in 1988 opened its banking system to all domestic comers; a decade later it had 240-odd banks. Although South Korea, China, Taiwan and India had at least partly closed capital accounts, and Singapore maintained a hawk-eyed vigilance on the speculative use of its currency by foreign bankers, Indonesia, Malaysia, Thailand and the Philippines opened their capital accounts completely (though the central banks in Malaysia and the Philippines kept a close watch on private foreign borrowings). A crucial element in the banking and capital-account liberalizations of 1987–97 in East Asia is that, contrary to the best expert theory, they were carried out before bank supervision and regulation were brought up to standard. In hindsight, the perils of allowing money to flow unimpeded to institutions with inadequate (or practically non-existent) official regulation were obvious.

Nothing better typified the let's-party era of international finance in Asia than the Bangkok International Banking Facility (BIBF). Set up in the early 1990s, the BIBF was designed to start building up Bangkok to take international lending business from other Asian financial centers, especially Hong Kong. For foreign banks the attraction was getting a toehold in a domestic market that looked increasingly appealing but where entry for foreigners had been highly restricted. But domestic banks, too, were allowed to sign up as BIBF banks. Once a bank had this status, it could borrow and lend without any geographic restriction, provided only that at least one leg of the transaction was offshore. What the government seemed to be hoping was that Thai-based banks would use the BIBF both to borrow and lend money outside Thailand, thus helping to turn Bangkok into an Asian financial center. This was a miscalculation. With virtually no restriction on the size or direction of transactions flowing through the BIBF, both foreign and domestic banks put most of their efforts into borrowing outside Thailand at low interest rates and lending inside the country at higher rates. By early 1997, some two-thirds of BIBF lending was of this type—aggravating the imbalances and risks that were building up anyway because of the nature of Thailand's (and most of the rest of Asia's) semi-fixed currency regime.

The composition of foreign capital flows into Asia also became more worrying as the 1990s wore on. In 1995 bank loans as a share of net capital inflows were above 100 percent in four Asia countries—China, India, Indonesia and Malaysia—and above 80 percent in Thailand and the Philippines. In the six years 1989–94 foreign banks' claims on Asia rose by about $230 billion; but in the next two and a half years alone, January 1995–July 1997, they rose by a further $200 billion. Unsurprisingly, foreign borrowings also accounted for an increasing share of domestic credit creation.

Several factors were behind this relentless rise in foreign bank lending to Asia. One is that, in the mid-1990s, rich-world banks had a lot of money sloshing around that they had to lend somewhere. Another is that Japanese banks in particular were making negligible returns at home and were following their industrial customers into the rest of Asia as they set up factories there. Third, many big European banks, with breathtakingly bad timing, decided in the mid-1990s that they had to go into Asia in a big way. Only the American banks kept a cool distance from the Asian fervor. All in all, by the end of 1996, according to the Bank for International Settlements, international banks had an exposure of $737 billion to East Asia. Of this the late-comer enthusiasts from Europe accounted for almost 45 percent ($318 billion), the Japanese for a little over a third ($261 billion) and the Americans for only 6 percent ($46 billion), with the other 15 percent scattered.

Whatever the causes, the growth and intensification of bank lending in Asian finance were bad news. As noted earlier, as a rule, banks are much less skilled than bond or stock markets at judging risk (but see the next section). Bank lending is very volatile (1) because bankers tend to hunt in packs, always prone to lend to the same companies and countries at the same time and to scurry out at the same time; and (2) because so much of the lending is short-term. The creditworthiness of borrowers (especially highly indebted ones, as most Asian borrowers were) is very sensitive to any quick or sharp rise in interest rates, which again puts a premium on lenders' getting their money out as fast as possible. Sure enough, the reversal of capital flows, when it came, was brutal. In 1996, some $90 billion in net private foreign capital flowed into Asia, and the figure rose in the first half of 1997 to $140 billion at an annual rate. In the second half of 1997, about $100 billion at an annual rate flowed *out* of Asia.

UNSTEADY, UNSAFE

An air of fantasy, fed by an astonishing degree of greed and arrogance, came to pervade every lender's perception of risk in Asia—including many who, though deeply familiar with Asia, foresaw nothing but endless smooth sailing. The most notorious example of this was the failure of a Hong Kong-based investment bank called Peregrine Investment Holdings. Set up in 1988 by Philip Tose, formerly of a brokerage called Vickers da Costa, and Francis Leung, ex-Citicorp, Peregrine boasted of being the first big-league Asian investment bank. Aggressive and fast-moving, it did establish itself by the mid-1990s as at least a match for the biggest American banks; Peregrine was always near the top of the underwriting league for share issues in Hong Kong, and in 1996 it was number one.

In 1994 Peregrine set up a fixed-income unit to underwrite and deal in local-currency bonds and other debt securities. Founded by Andre Lee, a 34-year-old American from Lehman Brothers with all of five years of financial market experience, the fixed-income unit quickly monopolized this business in Asia, taking big and hazardous positions for both itself and its clients. Backed to the hilt by Tose, Lee's 200-strong unit was in effect free from any internal risk controls—not that there were many at Peregrine anyway—let alone sophisticated ones of the sort American investment banks had come to use. In June 1997 Lee made a loan of $265 million of Peregrine's money to an Indonesian company deliciously named Steady Safe. The firm's only business was running a middling fleet of taxis in Jakarta—you can still see them on the road there in their cheerful yellow livery—but its 34-year old head had visions of building an Indonesian transport empire and (more important) allegedly had business connections with one of President Suharto's children. The loan amounted to more than a third of Peregrine's capital, and Lee mind-bogglingly made it without any security from the borrower and without taking any precautions against a possible decline in the Indonesian currency. Lee's thinking was to get the loan off Peregrine's books soon by floating securities in the bond market; but within weeks the rupiah had begun to collapse in the wake of the baht's fall, the Asian bond market was dead and Steady Safe had spent the money. In January 1998 Peregrine went bust with debts of some $1 billion.

Peregrine may have been unusually reckless, but whole global markets joined it in underestimating the risks in Asia. The difference in interest rates, or the yield spread, between U.S. Treasury bonds (the world's closest thing to a risk-free asset) and the bonds of other countries is considered the best measure of how risky the market reckons the other countries are. In 1996 the world's bond market was improbably rating the bonds of every Asian country about the same—making little differentiation between Hong Kong, China, Korea, Indonesia, or wherever. And the yield spread for all of them was a paltry one percentage point or so, suggesting that the market saw almost no risk in Asia—or at least that Asia was ten to fifteen times safer than Latin America.

This ignored not just the financial strains building throughout Asia but the fact that the region's economies were becoming less competitive. Between 1990 and 1996 hourly dollar labor costs in clothes manufacturing in East Asia went up by an average of around 10 percent a year (in Malaysia the figure was 23 percent). From 1985 to 1996 Korea's unit labor costs—a measure that compares increases in wages with increases in labor productivity—went up by more than 80 percent; in America in the same years the increase was about 10 percent. These changes had many local causes, like stronger labor unions and democratizing governments, but the biggest single one is that, ten years after the Plaza Accord and boosted by the power of the renascent American economy, the dollar began suddenly and sharply strengthening against the Deutschemark and the yen in 1995.

Yoked tightly to the dollar, Asian exchange rates began to appreciate (albeit modestly) in inflation-adjusted terms. Current-account deficits widened as, worst of all, the Asian export machine sputtered. For more than a generation, Asia's rise had been driven by year after year of double digit growth in exports. In 1990–95 Asian export growth averaged almost 16 percent a year in value terms. In 1996 growth was in single digits, often low ones, for every Southeast Asian country save the Philippines. This had complicated causes, including a slowdown in world semiconductor demand, but the fact was that the engine which had reliably driven Asian growth for 20 years had stopped working its annual miracle.

The other, more significant, fact was that, as in America 20 years before, Asian companies had stopped delivering even remotely adequate returns on the capital and assets they were deploying. The markets began shrieking that it was time to redeploy them.

The Annihilation of Value

Panics do not destroy capital; they merely reveal the extent to which it has been previously destroyed by its betrayal into hopelessly unproductive works.

—*John Stuart Mill*

The interplay of all the forces described in the previous chapter—abundant and cheap capital both domestic and foreign; institutional weaknesses; governments' industrial policies, cronyism and corruption; and a perception on the part of almost everyone that there was very little risk in the system—made it a sure thing that more money would be invested in Asia than could possibly make an adequate return. The resulting destruction of corporate and shareholder value is what will, over the next decade, compel the reform of Asian companies, financial markets and politics. Asia is going to have to find some way to deliver adequate returns on capital.

Asia hardly invented this process of boom, bust and reconstruction: it is the oldest story in the book. In fact, the very title of a nineteenth-century book on how the destruction of value happens—*Extraordinary Popular Delusions and the Madness of Crowds*—pretty much sums the matter up. The opening up of promising new regions, such as the Americas and Australia in the nineteenth century and Asia over the past 20 years, or of new industries, such as cars a century ago and the Internet today, invariably leads to a frenzy of overinvestment followed by a collapse and a retrenchment of capitalization to a level that makes economic sense. So much excess capacity was created during the American railway boom in the nineteenth century that it took 20 years to clean up, leaving uncounted British and other foreign investors with staggering losses. It started happening with the Internet in 2000, and in Asia three years earlier.

In Asia's case, the factors pushing excess investment began getting out of hand in the mid-1980s. Figure 3.1 shows how much faster investment was growing than economies were: between 1986 and 1997 East Asia's capital stock rose 420 percent while economies expanded by only 280 percent. Put another way, in 1980 Asia's capital investment as a share of GDP, at 27 percent, was only fractionally above the world average; just before the crisis broke, Asia's share was 36 percent of GDP, half again as high as the world average. You don't need an economics degree to understand that, when there is too much of even a good thing, its price sooner or later falls.

The "price" of a capital investment is actually the return on that investment. There are plenty of measures for returns and for additions to shareholder value—return on investment, return on capital employed, return on assets, return on equity, EVA (Economic Value Added), you name it—and it is hard to think of any such measure which did not deteriorate alarmingly

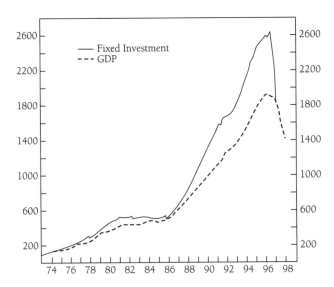

Figure 3.1 Asia: GDP and fixed investment. *Note:* Countries included: South Korea, Thailand, the Philippines, Singapore, Malaysia, Hong Kong, and Taiwan. Both series are denominated in U.S. dollar terms and rebased to 1974 = 100. (*Source: The BCA China Analyst,* February 1999)

for Asian companies between the mid-1980s and the mid-1990s. For instance, the World Bank has documented that, as the rate of capital investment grew in Thailand and South Korea between the last half of the 1980s and the first half of the 1990s, something called the incremental capital-output ratio increased sharply—meaning that to get each successive increase in output these countries had to put in larger and larger amounts of capital investment. There was less and less bang for each investment buck.

The most clear-cut sign of deterioration was in return on equity (ROE). Recall from Chapter 1 how important the movements in this relatively simple measure were in showing the decline and then the revival of the efficiency of American companies from the mid-1970s to the mid-1990s. Table 3.1 shows that, with few exceptions, over the same period Asian companies increasingly did worse than they had before. With American ROEs rising, this naturally meant that the gap between the corporate performance of America and that of Asia widened in the Americans' favor during the decade—often hugely.

This mattered in several ways. First, ROEs in most Asian countries fell so far in the early 1990s that the cost of capital was higher than the return on that capital. Like returns on capital, the cost of capital can be quite complicated to measure. Several elements enter into the calculation, including interest rates, various kinds of risk premiums including political and currency risk in the country where the company is located, and the relative shares of debt and equity in the company's overall sources of finance. But whatever the measure, it is clear that by 1995 large chunks of many industries in most Asian countries were paying more to finance their capital investments than those investments were generating in profits. It is obvious that, although such an imbalance can exist for some time, it cannot go on forever.

Second, corporate performance as measured by ROE is a strong guide to which companies will succeed and which will not. McKinsey & Company, a business consultancy, did a study of the 100 global companies that enjoyed the biggest increase in market capitalization in 1992–97. Market capitalization matters so much because, in a global economy, the size and value awarded to a company by the stock market allows the biggest companies to acquire other firms more easily and to exploit new markets with more of a cushion against the risk of expansion, while simultaneously protecting them against being taken over themselves. What the study found was that the growth in market capitalization of the

Table 3.1
Regional Financial Ratios, 1990–97

	Year	ROE (%)		Year	ROE (%)
China	90		Malaysia	90	10.8
	91			91	10.6
	92	12.8		92	10.7
	93	15.1		93	11.3
	94	12.7		94	12.5
	95	8.8		95	12.3
	96	7.5		96	12.0
	97	6.6		97	10.0
Hong Kong	90	11.4	Philippines	90	17.9
	91	12.2		91	16.7
	92	12.8		92	14.0
	93	12.0		93	19.8
	94	11.1		94	14.8
	95	10.8		95	13.8
	96	10.0		96	14.3
	97	12.0		97	11.4
Indonesia	90	15.3	Singapore	90	7.9
	91	13.7		91	9.1
	92	12.2		92	8.0
	93	12.4		93	10.0
	94	12.2		94	9.8
	95	13.4		95	10.2
	96	13.7		96	10.3
	97	9.7		97	7.5
India	90	23.4	Thailand	90	18.0
	91	13.9		91	18.4
	92	12.4		92	18.1
	93	11.9		93	14.4
	94	13.5		94	14.7
	95	15.5		95	13.5
	96	18.5		96	8.9
	97	19.5		97	−22.8
Korea	90	6.6	Taiwan	90	11.8
	91	8.5		91	13.3
	92	5.8		92	10.6
	93	5.0		93	11.0
	94	7.3		94	12.4
	95	8.6		95	12.1
	96	1.2		96	10.0
	97	−2.8		97	10.2

(*Source:* Rajiv Lall, Warburg Pincus)

world's most successful companies was due in only a minor way to increases in their book value—their mostly physical assets as reflected on the balance sheet. The lion's share of the growth came from a rise in the ratio of a firm's market value to book value. In a way this ratio is roughly a measure of how much better than average the market thinks a company is run. The rule of thumb used to be that the ratio should be about one, since a firm's value ought to reflect its asset base. McKinsey's 100 companies doubled their ratio to 4.2 between 1992 and 1997, or twice the average of listed American companies in the later year. (At one point in 1999 the ratio of market to book value for Microsoft was 24.)

Where did the doubling of this ratio come from? A bit of it from growth in the profits of these companies. Far more important, the McKinsey study found, was ROE. Companies with high ROEs vastly increased their market capitalization, whereas those with fast earnings growth but indifferent ROEs did only okay. Of course, if you can both grow profits fast and have a high ROE, "you can propel your market capitalization off the map"—you can be Microsoft or General Electric. This study did not bear directly on Asia—except that almost 60 percent of the world's best-performing companies were American and only 11 percent Asian, most of them Japanese—but it showed what Asia in general, with its dismally declining ROEs, was up against on global markets in the 1990s. Investors in a global economy do not smile on shrinking ROEs.

And globalization was indeed upon Asia. As explained in Chapter 2, much of East Asia in the 1980s and 1990s opened itself to global flows of capital as well as of goods and services. The openness of the world's financial markets is hard to measure precisely, but one good clue they have become more open in the last decade or so is that returns on financial assets worldwide, which used to diverge a lot, have started to narrow to a single level. As one analysis of the Asian crisis in 1997 put it, "Increased capital flows to developing economies have created pressure to narrow the variation of a country's risk-adjusted returns on capital with those of the rest of the world. Any excessive valuation of a country's financial assets relative to the 'world level' becomes increasingly unsustainable, provoking a converging process."

In such an environment, Asia's increasingly poor relative performance was bound to be punished—even for countries like China, India and Taiwan that traditionally have had more or less closed capital accounts, and Malaysia, which closed the door only in 1998. The reason is that it is not only inward flows of capital that matter. These countries, particularly China, have substantial excess savings; and while the bulk of the population, at least in China and India, have limited opportunities for sending money abroad for investment, there is substantial money at the margin that can find its way out if returns at home are not up to those abroad. In Taiwan, for instance, each person is free to transfer as much as $5 million out of the country each year. And despite China's supposedly strict controls on capital movements, the "errors and omissions" line its balance of payment accounts reveals that in recent years as much as $25 billion a year has been spirited out of China for investment elsewhere.

ROE is not a magic potion for any country. Hong Kong's ROEs are high by regional standards and it has a long history of good economic performance. Yet although the Philippines and India have ROEs at Hong Kong's level, over the past few decades they have turned in some of the worst records for economic growth and rising living standards. Taiwan, by contrast, which in many ways has Asia's best-balanced economy and an unsurpassed record for boosting incomes, has lower ROEs than India and the Philippines. Nonetheless, at the corporate level and as a basis for investment decisions ROEs have become a vital sign of competitiveness in the world economy.

Yet the attitudes toward shareholder value and the aim of the firm that are embodied in the pursuit of high ROEs have been conspicuously lacking among the big listed Asian companies that outsiders have heard of and governments have tried to promote. (As noted before, the story is entirely different for smaller firms whose efficiency is ruthlessly monitored by the informal financial markets where they tend to get their funding.) In May 1997, just a month before the financial crisis broke, Hugh Peyman, then the Singapore-based Asian strategist for the Dresdner Kleinwort Benson investment bank, did an interesting exercise. Arguing that the old Asian corporate model had outlived its usefulness and was going to have to be replaced, he put together a comprehensive list of Asian firms which at that point could meet the "value-investing" philosophy of America's Warren Buffett. The rough idea is to make a few big investments in well-understood and well-managed firms that substantially raise shareholder value over time with relatively little risk, and then hold them. Peyman's criterion was Asian "stocks that provide 15 percent to 20 percent earnings-per-share returns annually over five years without causing investors any loss of sleep." Among all the listed Asian companies outside Japan, Peyman found that only 13 Asian firms passed muster—and one of those, HSBC, although listed on the Hong Kong stock market, was really a western multinational with a big part of its business in Asia. Why were profitability and shareholder value of so little interest for so long to the overwhelming majority of Asian managers?

DAMN THE SHAREHOLDERS, FULL SPEED AHEAD

In January 1998 foreign investors with a sense of humor were delightedly faxing each other the text of an interview that "must be read to be believed." Kentaro Aikawa, the chairman of Mitsubishi Heavy Industries, told *Nikkei Sangyo Shimbun,* an industrial daily, that "we'll be in trouble if the theories of Harvard Business School are brought to Japan. . . . I have always said that Mitsubishi management values jobs before profit. Lately, I've become surer than ever that this thinking is correct. We don't give a hoot about things like return on equity." After all, Aikawa added, "It is essential that our business practices take social effects into consideration." When told that in America shareholders would complain about such a strategy, Aikawa responded, "That's why I openly brag that I don't cater to shareholders. . . . We don't need to advertise to get foreigners to buy our shares. If shareholders don't like us, they should hurry up and get rid of us."

It is all there: the commitment to workers and the indifference to shareholders, the concern with broader social goals and the xenophobia. To many minds, these are the qualities that define the Japanese corporate model—and indeed the Asian model more generally. Certainly, they remained predominant enough that, measured by ROE, Japan in the mid-1990s was the rich world's most inefficient deployer of capital. By 1998 the ROE for the Tokyo stock market was down to 3.5 percent. A year later the ROE for companies in the Tokyo market's Topix index (the most representative index) was 1.1 percent, less than one-twentieth the American level. In many Japanese industries, especially construction and property, returns were actually negative. By one calculation, at the end of 1997 just over 40 percent of the companies on the main board of the Tokyo Stock Exchange had book values higher than their market capitalization—in other words, close to half of Japan's blue-chip companies would have been worth more broken up and sold off than intact. A year later the proportion would have been even higher.

As explained in Chapter 2, this locking up of value within increasingly inefficient companies was made possible for so long by the availability in Asia of capital that was too cheap and abundant. But the fact that the credit taps were turned full on did not mean everybody had to keep drinking; there were plenty of Asian companies that obeyed the disciplines of global investment markets. They were few, however, and for the most part chose this route because a big slice of their shareholder base was western or their top management had American business experience. It is important to understand the motivations that drove the large majority who, like Mitsubishi Heavy's Aikawa, did not buy into the idea of shareholder value at all, since the forces that shaped those motivations are not about to disappear with a snap of the fingers. Three such forces were especially important: social consciousness, the priority given to sales and asset growth, and the strength of conglomerates in Asian business life.

The social component should not be underestimated, nor should it be thought of as peculiarly Asian. Recall from Chapter 1 that the head of America's blue-chip Conference Board spoke as late as the mid-1980s along lines that were virtually indistinguishable from, albeit less colorful than, those of Japan's Aikawa. Besides, the concern in Asian companies for the fate of the firm's "family" of employees has deep roots in the way all people think about social life.

Paul Romer, an economist at Stanford Business School, has been trying to bring a shocking amount of reality into economic theory by incorporating the obvious but hard-to-objectify idea that people put at least as much stock in "feeling" as they do in "thinking," and that any remotely plausible explanation of economic behavior needs to take account of this. He points out that the massive superiority of free markets of every kind for the efficient creation of wealth and higher incomes cannot erase the fact that markets operate on cold principles that deeply violate what people instinctively sense should be the ethics of behavior in social groups. Just think about the family, which has always been the fundamental unit of human society and even today everywhere on earth almost entirely rejects market principles (or democratic ones for that matter) in its internal workings. People can be persuaded that markets make sense from a broad perspective, but the cruelty of markets usually revolts them at a personal level. "No wonder the Asians are resisting [change]," Romer told me in the spring of 1998. "Bankruptcy is like throwing old people to the wolves." It should be kept in mind that, even as Asian companies are forced to change to deliver better shareholder value, the way they handle their human relations within the firm and often between the firm and outsiders will continue to reflect a particular cultural view of social duty and obligation.

Second, Asian companies have been obsessed with asset and sales growth. Again, this is an attitude that, however unfamiliar to American business in the 1990s, was commonplace in America of the 1960s, an era when a company's assets determined its market capitalization, when managers were rewarded by salaries and bonuses based often on company growth rather than by options whose value depended on stock prices, and when conglomerates were revered. In Asia the focus on growth, particularly of assets, had begun early, just as the region was taking off in the 1960s and 1970s, but became especially intense in the early 1990s.

A Boston Consulting Group (BCG) study of Asian manufacturing found extraordinarily high asset growth, often highest in lines of business whose return on equity was not only substantially below the cost of capital but falling further all the time—meaning the less profitable a business became, the more its managers invested in it. BCG's selection of Korean companies, all but one of which was unprofitable, grew their assets on average by 31 percent a year between 1994 and 1997. The comparable figure for Indonesian companies in 1993–96 was 42 percent a year, with the biggest and least profitable sector (cement) "enjoying" asset growth of 50 percent a year. Thailand's figure in 1994–96 was almost 40 percent a year. Moreover, cash-flow margins and asset turnover—the two sources of profitability—were shrinking. This meant that the 20 percent to 40 percent annual increases in capital investment during these years were vastly above what cash-flow from operations could have financed (26 percentage points below in Korea's case, 31 points below in Indonesia), so ever increasing amounts of debt had to fill the gap.

What could these businesses have been thinking (as noted before, investors in and lenders to them were not thinking)? One of the reasons for the focus on size and growth is that this was a central element in the industrial policies of many Asian governments—which helps to explain why there was so much bank credit to back it. Sometimes, as in Japan and Korea, the motive was to build an industrial base to compete internationally; in Malaysia it was to build a class of powerful businessmen for racial and political reasons; a strong influence in many countries, certainly in the early days of Asia's rise, was the thinking that fast capital accumulation was needed to raise income levels broadly and quickly. As an unsavory addendum almost everywhere, there was the desire to build a large source of ready cash for ruling parties or their leaders. Whatever the motive, fast asset and revenue growth rather than profitability seemed the best way to achieve it.

Yet for the companies themselves, there were also sound reasons for following this path. Owners, usually families (except in Japan), were getting plenty rich anyway and had a keen desire to build corporate empires. Managers' incentives, like those in America in the 1960s, were designed with scant attention to profitability or share-price performance. Perhaps most significant, during an extended period of fast economic and market growth it makes sense to pay more attention to expanding a business and grabbing market share in new businesses than to profitability; if the growth continues, profitability will often take care of itself provided a big enough market position has been secured. If this rings a more recent bell it should: this is precisely the business model America's Internet companies were following in the late 1990s when profitability counted for nothing and expansion of the business for everything. (The only difference between the Internet and Asia being that instead of buying their breakneck growth with bank debt, Internet companies have used their enormous stock-market capitalizations—Internet shareholders beware the fate of Asian banks.) If, as seems likely, Asia's economies and markets again start growing at two or three times the pace in the rich world, a lot of these reasons for fast asset and sales growth will again seem persuasive.

Lastly, many of these anti-shareholder tendencies were strengthened by the power of conglomerates in Asian business. By the time of the Asian crisis conglomerates accounted for 80 percent of Korea's market capitalization, 40 percent of Indonesia's and 25 percent to 30 percent of Thailand's and Malaysia's; the figure in America and Britain was about 10 percent. A conglomerate—which can roughly be defined as the collection of a large number of quite unrelated businesses under a single management—has become almost a dirty word among American investors. The glaring exception, of course, is General Electric, which officials of Asian conglomerates (particularly South Korea's *chaebol*) point to as proof that there is no reason they too can't keep a diversified fistful of businesses. But there are conglomerates and conglomerates. A study by McKinsey & Company in 1999 constructed a "conglomerate index" that multiplied together such factors as the number of "standard industry code" lines of business the firm is involved in, the number of subsidiaries for each, the revenue from each line of business and so on. The most diverse score possible was 100, the least 1. Focused companies like Microsoft and Canon had scores of 9. Rich-world conglomerates such as GE averaged 37. Asian conglomerates on average were about as twice as diverse as that, at 69, with the most focused about a third more diverse than a rich-world conglomerate and the five most diverse with stratospheric scores above 80 (see Figure 3.2).

Quantifying the extent of diversification—conglomerate index 1 to 100 with 1 the least diversified.

* BTR, GE, Emerson
** Canon, Microsoft

Figure 3.2   Corporate diversification. (*Source:* Annual reports, McKinsey analysis)

If GE's moderate diversity has clearly done no harm, the extreme diversity of Asian conglomerates has even more clearly done no good. In 1996, according to McKinsey, the spread between the return on capital and the cost of capital for almost every Asian conglomerate was negative—in at least two cases by double-digit percentage points. That year the same figure for GE was positive, by a huge 20 percentage points. It is true that conglomerates can do fine, provided they have extremely tight and sophisticated management disciplines from their centers. The modest share of conglomerates in America's market capitalization shows how hard it is, in even the most advanced economy, to meet those conditions.

In Asia the conditions were the reverse. The sprawl of businesses in an Asian conglomerate was at best very lightly controlled from the center. In fact, in the absence of most internal financial controls on what the various units were up to, the units of the conglomerate that were doing best were punished by having to support their weaker brethren through cross-shareholdings and off-balance-sheet cross-guarantees. The other side of this perverse coin is that the worst units did best in terms of capturing corporate resources. For example, the BCG study mentioned earlier found that at one Korean conglomerate in the early 1990s 75 percent of the investment was "allocated to underperforming businesses growing at unsustainable rates."

Yet, once again, in the Asian environment of 1965–1995 it is understandable that conglomerates should have thrived. In addition to the financial advantages and regulatory protections given by government patronage, conglomerates had an edge in acquiring scarce resources such as skilled labor (until just recently almost every top university graduate in Japan and Korea expected to go to a big firm and stay there). Conglomerates were also well-placed to realize operating efficiencies and economies of scale in countries plagued by weak institutions and small markets. This is why the McKinsey study found an exact negative correlation between a country's level of institutional development—measured by such things as an objective rule of law and transparent financial markets—and the dominance of conglomerates in the economy, with the institutionally weakest countries being the most conglomerate-intensive. In Asia a respected and recognized name mattered for all sorts of things from government contacts to consumer confidence to investor confidence—all of which were easier for a firm with size and scope to secure.

The power of such respect was immense: the McKinsey study found that in pre-crisis days conglomerates had much better stock-market performance than the index as a whole in Indonesia, Malaysia, Thailand and the Philippines. This was all based on trust, however. Investors' faith in the future growth of Asian conglomerates contributed an astonishing 76 percent to their pre-crisis stock-market capitalization, with current earnings accounting for only 24 percent. With the loss of faith following the crash of 1997–98, these positions were swapped: by late 1998 hopes for future growth accounted for only 23 percent of a conglomerate's market capitalization, actual performance for the rest. What this meant was that, to survive, Asian conglomerates would have to be run in a very different way so that they could deliver profits now rather than in the never-never. Nowhere would the shift have to be more radical than in Korea.

IN THE STRANGE KINGDOM OF THE *CHAEBOL*

Anyone who travels much in Asia knows that Koreans are the most extreme people on the continent: intense, proud, passionate, nationalistic, determined, hard-working but also hard-drinking, blunt, and with an undercurrent of violence that is not far beneath the surface. (It is the only place in Asia where I regularly see fist fights on the streets.) Connoisseurs of such matters add that Korean women are the most fiery and beautiful in Asia, their pugnacity perhaps not unconnected with the fact that they are the most discriminated against in Asia. Some Americans had an early taste of the Koreans' fierceness and toughness during the Vietnam war, when Korean contingents were sent to fight alongside the American army. One ex-GI told me that the only nights he could sleep well were when Korean soldiers were guarding the camp perimeter: the Vietnamese were so scared of the Koreans' bloodthirsty ferocity in battle that they just stayed away. It comes as no surprise, then, that Korea's economic development from the 1960s to the 1990s was also marked by extremism and willfulness: which is why the crisis presented it with perhaps the biggest challenge in Asia.

The story of Korea's rise is well-known. Formally colonized by Japan in 1910, brutalized during the Pacific war both by the fighting and by being forced to furnish labor (including sex slaves) to the Japanese, then flattened by the Korean war, South Korea in 1960 looked like it was on its deathbed. But in the 35 years after a military coup brought General Park Chung Hee to power in 1961, South Korea had one of the best economic records in the world. The economy grew by more than 8 percent a year in real terms, expanding 16-fold over this period and making the smallish country of 45 million people the world's eleventh biggest economy. This process lifted Koreans in 1996 to incomes of more than $10,000 each and gave their country the prestige of membership that year in the Organization for Economic Cooperation and Development (OECD), the rich-countries' club. It was an export-driven rise, with annual increases during 1960–80 of around 40 percent. The nominal value of exports in 1996 was almost 4,000 times bigger than it had been 35 years earlier, and by then South Korea was the world's twelfth biggest trading country.

All this was built on a government-led push to create businesses big enough to compete on the world stage—particularly against the Japanese, whose model of corporate development the Koreans had carefully studied. Firmly under the government's thumb, Korea's banks were directed to channel the country's large and captive savings (the capital account was largely closed until recently) to favored borrowers. The method Korea chose created one of the world's most concentrated industrial structures. Korean conglomerates, or *chaebol,* control unparalleled amounts of manufacturing industry (as well as of market capitalization, see above). Just before the crisis the top 30 *chaebol* accounted for 40 percent of value-added in manufacturing (a measure that eliminates double-counting at the different stages of the manufacturing process and so is more accurate than a raw figure for share of output—which would be over 60 percent). The top five *chaebol*—Hyundai, Samsung, Daewoo, LG and SK—alone accounted for almost three-quarters of that value-added figure, and for virtually all of corporate net profits.

As the crisis approached, the degree of concentration was rising: the top 30's share of value-added had doubled in ten years, as had the top 5's share of that share. The range of businesses in which each *chaebol* dabbled had also been swelling, until in 1997 each of the top five operated on average in 140 distinct lines of business. As the system became more concentrated, it also became more hostile to overseas influence. Chang Dae Whan, a businessman who heads Maeil Business Newspapers, told me that in the 1970s Korea was beginning to experiment with the idea of opening industrial parks to attract foreign direct investors and their expertise. By the mid-1980s all such ideas had been squashed, the victim of dinosaur syndrome and the rising power of labor unions (in an increasingly corporatist state they were good friends with the *chaebol,* theatrical street demonstrations by apparently angry workers notwithstanding. By the 1990s Korea was taking in less foreign direct investment relative to its size even than Japan.

Decades on steroids made the Korean economy increasingly less productive. The productivity of capital fell by an average of 4.7 percent a year from 1970 to 1995. Labor productivity by the mid-1990s was half as good as Japan's and a third as good as America's. Combine the two and, by 1998, whenever Korea applied the same amount of labor and capital as America did it got half as much output. Korea's position in service industries (a proxy for the efficiency of the domestic economy) and in technology was even worse. Korea's service industries were about 80 percent as productive as manufacturing, a figure not only vastly inferior to ratios in the rich world but below even Thailand's and Malaysia's. Distribution costs as a share of revenues were a third higher than in America (a much richer and more spread-out economy) and almost twice as high as China's. Korea's technology-trade ratio—license fees received from foreigners over those paid to foreigners—was 9 percent, compared with Japan's 43 percent and America's 406 percent. Perfectly understandable for a poor country, but Korea was no longer poor. Instead it was, as one study put it, caught in a nutcracker between high-wage but technology-intensive and high-productivity Japan and low-wage, low-productivity China. Korea increasingly combined relatively high wages with low technological prowess and low productivity. It was a disastrous combination.

It certainly was for Korean companies. In June 1997 (six months before Korea slipped into crisis) Rhee Namuh, now head of research at Samsung Securities, did a study of 38 prominent listed Korean companies to see how they performed on such measures of efficiency and value creation as return on capital and Economic Value Added (EVA, among whose fans is Jack Welch). The results were overwhelmingly negative. In the previous six years sales had risen by an average of 18 percent a year while earnings per share had gone up by a trifling 1 percent a year. Some 70 percent of the companies had a market value at or below their book value (i.e., they should be broken up), "which is not surprising given that most have destroyed value and should continue to do so." Every year in the 1990s the return on capital was below the cost of capital by 2 to 4 percentage points (or 30 percent to 45 percent), a huge gap that was projected to last as far as the eye could see. The EVA spread—which measures whether a firm is creating or destroying shareholder value—was also negative every year, even in the cyclical boom year of 1995. Since, over time, movements in share prices should closely track movements in EVA, it is no surprise that from 1992 to 1997 other Asian stock markets outperformed Korea's by half.

The heads of the *chaebol* were utterly indifferent to this. For one thing, their universal aim was to build business empires rather than reward shareholders. As long as debt was available to support this aim—and by early 1998 Korea Inc had managed to run up $500 billion in debt, equal to 165 percent of the country's 1997 GDP—shareholders were an irrelevance. The more so since they were powerless. Thanks to the loose organizational structure of the *chaebol,* to cross-shareholdings and to cross-guarantees, the *chaebol* heads were able to control group affiliates by holding on average only 5.4 percent of the shares in them. Competition from upstarts was never an issue (with the same business values and goals, other *chaebol* posed fierce operational competition but no financial competition at all). Even the old Korea did spawn some interesting business rebels (one will be discussed in Chapter 9) but they could mount no more than hit-and-run guerrilla raids on the vast conglomerates for which profitability was of no concern. Lastly, the peculiar sociology of the *chaebol* ensured that challenges from within to the traditional ways of doing business would be squelched.

Despite their often titanic size, all the *chaebol* were family firms under the autocratic control of the founder or his sons. In early 1998, of the top 30 *chaebol* 29 were under the chairmanship of a family member (and the one that was not was only the second in more than 30 years to have come, even temporarily, under a non-family chairman). The handling of even multibillion dollar businesses was often dictated by intrafamily rancor and rivalries that no soap-opera scriptwriter could have improved upon. An upstart businessman who had the temerity to divorce the granddaughter of the founder of one of the top *chaebol* found not only that he had to move the headquarters of his business outside the country if he hoped to do any more business, but that Korean newspapers would not carry advertising for his second wife's recordings (she was an actress and singer). At one fallen *chaebol* I know, an American-educated daughter with some moderately western ideas about how to run things was given joint responsibility for the business with an older brother. Thwarted at every turn, she appealed to her father, who told her "your ideas are right, but you have to obey your older brother because he is your older brother."

A more public example of fraternal bliss was the case of Milton Kim. In the mid-1990s he was the CEO of Ssangyong Investment & Securities, an affiliate of the Ssangyong Group, traditionally the sixth biggest *chaebol*. No visitor to his spacious modern office (as I was a few times), in Seoul's financial district in the south of the city, could doubt that the elegantly tailored

CEO, with his flawless English and a copy in hand of his latest speech to a group of financial analysts in San Diego or wherever, was American-educated. In fact, he was American-born and had spent 17 years in America and Europe, among other things studying international relations and French at Brown University and putting in a stint at Citibank.

As Milton was becoming cosmopolitan, the Ssangyong Group was being run by his brother Suk Won, 16 years Milton's senior. Suk Won, the eldest of three sons, had been chairman since their father's death in 1975; he was of the old mold and ran the group to grow it as fast as possible. In the two decades after he took over, sales expanded 18,000 percent in nominal terms and the number of subsidiaries rose from five to 22. In the mid-1980s Suk Won succumbed to the habitual vainglory of *chaebol* heads and decided that Ssangyong too must have a car company. This dream is what devoured most of the group's revenues over the next decade. Meanwhile, in 1990, Milton returned to Korea to join the group's brokerage arm, becoming its CEO five years later. To the horror of old Ssangyongers (including his brother), he began whipping Ssangyong Securities into American shape, bringing in merit-based pay and hiring a straight-talking American—who thought the Korean corporate system was a disaster waiting to happen—as head of research.

By 1997 the group's financial position was untenable. Milton had unsuccessfully been urging rationalization on the group; the Asian crisis made this, even for a Korean firm, unavoidable. First went the paper unit, sold to Procter & Gamble, then the car project. Oil refining and odds and ends were in the works when Milton moved in early 1998 to sell the brokerage to American interests. The brothers fought over this for most of the year, until Suk Won at last relented and allowed the transfer of the group's controlling interest in Ssangyong Securities to H&Q Asia Pacific, a unit of San Francisco's Hambrecht & Quist Group. Shockingly for Koreans, Milton stayed with the transferred firm instead of dutifully joining another unit of what was left of the family's *chaebol*. By this point the brothers were utterly estranged even as Ssangyong was unwillingly being yanked into modern form more than any other big conglomerate. Even if the restructuring works, Milton is finished as a *chaebol* hand—in fact in 2000 he left the securities firm to join a start-up—and his brother will feel like a failure.

In the midst of such strife, in Korea and elsewhere in Asia, what almost no one seemed to realize was just how extraordinarily strong a foundation for future growth had been laid by the apparently preposterous policies of the previous 30 years. Debates among economists can (and surely will) run endlessly about whether a largely free-market path to development, like the one Hong Kong followed, or a more *dirigiste* one, along Japanese or Korean lines, is best for a poor country to follow as it tries to drag itself out of poverty.

The fact is that, in all of the countries that composed the now momentarily derided "Asian miracle," two generations of very fast growth have created a lot to work with—accumulated capital and, far more important, human capital in the form of a better educated and experienced workforce than anyone would have dreamed possible 20 years ago. This is as true, at different levels, of China and Indonesia as it is of Japan, Korea and Taiwan. If Korea was as much of a buffoon at development as the details cited in this section seem to imply, why was it the place whose assets western investors were keenest to get their hands on as the Asian crisis unfolded? The solution to the paradox is this. The old Asian system created immense potential value, by whatever means, but that old system is finished. Which places in Asia can now make the transition to a new, more global and more market-based framework will be the ones that can most profit from the value created by two generations of hard work. Which will find it easier to remake themselves—the Koreas or the Hong Kongs—is still unclear (see Chapter 9) but, as always in modern Asia, Japan has had to cope with the question first. And, in the early 1990s, Japan led the way—backward.

PART TWO

THE RESPONSE

CHAPTER

4

The Japanese
Counter-Revolution

I t is hard to think of a recent subject about which more garbage has
been written, mostly by American journalists, than Japan in the second half of the 1980s. Mirroring the then fashionable belief that
America was in irreversible decline, the view of many of these observers
was that the tightly controlled Japanese system was going to be unchal-
lengeable and unchanging. America had better learn quickly or
would be left behind in the managed-economy era that was inevitably
coming. The Japanese, buoyed in their optimism by the late-1980s performance of their economy and stock market, shared this high opinion
of themselves.

At the thinking man's end of the scale stood Eisuke Sakakibara, a
finance-ministry bureaucrat who in the mid-1990s was to become famous as "Mr. Yen," the international-finance official who with the flick
of a word could move billions in the foreign-exchange markets within
minutes. Sakakibara, who ironically for a defender of the traditional
Japanese way is a cosmopolitan intellectual with a taste for public give-
and-take, argued forcefully that Japan should maintain its successful
and different system of "employee sovereignty" against any American effort to change it, especially since a "stable and successful society" feels
no need to reform. At the absurd end of the scale was a supercilious
Japanese stockbroker who in 1989 told a British journalist who had the
nerve to ask when stock prices would fall, "You must understand that
whereas other countries live in a Newtonian universe where the normal

laws of gravity apply, the Japanese market has learned how to function in an Einsteinian universe where they do not."

Everyone now knows what came next. The Tokyo stock market peaked on December 31, 1989 with the most widely quoted index at about 40,000. By its low point in 1998, the Tokyo market had fallen by 70 percent. Applied to Japan, Chris Wood's Jack & Bill index (see Chapter 3) showed that Tokyo's market capitalization was 48 times that of GE and Microsoft in 1990 but only 3.8 times in mid-1999, a 12-fold relative decline. For the Japanese economy the whole of the 1990s was a disaster. Despite occasional spurts of recovery, Japan's GDP grew during the 1990s by only about 0.5 percent a year, less than a fifth of the American rate and a third that of the European Union. During this period Japan never experienced a currency panic or sharp economic contraction of the sort that devastated the rest of Asia in 1997–98. But the slow-motion collapse of Japan in the 1990s, especially when put alongside America's accelerating rise, had a deep impact in Asia and beyond.

One reason is that in economics, finance and business, Japan has an overwhelming predominance in Asia and a bigger significance for the rich world than the rest of Asia put together. In dollar terms, its economy is the world's second biggest and accounts for about 70 percent of the Asian total. It is the world's third biggest trading nation (after America and Germany). It has $11 to $12 trillion in personal financial assets, about 80 percent of Asia's total, is the world's biggest exporter of capital, and in 1999 held more than $300 billion of U.S. Treasury bonds and $1 trillion of net overseas assets. On any numerical scale, Japan weighs heavily.

It also weighs heavily in Asia in terms of the example it sets. Japan was the model, copied consciously or not, for the economic development of much of the rest of modern Asia. By a full seven years Japan also prefigured the Asian crash of 1997–98. As Japan began to implode in the early 1990s Chris Wood, one of the best watchers of Japanese finance at the time in his role as a Tokyo correspondent for *The Economist*, wrote that the crash was sure to change Japan profoundly and for the better:

> The corporatist management of the economy that has prevailed in Japan since 1945 has not always done so; the country is not culturally programmed in some mysterious way to manage its affairs in this fashion. . . . [T]here are plenty of signs that Japan has again entered a period of convergence with the West, just as it did in the 1920s . . . It is the contention here that Japan will converge substantially with the West, though naturally it will do so in its own

fashion, and that the convergence will occur quicker than most expect, precisely because of the intensity of the economic slowdown, the shocks to the existing system that it will pose, and the market pressures that it will unleash in terms of the need for radical change.

The analysis was impeccable but the prediction was wrong. The system's powers of resistance were immensely strong. By 1999 a near-decade's worth of recession had seemingly budged the "corporatist management" of the country hardly at all. Japan's resistance to change, and the ways in which it at last did begin to change, show how difficult, complex but ultimately inevitable a transformation of the rest of Asia is likely to be.

BUBBLE AND PRICK

If the Plaza Accord of 1985 helped sow the seeds of the trouble that overwhelmed the rest of Asia more than a decade later, its harmful effects in Japan were felt almost at once. The Japanese fish-trap described by Andrew Sheng (see Chapter 2) was at its most powerful in its country of origin. As the yen began rising against the dollar, the Bank of Japan, the country's central bank, started lowering short-term interest rates to try to contain the yen's rise. In 1986 alone the official discount rate was halved to 2.5 percent. Since in those days Japan still had some modest inflation, this meant that real interest rates were close to zero. Moreover, with the stock market and the yen both rising, it was a simple matter for companies to raise equity capital cheaply at home—which they did to the tune of almost $650 billion from 1985 to 1990—and cash for expansion even more cheaply abroad by issuing dollar-denominated debt with stock warrants attached. Because the capital of Japanese banks consists substantially of shareholdings, the banks were in a position to expand their lending enormously. By the end of the 1980s the corporate sector's debt had risen to some 275 percent of GDP, half again as high as the comparable figure in America. Consumer debt went up seven-fold in the 12 years ending in 1991.

All this seemingly free money found its way into the usual repositories described in Chapters 2 and 3: the stock market, real estate and overinvestment in factories and equipment. By December 31, 1989, Japan's stock market capitalization equaled 150 percent of GDP, a five-fold increase in ten years (a frightening figure in those days, though the combined market capitalization of the New York Stock Exchange and NASDAQ in mid-1999 was almost 170 percent of America's GDP). As the 1990s dawned, the theoretical value of real estate in Japan was $20 trillion, five times as much as America's in a country with half as many people as the United States and a land area about the size of California. Throughout the 1980s Japan invested 18 percent to 20 percent of GDP in plant and equipment, compared with about 10 percent in other rich countries—and with a predictable effect on profitability. ROE declined continually in the two decades after 1980, falling from rough parity with the American level in the early 1980s to as little as one-twentieth of the American level at one point in 1999. Not once in the ten years after 1989 was the return on capital in Japan higher than the cost of capital.

The Bubble Economy, as everyone in Japan came to call the result of the late 1980s excesses, was pricked in January 1990. It was more than nine years before it at last seemed to stop deflating. The first casualty was the Tokyo stock market, which in the first nine months of 1990 lost almost half its value; in more or less the twinkling of an eye, some $2.2 trillion in paper wealth was destroyed. During the same period the bond market fell 15 percent. By the time the bloodletting in the property market was stanched late in the decade, the entire stock of real estate was worth perhaps 40 percent of what it had been a decade before and prices were down 85 percent from their peak.

Japan was the victim of a debt deflation the like of which had not been seen since the 1930s. Deflation—which is a fall in the overall consumer or wholesale price level in an economy—does not have to be damaging. During much of the last 30 years of the nineteenth century Europe and North America experienced deflation and strong economic growth at the same time; and the most familiar case of falling prices in the present day, the relentless decline of cost and rise of performance in computers and telecoms, is universally recognized as one of the greatest boons to the modern economy. A debt deflation, however, which happened pretty much worldwide in the 1930s and in Japan in the early 1990s, is both terribly destructive and hard to control. It takes place when asset prices, like those of stocks and property, increase far beyond what is justified by the fundamentals of profit growth and supply and demand. They need to be reduced, and the overcapacity of factories and the like that accompanies them must be shrunk, but this shrinkage is tricky to manage because companies and individuals have become heavily indebted and find they have to pay down their debts just when the collapse in asset prices has greatly reduced their wealth. In extreme cases, if prices are falling fast enough, the more a firm tries to pay off its debts the more its debt burden rises. The real value of its income cannot keep up with the growth in the real value of its debt, and a vicious downward spiral of falling prices and shrinking economic activity can ensue.

THE POLICY ENIGMA

The Japanese government's policy choices in this environment were disastrously wrong. As early as 1992 John Greenwood, a well-known monetary economist and Japan expert who designed Hong Kong's currency system in the 1980s, was warning that monetary policy was too tight for the disinflationary pressures the Japanese economy was coming under (eight years later, in the summer of 2000, he thought it was still too tight). The origin of the tight-money approach was the realization by Yasushi Mieno, the new Bank of Japan governor in 1989, that the bubble had to be punctured; sharp interest rate rises that year led directly to the asset-price falls of 1990. But in what Greenwood calls "a classic case of fighting the last war," the Japanese central bank continued to keep a lookout for danger signs of inflation, even while the deflationary storm was gathering strength. As for fiscal policy, between 1992 and early 2000, the Japanese government ladled out some $1 trillion in "extra" spending to give a kick to the economy; none of this stimulus had any effect for more than half a year or so before it petered out. In 1999 Milton Friedman, the Nobel prize-winning economist, described to me with astonishment the Japanese government's record:

> Japan has very great strengths, which they are absolutely dissipating and wasting. They have followed the most stupid policies you could imagine over the past eight years or so; it's amazing. It's also a fascinating parallel between Japan in 1985–89 and the U.S. in 1923–33. Incidentally, there's a third comparison, which is the United States from 1992 to 200X. We haven't seen the unfolding of that yet, but the first part is duplicating the 1920s in the United States and the 1980s in Japan.
>
> The 1920s in New York were a very profitable period, a good period in which you had stable prices of goods and services; on the other hand, the asset price index went up sharply. In Japan's case in the 1980s, you had

excessive monetary expansion which expressed itself less in the cost of living, though that went up too, than in the prices of assets. Once you had a so-called bubble, in 1989 in Japan and in the United States in 1929, the monetary authorities thought they had to burst the bubble and they stepped very hard on the monetary brakes. The bubble burst and, in both cases, monetary policy became very deflationary, in the United States to a far more extreme extent than in Japan, which is why, in my opinion, the American depression was much worse than Japan's. In the United States the absolute volume of money fell by a third between '29 and '33. Japan had only one year of absolute fall, I think in '92 or '93, but a rate of growth of 10 percent to 12 percent in the late 1980s fell on average to 2 percent a year over the next eight years.

The result was a very recessed economy. The bubble was burst, the stock market collapsed, the price level in general started going up less rapidly and then actually going down; and it stretched out over nine years what was compressed in the United States into three years. And in my opinion, in both countries, the monetary authorities were negligent in not expanding the money supply, because in a period like that the demand for money holdings as a fraction of income goes up because it's less expensive to hold money and because the world is so uncertain and you want to hedge. The appropriate rate of growth of the quantity of money is higher than it would be in ordinary times, and instead both kept it lower. I think that's the prime, immediate cause of what happened. Not the ultimate cause, because undoubtedly the structural weaknesses in banking and the interrelationships among corporations all played a role, but they were there during the eighties and didn't keep Japan from being a very prosperous and expansive economy.

But what more could the Bank of Japan do, having pushed interest rates to near zero?

It's crazy, the problem with interest rates. The point I have made repeatedly is that interest rates are a very misleading indicator of monetary policy because of the initial and the long-term effects of monetary growth on interest rates. The initial effect of an increase in the quantity of money is to lower interest rates, but it also stimulates spending and inflation. The long-run effect is that the higher the rate of monetary growth the higher the interest rates, and I don't understand why there isn't a wider recognition of that when it's so obvious. If you look around the world at where interest rates are high, it's in countries that are inflating, not in countries that are deflating.

The Bank of Japan is not alone in having put its major emphasis on interest rates. Every central bank in the world tries to use interest rates in a short-term way as the instrument through which they affect the economy, and all are going to pay for it with bad times which will vary depending on how sophisticated the central bankers are. Alan Greenspan will not fall prey to this fallacy because he understands the situation better, but in Japan it's terrible. They ought to pay no attention to interest rates at all. They ought to conduct their policy by buying assets in the open market, whatever they want to buy—let them buy dollars, let them buy houses, let them buy government bonds—and shortly, if the economy turns around, as it would under these circumstances, I believe that interest rates would start to go up.

In the past five years or so, Japan has tried to counter this by fiscal stimuli. They've all been failures and why should you expect them to be anything but failures? What does a fiscal stimulus amount to? It amounts to pouring in money to build infrastructure, much of which has a negative yield: it's not going to pay off in the long run. Why in infrastructure of that kind? Because the construction industry is such a big supporter of the [ruling] Liberal Democratic Party (LDP). And this was financed by borrowing—borrowing from the savings in the postal savings system fundamentally. Now if they hadn't engaged in that fiscal stimulus, those savings would have been used in some other way. What you did was to crowd out private productive investment for government unproductive investment. It was a stupid policy, they would have been far better off to cut taxes. But they made the mistake of raising the consumption tax in the middle of this [April 1997], so I think their fiscal policy has been misdirected throughout. Of course, I recognize that much of Japan's problem arises from the bad advice they've gotten from the United States. After all, it was the Treasury that was advising them to carry out these damn fiscal stimuli; it's only in the last year or two that Larry Summers has been talking a little bit about monetary policy.

Another factor, this one laid more directly at America's door (though with plenty of Japanese connivance), added significantly to bungled monetary and fiscal policy in contributing to Japan's lost decade: the perverse management of the yen/dollar relationship. Ron McKinnon, an economist at Stanford University, has pointed out that since the

1970s—and especially since the Plaza Accord in 1985—markets in Japan and elsewhere have expected that, whatever the short-term fluctuations, over the long run the yen will always rise against the dollar (which it did between 1971 and 1995 with remarkable steepness, going up from 360 to the dollar in the earlier year to 80 a quarter-century later).

The deeply ingrained expectation of an ever-rising yen is the result not of a fundamental relationship between the two economies, but instead grows out of America's habitual mercantilist tendency to get Japan to cooperate in pushing up the yen whenever Japan's bilateral trade surplus with the United States becomes politically sensitive in Washington. Japan's Ministry of Finance, as official keeper of the country's fish-trap, has been happy to go along quietly with this as a way of insuring that Japan's personal savings stay high and as much of them as possible stay in the country for investment in the government's bonds. Given such a united front, since the late 1970s the expectation of an ever-rising yen has driven long-term nominal interest rates (bond yields) in Japan persistently and substantially below those in America, because a constantly appreciating yen lowers both relative inflationary expectations in Japan compared with America and also the currency risk of holding yen.

As McKinnon sees it, this did not cause Japan serious trouble until the 1990s, when dramatically reduced inflation in the United States pushed down American interest rates and thereby helped force nominal Japanese rates toward zero. The external feature was critical: because capital could flow pretty freely into and out of Japan (today completely freely) long-term real (i.e., inflation-adjusted) interest rates had to be about as high in Japan as they were in America lest Japan suffer massive capital flight. Yet the only way real interest rates could be equalized between the two economies when nominal interest rates in Japan were so much lower was for the Japanese price level to be continuously pushed down.

The one way out of this would be a large depreciation of the yen against the dollar, but in view of Japan's already huge current-account surpluses and capital-account deficits this is unthinkable to both governments. McKinnon has various ideas for breaking the expectations of an ever-rising yen, including a mutual forswearing of the use of the bilateral exchange rate to try to tinker with the balance of payments. Meanwhile, Japan was left with nominal interest rates of zero, high real interest rates that choked off economic activity whenever it threatened to resume, and—despite a roughly constant consumer-price level during the 1990s—a very sharp 10 percent decline in wholesale prices, together with even sharper falls in asset prices, so that real interest rates could effectively keep up with those in the far more robust American economy.

GUARDING THE CONVOY

Japan's almost weird policy responses to its situation during the 1990s can be understood only in the context of its strong desire to preserve the system that had prevailed since 1945. Japan's "convoy" or "stakeholder" version of capitalism—the model, as described in Chapters 2 and 3, for much of East Asia's formal economy—was based on an interlocking set of ideas and institutions that were much more flexible when they began than when they reached their zenith in the late 1980s.

Using the captive pool of capital generated by high savings rates, banks (often acting under government guidance) allocated credit to favored companies and industries with little or no concern for cash-flow or credit-risk analysis and rather a lot for collateral like land and shares and an implicit government guarantee of the loans. Companies aimed for market share and asset growth rather than profitability, especially since most of their shares were held not by anonymous investors keen on returns but instead by their bankers or by affiliated companies which would never trade the shares. Firms often competed ferociously but also often within industries that were in many respects highly cartelized. Their employees, loyal thanks to a promise of lifetime employment, were faithfully prepared to share the firm's ups and downs. So, for that matter, were creditors and even competitors: stragglers in almost every financial or industrial "convoy" were given plenty of help from the others so that they would not perish.

This schematic diagram, so often accepted by westerners in the 1980s as a full depiction of reality, was full of myth. More than 90 percent of Japan's firms, for instance, are and always have been small businesses with no lifetime employment or indeed many protections of any kind; many were suppliers to the big firms which, in hard times, shoved their adjustments onto their weak and mostly invisible subcontractors. The evidence is mounting, moreover, that the things pro-interventionist Western pilgrims to Japan in the 1980s admired about the place were in fact drags on its progress. The best-known example is Japan's successful machine-tool industry, which from the 1930s onward got to where it did by defying rather than honoring government plans and directives. A recent book by Michael Porter, a Harvard Business School professor, and Hirotaka Takeuchi, of the Hitotsubashi University business school, argues that the more the government intervened in an industry, the more cartelized the industry was and the more cooperative R&D there was, the worse the industry did. The book also says that the famously successful Japanese exporting companies were operationally impressive but international laggards at strategy and organization; and that, as in America, companies performed best in industries driven by competition and an aim for profitability, though these tend not to be the companies that foreigners are aware of. In other words, Japan succeeded despite its model not because of it; and in the process surreptitiously created a much larger number of world-standard companies than most people realize that could fill the gap if the old-style Japanese firms were allowed to go under.

Nonetheless, the mythical model had in many ways institutionally entrenched itself in Japan by the end of the 1980s. Cross-shareholdings, the practice by which companies and banks hold large blocks of each other's shares inactively and indefinitely, is the essential tool of the profitability-indifferent school of corporate management. They rose from 55 percent of Japan's market capitalization in 1969 to 71 percent in 1988. On company balance sheets the value of stock and land holdings—which in constantly rising asset markets allowed companies to claim they were doing well even as their operational performance was declining—multiplied nine-fold between 1976 and 1989. By the time Japan's bubble burst, its establishment—ignoring reality just as America's had a decade earlier—was pleased with what it saw in itself. But it proved much more resourceful than America's had at defending itself from the forces of change generated both inside and outside the country.

The depth of the establishment's commitment to the convoy system is clear from the fact that, instead of turning away from the 1980s behavior that had plunged them into such trouble, Japan's government, companies and banks redoubled the madness. For awhile, this attitude could be put down to the widespread belief that the economy was merely going through a cyclical downturn and nothing was basically wrong with the system. But, in every respect, it continued throughout the decade.

The pork-barrel spending that had long been at the heart of the Liberal Democratic Party's (LDP's) money-politics rule was increased even during the 18 months when the ruling party lost power to a supposedly reformist opposition: public investment as a share of GDP rose by half from 1990 to

1996—when at almost 10 percent it reached more than twice the rich-world average—and it kept rising with each supplemental spending package after that. The banks spent the first part of the decade refusing to clean up their balance sheets—though eventually and under government duress-cum-largesse they wrote off about $500 billion-worth, but even then did not liquidate the loan collateral so the underlying property market did not clear.

Lastly, following on a full decade's-worth of overinvestment in factories and equipment, as recession deepened between 1989 and 1998 industrial Japan actually *added* 8 percent to capacity, driving down utilization rates in every industry save precision machinery and starkly lowering the efficiency of its use of capital (the incremental capital-output ratio tripled). Nor, despite a rise in the unemployment rate to an unheard-of high of almost 5 percent by 1999, were companies trimming their payrolls by nearly as much as the markets were telling them they should. Between 1988 and 1998 employee compensation as a share of national income rose from 65 percent to 75 percent, implying that firms were holding on to workers even at the expense of eating further into already meager profits. The result was that by 1998 Japan Inc had more excess capacity of both capital and labor, and was less profitable and more highly leveraged, than at the height of the Bubble Economy.

IT'S EVERYTHING PERSONAL

Apart from the natural human tendency to cling to the familiar—and the stability, conservatism and anti-individualist bent of Japanese society—why were so few Japanese politicians and businessmen prepared to catch the wave of globalization rather than wait for it to crash on them? The fairly simple answer is that the personal incentives for most people have been shaped in a way that, for any individual, sticking with the status quo has been more attractive than the alternatives, even when for Japan as a whole the lesson of the 1990s was that radical change was needed.

Take the case of a high-level corporate executive in a traditional company. Nicholas Benes, the head of Japan Transaction Partners, a firm that arranges agreed takeovers of untroubled Japanese companies by overseas ones, in 1999 pooh-poohed the idea that troubled companies would agree to significant restructuring, especially rationalization through mergers and acquisitions (M&A), without a lot more "continued pain and disruption." The directors who would make the decision, even if they understood the imperatives of global capitalism, grew up in a system heavily loaded against obedience to market signals. Initiative was penalized rather than rewarded. Collective responsibility and consensus were the guiding principles of decision-making. Laying off staff was not only excruciating but almost dishonorable. No manager had any conception of delivering adequate shareholder returns as a significant corporate goal. And, most important of all, no manager had his compensation tied in any appreciable way to the share price, and all were underpaid in the first two or three decades of their time with the firm only to be rewarded with high incomes and perks in the very closing years of their careers. The last point especially argued for sticking with the methods long in place or risk losing almost everything—even if, for the enterprise, the old methods were leading to disaster. This is why Japanese managers can seem so pigheaded in the face of reality: they are not stupid, it is their own bacon they are saving.

The structure of big Japanese companies, moreover, insures that even when top managers do run the firm in an attempt to produce shareholder value, their instructions usually go unheeded at the operational level. Tab Bowers, a consultant with McKinsey in Tokyo, points out that branches of a firm tend not to be organized so that their various functional units report to a single superior at headquarters. Instead, each branch is a complete integrated unit in terms of operations and personnel—almost a little firm of its own. Predictably, the incentives at this level to pay attention to shareholder value are even weaker than they are at headquarters. A 1998 survey of several Japanese companies by *Diamond Harvard Business Review* (a Japanese-American collaboration) found that, when a firm's financial objectives were oriented to gross margins and sales, they were closely followed by managers at the level of the profit center. When the emphasis at the top was on profitability, however, profit centers ignored them. In the survey, 73 percent of top managers reported using ROE as an objective, 72 percent EBIT (a measure of cash-flow) and 67 percent earnings per share; in the profit centers of the same companies 10 percent paid attention to ROE, 18 percent to EBIT and 7 percent to earnings per share.

Two Japanese who have the reputation of being shocking radicals agree that enormous disruption would be required to force through the needed changes in any volume. What would be shocking about these two to an American is that either could possibly be thought radical. Akio Mikuni, a quiet, scholarly but impish 60-year-old, quit Nomura Securities in the mid-1970s to set up his own company which, in the mid-1980s, became Japan's first independent credit-rating agency, Mikuni & Co. He went into credit-rating despite being told at the time by Ministry of Finance (MOF) bureaucrats that "credit ratings are un-Japanese." Mikuni had argued since before the bubble burst that the Japanese system of "socialization of credit risk"—every corporate borrower paid the same rates and enjoyed "an endless revolving credit facility for the benefit of Japanese industry"—would lead to disaster. By January 1999, when a bank bail-out plan at last seemed to be stabilizing what had threatened to be a systemic banking collapse, he noted that little had yet been done to reduce capacity or shrink banking assets. He foresaw no real improvement until 10 percent of the companies whose creditworthiness his agency tracked went bust: "the bureaucratic system can distribute goodies but not pain; only markets can distribute pain."

The other "radical," an ex-MOF pariah and somewhat disheveled Anglophile named Tadashi Nakamae, runs his own consulting firm, Nakamae Institute of Economic Research, and among other things advises the Singapore government on events in Japan. In early 1999 he too felt that an even more severe crash would be needed to force market disciplines on Japan. It had, he believed, taken nine years to get Japan near this goal and would take another year or two actually to get it there—nine years spent "wasting resources" in an effort to prevent the necessary destruction of overcapacity in the economy. However, he noted, the "positive thing about the past nine years is that it eliminated the resources that could be used negatively" to carry on the defense of the old system. What a lot of resources there were is shown by how long it took to come close to exhausting them.

CHAPTER

5

The Convoy and
the Snipers

The Japanese are famously frugal. In 1996 they had around $11 trillion in personal financial assets, and have since been adding to this pool at a rate of about $600 billion a year. With in addition a net foreign asset position of $1 trillion, Japan should, you might think, be able to finance almost anything. But it was only households in the 1990s that were net savers in Japan: companies and the government were huge spenders, to the point that all that massive accumulated wealth is now under a cloud.

Japan's financial problem in a nutshell was that from the beginning of 1990 to the end of 1998 around $4.5 trillion-worth of wealth in the stock market, and $11.5 trillion-worth in the property market, was destroyed without anyone—government, banks or companies—being prepared to recognize the losses. Recognizing the losses would have meant loans being declared bad, collateral being foreclosed, prices of assets (including whole companies) being driven to market-clearing levels, newcomers (including foreigners) taking over the resources that had been freed up, and a great deal of transitional disruption including high unemployment as the process of rationalization and reconstruction took place. It would, in other words, have meant a far bigger shake-up than America went through in its 1980s restructuring, but in a society far less flexible and accustomed to change. The convoy system would have been destroyed.

The lost wealth—equivalent to four years of GDP—was even more staggering than it sounds. Stocks and land, rather than cash-flow, underpinned most of the credit creation in Japan, so almost everything would have been affected if losses on them had to be recognized. The only way to avoid this was to borrow against the future, in the hope that an economic turnaround would lift the assets to their former value and allow business activity to resume without a shake-out. So banks, insurers, companies and especially the government went heavily into debt to forestall having to face facts, and did so in a time of economic stagnation and falling prices that made the real burden of the rising debt even heavier. Japan will spend years paying for its decade of denial.

THE COST OF THE CONVOY

The banking, corporate and government roles in the process were intimately entwined. At the height of the bubble in the late 1980s bank assets (loans) in Japan grew by an astonishing $1.7 trillion—or some 40 percent of a year's GDP—the lion's share of that secured by real estate. As Japan's economic stagnation in the 1990s continued, more and more borrowers were unable to meet payments on their loans. Rather than declare the loans bad and foreclose on the real estate—which would have meant having to take write-offs on already weak bank balance sheets and was anyway surprisingly often bad for the health since gangsters controlled a lot of the property—banks kept rolling over non-performing loans (NPLs) and the bad debts kept mounting. After years of denying there was much of a problem, and the failure of three of the country's 21 biggest banks, the government at last admitted in 1998 that "problem" loans might amount to as much as $500 billion to $600 billion. A $500 billion rescue package was put together in 1998–99 that provided public money for bank recapitalization, depositor insurance and nationalization of failed banks.

By the spring of 1999 the package seemed to have stabilized a situation that at times in 1998 threatened a systemic bank failure in Japan. However, the potential for a crisis remained because the government's calculation of doubtful debts was almost certainly an underestimate. Nakamae points out that, on the conservative assumption 10 percent of the $11.5 trillion loss in property values was tied to bank loans, bad loans at the end of 1998—not NPLs, of which some are recoverable, but actually dud loans—amounted to $1.2 trillion, more than four times the official estimate. Nakamae looks at it another way and comes up with the same figure. Since 1960 both money supply and bank loans as a share of GDP have about doubled in Japan. By contrast, America's money supply as a share of GDP fell slightly. What happened in America is what ought to happen in rich countries: money and credit should grow roughly in line with the economy. The fact that for almost two generations in Japan they increased almost twice as fast as the economy did suggests that an awful lot of credit was extended imprudently. Nakamae reckons that to restore a reasonable ratio of credit to GDP in Japan the banks will have to write off about 30 percent of their assets—which again translates into a shrinkage of bank loans of some $1.2 trillion. That in turn will equal around 25 percent to 30 percent of GDP. By comparison, America's S&L crisis eventually cost around 3 percent of GDP to sort out.

The life insurance companies were, amazingly, in even worse shape than the banks. With around $1.5 trillion in assets in 1999, ownership of 10 percent of the stock market and some $100 billion-worth of book value in real estate, the life insurers are a financial force in Japan second only to the banks. Yet by the middle of the decade they were losing money not just on the business of writing premiums (which is a common enough failing in this industry worldwide) but also, and hugely, on their investments. Not only did the stock-market and property price collapses cripple them—at one point in 1998 (thankfully) unrealized losses on stockholdings reached $13 billion—but they also suffered widening negative spreads between returns on their assets, like government bonds yielding 2 percent, and the 6 percent payouts they were obliged to make on many of the policies they had written or pension schemes they were managing. By 1998 the industry's liabilities were bigger than its capital—the whole life insurance industry, in other words, was technically bankrupt.

Japan's non-financial companies too had had better decades. Their declining profitability arose both from high costs and overinvestment. Despite falling wholesale prices, Japanese firms by 1996 still faced extremely high costs of doing business compared with companies elsewhere. A survey by the Ministry of International Trade and Industry (MITI) showed that Japanese manufacturers at home had to pay almost 50 percent more in salaries and rent, twice as much in shipping and distribution costs, and three times as much for R&D as the same firms did in their operations abroad. The overinvestment described in detail in Chapter 4 was so extravagant that, by one estimate, if marginal returns in Japanese industry were to be brought up to American levels some 20 percent to 30 percent of Japanese capital stock—the lower figure equals 70 percent of GDP—would need to be written off. Meanwhile, since cash flow from operations in this unprofitable decade were unable to support the assets that Japan's companies were nonetheless not cutting back, the firms went deeper in debt. By 1998 Japan's bigger companies had debt-to-equity ratios of 4 to 1, compared with 1 to 1 in America (which for the United States was a record post-1945 high). And, according to David Asher and Andrew Smithers, two experts in Japanese finance, even that horrendous figure understates the true indebtedness of Japanese firms. If you strip out cross-shareholdings from the equity of Japanese companies—which makes sense because no money changes hands in these transactions, only a mutual issue of shares that are then never traded—the ratio goes above 5 to 1, as bad as Korea's *chaebol* at their worst.

Yet even that is not the end of the corporate-debt nightmare. In common with the insurance companies (and the government, see below), Japan's non-financial firms have large unfunded pension liabilities. Providing enough for pensions is a concern everywhere—which is why Social Security is perennially one of the hottest political issues in the United States—but in Japan it is a life-and-death matter. Japan has the fastest-aging population in the world: the proportion of old people tripled from 5 percent in 1950 to 15 percent in 1995, years when America's grew modestly from 8 percent to 12 percent, and will rise to 25 percent by 2020, when Japan will have the world's oldest population. Public pensions are not as well-established in Japan as in America or Europe, so corporate schemes that are not fully paid up are a special worry.

Unfunded corporate pension liabilities were treated by companies as off-balance-sheet items until 2000, when new accounting rules forced firms to start disclosing them on their balance sheets. A full disclosure is likely to prove painful. Two things created an ever-widening gap between the money needed to fund pension schemes and the money set aside for that purpose. First, investment returns collapsed during the 1990s, so many of the corporate schemes began operating at a loss. Second, the government long ago set a rate of 5.5 percent for the assumed future return on pension-fund assets and did not revise this downwards even as government bond yields sank during the 1990s to 2 percent and even below 1 percent. Even though this unrealistic assumption started being corrected in the late 1990s, the effect was that companies built up a much smaller pool of assets than they would need to generate enough income in the future to meet their pension liabilities as they came due. In 1998 Kathy Matsui, the Tokyo strategist for Goldman Sachs, estimated that Japan's blue-chip companies had unfunded pension liabilities amounting to some $670 billion—equal to 60 percent of their equity and somewhat bigger than the government's figure for doubtful loans in the banking system.

Looming over all this like an Everest above the foothills was the government's own breathtaking mountain of debt.

THE WORLD'S BIGGEST SPENDTHRIFT

Its longtime reputation for fiscal prudence notwithstanding, Japan's government spent money wantonly during the 1990s. After years of running (apparent) budget surpluses, the government began running deficits that grew as the decade wore on. In the fiscal year that ended in March 2000, the central government may have had a deficit equal to 10 percent of GDP, with local governments chipping in another 3 percent-worth of deficit spending. But it was the cumulative debt that really mattered. Some observers, while admitting that the official figure for gross public debt of 105 percent in 1998 seemed uncomfortably large, noted that net debt (liabilities minus assets) was among the lowest in the rich world. This was misleading. Not only, as explained later, was net debt calculated in ways that much overstated assets; far more important, Japan has long run a huge part of its fiscal operations off the government's balance sheet. And these off-balance-sheet operations were astonishingly profligate.

What Japan did cannot properly be understood without a flow chart—in fact, two charts, shown as Figures 5.1 and 5.2—but the basic idea was this (all the figures in this account are as of mid-1998, translated into dollars at an exchange rate of 125 yen to the dollar; they would have grown since). A large part of Japan's retail savings are deposited in Post Office savings accounts; the Post Office is the world's biggest bank, with deposits of $1.8 trillion, equal to a little less than half of GDP. Public pension and other funds add another $1.4 trillion or so to the pot. About 17 percent of this money is invested in 10-year Japanese Government Bonds (JGBs), the government's main financing instrument, and in corporate bonds. The rest is deposited with the Trust Fund Bureau of the Ministry of Finance (TFB). The TFB has liabilities of $3.2 trillion, or 80 percent of GDP. The TFB invests 20 percent of this in JGBs. The rest—a massive two-thirds of GDP—is invested partly in public and semi-public corporations (described in the next paragraphs), but the lion's share goes to the Fiscal Investment and

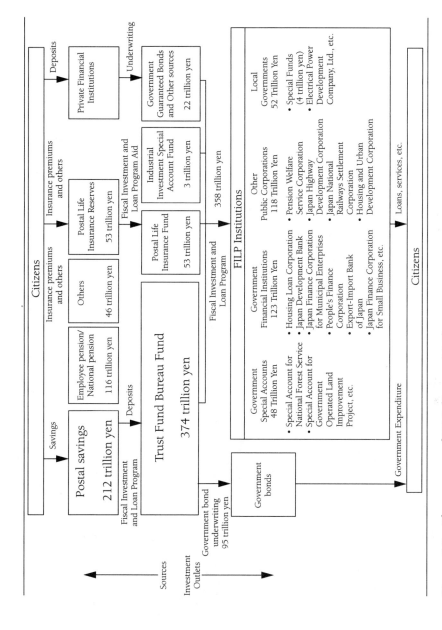

Figure 5.1 The structure of FILP. (*Source:* MoF)

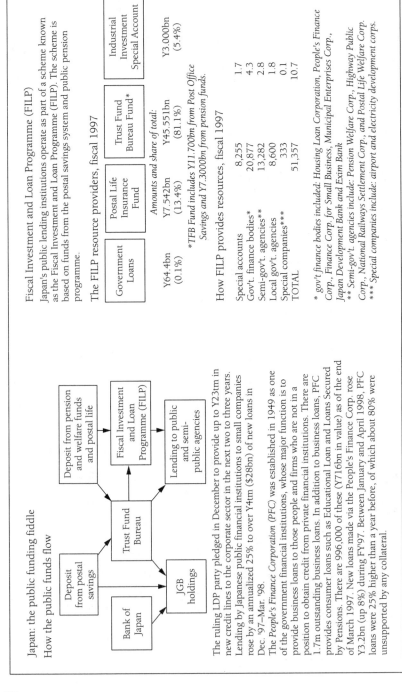

Japan: the public funding fiddle
How the public funds flow

Deposit from pension and welfare funds and postal life

Bank of Japan

Deposit from postal savings

Trust Fund Bureau

Fiscal Investment and Loan Programme (FILP)

Lending to public and semi-public agencies

JGB holdings

The ruling LDP party pledged in December to provide up to Y23tm in new credit lines to the corporate sector in the next two to three years. Lending by Japanese public financial institutions to small companies rose by an annualized 25% to over Y4tm ($28bn) of new loans in Dec. '97–Mar. '98.

The People's Finance Corporation (PFC) was established in 1949 as one of the government financial institutions, whose major function is to provide business loans to those people and firms who are not in a position to obtain credit from private financial institutions. There are 1.7m outstanding business loans. In addition to business loans, PFC provides consumer loans such as Educational Loan and Loans Secured by Pensions. There are 996,000 of these (Y716bn in value) as of the end of March 1997. New loans made via the People's Finance Corp. rose Y3.2bn (up 8%) during FY97. Between January and April 1998, PFC loans were 25% higher than a year before, of which about 80% were unsupported by any collateral.

Fiscal Investment and Loan Programme (FILP)

Japan's public lending institutions operate as part of a scheme known as the Fiscal Investment and Loan Programme (FILP). The scheme is based on funds from the postal savings system and public pension programme.

The FILP resource providers, fiscal 1997

Government Loans	Postal Life Insurance Fund	Trust Fund Bureau Fund*	Industrial Investment Special Account

Amounts and share of total:

Y64.4bn (0.1%)	Y7.542bn (13.4%)	Y45.551bn (81.1%)	Y3.000bn (5.4%)

TFB Fund includes Y11.700bn from Post Office Savings and Y7.3000bn from pension funds.

How FILP provides resources, fiscal 1997

Special accounts	8,255	1.7
Gov't finance bodies*	20,877	4.3
Semi-gov't. agencies**	13,282	2.8
Local gov't. agencies	8,600	1.8
Special companies***	333	0.1
TOTAL	51,357	10.7

* gov't finance bodies included: Housing Loan Corporation, People's Finance Corp., Finance Corp. for Small Business, Municipal Enterprises Corp., Japan Development Bank and Exim Bank
** Semi-gov't. agencies include: Pension Welfare Corp., Highway Public Corp., National Railways Settlement Corp., and Postal Life Welfare Corp.
*** Special companies include: airport and electricity development corps.

Figure 5.2 Another take on the Japanese government's slush fund. (*Source:* Independent Strategy)

Loan Program (FILP), in Japanese called *zaito,* also controlled by the Ministry of Finance.

FILP is the government's off-balance-sheet budget, and it is big: equal to about two-thirds of the "real" budget. Although FILP gets most of its money from the TFB, it gets about 25 percent to 30 percent from the Postal Life Insurance Fund and some miscellaneous sources. Its liabilities amount to around 75 percent of GDP, and each year in the late 1990s it invested about 11 percent of GDP in various public and semi-public bodies. Because its money comes from savings accounts, insurance policies and pension contributions on which interest and other payments must be made, FILP is required to lend profitably. The requirement is full of holes, however, since there is no proper accounting for returns and "policy" loans supported by interest-rate subsidies from the government are frequent.

Loans to bodies like the People's Finance Corporation (only 20 percent of whose borrowings are secured), the Housing Loan Corporation (which, with 40 percent of outstanding mortgages, is the largest mortgage-holder in the country) and the Finance Corporation for Small Business are unlikely to be of the soundest quality. For connoisseurs of government pork, FILP's activities make the United States Congress look like an implacable foe of special interests. The Ministry of Health's Environmental Hygiene Financial Corporation, for example, has borrowed $8 billion from FILP (this figure is not a misprint) for "vital public health related needs" such as "cockroach control at sushi, soba and udon restaurants and hostess bars." More seriously, because the sums involved are so huge, TFB and FILP loans have been the main conduit for politicians to pass public money to their political backers, especially in the construction industry (one investor has suggested that "Slush Fund Bureau" is a better name for the Trust Fund Bureau). Milton Friedman had no idea how much he was underestimating the waste in Japan's repeated fiscal stimulus programs when (see Chapter 4) he condemned them so mildly. Take, for example, a $150 million loan FILP made in 1995 to pay for a third of the cost of building a bridge to link a southern island town called Azumacho to the mainland, to provide "an agricultural path" for the island's residents so that they would have "easier access to markets"—all 353 residents, that is, or almost $500,000 of public money for each one.

Because the off-balance-sheet accounts are so opaque yet so large, the true debt of the Japanese government as the millennium turned could only be vaguely guessed at. David Asher of the MIT Japan Program figured that in January 2000 Japan's gross debt conventionally defined was 130 percent of GDP, already the highest in the rich world and rising. Add in the TFB and FILP borrowings, which the government is obligated to repay, and the figure rises to 200 percent of GDP. With unfunded public pension liabilities it rises to 400 percent of GDP. The net debt figures that some drew such comfort from were specious: on one side of the ledger they counted the 44 percent of GDP in surplus public-pension fund assets, but omitted deducting on the other side the 110 percent of GDP in unfunded future liabilities. Another, even more depressing, way of looking at the government's fiscal position is to see what annual spending was going for. Asher calculates that in the financial year that ends in March 2001, around 65 percent of available central-government revenue will go for debt service, and the amount of new debt issues will just about equal total revenues. The ratio of long-term debt (about $4.4 trillion, 100 percent of GDP) to available tax revenues is already over 15. The comparable ratio for America is 2, for Germany under 3, even for Italy under 4. Lastly, there is the question of how much of this debt is bad. In 1998 David Roche of Independent Strategy, a London-based investment house, reckoned that the public sector's bad loans amounted to 30 percent of GDP, about the same share as the banks had (and when added to the banks' bad debts making for a total that was three or four times the conventional estimate).

Faced with such spread-sheets, in the winter of 1998–99 some of the smartest financial observers—Nakamae, Asher, Roche—were predicting a Nikkei stock market index of 12,000 or lower, the yen at 150–170 to the dollar and JGB yields at 5 percent +. In other words, a meltdown.

THE GREEN SHOOTS

It did not happen, at least not in 1999. A tentative economic recovery took hold in Japan as 1999 unfolded. Foreign investors, thinking that the worst had passed, began buying Japanese stocks and pushed up the Tokyo stock market by more than 50 percent that year. After almost quadrupling the year before to 2.5 percent, JGB yields fell back to a shade under 2 percent and stabilized. And, far from going into free-fall, the yen rose against the dollar as the year went on, and more or less stayed put in the first half of 2000. Disasters that, on paper, look certain to happen have a way of fading—as those who, in the late 1980s, were predicting an American debt crisis thanks to perpetual government deficits should have been aware when, a decade later, the budget went into surplus and the debt began to shrink. Japan's fiscal condition is far more perilous than America's ever threatened to be, and a stock-and-bond-and-currency crisis of the sort predicted for 1999 could strike at any time. But just as America was being revamped from the bottom up in the 1980s, unseen by those who were fretting about the bleak macroeconomic picture, so Japan in the late 1990s was changing at the level of the firm and the household even while the powers-that-be continued their tenacious defense of the old order.

Part of the reason was that, despite the resistance of the conservatives, market forces were having an appreciable impact. The effect was not as dramatic as it ideally should have been, because the market for corporate control was (and still is) stunted in Japan. Junk bonds are mostly unknown and the tax laws have traditionally penalized restructurings (though legislation to amend this was introduced in 1999). Despite these handicaps, M&A activity more than quadrupled in value from 1998 to 1999, when $78 billion-worth of deals were done; foreigners quadrupled their acquisitions in 1999 to $24 billion. In the first half of 2000, M&A deals were another 6 percent higher than they had been a year earlier. By American standards these amounts are still trifling—Japan's 1999 M&A activity was equal to 5 percent of America's (though that was more than twice the share in 1998)—but by Japanese standards they are revolutionary. In 1994–95 Japanese M&A amounted to one-quarter of one percent of stock-market capitalization; in 1999 it was 7 percent.

The indirect signs that economic pressures were reshaping Japanese business mounted as the 1990s drew to a close. First, the unemployment rate would not have approached 5 percent and rising in 1999 if some serious restructuring were not taking place. Likewise, corporate bankruptcies rose from essentially zero in 1990 to a post-1945 high of above 3 percent of GDP in 1998 and were going up from there. Indeed, in 1999, for the first time since statistics became available in 1960, corporate Japan as a whole went into the red. Second, cross-shareholdings declined continuously through the 1990s, falling to 43 percent in 1998. Although up-to-date overall figures are hard to come by—companies go about the politically delicate and market-sensitive business of selling cross-holdings with great discretion—it seems clear that the pace of unwinding picked up in 1999–2000 as market buoyancy and the approaching end of the fiscal year made the practice more tempting. Third, by the end of the 1990s the bond market had started drawing sharp distinctions among the creditworthiness of different companies, as widening interest-rate spreads showed Mikuni's scolds from MOF that credit ratings were not so "un-Japanese" after all. In 1995, for the first time, Mikuni began publishing his credit reports in Japanese as well as English and two years later he had more Japanese clients than foreign ones. And, fourth, it was not just the bond market that was drawing such distinctions. As banks struggled to overcome their bad debts and poor returns, the bank index of the Tokyo Stock Exchange fell by 17 percent from 1997 to 1999; meanwhile, the non-bank finance index, dominated by Japan's upstart consumer-finance and leasing companies, rose by 50 percent and the shares of Takefuji, the biggest consumer-finance firm, quadrupled.

The economic hydraulics were so strong that their pressure would have been felt anyway, but a surprisingly robust program of deregulation reinforced their effect. One curiosity of Japanese politics in the 1990s was that it combined hidebound macroeconomic policies with an almost unnoticed agenda of supply-side regulatory relaxation. This agenda was pushed in the mid-1990s by Ryutaro Hashimoto, an unusually assertive leader who was the first LDP prime minister after the party's brief spell in the wilderness in 1992–93. He didn't last long (they seldom do), but meanwhile he appointed six advisory committees on deregulation whose recommendations his and succeeding governments dutifully enacted over the years 1995–98 without a peep. They dealt with everything from labor regulations to corporate holdings of farmland to distribution to transportation to telecommunications to housing to health care.

The simplest and perhaps most radical example of what a couple of rule changes could do came from the gasoline-retailing industry. In 1996, under the guise of an adjustment aimed at rebalancing prices between gasoline and hitherto subsidized kerosene and distillate, imports and exports of refined petroleum products were freed and prices decontrolled. The result was spectacular.

Ian Scoble, an Australian who in the late 1990s ran Mobil's Japanese operations, told me in 1998 that gasoline retailing in Japan used to be "regulated, comfortable and lucrative." Everybody made money on gasoline, so gas stations proliferated, service was lavish and productivity was low. The country's 60,000 service stations pumped only a quarter to a third as much as their American counterparts but did so at gross profit margins five to seven times as high. No wonder they could afford seven uniformed attendants at the average station; self-service pumps were banned until 1998. Between the spring of 1996, when deregulation took effect, and early 1998, gasoline prices fell and margins collapsed by half—though they still remained at two to three times their American level. Scoble guessed that by 2001 both the number of oil companies (then 11) and of gas stations would be halved. Of those that survived, he predicted, most would have some connection to a western oil firm.

This process was extremely painful. A lot of the gasoline stations were family-owned affairs in which generations had sunk their capital. At first, Japanese oil companies tried to find jobs elsewhere in their empires for retailers being squeezed but this eventually proved unaffordable. The survivors began doing things that had long been common in America or Europe—like selling food and other groceries along with gasoline, and otherwise marketing themselves to their customers—and foreign companies like BP came in to pick up distressed stations at bargain prices. Scoble tried to explain to his Japanese counterparts that "this is not a *gaijin* (white foreigner) way of thinking, this is the real world." They may not have been persuaded, but they had to face the fact that the government would no longer protect them from the market. Scoble guessed that in the two years following gasoline-retailing deregulation about $5 billion to $8 billion had been put back into gasoline-consumers' pockets. Even he seemed puzzled by the comprehensiveness of the deregulation: "Whoever did this was very astute. A couple of simple changes, supposedly to rationalize pricing between gasoline and diesel and kerosene, led to a wholesale deregulation without anyone understanding the implications."

Some higher-profile industries—glaringly telecoms—did not get such treatment, but a lot more deregulation was going on than is generally believed. Higher disclosure standards for company accounts alone have already begun to force changes in company policies such as cross-shareholdings and to provide investors with enough information to drive the already existing wedge between the market valuations of good and not-so-good companies even wider. In 1999 listed companies had to start preparing combined accounts—meaning that they had to include in their own accounts the financial reports for any subsidiary or affiliate which they controlled. Previously, they had had to do this only for subsidiaries of which they owned at least 50 percent. The significance of the change is that many groups were in the habit of shoving their problems (such as workers made redundant by the parent company) on to unlisted subsidiaries which were bleeding money that hurt the parent's finances but was never disclosed. As noted earlier, in 2000 companies were also required to disclose the market value of pension liabilities and to value securities they held at their market price (before they could carry these items at historic cost, which was a helpful accounting trick when the stock market had fallen by two-thirds).

The most influential piece of deregulation was a financial "Big Bang" that in the mid-1990s began liberating Japan's financial markets in ways that had happened in America 20 years earlier and in Britain in the 1980s. The Big Bang was actually a series of little bangs cautiously stretched out Japanese-style over many years and due for completion only in 2002. The complete abolition of foreign-exchange controls on April 1, 1998, the first significant departure, was followed by measures to make it easier for foreign financial firms to do business in the country and, in 1999, by the elimination of fixed commissions for stock-broking transactions. Yet it is the redeployment of Japan's huge accumulation of personal savings that will make the most difference for the way Japan Inc does business. Japan is about to go through a pension-fund revolution of the sort that overturned American finance in the mid-1970s. Disclosure of unfunded pension liabilities will begin to force companies to start paying more attention to shareholder return—their own employees will demand it as they realize their pensions depend on it—and one of the earliest results may be a further unwinding of cross-shareholdings since these are the most readily available securities for Japanese firms to hand over to their underfed pension funds. On top of this, in April 2000 a Japanese version of America's 401(k) personal pensions was introduced. Between then and April 2002 around $1 trillion in postal-savings deposits will mature, of which MOF expects only 55 percent to be reinvested in Post Office accounts (though in the first six months, at least, 75 percent surprisingly stayed put). The rest will go into higher-yielding instruments in private pension accounts, probably giving their biggest boost to Japan's still underdeveloped mutual-fund industry.

Economic changes combined with deregulation have already begun to create a dual economy in Japan, with new capital-unintensive service industries that boast higher returns expanding as old manufacturing concerns gradually wither. It's about time. Tadashi Nakamae reckons that old industries were shrinking themselves at an increasing pace in the last half of the 1990s by slashing capital investment; investment spending fell by 20 percent in 1998, alone lopping 3 percent off GDP growth. By Nakamae's calculation, with demand for the output of old manufacturing companies stagnant, the productivity growth needed to produce GDP growth of 3 percent a year could come only if employment in the old economy contracted by 3 percent a year. Since a large majority of Japan's 65m workers were still, by 2000, employed in manufacturing, this implied that around 2m newly unemployed people would be created each year. They can be absorbed only if a net 200,000 new companies (each employing 10 people) are formed each year.

Not impossible—in America in the 1980s 800,000 companies were formed each year, though 700,000 also went bust—but it will be a tall order for an economy where entrepreneurialism has been in relatively short supply. Still, it has begun happening as industries like computer hardware, software and services grew to some $140 billion a year in revenues as the century turned, and the electronic commerce market was expected by Anderson Consulting to reach $600 billion by 2003. Richard Li, a Hong Kong businessman who was trying in the late 1990s to build an Asia-wide Internet empire, said that by 1999 Japan was already the leading source of finance for such ventures throughout Asia (see Chapter 11). By MITI's own calculation, employment in the "new economy" will double to 20m by 2010, with output almost tripling to $5 trillion.

ROUND-EYES AND REBELS

The widening split in Japan's economy between old and new has two main (and related) sources: foreign influence and the rise of businesses run by outsiders to the traditional establishment. The conservatives tend to be large firms in well-established businesses with not too much need or liking for foreign markets and methods. Commercial banking, construction and large commodity businesses like steel, paper and cement are prime examples. The forward-looking firms, by contrast, tend to be in faster-moving businesses and—crucially—are much more internationalized in their markets and outlook.

Foreign influence on the shaping of business has tended to be indirect in Japan. Despite a late-1990s spurt in foreign direct investment and foreign M&A, especially in financial services (see Chapter 12), as late as 1998 cumulative FDI in Japan was a derisory $18 billion, or 0.4 percent of GDP. Even the Hermit Kingdom of South Korea had FDI worth 2.5 percent, and that was before a spurt of foreign buying brought on by Korea's economic troubles. FDI in Japan would need to rise by $500 billion to bring the share to middling levels by international standards. Yet in the best Japanese companies foreign influence, particularly American, is pervasive.

Shinichi Ueyama, a consultant with McKinsey in Tokyo, points out that the chairman or CEO of every reform-minded Japanese company—Sony, Toyota, Toshiba, Orix (a leasing-finance company that listed on the New York Stock Exchange in 1998) and Nomura Securities—has had overseas experience. Apart from its more substantial virtues, this can bring a welcome touch of informal bluntness to the customarily stuffed-shirt world of big Japanese business. In early 1998, for example, Junichi Ujie, the new CEO of Nomura Securities, blithely brushed off the sacrosanct subject of cross-shareholdings, saying Nomura was "seriously considering" dumping its huge portfolio of bank shares. Ujie explained, "We have a bunch of bank shares. Is this really a strategic portfolio for an investment bank? I kind of doubt it." Reformist firms also tend to attract overseas shareholders—40 percent of Sony's shares in 1998 were held by foreigners—drawn not just by higher returns but by greater corporate transparency and accountability; well before the year 2000 accounting changes imposed by MOF, two dozen blue-chip Japanese companies were already using American accounting standards.

Many Japanese companies are, of course, already global competitors and have often become so using methods as crisp and ruthless as those of any American business hawk. A good example is Aiwa, which makes low-end consumer electronics goods, like stereos and TVs. Aiwa is half-owned by Sony, but with a separate stock-market listing, and it almost went bust in the late 1980s when the yen rose sharply against the dollar following the Plaza Accord of 1985 and Sony's Betamax standard for VCRs lost out to the VHS format. Aiwa responded in a very un-Japanese way by massively shifting its production overseas; until then 90 percent of it had been in Japan. To a chorus of media abuse, Aiwa relied on early retirement—which can cost as much as $200,000 per retired worker to carry out, five times as much as in Europe—to cut 1,300 of the 3,600 jobs it then had in Japan. By the late 1990s, 90 percent of Aiwa's output was made overseas, overwhelmingly in Asia. Three-quarters of the staff were employed abroad and almost 90 percent of its sales made there. Instead of pursuing market share, Aiwa's managers specifically targeted ROE. The shift worked. By 1997 Aiwa made an ROE of 11 percent on sales of $2.7 billion—about twice the return of its nearest Japanese competitor (embarrassingly for the corporate family, perhaps, it was five times as high as Sony's own ROE that year).

If more Japanese companies are going to become globally competitive, they'll also need to adopt more sophisticated financial management practices. One firm that aggressively went about doing just that is Hoya, a Tokyo high-tech optics company with sales of about $2 billion in 1999. When I met him in 1998, Tetsuo Suzuki, then Hoya's chairman, was a white-haired 73-year-old who was reminiscent of Akio Morita, Sony's founder, in more than just looks. Like Morita in his day, Suzuki was considered a rebel by the corporate establishment. He was one of Japan's most outspoken advocates of the view that companies exist to increase shareholder value. Suzuki told me that traditional Japanese management style and objectives, which he described as based on the notion that shareholders were somehow "people outside the company" were "flatly wrong."

Hoya was founded in 1941 to make crystal products, and later moved into eyeglasses, computer disks and laser-surgery instruments. The company was badly hurt by the bursting of Japan's bubble in 1990. Suzuki, then Hoya's CEO (he became chairman in 1993), cut off unprofitable operations, sold peripheral assets like real estate and shifted some operations overseas. Employment in Japan fell from 5,200 in 1993 to 4,000 in 1997, growing overseas in the same period from 3,800 to 5,550. Behind these moves was a relentless drive to raise shareholder value and satisfy what Suzuki called "the logic of the market" and in particular the expectations of the 20 percent of his shareholders who were foreigners. It seemed to work. From 1993 to 1997, Hoya's ROE more than doubled to 11.2 percent and, in a generally declining stock market, its share price went up more than two and a half times. But raising ROE and dividends wasn't good enough for Suzuki. His goal from 1998 to 2002 was to double Hoya's version of "economic value added," which measures how much its business earns over the true cost of its capital. He also aimed to raise ROE to 15 percent, shift the business sharply into electro-optics (sales up from $1 billion to more than $2 billion) and reduce the share of the firm's total sales coming from Japan to 25 percent, down from 75 percent a decade earlier. Hoya was globalizing in almost every respect.

Other firms were changing, too, even some famous (and famously stodgy) ones. In a business culture where the idea of shareholder value was about as familiar as the theory of extra-galactic gamma-ray explosions, by early 1999 at least nine well-established firms—among them Fujitsu, Toshiba and Sanwa Bank—had publicly set ROE targets. A year earlier, gigantic Matsushita began offering its new recruits choices of the old lifetime employment system, including company housing and a two-year retirement bonus, or versions that offer less security but more cash; almost half have taken the untraditional options. Hitachi, another huge conglomerate with more than 1,000 subsidiaries and $65 billion in sales in the 1998–99 financial year (but $3 billion in losses, its first loss since 1963), under a new president began in 1999 to dispose of underperforming overseas assets by putting them into joint ventures with other companies, and to split the firm into ten more or less autonomous divisions. The new CEO also made ROE the new corporate performance target, with 8 percent as the initial figure (a big upwards jump for Hitachi). Yet, significant as these shifts at old companies were starting to become, it was the upstarts who showed the most promise for creating a new Japan.

SOFT BUSINESSES, HARD CASH

A good way to get an early feel for how new wealth was being created in Japan as the millennium drew to a close was to look at a list published each year by the National Tax Agency. The list shows which people paid the most personal income tax, and how much. (No nonsense about privacy laws in Japan.) Of the top 100 taxpayers in 1998, not only was the biggest from the consumer-finance industry—Takeo Hamada, the former chairman of Lake, a company taken over by GE Capital in 1998, paid $57m in income tax—but so was number two; and overall ten of these slots were claimed by consumer-finance entrepreneurs. Number three was Hitori Saito, whose company produces herbal diet-foods and cosmetics, number four was the head of McDonald's in Japan and number five the head of Nintendo, an electronics-games company. Conversely, traditional businesses were almost completely unrepresented. Only one car-maker was there—Shoichiro Toyoda, Toyota's chairman—and the number of real-estate tycoons was 13. In 1990, when the bubble burst, there had been 86 of them. Nor was the pattern about to change. The top taxpayer in 1999 was Kazuo Okada, whose company makes sophisticated gambling machines for Japan's purportedly unsavory but immensely popular *pachinko* industry.

Japan's rebels are a varied lot, but it is a good bet that their ranks will supply most of the growth in the Japanese economy during the first decade of the twenty-first century. At the charming end of the rebellious scale is a retailer named Sazaby. Set up in 1972 by Rikuko Suzuki, who was still CEO in 1999, Sazaby is unusual in several ways. For one thing, Suzuki does not show up for meetings in Japan Inc's regulation dark-blue suit: when I visited his headquarters, his spiky white hair (he was 55 in 1999) was offset by black boots, black leather trousers, a black silk shirt and a charcoal wool sports jacket. Headquarters staff do clock in at their elegant Tokyo building, but not until 10:00 A.M., the same time the firm's shops open and a couple of hours later than most salarymen drag themselves to their desks. Most important of all, Sazaby—which is listed on Tokyo's OTC market—understands what it means to be a modern service business, which is where Japan's future must lie if it is to rescue itself. Sazaby doesn't just sell products, but creates life-styles for its customers.

Sazaby's clutch of businesses includes purses and other leather goods, light-snack restaurants, home-furnishing shops, the Japanese and Hong Kong outlets of Agnès B. (a Paris-based maker of an upper-middle range of women's clothes) and the Japanese joint venture for Starbucks Coffee (which in early 1999 already had 40 shops). Suzuki wants his customers—mostly young women in their 20s—to feel at home in any of the outlets in which they find themselves. Most of the outlets are collected on the same premises in what the company calls "compound shops"; some of these are stand-alone but most are in cordoned-off areas in big department stores. To make something like this click, Suzuki applies his own style of brand management. The Sazaby name appears fairly infrequently. Instead, Suzuki makes sure that each of the outlets has a similar feel—simple lines and cool pastels prevail, and the sales staff is trained to be friendly and informal. Suzuki argues that applying this kind of uniform retail approach to different product lines builds customer awareness.

It seemed to be working. Japan's recession was particularly hard on traditional retailers—retail sales overall in 1999 were 5 percent lower than they had been in 1995—but Sazaby's target audience never really stopped spending since young working women living with their parents were still flush (the other retail segments that enjoyed good growth in the late 1990s were discount stores and "no-label" fashions). Sales in 1998 were $400m, a not-bad 10 percent increase in the worst year of the 1990s for the economy. In terms of size, Sazaby was a minnow. Revenues in 1998 were one-thirtieth those of Takashimaya, the biggest department store. But Sazaby's ROE was 10 percent, and its profits were more than half of Takashimaya's—or 15 times as much in relation to sales. Sazaby used the enforced downtime of the recession to revamp its internal operations, especially in personnel and other management systems and in technology. Suzuki doesn't lack ambition. He told me that when 7-Eleven's operations got started in the early 1980s nobody believed it would end up as Japan's biggest retail success. It did. He plans to emulate it.

The formal financial system was so arthritic that, even before the Big Bang started lowering barriers to entry, alternative sorts of finance—including foreign firms like Citibank—were beginning to nibble at the dominance of mainstream banks and insurance companies. Lease-finance companies started entering markets the traditional firms were withdrawing from. Orix, for instance, in 1993 gave up looking to banks for its own financing needs and started issuing commercial paper. In 1998 it got into trust banking by picking up a unit from Yamaichi Securities, which had just gone bust, and life-insurance premiums almost doubled between 1998 and 1999 to reach parity with leasing revenues as a source of income for Orix. It was one way, albeit oblique, for a bit of competition to Japan's stumbling financial giants to make itself felt. But Orix did not stop there. Late in 1999, facing growing competition from GE Capital in leasing, it kept expanding beyond its already 30 lines of business to make a joint venture with America's AIG for a property and casualty insurance business in Japan, and issued a sophisticated convertible-bond and equity issue internationally to raise more finance. It was beginning to behave more globally all the time.

But as the taxman's figures for Japan's super-rich suggested, it was consumer-finance companies that really boomed in this sector. The industry, which lends not just to consumers (often instantly through ATMs after a quick credit check) but also to small businessmen whom the banks can't be bothered with, has a rather unsavory past. It got going in the 1970s making usurious loans at rates of upwards of 100 percent, had ties to gangsters and used collection techniques that bordered on the extortionate. The taint of these beginnings stuck with the industry, still putting it off limits to many domestic investors (though not foreign ones), but by the 1990s the business had changed. Interest rates remained high, often at more than, 20 percent, and funding costs were low, sometimes below 3 percent, a yawning spread which helps explain the handsome profitability of the sector (as does the fact that default rates on consumer loans are only 5 percent in Japan, compared with 6 percent in America).

But the strong-arm collection tactics were a thing of the past. And the consumer-finance companies increasingly filled a role comparable to multiple personal credit cards in the United States in early-stage financing of small companies. Even the interest rates charged in both countries on these de facto business loans—consumer credit in Japan, limitless numbers of personal credit cards in America—were similar. With plenty of willing Japanese customers for these "loan sharks"—who, unlike the banks, would actually lend money to Japanese small fry, making them seem to their borrowers less like predators than saviors—Japan's consumer-finance business had become a force that only the ignorant or the excessively squeamish recoiled from.

This was also an interesting study in the attitudes of traditional Japan to upstarts. The founders of the finance companies are almost all self-made men who did not benefit from prestigious educations or comfortable slots in the lifetime-employment system. Yasuo Takei, the head of Takefuji, started in business selling fruit. Kenshin Oshima, the founder and head of Shohkoh Fund, the second-biggest finance company, spent a brief time at a low-level job with Mitsui Trading before setting up his own firm in 1978. Every year since then Shohkoh has enjoyed double-digit growth in profits. Oshima, whose boyhood heroes were the Rothschilds, had planned since he was 12 to be a billionaire.

"People think that I am bad as Scrooge," he said in a newspaper interview in 1999. Yet he pointed out that Japan's mainstream banks were simply not serving their smaller customers' demands—especially as the recession of the 1990s began to bite and the banks cut back lending—and his and the other finance companies were just filling a gap in the market. "To be successful you need a strategic niche with lots of demand. But you also need a sector with a bad image, because it attracts less competition." Comparing the profits of the banks and insurance companies in the 1990s with those of the consumer-finance companies gives a telling sign of how significantly Japan was changing at the grassroots even when it seemed immobilized at a higher level. Bank profitability consistently fell. But between 1991 and 1998 Shohkoh's sales rose six-fold to $500 million and profits more than tenfold to $250 million. Foreigners appreciate the finance companies' virtues more than Japanese investors—40 percent of Shohkoh's shares are held by foreigners—and they may be seeing more of them:

Takefuji listed on the London Stock Exchange in late 1999 and plans to invest in real estate and other assets globally. Oshima for one isn't concerned about his image in the old Japan. "The establishment never likes newcomers. I don't think that will change soon."

The newcomer who, as the century turned, exercised the greatest dominance over the emerging Japanese economy was, appropriately, an aggressive Internet entrepreneur whose war chest came from big early investments in some of Silicon Valley's most spectacular Internet successes. The whole of Chapter 11 is about the Internet in Asia. For now consider not the industry and its impact, but simply how different Japan's new captains of new industries are going to be. Masayoshi Son, aged 42 in 2000, is as much of an outsider as you can get in Japan. Although born in Japan and a Japanese national, he is an ethnic Korean, one of the country's most discriminated-against minorities. Marginalized by polite society, he didn't bother with a Japanese higher education, instead graduating from Berkeley in 1980. He returned to Japan in 1981 and, using as seed money the $1 million he had made from selling a patent while still at university, he set up Softbank to distribute personal computer software and publish computer magazines. Success did not come like a lightning bolt. Softbank made its first big international splash in 1996 when it bought America's Ziff-Davis, a computer-magazine publisher, for $3.1 billion. The same year, almost unnoticed, he paid $100 million for 30 percent of a fledgling Silicon Valley Internet company called Yahoo!. Ziff-Davis turned out to be a lemon; the Yahoo! investment, needless to say, did not. By the end of 1999 the 28 percent that Son still owned of Yahoo! was worth some $33 billion. On top of that, he made early investments in such American Internet stars as E*Trade, GeoCities and Buy.com. By the end of 1999 Softbank had investments in more than 100 Internet firms worldwide and, Son suggested, owned close to 10 percent of the world's Internet market capitalization.

Yet Son never intended to be a pure venture capitalist. His idea was to build Japan's dominant Internet company. The stunning success of his American investments freed him from reliance on Japanese bankers, for whose caution, conservatism and snail-like pace Son and his chief lieutenants have unbounded contempt. The first step was to set up Yahoo Japan in 1996 with start-up capital of $3.5 million (Softbank at first owned 60 percent and Yahoo! 40 percent).

By early 2000 the company's market capitalization was some $23 billion, around 7,000 times the original investment. Son repeated the model over and over, each time with Softbank taking about 50 percent to 60 percent of the shares and then in fairly short order taking the new companies public, generating more stock-market wealth to finance even more acquisitions and start-ups. By late 1999 there were dozens of Softbank Internet companies: Japanese versions of E*Trade and GeoCities, e-commerce firms and some ventures that promised even more innovations, such as three venture-capital firms and a deal with Nasdaq to set up a comparable exchange in Japan. Perhaps the most intriguing part of Softbank's Internet campaign is its broad-gauged assault on financial services. Led by Softbank's CFO, Yoshitaka Kitao, a former high-flyer at Nomura Securities who despises the old Japan Inc at least as much as Son does, the firm has taken advantage of the Big Bang's deregulations to move into every on-line financial services it can get its hands on. Ignoring protocol in the process—it never consults MOF because, Kitao says, "Why visit them? They're responsible for delaying Japan's financial revolution."— Softbank has gone into on-line stockbroking, insurance, currency dealing and personal loans. In 2000, together with Orix among others, it even bought a bust bank that had been nationalized by the government.

Son's dream was always to create a cyberworld *zaibatsu*—an electronic version of the great pre-war Japanese trading companies, which modernized and industrialized Japan from the time it opened up during the Meiji Restoration in the 1860s until the Pacific war wrecked them in the 1940s, but whose partially restored relics still exist as some of the country's biggest industrial groups. Whether he is up to the management or competitive challenge of realizing that ambition is an open question. Although, by one estimate, Son controlled 70 percent of Japan's Internet business in 1999, both local and foreign competitors are pouring in (especially in financial services); and Son's indifferent handling of Ziff-Davis after it was acquired makes many wonder whether his investment skills are not a lot better honed than his managerial ones. Moreover, the worldwide dot.com stock crash of the spring and summer of 2000 badly dented Softbank's seeming invincibility as well as his war chest. Still, as investors see it anyway, Son has pointed toward Japan's future.

Do you recall, from Chapter 3, Kentaro Aikawa, the chairman of Mitsubishi Heavy Industries? He said, among other things, that "I openly brag that I don't cater to shareholders." Look at Figure 5.3 to see how shareholders value his stewardship compared to Masayoshi Son's. In 1999 MHI underperformed the Nikkei 225 stock-market index by about half whereas Softbank outperformed it nine-fold—outperforming MHI, in other words,

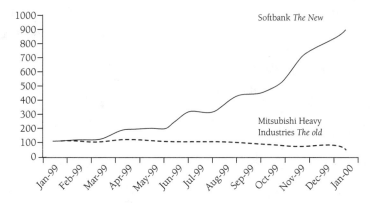

Figure 5.3 Softbank and Mitsubishi heavy industry stock price relative to Nikkei-225. (*Source:* Datastream)

18-fold. If the capital markets have anything to say about it, in another decade MHI and its ilk will have been torn limb from limb and the pieces sold, and Japanese industry will be dominated by insurgents who think like Son. It is another echo, this one resounding, of America in the 1980s.

WHAT THE FIRST TAUGHT

Japan's surreptitious thawing during the apparently frozen decade of the 1990s offered several important lessons for the rest of Asia. One is that the forces of conservatism are strong, especially when—unlike America in the late 1970s and the 1980s—a deep and multifaceted financial market does not exist to allow newcomers to raise funding easily and anonymously for their desirable but treasonable slaying of the old. Another is that, if a country has a fat cushion of savings, it will be fully used by the political-industrial establishment to forestall change.

The last is that the real world—especially these days thanks to globalization and supercharged information technology—intrudes at the bottom of societies and economies and transforms them much more deeply than anybody at first notices. This is because those who deliver the broad news about a place to the outside—mainly journalists, macroeconomists and investment-house analysts—tend to miss what's really happening by their focus on numbers and the big picture. These things usually reflect the past more than the future. Japan may yet be tripped up by its horrendous debt and its macroeconomic imbalances. My guess is that the forces rising from underneath will prove stronger—which is why Japan in the first decade of the new century could start to look as strong as it did in the 1980s, for much sounder reasons this time.

But how will the rest of Asia follow in Japan's footsteps?

CHAPTER

6

The Fall from Grace

Men go mad in herds, while they only recover their senses slowly,
and one by one—

Charles Mackay, Extraordinary Popular Delusions
and the Madness of Crowds, *1852*

The rest of Asia paid little attention in the early 1990s as Japan struggled with less and less success against its chronic ailments. In fact, the first half of the 1990s seemed to be the best years Asia had ever known (just as the last half of the 1980s had seemed to the Japanese). America was beginning its stupendous recovery, and its appetite for Asian exports only grew as the years passed. Economic growth rates throughout Southeast Asia were the highest ever. South Korea and Taiwan were thriving. After the political turbulence—the Tiananmen Square killings and their reverberations—and the economic austerity of 1989–91, China enjoyed one of its greatest booms as economic growth and foreign direct investment soared following Deng Xiaoping's visit to southern China in early 1992 and the relaunching of economic reform. Even former laggards got in on the act. After years of painful restructuring since the mid-1980s, the Philippines under President Fidel Ramos at last began to grow adequately and consistently. One of the biggest turnarounds came in India, which in 1991 abandoned its failed 40-odd-year policy of industrial regulation and protectionism and began to liberalize and open up its economy.

Yet if Japan's illness was chronic, that of the rest of Asia proved to be acute. In the 18 months between Thailand's devaluation of the baht on July 2, 1997 and the stabilization of most Asian currencies, stock markets and economies in the last few months of 1998, the region as a whole experienced its worst business and financial collapse since the end of the Pacific war in 1945. Like the lines on emergency-room scanners, Figures 6.1a and 6.1b show in detail how alarming the deterioration was. In country after country the value of the local currency against the dollar roughly halved before starting to recover. There were exceptions, of course: at one end of the scale, China's and Hong Kong's currencies did not budge; at the other end stood hapless Indonesia, whose rupiah at one point had lost 90 percent of its pre-crisis value against the dollar.

Stock markets fell even more precipitously than currencies did. From their highs to their lows, the markets of the Philippines and Indonesia fell by roughly half (in local-currency terms—the dollar terms don't bear thinking about); the markets of Hong Kong, Thailand and Malaysia by two-thirds or so; and Korea's market by almost three-quarters. For practically the first time in memory, GDP growth rates throughout the region—except in India, China, Taiwan and Singapore—had minus signs in front of them. Economies shrank in 1998 at faster rates than at any time since the 1950s. The carnage in Indonesia was especially brutal. Output fell 14 percent in 1998, a worse decline even than the Soviet Union suffered as it was falling apart. Significant social dislocation followed as city-dwellers throughout Southeast Asia and in South Korea—the people who had seen their living standards rise the most during the previous generation's-worth of economic growth—had the rug pulled from under them.

It is untrue that no danger signals were flashing before all this happened. Current accounts in many countries were going deeply into deficit. The stock markets in South Korea and Thailand—later two of the hardest-hit economies—had peaked in 1996, suggesting that investors had sensed something was amiss in Asian asset markets. But practically nobody had an inkling of the severity or breadth of the coming downturn.

In July 1997 the baht's devaluation was widely thought to be an unfortunate but unique sign of policy failure that would end the matter. When the Indonesian rupiah came under attack in August, the government and central bank were applauded for their textbook response of raising interest rates and tightening finances to deal with it. Indeed, in September, at the annual IMF and World Bank meeting in Hong Kong, George Soros, the famous American fund manager, declared that the rupiah had already been driven down too far and his fund was betting it would then go up. At the same meeting—which had been placed in Hong Kong as an optimistic celebration of the city's return to Chinese sovereignty on the previous July 1, a

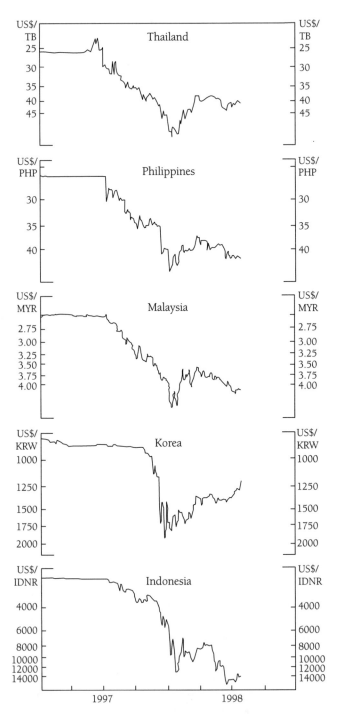

Figure 6.1a   Asian exchange rates. (*Source:* The Bank Credit Analyst Research Group)

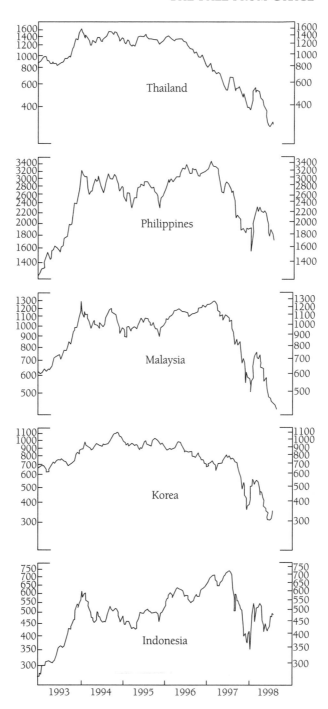

Figure 6.1b   Asian stock markets. (*Source:* The Bank Credit Analyst Research Group)

handover that everyone had firmly expected to be *the* Asian event of
the year—there was an entertaining clash between Soros and Malaysia's
Mahathir Mohamad: Soros called the prime minister "a menace to his
own country" and Mahathir bitterly blamed him in return for destroying
whole economies through his "immoral" currency speculation. But even
then there was no sense things were out of hand. When I flew into Kuala
Lumpur in October 1997, the first newspaper headline I saw, on the
lead piece in the *New Sunday Times,* was, "Currency problems will not
affect region."

Yet by then this was whistling in the dark, since every currency in
Asia that could be attacked by capital flight and speculation—including
the mighty Hong Kong dollar—had been attacked, and stock markets
worldwide were subject to violent and unpredictable downdrafts. By December the rupiah, ignoring Soros's expert opinion, had lost another
three-quarters of its value since he had declared it already undervalued,
and even South Korea had toppled into the arms of the IMF. By the end of
the year the IMF had pledged, in all, more than $100 billion to support
Thailand, Indonesia and South Korea.

The IMF was running out of money, and many held their breath.
Over the next eight months things went from bad to worse, as markets
spun out of control and governments fell (President Suharto in Indonesia, at that point Asia's longest-serving ruler, was forced by street riots
and pressure from the United States to resign in May). In August 1998
the Hong Kong government, abandoning three-decades'-worth of "positive noninterventionism," intervened with a vengeance to support the
stock market by buying billions'-worth of shares in every blue-chip
Hong Kong company—justifying this obvious share-propping scheme
by saying, to much derision, that it was needed to protect the currency
from speculative attack (the currency could not be successfully attacked
because, if left alone, the Hong Kong currency-board system was inherently invulnerable, see Chapter 9 for details). A couple of weeks later, in
September 1998, Malaysia's Mahathir threw out his IMF-friendly deputy,
Anwar Ibrahim, and had him arrested on lurid charges of homosexual
sodomy (a crime in Malaysia), and not incidentally imposed strict capital
controls on the country.

But that was it for the Asian "crisis." Between mid-August and mid-
September Russia went into a financial meltdown and defaulted on its
bonds, and an American hedge fund called Long Term Capital Management came close to going bust, threatening to take down major banks
with it. A bank-funded rescue of LTCM organized by the Federal Reserve

was followed, in September and October, by three swift cuts by the Fed in short-term interest rates. This is when Asia started recovering. To much amazement—six months earlier nobody was predicting this—in the first half of 1999 every Asian stock market performed well as both foreign and domestic investors started pouring back in. That should be kept in perspective: in dollar terms most of the markets save Hong Kong's were still vastly below their peaks of earlier in the decade; Thailand's, for instance, was still 80 percent off its 1994 high as the end of 1999 approached. Nonetheless, in local-currency terms the recovery was spectacular, with many indexes doubling or tripling in less than a year. Moreover, every country save Indonesia returned to positive GDP growth in 1999. Korea duplicated Mexico's "v-shaped" recovery almost perfectly (see Figure 6.2), and the comebacks elsewhere in Asia were almost as dramatic. By the summer of 1999 interest-rate spreads between Asian debt and U.S. Treasury bonds had fallen back to pre-crisis levels. The phony war was over. The real one was still in its early stages.

A BAG OF RICE IN A FAMINE

Economists draw a useful distinction between a panic and a crisis. In a panic—a bank run is a good example—the divergence between the

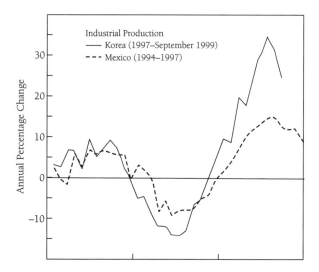

Figure 6.2 Korea's V-shaped recovery. (*Source:* The Bank Credit Analyst Research Group, 1998)

underlying economic or business reality and market signals becomes so pronounced that the signals become almost arbitrary. As Simon Ogus, a Hong Kong economist, remarked in 1998, the dollar values of many Asian currencies at that stage had no more meaning than "the price of a bag of rice in a famine." Particularly in Indonesia, where at least $60 billion in savings fled the country in late 1997 and early 1998 for safe havens like Singapore and Hong Kong, people would pay almost any price to get out of a currency they had lost all faith in. A crisis, on the other hand, arises out of deep structural flaws that have to be fixed before sustained growth can resume. Throughout the 1980s Japan was in crisis but experienced hardly any panic. In 1997–98 most of the rest of Asia suffered both. The panic dissipated just over a year after it began, while the crisis was set to continue for a long time—until Asia Inc brought its performance back up to reasonable levels of efficiency. The rest of this chapter is about the panic. The rest of the book is about Asia's crisis.

The panic had two main manifestations—a banking collapse and a currency collapse—and both were connected to the puncturing of asset bubbles. Much of the swift destruction of asset values in the stricken Asian economies was inevitable. Lester Thurow, an MIT economist, pointed out that "In the long run land values have to reflect the underlying earnings capacity (productivity) of the economic activities carried out in them. Bangkok, a city whose per capita productivity is about one-twelfth that of San Francisco, should not have land values much higher than those in San Francisco. But it did—as did other Southeast Asian cities. Land values had to come down." Yet, because of the way banks in Asia had run, the winding down of asset values created a vicious spiral of shrinking credit and declining loan value.

The reason, explained by another MIT economist, Paul Krugman, is that in most of Asia (Hong Kong and Singapore being notable exceptions) bank "liabilities were perceived as having an implicit government guarantee, but were essentially unregulated and therefore subject to severe moral hazard problems. The excessive risky lending of these institutions created inflation—not of goods but of asset prices. The overpricing of assets was sustained in part by a sort of circular process, in which the proliferation of risky lending drove up the prices of risky assets, making the financial condition of the intermediaries seem sounder than it was." The government guarantees were rarely formal. They were based instead on the perception of depositors in banks and other deposit-taking institutions like finance companies that, because of their political importance, depositors in these institutions would be rescued if anything went wrong; and, as it turned out, they almost always were. But the result of the system produced by this excessive and excessively risky lending was that when the bubble burst it produced "the same circular process in reverse: falling asset prices made the insolvency of the intermediaries visible, forcing them to cease operations, leading to further asset deflation. This circularity, in turn can explain both the remarkable severity of the crisis and the apparent vulnerability of the Asian economies to self-fulfilling crisis."

The evaporation of liquidity in Asia's financial markets sent interest rates to unbearable heights—by early 1998 in Southeast Asia real interest rates deflated by export prices were 100 percent—at the same time it sent asset prices to new depths. Borrowers quickly became incapable of paying their debts, particularly if they had borrowed in foreign currencies, and there was a sharp jump throughout the region in non-performing loans (NPLs) on the books of banks and other financial institutions. In the four hardest-hit countries (see Table 6.1) the total cost of recapitalizing the banks ranged from 11 percent of GDP in Malaysia to 90 percent in Indonesia, whose banking system was essentially destroyed.

A year after the panic began, in much of Southeast Asia and South Korea many borrowers were not even paying interest on their loans let

Table 6.1

Country	S. Korea	Thailand	Malaysia	Indonesia
Estimated system peak NPLs	153	87	21	55
Recapitalization:				
Funds raised by private sector	3	7	0	14
Funds raised by government	57	17	8	61
Nationalized banks	15	9	0	38
AMCs	17	0	6	20
Monetary injection (including				
bonds)	25	8	2	3
Total current recap cost	60	25	8	75
Debt servicing cost:				
Interest rates*	13%	8%	7%	21%
Estimated debt servicing cost	7	1	1	13
GDP (nominal; 1998e)	305	118	68	83
Percentage of peak NPLs recaptured	39%	28%	38%	136%
Total current recap cost as % of GDP	20%	21%	11%	90%
Debt servicing cost as % of GDP	2%	1%	1%	15%

Source: Warburg Dillon Read Regional Banking Team

alone servicing them on schedule. This contributed to the vicious circle, making it impossible for banks to lend (or sometimes even to stay in business) but also reluctant to throw their borrowers formally into default: even if it were possible to seize collateral like real estate or shares (remember, no bankruptcy laws), their value was so low it would have required banks to write off so much of their loan books that they too would have been wiped out. By mid-1998 much of Asia was in a curious limbo in which relatively few companies actually went to the wall since they had stopped paying their quiescent bankers anything at all. If a company does not have to pay anything on its debt, it has to be in pretty awful shape to be incapable of generating enough cash-flow to keep operations turning over. In Thailand even companies that could make payments chose not to because the banks were not forcing collections: these delinquent-by-choice loans were called "strategic NPLs" (see Chapter 7).

Asia's currency implosions in 1997–98 were also the direct result of the creation, and then the swift deflation, of asset bubbles. Chapter 2 explained why, with semi-fixed exchange rates in place in most of Asia, foreign and domestic investors figured there was basically no currency risk in borrowing abroad and using or lending the proceeds in the local-currency environment back home. This naturally created excess demand for credit, but the demand could not have been satisfied if the governments concerned had followed sound monetary policies. In circles that care about these things there was much debate in 1998–99 about whether semi-fixed exchange rates could ever work, with several people taking the view that the only sensible alternatives were either a rigidly fixed rate under a currency-board system like Hong Kong's or Argentina's (or even out-and-out adoption of the U.S. dollar as the local currency, which Argentina was considering doing in 1999). The reasoning of the skeptics was that a semi-fixed rate always invites destabilizing capital flows, because the illusion of stability causes too much money to flow in—and, when the currency threatens to break, then flow violently out.

In fact, says John Greenwood, the architect of the Hong Kong dollar link, any of the three main systems (fixed, semi-fixed or floating) is stable if the government chooses a single monetary target and sticks to it. A central bank has a choice of two: it can aim for a particular exchange rate and intervene in the foreign-exchange market to maintain it, letting domestic prices and interest rates find their own level; or it can influence rates, yields and prices through the domestic money market, letting the exchange rate find its own level. In the first half of the 1990s, in conditions of plentiful global credit, Hong Kong kept its exchange rate fixed and allowed domestic prices to fluctuate (especially asset prices). Singapore allowed its exchange rate to appreciate, hence discouraging capital inflows, but kept monetary policy at home fairly tight. Both city-states sternly regulated their banks and both escaped 1997–98 without a banking crisis.

In the rest of Southeast Asia, though, central banks decided they wanted the best of both worlds—stable exchange rates but also the freedom to adjust domestic monetary conditions to suit them. Money and credit in the domestic economy were allowed to grow far too fast in a semi-fixed exchange-rate regime. The result was swelling asset bubbles and strong economic growth but also rising real exchange rates and current-account deficits. That is why, eventually, the currencies started correcting themselves to make up for the distortions that their central banks' self-contradictory policies had fostered.

But the corrections overdid it, and in a big way—especially in Indonesia. The Indonesian overshooting was so extreme as to be almost inexplicable. In the universal scorn heaped on President Suharto when he was forced from office in 1998, it was universally overlooked that for all its faults of nepotism and venality the Indonesian government had turned in a highly creditable economic and social performance during the 30 years of Suharto's rule. Moreover, by the 1990s Indonesia was pursuing sound fiscal and monetary policies, with a balanced budget, modest monetary growth and only a slight current-account deficit. Inflation was a tolerable and steady 7 percent to 9 percent a year and to offset this the rupiah declined against the dollar by 5 percent to 6 percent a year. In such circumstances, and with Indonesia's totally open capital account, the sudden loss of as much as 90 percent of the value of the currency should be impossible: money flows across borders and interest-rate differentials should quickly haul a currency with such sound economic fundamentals back from the brink. It is only in cases of hyperinflation, and usually with capital controls, that a collapse of this magnitude takes place.

When I told Milton Friedman about this, he was incredulous: "The only way that the exchange rate could have fallen that much is if the initial rate was a wholly artificial rate." Which it wasn't, since the capital account was open and a third of domestic bank deposits were in dollars, so Indonesians had long been free to put their money in whatever currency they wanted. "Then how could the exchange rate have fallen so much? I have never heard of anything like this." No one had (recall Soros's miscalculation) and even now nobody has given a persuasive explanation of what happened. The rice-in-famine theory probably points in the right direction, which is comprehensive political breakdown. It seems plausible that, amid the disorder and instability that accompanied Suharto's drawn-out fall from power, Indonesians lost all faith in their government's ability to function (see Chapter 15 for details on all this).

Mahathir's Gamble

Yet not everybody in Asia suffered the same punishment. Singapore's currency fell far, but although GDP growth was slashed it remained mildly positive even in 1998 and there was no bank crisis. Four countries—China, India, Taiwan and the Philippines—got off lightly or (in the cases of Taiwan and India) almost scot-free. China's currency did not weaken at all, and while those of the other three did it was not in a sickening free fall: for reasons of export competitiveness, their governments were happy to see them slide. Economic growth in China and Taiwan, while not quite as robust as before, remained solidly positive throughout 1997–99, while India's GDP growth actually rose and that of the Philippines barely slipped into negative territory. Various things accounted for this relatively good performance. Unlike the rest of Asia, India traded little within the region and so was not dragged down by falling export demand. The Philippines got a very late start in East Asia's dash for growth and so did not have time to inflate its asset bubbles nearly as much; besides, its banks were more profitable. Taiwan has Asia's most flexible economy, dominated by small and medium-size businesses that respond adroitly to shifting markets. What the four shared, however (this was not true of Singapore), was that all had controls on the flow of foreign capital intended for investment in stocks, bonds and currencies. In China and India the controls were rigid, in Taiwan sticky (see next section) and in the Philippines light but carefully administered by the central bank.

This common fact did not escape the notice of Malaysia's Prime Minister Mahathir Mohamad. Mahathir is a difficult, even unpleasant, figure for most westerners to come to grips with. "Our prime minister," a Malaysian once told me, "is a well-balanced man, with a chip on each shoulder." Mahathir's neighbor and frequent antagonist, Singapore's Lee

Kuan Yew, may put off some westerners with his frankly authoritarian streak, but Lee was educated in the West, speaks with a refreshing bluntness in words of one syllable, does not have an ounce of self-doubt and is an intellectual powerhouse ("practically the smartest person on the planet," as Citibank's Walt Wriston put it to me). Mahathir, still trapped in post-colonial resentment, radiates grievance, a sense that is accentuated when he speaks English in what sounds to western ears like a sort of oily whine. In fact, I am told by Malaysians, when he speaks *bahasa Malaysia* he is eloquent and powerful. You can sense that in the English text of his classic book (which he actually wrote himself), *The Malay Dilemma,* published in 1970 and still striking for its penetrating analysis of social and economic relations between the majority but underachieving Malays and the commercially successful Chinese minority in Malaysia. And, hardly least, as prime minister since 1981, Mahathir presided over one of the most successful economic transformations in all of East Asia.

Since the panic broke in the summer of 1997, this complicated man increasingly seethed over what seemed to him the wanton destruction of so much economic accomplishment by arbitrary surges of footloose foreign capital. He saw the malevolent hand of Soros and other western speculators in the currency attacks (even straying at one point into talking about "Jews" being darkly behind it all) and believed the "remedies" being prescribed for other Asian countries by the IMF were worse than the disease. Much of this, and not just the xenophobic and racial overtone, was nonsense. Everywhere in Asia as tensions mounted it was local investors—who had a much better idea what the score was—who quietly made for the exits before the relatively clueless foreigners made their noisy stampede. But not all of what Mahathir perceived was nonsense.

Meanwhile, Mahathir's disputes with his deputy and finance minister, Anwar Ibrahim, worsened over the months. Malaysia had no need to turn to the IMF for help since, though its domestic debt was large, it had a modest foreign debt and adequate foreign-exchange reserves to cover it; but on his own Anwar pushed the same sort of policies that the IMF tended to favor in currency crises, tightening both fiscal and monetary policy in an effort to support the currency and keeping the capital account wide open. Anwar had also been champing at the bit politically, eager to take over as prime minister from the long-serving Mahathir, and allowed his supporters to make thinly veiled attacks on government "cronyism" at a ruling-party convention in the summer of 1998. But at the last minute Anwar pulled back from a direct challenge.

This hesitation was fatal because it opened the only way for Mahathir to do what he wanted: get rid of Anwar—who was arrested in mid-September after police investigations into his alleged crimes were accelerated following the abortive party convention—and impose capital controls to insulate Malaysia from the pressure of international money flows. On September 1, 1998 Malaysia fixed its exchange rate to the U.S. dollar and installed strict capital controls that outlawed the use of *ringgit* outside Malaysia, forbade the repatriation of capital owned by foreigners (e.g., from the sale of shares) for one year and set up a system requiring registration and government approval for the export of currency. In late September financially sophisticated opinion in Kuala Lumpur was that the controls would lead to a catastrophe of rising inflation (interbank interest rates had already fallen by three percentage points, banks were being told to expand lending by 8 percent a year and the government fiscal taps were being opened), a current-account deficit, falling foreign-exchange reserves, a currency black market and eventually a complete collapse of the currency.

By late spring of 1999 financially-sophisticated opinion in Kuala Lumpur was eating crow. The stock market rose threefold in value in eight months (indeed an extra $100 billion in foreign portfolio investment gushed into the country in just two months early in 1999), foreign-exchange reserves rose by half in six months thanks to a huge current-account surplus of 15 percent of GDP in 1998, the currency was steady at its fixed rate, there was no black market in the currency and no capital flight, international credit-rating agencies had restored Malaysia's investment-grade status, and it was about to be announced that Malaysia's stock market would be restored to the main international benchmark weighting index. What happened?

For one thing, Malaysia's government did not use the breathing space it got from the pressures of the international capital markets to go on a spending spree: monetary and fiscal policy were prudent (some even say too tight). Second, and confirming Mahathir's suspicions, foreign direct investors in the country rather liked the stability their operations were given by a fixed exchange rate—especially since Malaysia honored its promise and allowed them freely to repatriate their profits even while stock-market "speculators" were tied down. So the FDI which accounted for much of Malaysia's manufactured exports was unimpaired. Third, Malaysia tackled bank restructuring in a fairly professional way, setting up one body (called Danaharta) to buy NPLs from banks and restructure the loans and another (Danamodal) to recapitalize the banks and inculcate them with such novel concepts as credit and risk assessment even while they merged and streamlined them. Not everything was done by the book. Later in 1999 political considerations seemed to be seeping into the process of bank consolidation, and the restructuring of non-financial companies—where the crony capitalists make their homes in Malaysia's highly politicized corporate system—was producing few obvious successes and one clear failure: the rescue, using minority shareholder and pension-fund money, of a ruling-party darling called Renong.

Malaysia's experience fell far short of proving the case for capital controls. They were imposed just when interest rates began falling, exports shooting up and currencies stabilizing throughout Asia. As in the case of Hong Kong with its ill-advised but brilliantly timed stock-market intervention two weeks before Malaysia imposed capital controls, a bold action may well have appeared to have beneficent consequences that were in fact purely coincidental, caused by the movement of much bigger forces. Moreover, they clearly damaged the government's credibility with foreign investors. Malaysia outrageously seized the shares of Singaporean investors who had bought Malaysian stock on a parallel market that was active in Singapore in the years before the imposition of capital controls; it took until the middle of 2000 before a plan was in place providing for the gradual release of the Singaporean shores. The government's arbitrary changes of the investment rules also created mistrust among foreign portfolio investors of all types. When, in September 1999, after the exit tax on repatriated principal of foreign portfolio investment was abolished, inflows pretty much dried up. Lastly, with much longer hindsight, Malaysia's capital controls may prove to have been nothing more than a way of unfortunately putting off much needed reckonings and changes in business and the economy. But after a year's-worth of controls in Malaysia, only a pedant could argue that they had plainly failed as an emergency measure.

Mahathir does neither himself nor Malaysia any favors by always leading with his chin, but on the substance of his critique of unfettered capital flows he had plenty of respectable support (particularly—how ironic can you get?—from George Soros). Jagdish Bhagwati, an economics professor at Columbia University who is one of the world's most ardent proponents of absolutely free trade in goods and services, said in 1998 the case for absolutely free flows of capital is pretty weak. One reason is that the benefits are unproven: to take the biggest example, under the Bretton Woods international financial regime of roughly 1950–71 the world operated on a system of fixed exchange rates and highly regulated capital accounts but also enjoyed the best sustained global economic and trade performance in history.

A second reason is that the costs can be enormous. When prices or quantities of goods and services shift, the interplay of supply and demand tends to make for a smooth adjustment even across national borders. Not so with financial markets. The volatility of capital flows and the herd-like behavior of lenders and investors can, in the case of currencies and securities, easily destroy the self-corrective market-clearing function of price changes; indeed, this is what a panic is all about, as the epigram which opens this chapter suggests. Eventually prices of financial instruments again start reflecting reality, but meanwhile the damage done first to wealth and then, through the credit mechanism, to the real economy can be staggering, unwarranted by the economy's true condition and much longer-lasting than the panic itself. This is serious stuff. The IMF has guessed that over the four years 1999–2002 Indonesia will have lost a cumulative 82 percent of its potential output in those years, Thailand almost 60 percent, Malaysia almost 40 percent and South Korea 27 percent. For still immature countries, potential output loss on this scale is devastating. Unemployment roughly tripled in Indonesia and South Korea and doubled in Hong Kong and Thailand. Poverty rates roughly doubled in Indonesia and urban Korea. It is no wonder Bhagwati, among others, thinks some capital controls are justified.

As they watched with mounting horror the havoc Asia's financial panic was wreaking in 1997–98, many of the region's most internationally-minded leaders began to have their doubts about the wisdom of Southeast Asia's decision over the previous decade to open capital accounts fully—at least without first creating strong enough banks, and appropriate instruments of bank regulation and supervision, to cope with an open regime. Washington Sy Cip, a well-connected Philippine businessman and financier, said in early 1999 he thought that, once the IMF's tutelage had ended, most Asian countries would install some sort of capital controls. He did not necessarily buy Malaysia's after-the-fact controls but said that "as long as the rules of the game were there from the beginning, were consistent and predictable, then it doesn't hurt" a country's ability to attract foreign investment. Even Lee Kuan Yew had been shaken by the unprecedented devastation:

All the faults were there and they were making this phenomenal 8 percent to 11 percent growth despite all these faults. The difference was they had opened up their capital accounts, and had borrowed in foreign currency expecting the exchange rate to remain unchanged. I'm not saying that they wouldn't have come up against a brick wall; they still would have, but at different times and with different results. As it was, one collapse (Thailand) led to another (Indonesia) and brought down the whole of East Asia (South Korea). The herd instinct caused foreign investors to exit from all the East Asian emerging markets. Whether a country is sound or unsound, we were all under the category "emerging markets," from which the fund managers ordered their funds out. So Singapore and Hong Kong went down with the rest, although we had sound banks and no foreign debts. Taiwan was saved because it had partially closed its stock market, and had foreign-exchange controls. The lesson of this crisis is that those with partial or full capital controls—Taiwan, China, India—have done better.

Without the large capital flows there wouldn't have been a meltdown. Some of their banks would have gone bad but not all banks at the same time. All the banks in Jakarta, over 200 of them, were demolished at the same time. So too in Thailand. Once foreign fund managers pulled out simultaneously, they rubbished the domestic currencies.

The Indonesian rupiah fell from 2,400 to the dollar before the crisis to 17,500 in February. When you rubbish a country's currency like that, you demolish the whole system. That wouldn't have happened if they had an internal domestic currency crisis. The rupiah wouldn't have gone down to a quarter of its U.S. dollar value. Some banks would have collapsed, but not all banks. Companies that had borrowed in their domestic currencies and invested unwisely, building resort hotels, office blocks, etc., would have been bankrupted. But there would have been good companies in their midst that would have absorbed them and taken over. But here good companies also went down the drain.

So do capital controls make sense?

Not for the efficient use of capital worldwide and proper allocation of resources. But if I've got a weak central bank, badly run banks, poor corporate governance, I would not open up the capital account. I will suffer disadvantages, but my financial system will not be demolished. If I have a weak economy, how can I defend a peg or semi-peg for my currency when there are such huge flows of capital? It's better if I can control big sums moving in and out.

   If I were an underdeveloped country I would not join this system of free movement of capital in and out of my economy. I've been alarmed at the devastation it has wrought in Indonesia and, to a lesser extent, in Thailand. The Indonesians would have continued their growth if they had not freed their capital account. And Indonesia might have needed stricter controls than Taiwan.

Capital controls or none, Taiwan proved the most resilient of Asia's economies. Why?

THE PARAGON

Taiwan has long had a plausible claim, along with Hong Kong, to being the best economy in Asia. The meltdown of 1997–98, which revealed some surprising structural rigidities in Hong Kong (see Chapter 9), suggests Taiwan may be ahead in this hypothetical race. Part of the reason Taiwan shrugged off the Asian flu is that, unlike everywhere else in Asia, it had precious little crisis for the panic to latch onto—its businesses were less stuck in an unprofitable and increasingly untenable past, and so less exposed to a market-based shake-up. The other reason is that Taiwan had an intelligent system of capital controls that worked with the grain of the market to prevent destabilizing surges of foreign capital while also avoiding the distortions that controls often entail.

   Although Taiwan has its share of government-owned banks and ruling-party-backed companies, the economy is dominated by small and medium businesses, often family-owned, that get no favors from the government. Taiwanese firms tend to have relatively low debt loads, partly because interest rates have been kept close to world levels. In the late 1990s Taiwan had a property bubblette of its own, and some construction companies were teetering (though more because of unwise stock-market speculation than property defaults), but the island's real asset bubble—like Japan's—was formed and burst in the late 1980s. In the space of two years the main stock-market index fell from 12,000 to 2,000. Unlike Japan, however, Taiwan did not try to resist the dictates of the market. Taiwan's greatest advantage, as the Asian storm broke in 1997, was that it had already been restructuring for ten years. Yang Shih-Chien, a Taiwanese minister who specializes in science and technology, explains the process.

Beginning in 1987, the central bank allowed a drastic appreciation of the New Taiwan dollar (NT$) from 40 to the U.S. dollar at the start to 25 by the early 1990s. The impact on export-based and cheap-labor industries was huge. In the ten years after 1987 Taiwanese firms shifted 30,000 factories to mainland China, where total Taiwanese FDI may have reached $40 billion by 2000, and another 10,000 factories to Southeast Asia. Production in Taiwan itself was shoved rudely up the value-added scale. In 1986 the factory cost of shoes made in Taiwan was $3 a pair, and 800m pairs were exported from the island. In 1998 as few as 60m pairs were exported from Taiwan itself, but at a factory cost of $20 a pair.

The shift over this decade was helped, says Yang, by a partial liberalization of markets for banking, airlines, telecommunications and power. The capital markets also grew in breadth and depth—particularly, and almost uniquely in Asia, the market for venture capital. By the end of the 1990s there were some 125 venture capital firms operating in Taiwan, and they had invested $3 billion in 1,500 high-tech firms. Lastly, during this decade of adjustment the government invested heavily in public infrastructure, which helped smooth the transition by boosting domestic demand and keeping growth at comfortable levels. Among other things, all this helped push Taiwan toward being the most high-tech manufacturing economy in Asia (of $230 billion in manufacturing sales in 1998, 40 percent was in high technology, a share Yang expects to rise to 50 percent early in the 2000s). There will be more on the high-tech aspect in Chapter 10. The point here, as Yang notes, is that alone among Asian countries pre-crisis Taiwan followed the United States in undertaking an across-the-board reform of its economy.

In other words, Taiwan had fewer of the fundamental weaknesses to make it prone to investor suspicions than any of its neighbors did. Perhaps just as important—and in the fevered atmosphere of 1997–98 closely linked to this basic strength—it was less vulnerable than most to an attack of foreign nerves or speculative predation. Not only did Taiwan's economic growth dip only slightly, the stock market's value fell less than half as fast as that of the rest of Asia in the year after the crisis broke; and the currency fell only as far, and then gradually, as the authorities thought necessary to keep the export engine firing. This was thanks to the fact that the Taiwanese managed to modulate capital flows without interfering with free-market forces. Taiwan did this not through heavy-handed Malaysia-like controls, but instead through what one investor calls "capital stickiness" and another "administrative friction."

Here is how it worked as of the end of 1998. Taiwan has no restrictions on the use of foreign exchange for trade in goods and services. The authorities have to be notified of incoming FDI, but no permission is needed either to bring it in or to take capital or profits out. Taiwanese who want to make direct investments overseas are free to do so, with one national-security exception, China itself. But even there—and this is typical of the Taiwanese approach—small-fry investors are in practice free to set up factories. It is only high-profile projects that attract government pressure.

As for pure capital flows, each man, woman and child in Taiwan can send up to $5 million out of the country each year, no questions asked (often in cash, as bemused Hong Kong customs officers discovered at their airport in 1992 when, during blanket searches after the robbery of an armored car, they opened the carry-on bag of a polyester-trousered, highly-permed Taiwanese grandmother and found she was carrying—entirely legitimately—$2 million in $100 bills with her). Each Taiwanese company can send out $50 million a year. Foreign banks are not allowed to open offshore accounts for Taiwanese. Foreign mutual funds can be sold in Taiwan but not advertised.

Foreign institutional investors are allowed to set up shop in Taiwan but are subject to capital requirements. A single investor can own up to 15 percent of a company, foreigners in total, up to 30 percent (all these limits were to be abolished in 2000). Foreign investment in stocks can be taken out under a variety of restrictions, from none to heavy, depending on how it was put in. Foreign banks (provided they are among the world's 500 biggest) can open branches, but not many, and their deposit base is limited.

Turnover in the foreign-exchange market is often only $150 million to $200 million a day, and banks are limited in the extent to which they can lend NT$ for foreign-exchange dealing. When combined with a trifling foreign debt, equal to 11 percent of GDP at the end of 1998, this has allowed the authorities to let the market pretty much determine the level of the currency while they adjust interest rates to domestic business conditions—without having to worry about the machinations of hedge-fund speculators, who can't get a toehold in such a thinly traded market.

This may sound like a complicated mess, but that was precisely its virtue. Clean-cut capital controls run the risk of creating political favorites, corrupt constituencies and market distortions that lead inevitably to black-market trading. Taiwan's vague method offered enough scope for individuals and companies to do most of their business unhindered by bureaucrats, for foreign portfolio capital to enter and leave in adequate volumes to reflect true market signals for both equities and the currency and—most important of all—for financial transactions not to distort the allocation of resources in the real economy. It was as perfect a marriage as could be hoped for of a free market for goods and services and a market for capital that reflected fundamentals rather than whims.

Not that you would ever hear about it from the two "guardians" of the world economy. Because of the festering dispute between China and Taiwan, the World Bank does not even publish statistics about Taiwan. Nor, for the same reason, does Taiwan enjoy the "benefit" of advice or cash from the IMF—which, in the Asia of 1997–98, was a blessing mostly without disguise.

A BUNCH OF SOCIALIST FRENCH

Bill Kaye is a lanky Mississippian whom Bear Bryant, the University of Alabama's legendary football coach, turned down for a slot on his team because "unlike these black kids, you've got options for what to do with your life." One of the options Kaye took was to move to Hong Kong in 1991, set up an Asian hedge fund and participate in a direct-investment fund for China. He shut everything down in 1997, only to reopen a year later with a private-equity firm to invest in new industries in Asia. He has no doubt about the root of Asia's problems in the mid-1990s. The IMF, he says, advised every regime in the region to link its currency to the dollar, a step that made the markets think currency risk had been taken away so the cost of capital was too low. "Only a bunch of socialist French," he says (referring perhaps to the IMF's managing director Michel Camdessus), could believe this would help.

It is a sentiment widely echoed—though with less entertaining pungency—by some very heavyweight opinion. Steven Radelet and Jeffrey Sachs of Harvard attacked the IMF's handling of Asia's problems with great vigor in 1997–98. In early 1998 two ex-Treasury secretaries, George Shultz and William Simon, and Walter Wriston (ex-Citibank) called for the abolition of the IMF. And in a conversation with me in 1999 Milton Friedman, though in a kindlier way, repeated Bill Kaye's view about the IMF:

Oh, well, what was behind the Asian crisis was the IMF. This was a banking crisis in all these countries, and the banking crises became severe because of the system of pegged exchange rates with independent central banks. In all of these cases, whether it's Korea, Thailand, Indonesia, what you have is a system of exchange rates pegged to the U.S. dollar and independent central banks, which were very much concerned with trying to promote growth internally. A system like that is a disaster waiting to happen, whether it be in an underdeveloped country or a developed country. If you think of what happened in Britain in the late sixties or early seventies, or in 1992–93, or in Italy at the same time, the system was particularly dangerous.

Then take the way Mexico was handled. The handling of Mexico [in 1995] created, as you are well aware, the problem of the bankers around the world thinking that if any currency collapsed the IMF would bail them out. That's stage one. And so you had an excess inflow of capital, short-term capital in particular, from abroad. It came because it seemed it was a no-risk deal, interest rates were very high because there was internal monetary expansion, you had pegged exchange rates so there was no exchange risk, if the exchange rate went the IMF would bail you out, so money flowed in. And sooner or later that system was bound to collapse. And when it collapsed the IMF made it worse by treating the East Asian problems as if they were Latin American problems, as if they were problems of extravagant governments that had engaged in excessive spending and run deficits, when they weren't. They were all banking crises, not fiscal crises, and what was needed was to maintain internal expansion as best you could, while trying to repair the bank crisis.

Now, I think the IMF has a problem in a much more fundamental sense. There are three kinds of system you can have for exchange-rate arrangements. One is a currency board or dollarization. Panama is the extreme case of dollarization, Argentina and Hong Kong are different cases of currency boards. Next is pegged exchange rates with independent central-bank policy. Finally freely floating exchange rates.

Now it's obvious . . . first of all as far as East Asia is concerned, note that Australia and New Zealand were not affected. Why? Because they have floating rates. Japan has a serious internal problem but no external problem. Why? Because it has a floating rate.

The countries that were affected were those that had pegged rates. But now you're the IMF. If a country has a currency board, what role is there for the IMF? Zero. If a country has a floating exchange rate what role is there for the IMF? Same. Then it's not surprising that the IMF encourages countries to peg exchange rates. So if there had been no IMF, I don't think you would have had an East Asian crisis.

The appropriate response to the initial crisis would have been to let the exchange rate go to wherever it would have settled. Do not contract internally any more than you have to. The problem is a problem of debt abroad, not internally, and so you ought to maintain the banking system, you ought to maintain domestic monetary growth at the same time you try to get debt arrangements, to solve your foreign debt problems, but what you don't want to do is raise taxes internally, cut general spending internally, and put a domestic collapse on top of the foreign collapse.

Why was the U.S. Treasury so supportive of the IMF?

It enabled the Treasury to conduct foreign policy. Given the propensity of every agency to want to have more power, the real problem in there is the Exchange Stabilization Fund, which all by itself enables the Treasury to conduct foreign policy without Congressional approval. You ought to abolish it, but the Exchange Stabilization Fund enables them to cooperate with the IMF in conducting foreign policy. I can believe that the IMF does not take any emergency decision without consulting the Treasury. You know, self-interest is really a very important thing. Would people who run the IMF be in favor of the IMF if they weren't in it? I find it very hard to believe that Mike Mussa, for example [then the IMF's chief economist], would be in favor of the IMF if he were in the academic world, or Stan Fischer [then the IMF's deputy director]. Both of them are very good economists, they're first-rate as technical economists. But if you want to see self-interest operate in a naked way. . . . You're right, the IMF right now has almost no friends, but the ones it has are very important.

As all these remarks suggest, there are two main charges leveled against the IMF. The first is that, pre-crisis, it encouraged the crisis by creating "moral hazard"—all the commercial bankers thought the IMF would bail them out if anything went wrong, as they had been bailed out of Mexico—or fostering an inappropriate exchange-rate regime. The second is that, once the panic broke, the IMF did not understand what it was dealing with and prescribed the wrong medicine.

As for the first charge, it seems pretty likely that bankers figured they had a free ride—why not after Mexico? On the other hand, as pointed out by John Greenwood, semi-fixed exchange rates do not have to be inherently defective, though it takes a well-disciplined central bank to make them work. So it may have been bad advice from the IMF to adopt such a scheme, but the self-indulgent countries were hardly blameless either.

The IMF's (and the U.S. Treasury's) behavior once the crisis broke seems more dubious. The misdiagnosis, as Milton Friedman pointed out, was clear almost at once. The IMF seemed not to grasp the elementary point that by its nature a private-sector debt and overcapacity problem would lead quickly to deflation as companies tried to deleverage themselves and banks rolled in their lines of credit. It was not a situation in which the gung-ho deployment of the inflation-fighting tools of fiscal stringency and high real interest rates made much sense. Six months or so into the panic the IMF appeared to realize this and relaxed some of its earlier requirements, but by then a lot of damage had already been done to the real economies to which its remedies were applied. The IMF could also point out with some justification that, even if high interest rates were inappropriate from the viewpoint of the domestic economy, they were needed externally to shore up the value of the currency. The trouble with that argument is that the price of the currencies—the real interest rates paid to the holders of them—was almost irrelevant in the midst of the panic: remember the point about the bag of rice in a famine.

A deeper charge about the handling of the panic is political. One of the most vivid images to emerge in the first few months of the panic was a notorious photo of a looming Michel Camdessus standing with arms folded above Indonesia's diminutive President Suharto as he signed one of his country's deals with the IMF in January 1998. Even to western eyes the gesture and posture looked for all the world as if Camdessus were displeased with a truant schoolboy; in Javanese culture the arms-folded posture is a lot ruder than that. As events unfolded, the tendency of the IMF and the U.S. Treasury to use the leverage of financial need to extract political changes—more democracy in Indonesia, say, or an attack on "cronyism"— became more pronounced. It was a form of financial diplomacy that made more than a few people nervous, among them Martin Feldstein, an economics professor at Harvard, who wrote in 1998 that "the IMF is risking its effectiveness by the way it now defines its role . . . its recent emphasis on imposing major structural and institutional reforms as opposed to focusing on balance-of-payments adjustments will have adverse consequences in both the short term and the more distant future. The IMF should stick to its traditional task of helping countries cope with temporary shortages of foreign exchange and with more sustained trade deficits."

Lee Kuan Yew's view is that the picture is mixed:

[The IMF and the U.S. Treasury] did both good and harm. I will not join Jeffrey Sachs to say the IMF was stupid or wrong-headed. IMF officials came with good intentions but inadequate understanding of what had happened.

The critical factor needed to restore the currency markets in Indonesia and Thailand was confidence, market confidence. If the U.S. Treasury had shown that they backed Thailand and Indonesia as they showed they were behind Korea, Thailand and Indonesia would not have gone down so badly. Korea would have suffered more if the U.S. Treasury had not told the lending banks, "Hold it. Talk and roll over the debts. We cannot allow Korea to go down the drain."

In the case of Indonesia, every market player knew the U.S. wanted Suharto to reform or perish. So they had to reform or perish. Right or wrong, that's the way it was.

Setting high interest rates for the rupiah to restore its exchange value did not work because the critical factor of confidence was lacking. The market knew the U.S. position that it wanted to change the way President Suharto ran his government. The old man did not want to change. So the U.S. and the IMF folded their arms and allowed the market to sell the rupiah down. The stock market collapsed. Indofood, a company worth billions of dollars before the crisis, was suddenly insolvent.

This didn't happen in Thailand's case because Thailand was IMF-compliant. Then they said, "Okay, you are a good boy." Thailand and Korea became two good boys and Indonesia became the bad boy. Malaysia was a potential bad boy, so Mahathir decided to disconnect his capital account.

However, once the debris started being cleared throughout the region toward the end of 1998 (except in poor Indonesia), the question was no longer how the damage should have been contained. Instead it was how Asia was going to rebuild. The struggle over that was intense from the start, and the outcome will shape Asia for at least the next ten years.

CHAPTER

7

The Fight for the Future

On a blazing hot Friday afternoon, November 13, 1998, I sat for an hour in a conference room at Deloitte Touche Tohmatsu's offices in Bangkok listening to a bluff 58-year old Australian bankruptcy specialist called Mike Wansley tell me about the frustrations he had trying to work out business restructurings in Thailand. The economy, he rightly guessed, had bottomed and the government was as reform-driven as it could be given the Byzantine political system (including an oligarchical, albeit elected, Senate whose members were fighting tooth-and-nail against a proposed bankruptcy and foreclosure law, among other things because many if not most of them had given personal guarantees against their companies' debts and stood to be ruined if creditors could enforce them). At the moment, he said, it took about 10 years in Thailand to foreclose on collateral for a loan. Of course, it never happened. There is, supposedly, a Thai saying that "It is better to eat dogs' dung than to go to court."

The attitude of company owners was that pain had to be shared equally, even by people—i.e., creditors—who had not bargained for that when they gave their loans. The defiance of the head of Thai Petrochemical Industry (TPI), which with $3.5 billion in debt in late 1999 was Thailand's biggest debtor, was typical. Prachai Leophariatana, who was also a member of Thailand's Senate, told a reporter in late 1998 that "This is Thailand. This sort of law [providing for creditor-enforced bankruptcy or foreclosure] is unfair to the debtor, to the people." Bankers, he scoffed, are like lawyers or accountants, with no right to take away a company that had been built by businessmen like himself who worked for decades

130

to create a going concern. At that point Prachai's negotiations with his creditors had been dragging on for a year. Because TPI and its affiliates were not making any payments on their huge debt, they actually went back into the black midway through 1998. Some creditors were calling for Prachai's ouster from the company, but he not only ignored that and kept running the companies as he saw fit—he also had TPI repay some $25 million to a company he was connected to, a clear violation of an agreement with TPI's creditor committee that payments to all creditors would be suspended until an overall deal was reached. When told by the creditors' committee to stop these payments, Prachai simply brushed off the request and kept making them.

Wansley, who had been in Thailand for only a year, said that the attitude of debtors was changing slowly toward recognizing they could not simply stonewall their bankers. (TPI, for instance, was moving toward an agreement with its creditors in late 1999 despite Prachai's views a year earlier, see next section.) Among Wansley's firm's involvements was a company called Thai Modern Plastics, which he said had engaged in massive fraud that led to the suspension of some directors. Creditors were almost as problematic as debtors. Most lending was syndicated, and large, usually national, divergences existed among syndicate lenders. Thai bankers wanted modest debt-service payments rather than write-offs, Japanese banks didn't want to write off anything, the Europeans and Americans just wanted to cut bait. Standstill agreements—meaning each bank would not press claims provided the others did not—was a common practice in the West but hard to come by in Thailand. Supplier-creditors just stayed away from formal talks. Record-keeping in the companies was "bizarre," with multiple sets of books the norm. Often, Wansley said, there would be 30 Thai banks on the creditor side of meetings, each represented by somebody so junior he would say nothing. The foreigners attended at first and then gave up. By late 1998 they were coming back, though as possible purchasers of assets rather than creditors, and represented by operations rather than financial people.

Still there was a wide gap between what the Thais and the foreigners thought. Reflecting the view of TPI's Prachai, Thais "looked at the top line and total assets, the rest of the world at the bottom line and net assets" when valuing a company. When shareholders' equity was already gone, said Wansley, the owners and managers of a Thai company still thought they had a lot of value; they expected to keep 30 percent to 40 percent of the business at worst. Much money had been lent by Thai banks without the remotest stab at due diligence; some bankers never even saw the factories they were lending to. Foreigners, he said, were no better, lending in recent years even without bothering to get collateral. Assets were hard to trace, with myriad companies to hide transactions and much money placed in banks in the Cayman Islands or Switzerland. In Thailand itself they didn't even try to trace assets.

As you must suspect, Wansley told me almost all of this off the record. I can write it now because he is dead. Almost four months to the day after I talked with him, he was murdered at gunpoint in broad daylight on an open road in the countryside near Bangkok. He was riding in a van at the time and was shot eight times by a gunman on a motorcycle. It was an assassination, arranged for not much money by executives at a nearby sugar mill where Wansley had uncovered a lot of corruption. It was emblematic, despite the amazing progress Asia has made over the past 40 years, of the gap between what rich Westerners expect of modern business and what most Asians used to be resigned to. The rest of this book is about how that gap is going to be closed.

DRIVERS OF CHANGE

As recovery spread through most of Asia late in 1998, five things helped drive growth forward and offered a glimpse of how Asia's future would be shaped. The five were a rising tide of exports, especially within the region itself; the makings of a consumer boom; the beginnings of a shift from old industries and business dynasties to new ones; financial restructuring; and the early days of corporate restructuring. There were big differences from country to country in the way these forces interacted, some of which will be discussed in the next two chapters, but also quite a lot in common.

Begin with exports. If there is a single trend that defined how Asia succeeded in 1960–95, it is the region's openness to the outside world. The more trade, and the freer, the better for any economy, but East Asia's export orientation over two generations was unusually strong for a mostly poor part of the world. Between 1965 and 1990 South Korea's exports grew ninety-fold in real terms and Taiwan's thirty-fold, in the process driving both up the economic ladder from farming to light and then advanced manufacturing. The export, in the early days, of labor-intensive goods like textiles and toys greatly boosted labor productivity and wages, and stimulated further investment. Just as important, the productivity increases in export industries that came from exposure to world standards of quality and technology were quickly transmitted through the whole economy thanks to the export firms' demands for intermediate inputs like cloth to make the shirts or plastic to make the toys.

Asia's export machine began sputtering in 1996 and in the months after the financial panic began it alarmingly did not seem to reignite. However, this was a statistical illusion brought about by the initial steep fall in Asian currencies and the inability of many Asian exporters to secure lines of credit for a few months. The volume of exports (as distinct from their dollar value) began shooting up almost immediately, while imports slumped even faster. In the first quarter of 1998 imports in volume terms fell by double-digit percentages everywhere in Asia except China, whereas exports jumped by double digits everywhere except the Philippines and Japan. One of the surest signs of this was the shattering of a 20-year trend in the price of chartering freight ships. Before the crisis it always cost more to charter a ship to carry goods from Europe or America to Asia than to charter one going the other way. In mid-1997 it cost $3,500 a day to charter a ship heading from Asia to the West. A year later it cost $7,000 to $8,000. Conversely, in 1997 it cost $7,000 to $9,000 to charter an Asia-bound ship; a year later it was $5,000 to $6,000. Nor were Asian exports picking up steam solely westbound. Pre-crisis it cost $4,000 to $5,000 to charter a ship for intra-Asian trade. A year later it was $5,000 to $6,000.

And sure enough, when the macroeconomic statistics at last came in they reflected what the market had long been telling shippers rather than what hand-wringing analysts had been reading in out-of date balance-of-payments figures. In 1998 the Asian "crisis" countries—Indonesia, Korea, Malaysia, the Philippines and Thailand—pulled off one of the most remarkable trade turnarounds ever recorded. In 1996, the last year of their binge, they had a collective current-account deficit of $53 billion. In 1997 they had a deficit of $24 billion but in 1998 a surplus of $69 billion—a swing into surplus of $93 billion in one year and $122 billion in two years. When Mexico had to adjust in 1994–96, it went from a deficit equal to 7 percent of GDP to a deficit of 0.7 percent. In the two years 1996–98 Korea went from a deficit of 4.4 percent of GDP to a surplus of 12.4 percent, Thailand from a deficit of 8 percent to a surplus of 12.5 percent, Malaysia from a deficit of almost 6 percent to a surplus of more than 13 percent. On top of this all the Asian countries had by 1999 resumed economic growth that was at least respectable and in Korea's case as strong as it had been pre-crisis.

One thing this speedy adjustment tells us is that the flexibility and adaptability of Asia's economies was every bit as strong during the panic as before it—or as Martin Wolf, a British financial journalist, put it, "the notion that these crisis-hit economies were basket cases was quite ludicrous." Another is that Asia's growth—and more significantly its efficiency—is still driven first by its export-orientation, its seemingly innate willingness to be plugged into the world economy. A less obvious but perhaps more telling point for the future is how relatively fast the trade of Asians among themselves has been growing, compared with their trade with the rich countries of the West. The numbers are hard to get straight, because so much intra-Asian trade is in intermediate goods that are eventually sold in their final form in the West, but the trend does not seem to be in doubt. In 1990 intra-Asian trade excluding Japan accounted for 28 percent of Asian exports. By 1997 that had risen by a quarter, to 35 percent. The collapse of 1998 slowed that shift but by early 1999, with Asia's recovery seriously underway, it had resumed: to take one example, Singapore's export growth to America and Europe in the second quarter of 1999 increased by a modest 10 percent or less, whereas its exports to Taiwan and Korea rose by more than 20 percent. The same was true of other Asian countries. Moreover, contrary to popular opinion, Japan in some ways depends on the rest of Asia more than its neighbors do on Japan: it sends almost four times as many of its regional exports to them as they do to it.

The trade of Asians among themselves is worth watching because of the second trend the evolution of the crisis has revealed.

NEW SPENDERS, NEW SPENDING

As the disaster unfolded in Asia in 1997–99 household savings rates rose everywhere, just as they did in Japan during the whole of the 1990s. Falling retail sales overall convinced many people that stimulus for the revival depended crucially on the United States and Europe. What the high savings rate probably means instead, as Chris Wood of ABN-Amro has pointed out, is that the next phase of Asia's growth will be driven by household consumer spending rather than by company investment.

Throughout 1998–99 companies (except in some cases in Korea) were slashing borrowings as they tried to salvage their balance sheets and get rid of the excess capacity they had built up over the previous decade. The other side of this coin was that banks were cutting their loan books just as eagerly as companies were cutting their borrowings.

All of this suggests that consumer rather than corporate lending is what banks in Asia will be pursuing in the early years of the new century, and that they will find a ready audience in a new generation of Asian consumers. The (for good reason) scared middle-aged may not buy, but their children will. The divergent consumption patterns coming out in Japan—older people hoarding, younger ones buying pretty freely but not at all the same stuff that was being bought before—was described in Chapter 5. It is a pattern likely to be repeated throughout Asia, and one that augurs well for new Asian companies of all kinds. It is startling, for instance, that while retails sales overall were falling in 1997–99, mobile-phone ownership in those years rose from 24 percent of the population in Hong Kong to 52 percent, in Singapore from 18 percent to 38 percent and in Taiwan from 7 percent to 35 percent. The meltdown of 1997–98 will prove to have been a crisis for the old but a great boon for the new.

NEW INDUSTRIES, NEW PEOPLE

As the evolution of corporate Japan has already suggested (see Chapter 5), one result of Asia's restructuring will be to create fast-growing companies in industries that have not shone brightly in the past. They will begin to displace, first in profitability and later in size, the commodities-based and manufacturing firms that dominated Asia's rise in the two generations after 1960. Some of the new stars will be big surprises: who 20 years ago was predicting the sway that Japan's consumer-finance companies would have in the mid-1990s?

One clue about the near-term changes can be found by looking at which companies did best and which worst in the buffeting of 1997–99. Among the best performers were companies like Jollibee, a Philippine-based fast-food outlet with branches wherever Philippine emigrants tend to congregate—meaning throughout Asia and in parts of North America. Another success was a group in Thailand run by an American émigré called Bill Heinecke that deals in food, drink and hotel outlets and other

consumer businesses (Heinecke has, e.g., the Pizza Hut franchise for
Thailand). As with Jollibee, Heinecke's fast-food and hotel businesses had
been plagued during the boom years by high land costs and labor shortages; those impediments disappeared with the crash. Some of the firms
that did worst in Asia were property companies, whose share prices may
take years to recover. One of the most striking broad changes came in the
Hong Kong stock market, whose capitalization had long been dominated
by the shares of property companies. In 1997 property shares accounted
for 31 percent of market capitalization; in the fourth quarter of 1999 the
figure was 15 percent and still falling. There will be more on all this in
Chapters 12–14, which are about the market for corporate control in Asia
and the reshaping of the Asian corporation. The single biggest shift,
though, is likely to take place in information technology, a business Asia
has tended to neglect but where its biggest opportunities over the next
decade—and the world's biggest threats to western (especially American)
Internet dominance—probably lie (Chapters 10 and 11).

Bill Kaye, the IMF-friendly Mississippian you met in Chapter 6, runs
a direct-investment firm out of Hong Kong that is designed to look for
new industries in Asia to invest in. Originally, in the early and mid-
1990s, he had run an Asia-only hedge fund but switched in 1999 to one
that invested in emerging markets generally. In Asia itself he also began
taking direct equity stakes in private firms. The first reason for his switch
was that publicly-listed companies in Asia were "not impressive" and the
shallow liquidity of the markets made hedge-fund investing in Asia alone
very risky. The second reason was that he felt that over the years
2000–2005 the most promising sorts of Asian restructuring would be
debt/equity swaps, and that the inefficiency of capital allocation in Asia
should open large market opportunities that a direct investor could take
advantage of. But unlike with hedge funds, a direct-investment fund
needed to operate with a focus on sectors rather than countries. Kaye
had no doubt what would count in choosing the right Asian sectors over
the next five years:

> An ability to access technology or an understanding of technology. This re-
> gion has been extremely weak in industry expertise and technology. They're
> ideas whose time has come. It couldn't be done a few years ago because
> they had plenty of capital and the patriarchs could resist all change. You
> couldn't even talk to them in 1992. Their balance sheets were strong and
> they had an incestuous self-feeding mechanism with politicians.

No longer. The bubble years of fixed-asset inflation "rescued a lot of morons," Kaye says, but with that slammed into reverse by the events of 1997–99 the qualities that used to be rewarded will no longer be and those that used to be punished should now flourish. Kaye thinks Asia may even be better positioned to take off now than America was at the end of the 1980s. The reason is that, whereas America only had productivity gains to set it off, Asia should have both that and significant cost declines thanks to the deflation of fixed-asset prices: "a potent combination once you get over the hump." But very little of the coming bright future ("I'm an optimist about Asia remaking itself") will be found in publicly-listed stocks, which are still too dominated by banks and property companies, "where there is a lot of detritus still around. Price isn't the issue. It's the future structure of the business." Kaye's vision of Asia's future over the next ten years is: telecoms, media, Internet, fast food, advertising, accounting services.

These tend not to be the hunting grounds of the "patriarchs," but the old-timers may be in more trouble than is generally realized. One of the little-noticed facts about the crisis is the extent to which the wealth of the old guard was destroyed. Again, Japan's experience is somewhat instructive. The country's great personal fortunes in the 1990s were amassed in consumer finance, software, even parking-lot operators. Toward the end of the decade, of course, these earlier and sometimes quirky successes were widely eclipsed by software, telecoms, and Internet firms (see Chapters 10 and 11). Because entrepreneurial capitalism has been relatively underdeveloped in Japan it is a bit harder to identify the losers. At the very top, those losing ground fastest have been property developers and the managerial barons of traditional industrial firms. But Japan's mountain of unfunded private pension liabilities also suggests that a broader if invisible erosion of private wealth among middle to high managers is taking place as the security of their retirements is undermined.

The casualties in Southeast Asia's family-based capitalism are easier to single out. The combination of bad debt, stock-market declines and real-estate depreciation in the crisis-hit Asian countries could easily have surpassed $1 trillion. Of course, not all of that loss will have to be realized but much of it will be. And the losses are having a deep impact on the families that dominated Southeast Asian business for two generations because business power there has been so concentrated. One study by the World Bank and the University of Chicago found that, pre-crisis, in Indonesia, Thailand and the Philippines the top 15 families in each country controlled half of the business. In Hong Kong and Korea the figure was 35 percent, in Malaysia and Singapore 30 percent. One guess is that in Thailand by mid-1999 the wealth on paper of the top 20 families was only 20 percent of what it had been two years before. In Indonesia losses running into billions of dollars—especially when added to the political purging of certain business influences following the fall of President Suharto—have shorn many families, notably the Salims and the Bakries, of large parts of their corporate empires. Thailand's Heinecke, who has been doing business in Thailand for 35 years, says flatly, "I have never seen so much wealth wiped out completely in my entire life—and the losers won't be back." It thus seems certain that, to parallel the growth of new industries and companies in Asia over the next decade, a new class of entrepreneurs will rise to take the place of the old. A transitional example is Thailand's Thaksin Shinawatra, a likely candidate at some point to become the country's prime minister. Almost alone among Thailand's pre-crisis tycoons, he emerged from the crisis almost untouched: his business is telecoms.

REMAKING THE BANKS

By early 2000 financial restructuring had made a lot more progress than restructuring Asian companies had, but in some important respects the progress in bank reform was illusory. One of the biggest defects in the earlier Asian model was the intertwining of industrial and bank ownership. Throughout Asia it was common for industrial groups to own banks, which they used as a ready source of credit for their industrial operations. Many times, particularly in Southeast Asia, banks also lent to their industrial owners on their personal accounts—to buy shares, for example, or make other investments. These arrangements were often corrupt, especially in Indonesia, where (as noted in Chapter 2) wholesale liberalization in the late 1980s combined with virtually no regulation allowed the proliferation of more than 200 private banks, most used as piggy banks for their owners and their industrial conglomerates.

Even when the arrangements were not strictly speaking corrupt, they inevitably created a conflict of interest between the banks and their controlling owners and even top managers. At the very least, they made scrutiny of loans to interested parties even more superficial than it normally would have been. As Chatumongol Sonakul, Thailand's reformist central-bank governor, contemptuously put it in 1999:

Thai banks lose money because major shareholders borrow money from their own banks. Top managements borrow money from their own banks and go sit on their borrowers' companies until they don't know where they are working or for whom they are working—the borrower or the lender. How can you have good risk control when for a substantial part of it you yourself or your superiors are the borrowers?

In the early clean-up phase of Asia's banks, the result was that, while banks were merged or shut and their balance sheets cleared of bad loans and recapitalized, little was done to sell off the assets and let prices of the underlying collateral (like land and buildings) fall to market-clearing levels. Nor was enough done to sever the links between the surviving banks and their industrial owners. That would have to await more progress on corporate reorganization (see below). Still, Heinecke for one thinks that people are simply being too impatient—it does take awhile for a bank to muster the will to foreclose on borrowers many of whom sit on its board of directors—but that already by 1999 new loans were no longer being made on the basis of personal guarantees or relationships, and that in the next year or so a sweeping clean-out of the bad old stuff will have begun.

Backing up his optimism is the fact that recapitalization had made more progress than many had expected. In the first half of 2000 the share of NPLs on the books of Thai banks had fallen to around 35 percent, down from a peak of 50 percent; this shoring up of balance sheets at last allowed the banks to start foreclosing in earnest on their assets.

Even the initial reorganization of banking systems boasted some real achievements. One of the clearest was to tighten—or in some cases just create—bank supervision and regulation. In South Korea supervisory and licensing powers were stripped from the hopelessly inadequate Ministry of Finance and entrusted to a tough and independent Financial and Supervisory Commission, which also was put in charge of restructuring the financial system. The Bank of Thailand remained in charge of overseeing Thai banks; but a clean-out of its upper ranks, their substitution with more competent and professional technocrats, and hiring the Singapore central bank's famously tough former top civil servant as an adviser all raised the quality of supervision in Thailand enormously. Malaysia's central bank, which even pre-crisis had a good regulatory reputation, also retained its supervisory role. This was reinforced by the bank recapitalization agency, Danamodal, which when it injected capital into ailing banks always took seats on the board of directors and helped crack the whip from there.

Another chunk of progress was made—including in Japan, see Chapter 5—in starting to wipe bad loans off bank balance sheets. Even well over two years into the crisis nobody had a clear idea how much it would cost to recapitalize Asia's financial systems (one guess was given in Table 6.1 in Chapter 6). Part of the reason for this vagueness was that record-keeping had not been of the best almost anywhere, and part that it was impossible to predict how many questionable loans would eventually be rescued by faster-than-expected economic growth. A more unsettling reason, however, and one with all too much precedent in Japan, was that it remained unclear until corporate restructuring was further along how much of the burden of that would be borne by shareholders of ailing companies and how much by continued bank support paid for with more slices of taxpayer-funded bank recapitalization.

Even so, much was being overhauled (see Figure 7.1). Thailand's Financial Restructuring Authority (FRA), headed by Amaret Sila-On, a former businessman of unquestioned probity, shut 56 finance companies in 1997 and over the next two years auctioned off their assets at anywhere from 10 to 50 cents on the dollar. By the end of 2000 foreign investors were expected to be in control of half by number, and of a third by assets, of the 12 commercial banks still in business. In Korea a fifth of the commercial banks were shut down within two years of that country's IMF

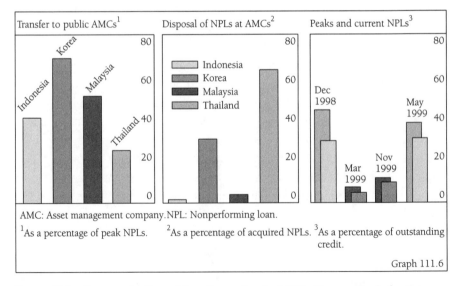

Figure 7.1   Progress in financial restructuring in 1999. (*Source:* Bank for International Settlements)

bailout, one (Korea First Bank) had been sold to an American-led foreign consortium and all the others were being shaken up in operational as well as financial ways. By the end of 1999 a quarter of the system's workforce had been cut, salaries of the remaining had been slashed and there had been substantial branch closures. The clean-out of Indonesia's system was even more thorough—as it needed to be since its problems (however defined) as a share of GDP were two to three times worse than those of the other three "crisis" countries. The Indonesian Bank Restructuring Agency (IBRA) was given powers so sweeping to force owners of bust banks to hand over assets that by mid-1999 it owned shares and real estate equal in value to 25 percent of the country's GDP. How effectively IBRA was using its clout to reshape Indonesian finance and business was called into question in late 1999 as the agency got sucked into the slipstream of a political scandal involving the repayment of loans made by one of its wards, Bank Bali, but given the scale of its powers and holdings its importance seemed unlikely to be much diminished.

There remained considerable doubts about whether any of this would go far enough to break the distorting links between finance and industry or put Asian finance on a commercial enough footing. One skeptic was Philippe Delhaise, then Thompson BankWatch's Asia specialist, who felt endless taxpayer-financed bailouts were such a danger that most existing banks should be nationalized, after their liabilities were set off against all available shareholder equity, and entirely new ones set up. A more interesting possibility is that, as Asian bond markets grow fast in importance both for corporate borrowers and private investors (see Chapter 12), the competitive pressures this will put on banks will force them to shape up more effectively than any government-directed plan could do. That in turn could give corporate restructuring just the jolt it needs.

ONE CROOK AND ANOTHER

Marc Faber, a mischievous Swiss contrarian who until 2000 ran his investment fund out of Hong Kong (he then moved it to Chiang Mai, in northern Thailand), liked to say this when he was asked at conferences in 1998–99 how the crisis would change Asian business: "Reforms in Asia amount to one crook replacing another." I don't think he will be proven entirely right, because very different industries will now be rising in Asia operating in a very different financial and business climate (see Part Three). But he has a serious point: "I very much doubt that the economic crisis will change the way business is conducted in Asia. In fact, I would argue that the various IMF bailouts have, as in the case of Russia, perpetuated the corruption and 'crony capitalism' because the loans allowed so many rotten businesses and business practices to survive, which might otherwise have been thoroughly cleaned out."

Certainly by the end of 1999, the products of corporate restructuring in Asia appeared to be a lot more meager than those of financial restructuring. Amaret Sila-On, of Thailand's FRA, said in a speech in Hong Kong in May 1999 that, although NPLs in the Thai financial system had stopped growing, they still amounted to half of total loans. Despite the FRA's having disposed, at that point, of 60 percent of its $22 billion loan portfolio through auction (almost all of that from finance companies rather than banks), Amaret guessed that even so no more than 10 percent of the country's total bad debt had been restructured in the sense of underlying assets and businesses being disposed of at market prices. The reforms, he said, were fragile, especially thanks to the recent stock-market rally. Social attitudes had to be changed. Thailand was still plagued, he said, by the four evils of "cronyism, collusion, corruption and complacency." He said that, above all, "social values need to change." He explained how it would be considered normal if a man in his position, say driving alone drunk late one night, got a traffic ticket, next day to send his chauffeur to the police station to "take care of the problem" with some money for the police officers concerned. He thought the new bankruptcy law would help: "The most powerful human emotion is fear; you can't get a banker to change his behavior through love." He also thought raising the bogey of western imperialism to criticize the reform process was pure demagogy: the real fight was within Thailand, between those who supported and those who resisted change.

Nowhere in Asia was changing business habits going to be a clear-cut operation. It began, in Southeast Asia at least, mostly through attempts to set up a modern institutional framework through bankruptcy laws and the like. But, as explained before, these institutions were very much in their infancy and the real work of corporate restructuring was carried out informally and piecemeal. Even those company heads who were voluntarily bent on reform found the process agonizingly slow. One of them, Rini Soewandi, a western-educated and politically well-connected woman who took over Indonesia's Astra International in 1998, found that it took a year to put together a restructuring deal that would focus the company's business (it was mainly a car-distribution firm but had strayed into much else besides) and permit a debt workout with its creditors. Even with asset sales and staff cuts—she slashed the workforce by 25 percent during the summer of 1998—the firm was hard-pressed to keep going. One reason was the utter political drift in Indonesia, which started in late 1997 and went on and on (see Chapter 14). The country, she said in the autumn of 1998, was like a sinking ship peopled with "crooks, priests, mullahs and murderers" who refused to understand that for the sake of all they needed to suspend their quarrels and pull together until the ship was saved. But in addition the firm's creditors, many of them Japanese banks, balked at taking any losses until meeting after meeting with the bankers at last persuaded them. Soewandi's clean-up of the firm finally got it into good enough shape for it to be sold at a handsome price, in the spring of 2000, to an international consortium, though her efforts brought her politically foul of the government and she was sacked before the sale.

For all the headaches, things did change, sometimes in surprising ways. Despite the reputation of Thai companies for arrogance and intransigence, for example, by the autumn of 1999 three of the biggest debtors had started remaking themselves. Siam City Cement, the country's second biggest cement-maker, sold 25 percent of itself to Switzerland's Holderbank and brought in a new Swiss managing director who negotiated a restructuring of more than $500 million in debt that involved the loss of 800 jobs, a quarter of the workforce. Since mid-1997, Alphatec Electronics has had an American CEO who gradually won the trust of foreign creditors for a restructuring deal by bringing more transparency to what had previously been a pretty murky operation.

Even TPI's Prachai (see first section above) was forced in early 2000, after more than two years of haggling, into a deal with creditors that set strict targets for the firm's operations and financial performance after one of the main creditors, Bangkok Bank, brought in a group of Australian advisers to get its problem-loan portfolio sorted out and the creditors set a firm deadline after which they would formally file for bankruptcy. A stone-faced Prachai capitulated on the last day, agreeing not only to the supervisory controls but also to a slashing of his family's equity stake in the company from 60 percent to 30 percent. Tough pro-reform attitudes from both the central bank and Amaret, the FRA's head, undoubtedly played a part in such deals. Even more encouragingly, in the case of TPI, the threat of resort to the bankruptcy court seemed to be what tipped the scales. The TPI deal may, in fact, have marked the turning point in the resolution of the Thai crisis: alone, it disposed of 5 percent of the country's NPLs and, since it was agreed to by Thailand's most notoriously recalcitrant debtor, it set an example for the wholesale restructuring of the country's bad-loan portfolio.

There is no denying the trench-warfare aspect of corporate change in Asia in 1997–2000, borne out by the fact that, two years after things blew up, only 10 percent to 20 percent of corporate debt had really been restructured. Nonetheless, the TPI deal was the harbinger of a faster pace of restructuring that gathered momentum in much of Asia throughout 2000. Institutional changes were an essential part of this, but it was the squeeze on profits, which began in Japan in the early 1990s and hit the rest of Asia with typhoon force in 1997–98, that really made old business practices impossible to continue, even for family-run companies whose interest in stock-market opinion had generally been negligible. More on this in Part Three. What the margin squeeze was also doing, however, was forcing whole countries to revise their economic and business policies—whether they were huge and relatively insulated countries like China or small and internationalized islets like Hong Kong or Singapore. The responses suggest just how different a chapter was being opened in Asia's modernization.

CHAPTER

8

The Giant's Delicate Dance

In September 1999, just a couple of days before the fiftieth anniversary of the founding of the People's Republic of China on October 1, 1949, *Fortune* magazine held a conference in Shanghai on China's next 50 years. The conference was notable for many things: the sheer number of high-powered American and European chairmen and CEOs who came (Shanghai opened its new airport a little early for the exclusive use of the 60 or so corporate jets that flew some of them in and out); the shameless fawning of many of these CEOs on the Chinese leaders on hand, who to hear America's captains of industry tell it not only could do no wrong but in fact never had; conversely, the balanced weighing of China's prospects in speeches by Henry Kissinger and Lee Kuan Yew. What I found most interesting, though, was a small side session on the reform of China's state-owned enterprises (SOEs).

Most of these side sessions, on subjects like intellectual-property protection or China's financial system, were attended by a couple of dozen delegates, overwhelmingly Western. The session on SOE reform was packed with 120 or so people, almost all of them Chinese. For the Chinese delegates other subjects were of academic (i.e., no) interest. SOE reform was a matter of life and death. The week before, the Communist Party's Central Committee at its annual meeting had adopted yet another murky statement about policy on SOE reform, and the SOE managers who were in Shanghai wanted to hear from the horse's mouth what it would mean for them. Among the three panelists was Sheng Huaren, head of the State Economic and Trade Commission (a cabinet-level government post) and a Central Committee member. When the

145

session was opened to questions from the floor, I was astonished to hear the vehemence with which—in what amounted to a public setting in front of foreigners—Sheng was assailed by SOE managers in the audience. One complained bitterly, "Why are you attacking the SOEs, which are the backbone of the Chinese economy and which built socialism in China? You are making us compete with the Americans. It's like making a baby fight Mike Tyson." Sheng gave as good as he got, waving a copy of the Central Committee's SOE decision document at the questioner: "China is no longer a socialist economy. It is a 'socialist market economy,' [the latest official phrase for moving-to-market] and if you can't cope with that it's your problem not mine."

In addition to the lack of deference and the openness of the debate, what struck me was the thought that, if this was the sort of talk you heard in the polite and luxurious surroundings of a high-profile international conference in Shanghai, what was it like in the more bare-knuckled parts of China? Being a top leader in China was not high on my job-search list—especially not as Asia's financial crisis unfolded.

FROM GOOD TO WORST

Along with India, Taiwan and Singapore, China was one of the handful of Asian countries whose economies kept growing in 1997–98 (see Chapter 6). During the panic phase it came to be seen as the pivotal country in East Asia: if China went down, it was feared, there would be no stopping wave after wave of devaluations and economic destabilization throughout the region. The irony of China's brief role as the bulwark of Asian stability was that, despite the relative isolation of its economy, China offered perhaps the most intractable example of the structural ailment that Japan invented and most of the rest of Asia copied: the intertwined failure of banks to lend wisely and of companies to put the credit to profitable enough use.

During the panic, though, China did hold the line. The great fear in the spring of 1998, about six months before Asian stock and currency markets hit bottom, was that China would devalue its currency, the renminbi, unleashing a series of competitive devaluations everywhere else in Asia and perhaps in other emerging markets too; a global financial crisis did not seem too far-fetched a result. A theory that became popular around this time was that a big part of what lay behind the whole Asian crisis was a sharp Chinese devaluation in 1995—when the renminbi was fixed at about 8 to the dollar, up from almost 5—leading to a burst of Chinese export growth that undermined its neighbors' current-account positions by taking trade business away from them. The theory made no sense. Before 1995 China ran a two-tier exchange rate, with an official rate substantially higher than the unofficial one. But most of China's foreign trade was already conducted at the unofficial rate so the "devaluation," which could more accurately be described as an exchange-rate unification, had little competitive impact. That did not stop this myth from haunting Asian and other nightmares about what a repeat Chinese devaluation could mean in 1998.

Nonetheless, there were a couple of more persuasive reasons for thinking the Chinese might devalue—which, remember, they could do at will, or refuse to do more or less at will, because the capital account of the balance of payments was closed (albeit leaky thanks to capital flight). First, the Japanese yen was crashing against the dollar in the spring of 1998. A weakening yen made Japan's exports more competitive, and imports from the rest of Asia less attractive to Japanese consumers. Unsurprisingly, this helped push down Asian stock markets because the earnings prospects of export-dependent Asian companies were thrown into doubt. In the normal course of events, a weakening yen also tends to drag other Asian currencies down with it, and if they did start going down it would have put increasing pressure on China.

China's trade performance already seemed to be suffering. Particular industries—mostly heavy ones like steel and shipbuilding—were badly hit as they lost overseas orders to competitors like the South Koreans and, adding insult to injury, domestic orders as well to the same competitors (whose products were often smuggled into China in massive quantities). These industries, many of them politically well-connected, were squealing loudly to Beijing. They seemed to have a point. Export growth in 1997 generated almost 30 percent of total economic growth, and a big cut in that would be a lot to lose. Ordinary people's faith in the renminbi seemed to be weakening, as black-market exchange rates fell to a 9 percent discount to the official rate and as much as $39 billion was illegally sent out of the country in 1998 (another $24 billion fled in 1999).

Yet there was less to this than met the eye. China's current-account surplus may have been shrinking but it was still there. Moreover, whatever the exchange rate (within reason) many of China's exports simply had no effective competition: for instance, in 1997 it exported 22 times as many shoes to America as the rest of Asia combined. Intra-Asian trade had hit a rough patch for China, but its exports to the West were holding up well. Besides, since about half the inputs that went into making China's exports were imported a significant part of the export-boosting benefit of a devaluation would be offset. The upshot was that trade was not such a big issue in the decision on devaluation.

Deflation, however, was. In common with the rest of Asia, China in 1997–98 faced a situation of vast overcapacity in most of its industries and a falling price level: by mid-1998 retail prices were falling at a rate of 3 percent a year. With economic growth slowing, this threatened to turn into a vicious downward spiral of the sort Japan had endured during the 1990s. In 1997–99 China repeatedly lowered interest rates and increased government spending to try to give a jolt to the economy. The government was worried enough about the deflationary threat that in 1998 it imposed price controls that set a floor under the prices of several goods to stop them from falling too far. A devaluation could have made a handy contribution to the anti-deflation effort by raising the prices of imports and so the economy's general price level.

However tempted China may have been at various points to resort to a devaluation, in 1997–99 it never did so. By mid-2000, with Asia stabilized and China itself pulling solidly out of deflation, a sudden Chinese devaluation was no longer a realistic threat. What mattered more for China, for foreign companies investing there and for its neighbors was instead how vigorously and how quickly China would tackle the structural flaws that presented a bigger long-term threat to its future than deflation did: the banks and the SOEs.

SOE SORRY

Ever since Deng Xiaoping inaugurated China's economic reforms in 1978, the process has moved ahead in fits and starts depending on the political mood, the balance of power in the leadership and the country's economic cycles. One spurt of reform that began in 1992 was held back in 1994–96 by the need to keep the inflationary pressures then building up from getting out of hand. Subsequent events showed that, from a macroeconomic point of view, this tightening may have been done a bit too thoroughly. But the man in charge of the economy since 1994, Zhu Rongji, a blunt Shanghainese, became China's prime minister in March 1998 and started pushing a structural reform program whose fate will have more significance for China than whether in the late 1990s he was managing fiscal or monetary policy in the best possible way.

The central problem in China is an exaggerated version of the one found in Japan and much of the rest of Asia: banks lending badly to companies spending badly. It is exaggerated in China because the Asian model was overlaid with the apparatus of a Communist state. The banks in China did not just follow the government's policy guidance: they were all owned by the government and were automatic instruments of whatever industrial policy the government happened to be pursuing at the time. The SOEs, long the sole customers of the banks and even as late as 1999 still the recipients of as much as two-thirds of bank loans, were also instruments of government policy. For decades the policy was simply to produce given quantities of goods with no regard to quality or profit. Even when that began changing in the 1990s, as SOEs were expected to start functioning like real companies, there was immense confusion about the incentive structure for managers, about their relations with the owners (i.e., the government) and the Communist Party, and about the social function of the SOEs—the provision of schooling, housing, urban workplaces and pensions for as many as 120 million urban workers and their families.

During the first 15 or so years of China's economic reforms, the growing inefficiency of the bank-SOE nexus was masked by the stunning performance of the real economy. During that period the economy grew by almost 9 percent a year and at the end was almost four times as big as it had been at the beginning. Between 1978 and 1985 alone the number of people living in poverty was cut by two-thirds, to 10 percent of the population. China became increasingly plugged into the world economy: by the mid-1990s its share of world trade had quadrupled, and by the late 1990s the stock of foreign direct investment in the country approached $300 billion, by far the biggest share of any poor country in the world. Partly because of the influx of foreign investment but mostly because of the super-fast growth first of semi-private township and village enterprises and "collective" enterprises in the 1980s and then, in the 1990s, of truly private firms, a significant share of the economy passed into the hands of companies that were guided almost entirely by market signals. By the end of the 1990s, purely private firms accounted for as much of China's GDP as state-owned firms did. In many cases, non-state companies performed extremely well. One study of private Chinese firms in the late 1990s found that their return on equity averaged almost 20 percent, among the highest in Asia. And by early 2000, private firms seemed poised for further robust growth. In January the government's chief planner publicly announced that henceforth (and for the first time since the Communists came to power), private enterprises would be put on an "equal footing with state-owned enterprises," and that tax, land-use, stock-listing, foreign-trade and other regulations that discriminated against private firms would be scrapped.

Yet even while the rudiments of a private economy were beginning to take shape, the central problem of inefficiency in corporate China remained largely untackled. At the level of the firm, the scale of the problem was staggering. In northern China, the part of the country where SOEs are most heavily concentrated, one state-owned steel firm employed 400,000 people in 1998 but had a smaller output than a Japanese firm with 30,000 employees. At the *Fortune* SOE session mentioned above, another of the panelists was Liu Benren, the reformist head of the Wuhan Group, which owns the Wuhan Iron and Steel Company in central China. Although he has been doing his best to trim the workforce and rationalize production, in 1999 he still had 100,000 employees producing some $2 billion in steel output. The significance of these numbers did not register until I recalled an earlier panel where the head of Royal Dutch Shell mentioned that his globe-spanning firm employed the same number of people but had revenues in 1998 of $95 billion—about 50 times Wuhan's worker productivity.

Overall, the SOEs were colossally inefficient and got more so as the 1990s wore on. By the end of the decade, they still swallowed 70 percent to 80 percent of bank credit, owned 70 percent of industrial assets, and employed 70 percent of the 150-million industrial workforce. But they produced no more than 30 percent of industrial output, and at least two-thirds of them lost money. Return on investment in the state-owned sector as a whole fell from 15 percent in 1987 to 5 percent in 1994. The profits generated by the sector fell from 7 percent of GDP in 1987 to 2 percent in 1994, and went negative in 1996.

Almost all of these mounting losses have been underwritten by China's banks, of which four—all state-owned—dominate the banking system. Their financial condition is awful and has been worsening. Nicholas Lardy of the Brookings Institution in Washington, an expert on China's banks, has quoted an estimate from a Communist Party think tank: As of 1994, the banks' main SOE customers would need to slash their indebtedness by the equivalent of 25 percent of GDP before their cash flow would be big enough to meet their interest payments to the banks. The usual estimate of the number of NPLs in the banking system is 20 percent to 25 percent, though many analysts think it may be twice that. Lardy's estimate was that, by 1998, given any Western definition of the term, all four main banks were insolvent, and recapitalizing them could require as much as 35 percent of GDP.

If some of these percentages vaguely ring a bell, they should. The figures for NPLs and recapitalization costs are quite similar to those of the panic-struck Asian countries—with a crucial difference. China has not been through a panic, which naturally causes a bad deterioration in any country's financial condition. Nonetheless, until the middle of 2000 the usual thermometers are showing levels of fever as high in China pre-crisis as they were in most of the rest of Asia post-crisis. The first question this raises is whether over the next few years China is in significant danger of going into the kind of tailspin much of the rest of Asia did in 1997–98 because, if it does, its current financial condition suggests it would have more trouble than the other countries in pulling itself out before a real crash.

The short answer is that the danger is slight and dwindling in the short run (say 2000–2002), but will progressively grow the longer the SOEs remain unreformed. One of the reasons the risk is not too big right now is familiar: China's external financial position is strong. The closed capital account means that opportunities for a destabilizing rush of capital are small. Moreover, by mid-2000 China's foreign-exchange reserves had climbed to more than $150 billion and short-term foreign debt as a percentage of reserves was less than a quarter, one of the world's lowest ratios. The debt-service ratio—the share of export revenues needed to pay debt as it became due—was under 10 percent, again exceptionally low.

However, as Malaysia proved in 1997–98, a sound external position is no warranty of a trouble-free existence. Yet parlous as China's internal finances look, there is little short-term risk of a blow-up. Although the government's budget deficit and its debt were rising in the late 1990s as it applied repeated fiscal stimulus to try and ward off deflation, government debt—which was 5 percent of GDP in 1998—was tiny. Increasing it to, say, 40 percent by issuing bonds to recapitalize the banks would certainly be feasible. Because China's banks are almost all state-owned, there is no problem with wiping out "shareholders'" equity as part of a restructuring. For the same reason—and because they have almost nowhere else to put their money—depositors are not worried about the safety of their savings. China does have bank runs, but they are traditionally caused by inflation, which has not been a worry for years. The result is that, although some financial firms in China may go bust (many did in 1998, though they were not banks), a systemic banking crisis remains a remote risk.

That would change if the economic recovery that began taking hold in the middle of 2000 fizzled out, especially if it did so in connection with another outbreak of inflation. This is where SOE (and bank) reform comes back in. China's longer-term prospects will remain clouded until something significant is done to get the growing burden of the SOEs off the economy's back. Because corporate governance—and indeed the distinction between public and private ownership—is so tangled and murky in China, three examples of different kinds of reform may be the easiest way to point to the likely overall outcome.

IN, UP, OUT

In late 1992 I visited a dingy small factory in a rural county called Fengxian about 30 miles south of Shanghai. One thing that stood out in the dreary surroundings was the delicious lunch of Shanghai fresh-water crab whipped up in the staff kitchen for the board of directors meeting. The other was the determination of the factory boss to make money. The company, then called Sail-Star Commercial Machinery, was owned by a bureau of the county. It had started out making barges for use on Shanghai's Huangpu river and the canals and tributaries that fed it, but had gone bust in the early 1980s. By the time of my visit it was making commercial dry-cleaning machines. It also had sold half of itself to Morningside, a Hong Kong-based private-equity fund, for $300,000. It had brought in western accounting and management methods and, spurning the wretchedly bad state-owned distribution system, had set up a nationwide team of salesmen who made most of their money from bonuses and commissions. Despite the fierce competition—25 Chinese companies were then making dry-cleaning machines—Sail-Star had just gone into the black.

That year the company's sales were about $3 million. In 1998 I paid a return visit to what was now called Shanghai Sail-Star, with a new logo. Sales had risen to almost $45 million, with operating margins of 15 percent. The shabby premises of half a decade before had been exchanged for a spectacularly tasteless but expensive neo-something 44,000 square-foot headquarters building and 300,000 square feet of tidy and clean factory space. The firm was not only the biggest commercial dry-cleaning machine-maker in the world in volume terms but had also branched out into making boilers and electrical panels for power-supply controllers. It had acquired half of a dry-cleaning maker in Italy and was shopping for partners in America. The CEO, a Communist Party member, was just as direct as ever—railing this time at the government for refusing a devaluation, a refusal which he thought was crushing exporters, and at the unreliability if not outright fraud of government economic statistics—but new-product development is what was really on his mind. The distribution issue had long ago been settled, he said, with independent subsidiaries set up to take care of distribution and sales. Now R&D and new products were the priority to allow the firm to expand and become more profitable. Significantly, ownership had changed. The government was entirely out: it was a private company, 80 percent owned by Morningside, the rest by managers and employees. It is hard to tell how much of the old state or quasi-state sector is being sold off to foreigners but, as Sail-Star shows, when it happens the effects can be dramatic. And however many may already have been sold, it is not a trivial number and it is going to increase (see next section).

If bringing in foreigners is one way of reform, building up the companies without changing ownership is another. By far the best-known example of this is a company called Haier. Haier is categorized as a "collective enterprise," of which China had some 25 million in 1997. Collectives are not strictly speaking SOEs: unlike them, collectives are "owned" by their employees not by government and the government agencies supervising them are entitled only to taxes from them, not to their assets or their profits. On the other hand, they are under the control of a government agency—usually a bureau of a city government—which has the power to appoint and dismiss the CEO, set ceilings on the distribution of profits and require the collective to provide unemployment and other welfare benefits to its workers (if it allows any to be dismissed, that is). "You have to have three eyes," says Zhang Ruimin, Haier's CEO, "one on the market, one on the workers, and one on the government."

Zhang, today one of China's most famous businessmen, took over in 1984, when he was a functionary in the Household Appliance Division of the municipal government of Qingdao, a northern city best known in the West for a beer made there named Tsingtao. The firm was then known as the Qingdao General Refrigerator Factory, a down-at-heel unit that made refrigerators of (for China) typically poor quality (they were usually scratched and often the doors would not even fit properly), and "marketed" them by letting consumers line up to buy them. Zhang, who had read a lot of Western business books as well as Chinese classics, believed that in the longer run, as China's consumer market became more sophisticated, competing on price alone would be suicidal. He had several radical ideas for turning around the factory's business. He wanted to instill a sense of personal responsibility in the workers, getting them to focus on quality and on process improvements; to bring in work evaluation systems that would relate pay to performance; to set up thorough organizations for marketing and after-sales service; and to begin a program of expansion that—absurd though this seemed—would one day put the firm (whose name Zhang changed to Haier, meaning "dear sir") in the Fortune Global 500.

To drive home some of these themes to the workforce, for whom they were at first gibberish, early on in his tenure Zhang one day went to the stock of refrigerators fresh off the assembly line and pulled aside 76 of them that had visible defects. With a sledgehammer he smashed the first, and ordered the workers involved in making the others to smash all of them in succession. This was an almost incomprehensibly shocking act: the sales price for each of the refrigerators was about the same as the average annual wage of a Haier worker. They got the point, especially when the worker responsible for each defect discovered each day thereafter was identified and had to explain himself to his co-workers.

Zhang was equally determined to make Haier bend to the consumer instead of vice versa. "When aiming the gun," he said, "you have to follow the target." Through substantial product differentiation, the company began showing an acute sensitivity to customer tastes and local variations, which in China are vast. The washing machines Haier sells in Shanghai, for instance, are smaller and have gentler cycles, because the weather there is warmer (people want to wash their clothes more often and so in smaller batches) and with the higher incomes of Shanghainese their clothes are of finer quality. But that is a relatively tame variation. When Haier began selling washing machines in rural Sichuan province, in southwestern China in the early 1990s, it was puzzled to receive frequent complaints that the machines would not work because they were clogged with mud. On inspection, it turned out that the peasants had been using the machines to wash their vegetables as well as their clothes. Local officials told Haier to teach the peasants what the machines should and should not be used for. Instead, Zhang told his engineers to develop a machine that could handle dirt-caked vegetables as well as clothes. They did, and sales soared.

Today the sledgehammer hangs on the wall of Haier's boardroom. Through internal growth and a lot of acquisitions the Group has expanded from its original 700 employees to 20,000, its product lines from one to more than 2,000, and revenues from $500,000 to near $1 billion. Zhang is now busy expanding overseas, where he hopes to make the brand—which now also covers air conditioners, washing machines and microwave ovens—in the rest of Asia at first, and then in the West, as well-known as it is in China. What is most startling about this story is that Zhang did it without changing the firm's ownership, but instead bringing in management methods that allowed world-class results to be achieved despite the absence of any clarity about property rights in the firm. The secret seemed to be that he kept the firm almost always in profit, which generated the taxes and other benefits the Qingdao government wanted, while the government was enlightened (and uncorrupt) enough to let Zhang run the firm without interference.

That, of course, represented an unusual combination of qualities, and a third method of SOE reform is needed: destroying capacity and jobs and thoroughly restructuring a business. This is the painful one, and the method most torn by politics. When the firm at issue is prominent or well-connected enough, it can be very hard to get results. Liu Benren, the head of Wuhan Group mentioned above, is known as one of the toughest reformers in a big SOE. Yet though he has managed to rationalize the workforce by sending 20,000 to 30,000 core-company workers into affiliated subsidiaries or service businesses, he has made little headway in actually getting the drag of such surplus workers off the Group's overall income statement. The central government has recognized his cost-cutting and modernizing efforts by paying for more than $1 billion in capital spending and technological upgrades at the steel plant, but profits are as elusive as ever. Wuhan is an important city, at a geographically strategic position on the Yangzi river in the middle of China and with a big military presence and a historically restive workforce. Wuhan Group is by far the most important employer in the region and, by the end of 1999 at least, the government had settled on no way that would give Liu the political latitude to do what he knew was needed for business reasons.

Out of the glare of publicity, however, the government can be as ruthless as any American corporate raider in slashing capacity, jobs and costs—which is why all those SOE managers at the Shanghai symposium were so anxious and angry. There were important indirect signs of this in the rising unemployment of the late 1990s and a collapse in industrial profits in 1998. Both of these could have had something to do with the cyclical downturn, but they are more likely the result of a sharp squeeze on underperforming SOEs. The first signs of significant corporate re-structuring often come in this form, as they did in America in the early 1980s and Japan in the late 1990s (and recall in Japan's case that a near-decade's worth of recession did not produce a real rise in unemployment, it took the beginnings of restructuring toward the end of the 1990s to do that). In particular industries there is direct evidence of serious restruc-turing. In 1998 the government ordered 500 million spindles in state-owned textile firms to be destroyed, which reduced capacity by half. Around the same time, China closed more than 60 percent of its coal mines in just twelve months even though among the most unproductive and politically powerless groups in the country. Likewise, in 1998–99 the government shut down 25 steel firms and forced the merger of 51 others, thus cutting capacity by nearly 3 million tonnes; Lin Benren of the high-profile Wuhan Group may feel frustrated, but his more anony-mous counterparts do not.

The government was also turning to professional dismemberers, often with foreign connections, to take on certain recalcitrant SOE cases. One of the professionals was J.P. Huang, a native Chinese with a Ph.D. in finance from Rutgers University. His Beijing-based JPI Group acted as a sort of holding company plus investment bank to set up and run a variety of busi-nesses—including education, textiles and telecoms—with foreign private-equity partners and advise them on how to do business in China (see Chapter 12). Part of this entailed doing privatization deals, of which, said Huang, there were plenty because "when it comes to SOEs, most are al-ready dead." In the case of the state-owned Zhuzhou Gear Works, which made gears for Volvo and Rockwell among others, Huang put together a buyout deal that involved firing two-thirds of the workforce and paying the local government a small sum to take over responsibility for them.

Some of the privatizations were quite large. In late 1999 Huang was working on a deal to take over the China New Building Materials Corpo-ration, one of only a hundred firms significant enough to be under the di-rect control of the State Economic and Trade Commission (headed by the fearsome Minister Sheng, see above); one of the group's subsidiaries was China Cement, the number-four supplier of fiberglass in the United States. Huang was in negotiations to tear the firm limb from limb, handing over dud assets to the government to do what it wanted with them, getting the group's loans off its banker's books and transferring them to an asset-management corporation (see next section), completely reorganizing the reporting lines and management and firing one-third of the workforce, whose welfare benefits would be paid out of taxes that the newly profitable private group would generate. With a clean balance sheet and rational organization, Huang expected to have no trouble bringing in foreign partners up to the 25 percent limit the government had agreed to allow.

Two Steps Forward, One Feint Back

Drawing general conclusions about what the government is up to with SOE reform is always difficult. Wu Jinglian, probably the country's most prominent pro-reform economist, said that, despite his decades of experience with SOE reform efforts, the September 1999 Central Committee decision document was "hard to understand." The opacity of the process arises partly, as noted before, from the ambiguous state of property rights in China but also because the political sensitivity of the issue makes deliberate obfuscation inevitable. After all, SOE reform means facing almost every fraught economic and political issue in the country: not just the banking system but also relations between central and local governments, urban unemployment and social welfare and last (but foremost) the role of the Communist Party and the power and privileges of party members. There is a school of thought that thoroughgoing reform simply will not happen while the party remains in power because it derives its influence from a top-down ability to command and direct economic resources and to make as many people as possible depend on government favors—which also carries great risks of instability since all of China's success over the past 20 years has been bottom-up, and if both approaches are maintained they will collide more and more violently. My guess is otherwise. I think the leadership is determined on a complete overhaul during the next decade and, although it will happen in a messy and almost incomprehensible way, it actually will come to pass. Here, roughly, is how.

What the government intends to do about the banks is the clearest and simplest part. It is simple because the banks are not really an independent problem: they can be fixed if and only if the problem of the SOEs is fixed. There are three steps to fixing the big four banks (Industrial and Commercial Bank of China, China Construction Bank, Bank of China and Industrial and Commercial Bank of China), which together account for some 90 percent of bank assets (outstanding loans). Bad loans have to be taken off their books, the banks have to be recapitalized, and their operations have to be put on a commercial footing—primarily meaning that they make no more "policy" loans to SOEs. Otherwise, the first two steps are pointless.

The removal of bad loans got underway in earnest in 1999 with the establishment of four asset-management companies (AMCs), one for each of the big banks. The job of the AMCs is to take on NPLs in exchange for AMC bonds that are implicitly guaranteed by the finance ministry. AMCs will have a crucial role in restructuring the SOEs. The dud loans they acquire will be disposed of by debt/equity swaps (the AMC will write down the loan in exchange for stock in the debtor), bundled loan sales and the introduction of strategic investors—like J.P. Huang, whose proposed buyout involves loans from China Construction Bank. Cinda Asset Management, the first AMC (for China Construction Bank), got off to a fast start. In a typical deal, in September 1999 Cinda acquired the debt owed by the Beijing Cement Factory to China Construction Bank and, in exchange for writing down about 70 percent of the value of the loans, got a 70 percent equity stake in the company. The firm, whose operations were not bad though its financial position was, now was able to service its remaining debt. It has the option of buying back Cinda's stake within three years, but if it cannot raise the money Cinda can dispose of it at will. Meanwhile, once the AMC has relieved a bank of most of its bad-debt burden (Cinda, for instance, is committed to taking over all $30 billion-worth of China Construction Bank's NPLs), the bank can actually begin to lend again because the quality of its remaining assets is high.

Second, however, the banks need to be recapitalized and not just with AMC bonds. Most of the money to pay for taking the NPLs off the banks' books and to shore up their capital base has to come sooner or later from the government. This, as noted above, is in theory not a problem since the government's debt is relatively low, and already in 1999 the government had issued some $30 billion in bonds for bank recapitalization. A more intriguing way to raise capital would be equity-raising through partial privatization of the banks. Dai Xianglong, the central bank governor said flatly (though not publicly) in 1999 that there were no political or ideological obstacles to this but that it could not be done until bad debts were removed and the banks had time to prove that they could be run on commercial lines. The reason? The average retail depositor knew full well that all the banks were insolvent but was content to leave his money there anyway because the central government's implicit backing could be counted on. China would risk a bank run if the government seemed to be withdrawing from bank ownership before it became obvious the banks could run themselves.

Lastly, none of this would have any meaning unless, after balance-sheet clean-up and recapitalization, the banks started behaving like banks instead of government departments. Moving the loans to the AMC without subjecting the debtors to market discipline would be paper shuffling, and giving the banks more money without changing the way they lend would just create a new stack of bad loans. Fang Xinghai, a young Stanford PhD in economics who until 2000 worked as the chief of staff for the president of China Construction Bank, told me in 1999 that their bank was feeling no pressure to run their business to suit government policy. They were in the midst of strengthening internal controls, putting in credit-assessment systems and installing a system of incentives for branch managers and loan officers to reward them for making good credit decisions. Fang expected less and less of the bank's business to come from loans to SOEs ("let them go to the capital markets") and more and more from loans to private firms, foreign-invested firms, credit cards, car loans, consumer loans and mortgage loans. He especially liked the mortgage business, in which China Construction Bank had taken the lead: excellent security, low default rates and good lending spreads (see last section of this chapter). Whether all this will be allowed to reach its logical conclusion across the whole of the banking system, however, still ultimately depends on how far SOE reform goes.

THE PARABLE OF SHANGHAI

By the end of 1999 China seemed to have the outlines of an SOE reform program that could work if it were actually carried out. That it would be carried out became far more likely when, in November 1999, China and America at last reached a deal providing for China's entry into the World

Trade Organization, a step that will help open the Chinese economy to greater competition and make it more efficient across the board (see Chapter 13). That deal was welcome on its own, but also because it suggested that after months of seeming retreat the forces of reform in the Chinese government had regained the initiative. This is vital because SOE reform remains the key to China's economic future.

The main elements of China's SOE plan as of end-1999 were to put credit-granting decisions on a market-rather than a government-directed basis; allow firms that can't make the grade to go out of business; change incentives so that SOE managers try to reach profit goals rather than all sorts of other ones; set up a social-welfare system—education, unemployment insurance, pensions—independent of the SOEs; and (though the word dare not be used) privatization. The last is the one that matters most. China's leaders have been wrestling for a couple of decades with the question of how to maintain state control yet also get managers to obey market signals and manage in the interest of the shareholders (mostly the state itself). These repeated efforts have failed almost totally. No wonder, points out one observer: if Margaret Thatcher, of all people, couldn't get British Steel's managers to act in the shareholder's interest before privatizing it in the early 1980s, how do you expect Zhu Rongji to keep state ownership but still root out a market- and shareholder-unfriendly culture that is much more deeply entrenched?

In fact, from what could be divined of the 1999 Central Committee decision, the most bullish sign is that it expanded the scope for privatization. It declared that the only lines of business where sales of the government's stake in SOEs would be off-limits were in those related to national security and certain natural-resources industries. Partial or full sales were permissible everywhere else. Encouragingly, that included sales to foreigners, which are already picking up smartly. It is likely that, market conditions permitting, some $30 billion-worth of shares in big SOEs will be offered to foreign buyers in 2000; that would be a larger amount than was offered in the whole of the previous seven years. Of course, the possibility that such a wide range of privatizations is now possible does not mean they will happen—that still depends on political will—but the 1999 decision marked the first time the party was willing to spell out the criteria by which privatization would be judged as an acceptable option or not.

Much, however, remains problematic. Wu Jinglian noted that the 1999 decision almost wholly missed the main point that corporate governance needs a radical overhaul. SOE managers almost uniformly assume that the company is theirs rather than the owners'. In the worst cases this leads them to loot the assets of the firm; at best they act for themselves, their workers, their locality, instead of trying to maximize the value of the firm. Proposals are in the air about how this might be changed—for example, by bringing SOEs under Singapore-style holding companies whose boards would not need to steal from the owner to get their financial and other rewards—but this is a nettle the party has yet to grasp. Then, as always in China, there is the matter of implementation. In one stab at reform in the late 1990s the government decided to allow foreign investors to take on local SOE monopolies, so as to sharpen up their performance through competition. One Hong Kong industrialist decided to take up this offer and set up a factory in a remote province, only to discover that regulations required that, "to prevent abuses," any application to establish a competing enterprise would need approval—from the SOE with which it proposed to compete. This being China, the story would not be complete without the twist that the unfazed Hong Kong investor eventually got the approval by allying with a faction in the local government that was at odds with the SOE's managers.

To get a clearer picture of what may happen at the national level, it is worth a glance at Shanghai. China usually (and sensibly) experiments with its reforms in a couple of localities before rolling them out nationally, and Shanghai is in the vanguard of SOE reform. In mid-1998 I talked about SOE reform with an official who is very high in the Shanghai Communist Party. The precision of his answers suggested that on this subject the leadership was less divided and more committed than it let on in public. His general point, commonly made in private by top party men, was that reform was essential. "The difference between a market economy and a planned economy is that in a market economy bad companies will be kicked out. In a planned economy they survive. That must change." China had to maintain its reforms. "If you have cancer of the arm, you cut off the arm to save yourself. Let the losers go bankrupt; that way we can prevent the loss of our social treasure."

The official said that the aim for Shanghai in three years and China as a whole in five years was for bank credit to be available only to SOEs that met four tests: (1) debts less than 50 percent of gross assets; (2) no more than 10 percent of the workforce surplus to requirements; (3) annual output of at least $50,000 per worker (for comparison, Haier had already beaten this figure in the late 1990s, whereas Wuhan Iron and Steel fell far short with only $20,000 per worker); (4) return on assets of 10 percent.

He claimed that the average Shanghai SOE was within striking distance of these targets already, with a debt figure of 60 percent, 20 percent redundant labor, output per worker of $40,000 and an ROA of 5 percent. It would be tougher going in China as a whole for the average SOE to make it in five years, but averages could mask wide variations in performance anyway and all those that don't meet the tests "will be starved." Success of SOE reform, the official went on, could also be counted in fours: whether (1) the principle of survival of the fittest has been widely introduced; (2) credit allocation is market-based and has been broadened from state-owned Chinese banks to private and international ones and to bond and stock markets; (3) the system allows for free movement of labor from one firm and one region to another; (4) an adequate social safety net has been put under 90 percent of the urban population.

Naturally there are forces in the party and government fighting against this line as hard as they can—the Shanghai official was in the camp of Zhu Rongji, whose proteges appeared to be under serious attack as 1999 drew to a close though they later bounced back—but even if China gets only partway to these goals the change could be profound. Some of the deepest changes could come, perhaps surprisingly, out of welfare reform. The creation of even a bare-bones pension scheme, for example, would have huge effects on the financial industry—insurance firms and (as yet nonexistent) mutual funds in particular—and on the capital markets. Yet to track the most sweeping changes in China over the next ten years, keep an eye on housing reform.

A NATION OF WARD CLEAVERS

Why will this seemingly mundane subject matter so much? Because if China's housing reforms succeed, hundreds of millions of Chinese over the next decade will become latter-day Ward Cleavers. For those whose memories need jogging (or who have no recollection of this at all), Ward Cleaver was the mythically steady and reliable suburban household head in a 1950s American television series called "Leave It to Beaver." But he represented more than the ideal husband and father of that era. The huge growth of America's home-owning middle class from the 1930s to the 1960s—boosted among other things by tax breaks on mortgage interest payments, federal guarantees for mortgage loans and the rise of the savings and loan industry—was one of the most powerful forces shaping American business, finance, and social and political life in the second half of the century. The housing reforms unveiled in China between mid-1998 and mid-1999 have the potential to revolutionize China just as deeply, and very much along American lines. The Chinese leadership realizes this, and is pursuing the policy quite deliberately.

Until the late 1990s, when a big enough upper-middle and rich class had been created to justify relatively high-priced private housing, almost all urban housing in China was built by the state and owned by state "work units" including SOEs and government departments. These Communist landlords let apartments to their workers for a peppercorn rent that did not come close to covering costs. There was precious little maintenance of the premises either, whether inside or outside the flats. Beginning in 1999, however, no more housing was handed out to SOE workers as perks. Those already in such housing could remain as tenants but would gradually have their rents raised to market levels. But the real aim was to convert existing tenants to homeowners and to encourage newcomers to make home ownership their goal and meanwhile require them to pay market rents for their premises. In late 1999 the government set an "at-cost" price of about $15 a square foot for sales of units built before 1999 to their tenants.

Most people can afford that, but the new-housing price of as much as four times that would be beyond the reach of most city-dwellers. So a program of subsidies was set up, along with permission for a secondary market in housing—meaning, with some restrictions, that anybody buying previously state-owned units could resell them to others and use the proceeds to help haul themselves up to better accommodation. Further encouragement for home-owning was provided in late 1999 by a package of tax breaks for housing transactions, by government backing for an increase in mortgage loans and, in smaller cities, by the establishment of housing-finance companies. By mid-2000, official figures showed that real-estate investment was a third higher than a year before, and 70 percent of public housing had already been sold to its occupants at heavily discounted prices.

There are three predictable consequences of this pro-homeowner policy thrust. One is the boost it will for years give to the economy. China's city-dwellers, with a surfeit of consumer goods like air conditioners and color TVs, are starved for space. On average they have only 90 square feet apiece, less than half as much as the average middle-class Hong Konger (whose personal living space would in turn seem like a jail cell to almost any Westerner). Urban Chinese have big pools of personal savings and, after spending on education (see next section), would be most inclined to use them to buy and then refurbish apartments of their own. The scare of 1997–99 may have deflected this trend but that was over by 2000. Even between 1998 and 1999, the worst year of China's relative contraction, consumer spending rose by close to 9 percent. Lower-quality producers and retailers, moreover, were hurting far more than higher-end ones. The Beijing business of Ikea, for instance, the Swedish household-furnishing retailer, was booming in 1999, and the company had plans to open stores throughout China in the next five years. Housing privatization can only accelerate this movement: by one guess, the reforms could generate household-related spending equal to as much as 10 percent of 1998 GDP over the next several years.

Second, the growth of a mortgage market will help shake up the financial system. As noted above, China Construction Bank has already spotted how lucrative mortgage lending is. Others will follow, further spurred by the permission granted in 2000 for financial firms to issue mortgage-backed securities. Already, in the first half of 2000, mortgage lending was two-and-a-half times bigger than it had been in the whole of 1998, and officials expect mortgages as a share of total bank lending to jump five-fold to 10 percent by 2010. The opportunities will not lie in the privatization of SOE housing units as such—the old ones have been offered too cheaply to require mortgage financing—but rather in the secondary and tertiary markets as tenants-turned-owners trade up.

Third, widespread home ownership will shift Chinese society and politics toward liberalization. The party's vestigial control over people's lives will wither, and once a private market in housing gets going, the ability of Chinese to move from place to place will rise. And, as California's Proposition 13 tax revolt of 1978 showed, there is nobody like a homeowner for telling the government to get off his back. It seemed to me no human-rights activist could have designed a more orderly plan to spread freedom and democracy in China than the housing privatization scheme. When I gingerly asked that Shanghai party official in 1998 what the social consequences of housing reform would be, he replied, "The only social impact will be to make society more stable. People who own their own property will want to keep things stable. We want 80 percent home-ownership [an ambitious target even by American standards]. People who work hard for 15 to 20 years to save for a home will treasure it and will treasure work, and will fight to keep their house and to keep society stable."

Scylla and Charybdis

For hard-to-fathom reasons, Westerners seem to find it difficult in talking about China to avoid falling either into sycophancy—which is ridiculous since China's leaders are some of the intellectually and politically toughest people on earth and can take it as well as dish it out—or into visceral hostility. China's problems are breathtaking in their scope and depth. The mind boggles at trying to run a country of 1.3 billion individualists, living mostly in poverty, with almost no developed instruments of law or objective governance. Yet equally impressive, in my experience, has been the determination of the people at the top to modernize their country using every means they can—they are as aware of global trends as anyone—that will not make them and their families end up one day under house arrest or worse.

Maybe the confusing gradualism, which has been the hallmark of Chinese reform since 1978, won't work. But so far it has worked, for the most part brilliantly and far better than the gangster-led anarchy of the ex-Soviet Union, and if the tight-wire act can be maintained the underlying strength of China will eventually prove itself. This is a country with so much faith in the future that fully 35 percent of urban disposable incomes are spent on education. It is also a country where, according to one Hong Kong executive in the textile business who has plants scattered all over the world, labor productivity under exactly the same management methods and using the same equipment is twice as high as it is anywhere else on earth.

Of this paradoxically super-capitalistic environment run by Communists, it may therefore not be so surprising to hear the arch anti-communist Milton Friedman say:

> It seems to me that once you get a movement going in that direction, where you have an increasing number of individuals who are engaged in private activity and private enterprise, it has a momentum that is very hard to stop. You're going to have ups and downs, of course, but I find it hard to believe that you're going to reverse the momentum towards a larger and more productive economy. These government ventures are slowing it down and

they're going to be very troublesome, you may get a severe recession or depression in China, but I find it hard to believe that ten years from now Chinese aggregate income will not be a good deal higher than it is now.

Of course, nobody with eyes and ears doubts that this has been carried out through a process that has been violent and disturbing in many ways; but some toughness of mind and historical perspective are needed to judge it properly. Lee Kuan Yew explains why when he contrasts the paths of the Soviet Union and of China:

> The day Gorbachev said to the masses in Moscow: don't be afraid of the KGB, I took a deep breath. This man's a real genius, I said. He's sitting on top of a terror machine that holds the damn pile together, and he says don't be afraid. He must have a tremendous formula to democratize—until I met him, and I found him completely bewildered by what was happening around him. He had jumped into the deep end of the pool without learning how to swim. That's why I didn't follow the Russians, because I expected that to go down from the very beginning. I don't know why George Soros and all the big American banks went into Russia. I've never believed that they would get off the ground.
>
> But I understood Deng Xiaoping when he said: if 200,000 students have to be shot, shoot them, because the alternative in China is chaos for another 100 years. Deng understood and he released it stage by stage. Without Deng, China would have imploded.

Which is why I still guess, contrary to almost all Western opinion, that—despite Tiananmen Square in 1989 and various other bloodlettings—come 2050, Deng Xiaoping will be thought to have been the greatest man of the second half of the twentieth century for what he did to push China irreversibly onto the course of modernization and prosperity.

Structures, Cycles
and Strengths

China was hardly alone in having its foundations shaken by the
forces of globalization in 1997–2000. But, like buildings in an
earthquake, different places were differently affected. John Greenwood, mentioned before as the architect of the Hong Kong dollar peg,
draws a distinction between Asian countries whose problems at the outset of the crisis were deep-seated (structural) and those whose troubles
were mostly due to the business cycle. Those with the most severe structural problems, because of the rigidity of their economies and industrial
systems, were Japan and South Korea. By contrast, in Greenwood's view,
most Southeast Asian countries were overwhelmed when a cyclical wave
crashed on top of them in 1997 but their economies were basically
sound. The reason is that these smaller places were more export-oriented, and serious distortions were thus not institutionalized because so
much of the economy was attuned to global market signals. Indeed, in
1998 the world's top seven exporting countries (measured by exports as
a share of GDP) were all East or Southeast Asian: Singapore, Malaysia,
Hong Kong, Indonesia, Thailand, the Philippines and Taiwan. Yet all had
adjustments to make, and the question is whether those adjustments will
be enough to allow Asia's underlying strengths to assert themselves and
produce another generation of growth. Begin with South Korea, the most

structurally challenged place in Asia, before moving on to the cyclically challenged: Singapore, Hong Kong, and Thailand.

THE HERMIT PEERS OUT OF THE CAVE

Purely by chance, just as South Korea, the last and biggest of the Asian dominoes, toppled into the arms of the IMF in December 1997 the country held a presidential election. The winner was Kim Dae Jung, a 73-year-old former dissident, political prisoner and assassination target in the days of military rule. It was Kim's fourth try at the presidency, and the fact that he won during the worst financial turmoil the country had been through since the Korean war did not please many economists or businessmen. Because of his past and his close ties with organized labor, Kim was thought to be a populist left-winger—hardly the ideal choice for a country in crisis whose main need was for a radical restructuring of industry and deregulation of the economy. Those dismayed by his election, however, had overlooked something important. Because of his union connections Kim may have had what in Europe would be called social democratic leanings (though even that is doubtful since all his overseas experience had been in America and his writings on economics usually displayed a pro-market mentality), but above all else he was an outsider. Politics in Korea is heavily influenced by regionalism, and Kim hails from Cholla in the southwest, a region traditionally downtrodden and dominated by other parts of the peninsula—and, crucially, a place where none of the heads of the major *chaebol* came from. Unlike all his predecessors, Kim owed nothing to the *chaebol* for campaign financing or other help, and, if anything, would have been innately hostile to them. He was just what Korea needed.

Kim Dae Jung's immediate predecessor, Kim Young Sam, was already marginalized by December 1997 and in any event seemed paralyzed. In January 1998, a full month before his inauguration, Kim Dae Jung went on television to tell Koreans that they had to accept the IMF's medicine, that serious reform and deregulation must be undertaken, and that "unemployment is going to be inevitable." He then convened a commission with government, business and labor representatives to work out an agreed program of layoffs with the country's notoriously obstreperous unions. It all made for a convincing piece of leadership that allowed Korea to endure its worst post-war recession—GDP fell 6 percent in 1998 and unemployment rose from negligible levels to more than 6 percent—with surprisingly little social turmoil. And the next year, in Asia's most spectacular recovery, South Korea's economy grew by an astonishing 11 percent, boosted in part by a powerful export performance that produced a current-account surplus equal to 12 percent of GDP in 1998 and 6 percent in 1999. Foreign-exchange reserves, which by December 1997 had sunk to $9 billion had recovered by mid-1999 to $60 billion, and net external debt, which stood at $53 billion at the end of 1997, was zero just two years later.

If nothing else, this proved that even deep structural flaws are no impediment, in the short run anyway, to a strong cyclical recovery. Whether the recovery could continue, however, was another question. Even after two years of effort, it was unclear just how much the dense tangle of corporate shortcomings described in Chapter 3 had been unpicked. Korea had shown a surprising willingness to change—which is one reason why it became the darling of foreign investors in 1998–99—but will and results were two different matters.

On the plus side, the government was quick to tear down barriers to foreign involvement in the economy that had been among the highest in Asia. Whereas before it had been virtually impossible for foreigners to buy more than minimal stakes in Korean firms, even when the sale was friendly, by the end of 1999 almost nothing was off-limits, even hostile takeovers. Second, financial restructuring proceeded at a fairly fast clip. The Financial Supervisory Commission (FSC), which oversaw *chaebol* borrowings as well as supervising banks, shut down five banks and, in 1999, sold one of them, Korea First Bank, to an investment consortium led by America's Newbridge Capital. Failed insurance companies were also put on the block for bidding by foreign investors. So-called merchant banks, which were short-term finance houses with few risk controls and not much rationale (the intelligent young head of one of them told me in 1997, "we have no reason to exist"), were shut down in short order. And Korea Asset Management Corporation (KAMCO), the bank recapitalization agency, by late 1999 had bought some $50 billion-worth of NPLs from the banks, around 40 percent of the estimated face-value total, and had even managed to sell a third of them.

The government also demolished many of the laws and regulations that had allowed the *chaebol* to metastatize into the sprawling messes that they were. Recall that cross-shareholdings among *chaebol* affiliates and cross-guarantees of their debts had given the family founders of the conglomerates immense leverage over their groups despite their owning very little of the equity: by one calculation, among the top 30 *chaebol,* family equity holdings worth just $3.5 billion (one-tenth of shareholders' equity) gave control of $255 billion-worth of corporate assets. In 1998 cross-shareholdings were limited to 25 percent of the companies' net worth. The same year restrictions on foreign M&A bids were lifted. Beginning in 1998 no new cross-guarantees were allowed among members of a group, and beginning in 2000 old cross-guarantees are supposed to be phased out. In 1999 the amount of *chaebol* bonds that financial institutions were allowed to hold was capped. Also in 1999 at least a quarter of the board of directors of each *chaebol* company were supposed to be outsiders. And in 2000 all companies are required to combine and publish accounts for all their subsidiaries (meaning accounts for any company they effectively control). The sum total of these changes should be to make each company in a *chaebol* stand on its own feet, and to disclose enough financial information to shareholders so they can see plainly whether it is actually standing or instead staggering.

The transformation was real enough, but its effects have been hard to judge because in the process three Koreas have been interacting. The first, and least visible, is upstart (or start-up) companies in new lines of business whose existence would be commonplace in America or Taiwan but which had been suppressed in Korea for three decades because of the government's pro-*chaebol* financial and industrial policies. Second are the *chaebol* below the first rank (i.e., the top five), most of which have been forced to change or which have changed themselves in response to the new environment. Then there are the top five—Hyundai, Daewoo, Samsung, LG and SK—which are so large that they account for appreciable shares of GDP. Their handling has implications for the nation as a whole rather than just for shareholders or their own workers.

THE REBEL

The hope for Korea, as for the rest of Asia, lies in the new industries—technology, distribution, retailing, life-style, entertainment and other services. In 1997 I saw one example of what this could mean. Park Kyung Hong was then president of 39 Home Shopping Television, a lean, focused and fast-moving company with ownership incentives for staff and no room for either corporate bureaucracy or labor unions. Park's father founded the company, then known as Samkoo (Korean for 39) and eventually took it into the business of exporting silk textiles. Park joined in 1986. Two things impressed him. One was visiting a Hong Kong textile company whose 60 employees generated $300 million in annual export revenue, compared with the $30 million that Samkoo's 100 employees produced. The second was visiting the United States and seeing QVC, the home-shopping channel, to which Samkoo was then supplying clothing. TV shopping seemed to Park a perfect sales medium for South Korea, where TV ownership was spreading, traffic jams worsening, and retail channels old and consumer-unfriendly.

When the Korean government auctioned licenses for 29 cable channels in 1994, Samkoo got one and (eventually backed in part by foreign private equity) went into head-on competition with a home-shopping channel run by LG Group, one of the top five *chaebol*. LG naturally assumed that it would easily brush aside its upstart rival. Park was not worried. Clearly a rebel himself, he turned for recruiting either (for his senior people) to Koreans with experience working for a western firm or (in the case of the junior ones) to high-school graduates who were bright but misfits, improbable candidates for the suffocating world of the *chaebol*. He also kept costs tightly under control ("It is easier to save money than earn it," he exclaimed) and emphasized strong management systems and technology. In 1997, 39 Home Shopping had about 160 employees (average age 28) putting out 24 hours a day of content, compared with 250 at the rival LG channel. Its signals were digitized, and it used robotic cameras controlled by one software technician (other channels would use three cameramen). It also had sophisticated tracking systems for orders and customer feedback, as well as (rare for Korea) a no-questions-asked return policy. It seemed to be working: Park said the company had never had an annual loss, and by 1997 it had revenues of $100 million with profit margins of about 10 percent.

Racing from floor to floor showing me the television studios, the high-tech control room, the banks of telephone operators taking orders, and the storage rooms for the samples of goods they would sell, Park could hardly contain his excitement. And, in this atmosphere much more reminiscent of Silicon Valley than of the formal and somber surroundings of a *chaebol* headquarters, it was easy to agree with Park that "Korea is entering a new paradigm." His own contribution to it was cut short by his untimely death a year later, but it is clear there is now appreciable space in Korea for the small and mid-sized firms that have added so much to the American and Taiwanese economies. That space would be considerably enlarged if less of Korea's savings were hogged by the big five *chaebol* (see below), but at least it now exists.

THE VOLUNTEERS

What went much underestimated during 1998–99 was the degree of change, too, among second-tier *chaebol*. The pressure on them, as well as on smaller companies whether suppliers to the conglomerates or not, came from the interaction between a severe credit squeeze and Korean firms' notoriously high debt levels. In the first half of 1998 gross expansion of credit was 40 percent lower than it had been a year earlier (meaning, since bills were being repaid, that the net expansion of credit had shrunk even more). This is even worse than it sounds for most of the economy since the big five *chaebol* as a group actually *increased* their debt in 1998, whipping it out of the hands of everybody else. Even before the IMF was called in late in 1997, eight middling *chaebol* had gone into some form of reorganization, and in 1998 some 900 companies filed for court protection, ten times the pre-crisis rate.

Granted, this was not always what it seemed. Even a pro-reform government showed itself sharply divided about how far to go in letting the market's powers of creative destruction do their work. For instance, before at last giving up on Korea First Bank and SeoulBank, the government wasted $1.2 billion trying to save them through a recapitalization that spectacularly failed when the banks lent the money to firms that then defaulted. Then there was the amazing case of Hanbo Iron & Steel, which presaged the crisis by going bankrupt in January 1997. But during its two-and-a-half years of court protection before an American consortium proposed a takeover in mid-1999, Hanbo continued—under the same management that had led it to destruction in the first place—to churn out loss-making steel in an oversupplied industry even though it was already $5 billion in debt. As noted many times before, functioning bankruptcy laws have not been Asia's strong suit, and their lack in Korea has no doubt prevented a clean-out as thorough as the situation warranted.

Despite this, there has been a significant shake-up—though in all the high-profile instances led by managers with some foreign experience and often involving asset sales to western buyers. One of the most instructive examples (and one of the biggest foreign deals) came from Daesang, by mid-1998 only the number 29 *chaebol* and (not coincidentally) at that point the only one of the top 30 not to be headed by a member of the family that owned it. Ko Doo Moo became Daesang's chairman only in August 1997, after a long time running the firm's operations in Indonesia. He concluded that with profitability low, debts high and (by December) bank credit gone, he had to act quickly. Partly to impress on the workers how serious matters were, he moved the headquarters out of a posh high-rise district in one of Seoul's financial centers and into a plain old building in an unfashionable low-rise area of small shops and workshops. Rather than try laboriously to sell real estate or slightly profitable businesses, he went for a quick sale of a profitable "core" but "not a priority" business. He hired Morgan Stanley as the firm's investment adviser and within 8–9 weeks (compared with the usual 6–8 months for such a deal in Korea) had sold Daesang's lysine business to Germany's BASF for $600 million. (Lysine is a hormone-derived chemical used in animal feed.)

It was a sweet business, with 90 percent of its output exported and a market share of 30 percent in China, and when Ko made his revolutionary decision to sell it, the financials were also excellent: on sales of $221 million in 1997, the company got cash-flow of $94 million and net income of $57 million (a net margin of more than 26 percent). The price was six times cash-flow, and Ko came in for heavy criticism for selling such a jewel to foreigners. Ko says Morgan Stanley told him that the price, arrived at after a bidding process that at one time included 10–15 interested parties, was fair. And though he himself felt $800 million should have been more like it (and Daesang's owners $1 billion), Ko had no regrets and the founding family never tried to interfere with his decision. Ko's aim with the lysine deal and the sale of some $300 million-worth of real estate was first to cut the company's debt in half, then to improve its "priority" fermentation businesses such as MSG production. Uninterested in "meaningless" activities to increase turnover, Ko aimed for "value-added" targets like profitability.

Also percolating through the mid-sized *chaebol* during 1998–99 was an idea that change had to come even if it was not compelled by the state of the firm's finances. Lee Woong Yeul, the chairman of Kolon, said he had decided on a full-blown restructuring of his family's conglomerate even before the IMF showed up in Korea. Educated at George Washington

University Business School in St Louis, Lee put in stints in American and Japan before returning home to run one of the firm's factories for a year, at which point his father decided to appoint him as the *chaebol*'s chairman. He was shocked at how "unscientifically" the firm's accounting and personnel systems were managed. He set a goal of raising net profit margins to 10 percent over five years. A lot of the problem, he said, was not operational inefficiencies but just sloppy management. The textile department, for instance, did not even know how much bad inventory it had warehoused. The manager told him $1 million or $2 million-worth. An audit disclosed that it was actually a ten-year accumulation of bad inventory worth $20 million—which had not only not been written off financially but not even physically cleared off the premises. Once that was done the textile factory, which for reasons no one could understand had previously been one of the worst performing parts of the group, suddenly became one of the most profitable ones. Lee demanded contracts with the president of each subsidiary for "clear" management so that he could see what was actually going on in each. He also planned over a 2–3 year period to slim down the empire from 25 companies to about half that number in four lines of business, and to cut the debt load by a third. Lee's view was that "Koreans caused this crisis, so we must suffer to recover from it."

EVOLUTION AMONG THE DINOSAURS

That was not a view widely shared by the top five *chaebol*. Still led by founders or sons of founders, the instinct of the top five was to think that the crisis was an opportunity for more aggressive expansion rather than for a reorientation of the business philosophies that had brought them so far. Handling the top five was the central challenge for President Kim's government. They represented so large a part of the economy that, if their powers and ways of doing business remained unchecked, the financial and human resources needed by upstart firms and reformist mid-sized *chaebol* for their more profit-driven growth would simply not be freed up in adequate quantities. And as late as mid-2000 it remained unclear how much progress the government was going to make in severing what one top economic adviser to President Kim described to me as the "incestuous ties" that bound members of the *chaebol* "families" together.

There was no uniformity of attitude among the top five. Hyundai and Daewoo, the biggest, were also the most recalcitrant. They embodied what one analyst called the traditionally "reckless megalomaniacal pursuit of market share and sheer size with little concern for return in investment." Both groups, still run by their founders, went on spending sprees as soon as the crisis got underway, Hyundai bought bankrupt Kia Motors for $1 billion, thus adding to the already inflated car-making capacity of Hyundai Motors, took over LG Semiconductor for $2.1 billion and absorbed it into Hyundai Electronics, and started a $1.3 billion project to build a tourist resort in North Korea. Daewoo's expansion and its more disastrous effects are described below. Hyundai had not by the end of 1999 gotten into a Daewoo-like life-threatening situation because it still had reasonable cash flow and, besides, the government could not face the simultaneous bankruptcies of the country's two biggest companies. But by mid-2000 its position was precarious enough that the government was able to force its octogenarian founder, Chung Yu Jung, to resign and sell a big chunk of his shares in Hyundai Motors. Meanwhile, the two smallest of the five, LG Group and SK Group, made middling efforts at restructuring themselves, easier in SK's case because of its cash-rich mobile phone subsidiary, SK Telecom. Only Samsung was showing clear evidence of a move away from the old model.

Samsung had long seemed to be the most forward-looking of the top five. The chairman, Lee Kun Hee, took over in 1987 on the death of his father, who had founded the firm in 1938. Until Korea got in trouble in 1997–98, Lee had gone along with conventional Korea Inc thinking about how to run a business—he even invested $3.5 billion in an effort to build a car company from scratch whose factory didn't begin operations until (talk about bad timing) the spring of 1998—but then changed direction sharply when he saw how circumstances had changed. It helped that some of Lee's most influential lieutenants were, highly unusually for a *chaebol,* not lifers with the company and had had considerable western experience. Hwang Young Key, for example, who in 1998 was put in charge of managing Samsung Life Insurance's $15 billion stock portfolio, and a year later was shifted to run the group's troubled mutual-fund arm, had spent several years with Bankers Trust before joining Samsung. In late 1998 he told me the group's strategy was to get rid of most of the scores of companies that had been built up over the decades and to concentrate on only two lines of business: finance, especially Samsung Life with $30 billion in assets, and the hugely profitable Samsung Electronics, which accounts for 10 percent of all of Korea's exports. He expected these two lines to account for 80 percent of the group's business. Unrelated lines might be kept, but only if they were profitable on their own merits.

Samsung was slimming itself in various ways. It sold its loss-making white-goods division to its employees, who now with a far greater incentive for efficiency made it profitable within a month. It sold the construction-equipment division to Volvo. In all, by the end of 1999 the group had sold $3 billion-worth of assets and reduced its workforce by 30 percent. Even Samsung Electronics, which aims to increase its revenues fourfold between 1999 and 2005, is intent on doing so with much greater efficiency: despite the fast growth it cut its workforce by almost a third between 1997 and 1999. By international standards Samsung still has a long way to go with its restructuring and in meeting profitability goals, but the market was clearly impressed with its moves. By late 1999 Samsung had about a fifth of the total assets of the top five *chaebol,* but commanded half of their total market capitalization. The only thing nagging at Hwang in late 1998 was that he was "very worried about Daewoo; if it goes under, the government may make us take large chunks of it and we don't want them."

Less than a year later it looked as though that nightmare might come true. Daewoo's rise coincided with, and in many ways symbolized, South Korea's heroic age. Founded, in 1967, as a textile trading company by 30-year old Kim Woo Choong with some $10,000 of borrowed money, Daewoo ("great universe") grew over the next three decades into Korea's second biggest conglomerate, ringing up $50 billion in sales (more than 10 percent of GDP), employing some 80,000 people on its own payroll, sustaining a vast network of 10,000 major subcontractors employing perhaps 1.2 million more people, and single-handedly accounting for around 15 percent of Korea's exports. Kim was driven by only one aim, relentless expansion, and he was fearless in going for it (an intrepidity that was no doubt aided by the willingness of successive governments to write blank-check guarantees for however much debt he wanted to raise). Whether it was cars, electronics or shipbuilding at home, Middle East construction projects in the 1970s (when Daewoo had no experience of either the region or the business), Siberian timber and mineral extraction in the 1980s, car plants in Poland, India and Uzbekistan (!) in the 1990s, and mini-conglomeration in Vietnam also in the 1990s, Kim was always game.

Nothing in the events of 1997–98 made him change his mind. He told group employees early in 1998: "Daewoo will overcome the crisis through expansionist measures. We cannot embrace the future if we flinch at a time of recession." Daewoo immediately snapped up heavily loss-making Ssangyong Motors despite already having its own car company. In all, during 1998 Daewoo added 14 firms to its existing stable of 275 even though it also lost nearly $500 million that year. Also during 1998 Daewoo added 40 percentage points of debt to a debt-to-equity ratio that was already around 500 percent, in a year when the government had ordered the *chaebol* to cut this ratio to 200 percent and every other conglomerate had begun to do so. It raised the extra debt through both bank loans (even though the government controlled the banks) and by issuing bonds. Everyone felt Daewoo was far too big to be allowed to fail.

That depends, as Bill Clinton might have put it, on what "fail" means. One seemingly clear thing is that Daewoo's founding family was not going to remain in control. By July 1999 the government had to mount a rescue operation to prevent the formal bankruptcy of the group, but did so on condition that a radical restructuring of 12 of the group's main companies would take place. In the summer it was thought that Daewoo's debts amounted to some $47 billion. Updated (and probably still understated) figures in November showed the group's debt to be about $73 billion (about 17 percent of GDP), some $10 billion owed to foreign creditors, and its negative net worth at more than $21 billion. It was the biggest bankruptcy in history. How Kim Dae Jung's government eventually handled Daewoo would be the president's biggest test. By guaranteeing Daewoo bonds held by investment trust companies in late 1999, the government in effect nationalized the group. Disposing of the assets and bad debt would be an immense problem. If other groups such as Samsung were forced to participate in a bailout, the restructuring taking place elsewhere in Korea Inc would be jeopardized. But a market-clearing wipe-out, surely including mass layoffs, just before legislative elections in April 2000 would have made any politician blanch. Still, by mid-2000, the government had gone some way to cleaning Daewoo up. The two most important steps were to put Daewoo Motors on the block after a bidding contest that involved mostly foreigners (see Chapter 13); and to get foreign creditors to accept a restructuring plan that involved write-downs of between a third and two-thirds on their loans. It may not have been a surgically precise solution—the surviving bits and pieces would still carry too much deadweight—but nor were other groups like Samsung forced at the expense of their own efficiency to participate in a bailout.

Whatever the exact details at the end of the day, what counted was that pro-market measures which would have been unthinkable in early 1997 had become commonplace three years later. Foreign investors were swarming over Korea, companies were reshaping themselves (or being reshaped) and bank balance sheets were being cleaned up. A really clean break-up of Daewoo, with assets mercilessly going on the block, would prove a revolutionary turning point. The changes that had already come about regardless of that were, in light of Korea's recent history, still remarkable. That's why the foreign investors were swarming over Asia's best industrial assets. But Korea's weren't the only good assets available in Asia.

A TALE OF TWO RIVALS

The game of comparing Hong Kong and Singapore is an old one, because the two city-states have followed such different paths of economic development and different models of government yet nonetheless enjoyed just about the same astonishing economic success from the mid-1960s to the mid-1990s. While the game has always been fun, it was in fact never much of a contest. The openness and suppleness of Hong Kong's economy, which despite some troubling cartels was still the freest on earth, made it by far the favored site for multinationals wanting a regional headquarters for Asia. Moreover, Hong Kong firms created vastly more shareholder value than Singapore companies did (see Figure 9.1, which shows that in 1969–99 Hong Kong's stock market rose 63-fold in U.S. dollar terms whereas the Singapore market went up only nine times, a little less than the Dow Jones Industrial Average).

Then came the crisis of 1997–98. Michael Enright, a Harvard business professor on leave in the late 1990s at the University of Hong Kong, sums up the almost universal view of observers and businessmen: "Hong Kong had better cards, but Singapore played its cards far better than anyone else." Foreign businessmen in particular took notice, and began to make comparisons that would never before have occurred to them. Lurking behind Enright's observation are two more precise questions. The first is that, whereas Hong Kong now has a decidedly better economy than Singapore, Singapore has a decidedly better government than Hong Kong: which will matter more? Second, Hong Kong is now part of China. Will this be an advantage or a disadvantage for Hong Kong's status as Asia's managerial

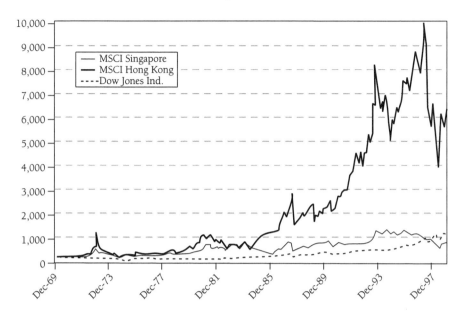

Figure 9.1 MSCI Hong Kong versus MSCI Singapore market performance in US$, 1969–March 1999. (December 1969 = 100) (*Sources:* Datastream, Morgan Stanley Dean Witter Research)

and services hub? If Korea's future will be decided by its success at restructuring, the relative performance of Hong Kong and Singapore will depend on which city bends more flexibly with the global winds of change that have started blowing through Asia.

In the past the outcome would have been a foregone conclusion. "Flexibility" was a word that nobody associated with Singapore. The Lion City was well-run, both at a strategic level thanks to the clairvoyance of Lee Kuan Yew and at an operational level thanks to a disciplined civil service, and it was clean in every sense of the word. But it was also an authoritarian place with tight controls on information flows and political activity and a dearth of the entrepreneurial verve that Hong Kong breathed from every pore. In 1998–99 that began to change perceptibly, and did so because a few years earlier Lee Kuan Yew saw which way the wind was blowing, understood that Singapore had to bend with it, and had a vision of how changes in the world economy and in Hong Kong's own situation would make the Chinese city more vulnerable to a well-aimed attack from its smaller rival.

In Lee's view, two things will matter for making Singapore competitive in the coming decade. One is technology—partly, attracting western technology companies but, more important, raising the educational levels of the workforce. On this, he notes, an adequate number of trained people are being produced: 30 percent to 35 percent of young people are university graduates, and 35 percent to 40 percent graduate from polytechnics or technical institutes. The second point is the internationalization of Singapore, and that begins with the reform of finance:

> When I resigned as prime minister in 1990, I joined the international advisory board of J.P. Morgan. I suddenly realized that our banks were light-years behind. The banking industry was changing. We had been ultra-conservative with strict regulations to build up our credibility.
>
> By 1993–94 I could see that we had to change. We cannot wait until a financial product is proven to be safe elsewhere before we adopt it. We've got to take some risks. These new financial products were coming on fast and we had to take some risk in marketing them. The foreign banker says, "I've got this product. It's a risk, but do you want to wait for two, three years, after it's proven to be not so risky?" I had a difficult problem changing the mindset of the staff at the Monetary Authority of Singapore. Our top regulator Koh Beng Seng, who's now helping the World Bank with their work in Thailand, resigned in protest. He had built up our reputation and credibility and did not want to see it endangered. So I had to put in a new team. I couldn't get Koh to change. He was totally reliable, completely competent and honest. He had good relations with the BIS, the Fed, and the Bank of England. They trusted him. He wanted to resign. I had to let him go.
>
> With the prime minister's [Goh Chok Tong's] agreement, I got my son [Lee Hsien Loong, now head of the central bank and deputy prime minister] to take on and assemble a new team. Koh stayed on another six months for the transition. We assembled a team which we sent to the New York Fed and BIS. With this new team the mindset changed. The financial crisis forced the pace of change. We could go in one of two ways: just stand still and wait for the crisis to be over, or say, "Look, no, take the bull by the horns. Let's proceed. The crisis will blow over and we will be better placed. Let's move."

And how. Under Lee Hsien Loong (a smart and tough man in his 40s whose becoming prime minister is only a matter of time), the Monetary

Authority of Singapore began to shake up the protected domestic banks, allowing in much more foreign competition and driving the overextended sector toward consolidation. Lee brought in John Olds, an American and ex-J.P. Morgan man, to run the Development Bank of Singapore (DBS), the country's biggest bank. Olds started disclosing the true state of DBS's bad-loan portfolio, a rare piece of transparency by Singaporean tradition, and then fired a lot of civil servants who had been snoozily manning some of the bank's highest positions. The snail-paced processing of applications by foreign financial firms to do various kinds of business in Singapore was suddenly speeded up. One western fund manager told me in 1998 that an application she had expected to remain unanswered for several months was approved in ten days; by 1999 some western investment bankers in Hong Kong were saying they thought the regulatory climate in Singapore was in some respects less onerous than that in Hong Kong. Lastly, the Singapore government also began slamming heads and companies together in the state-owned corporate sector, forcing mergers and rationalizations that would have been inconceivable just a few years before.

Consider just what is being done with the GLCs, or government-linked corporations,the state-owned firms which together with western multinationals have dominated the Singaporean economy for more than 30 years. Temasek Holdings, the outfit that manages the government's investments—usually controlling ones—in industries ranging from telecoms to shipping, had assets worth some $40 billion in mid-2000; that then represented a third of Singapore's total market capitalization. Reforming the GLCs has become a top priority. Part of the plan for making the GLCs more competitive will be a faster pace of deregulation (telecoms were completely deregulated on April 1, 2000, two years ahead of schedule). There will also be substantial sales of government stakes in the GLCs.

None of the GLCs better illustrates the drive for change than Semb-Corp industries. Once known as Sembawang Group, this firm was a slow-moving and unfocused conglomerate with at least 150 companies in ten often amazingly unrelated lines of business (like supertanker ship maintenance and a fast-food chain). K.S. Wong, SembCorp's wiry CEO, put in a stint at Singapore Technologies (another government holding company) and then ran Nomura's Singapore operations before being handed the conglomerate to whip into shape. Luckily he had the government's cooperation. Singapore's officials had looked at the Asian crisis and the megamergers in Europe and America and realized that the old Asian conglomerate model would no longer work. Among other things, they concluded global giants would be coming into Asia more and more because it would remain the world's fastest-growing region. As Wong put it, "The old GLC model was okay when we were in a lagoon, but when you get linked to the ocean you have to deal with sharks."

Wong came up with three strategies for swimming with sharks. One was to clean up the group's organization, selling most of its companies and reducing its focus to three core businesses: infrastructure (mainly construction, engineering, and logistics); marine engineering, and information technology. Another was to form strategic alliances with Western firms that would allow SembCorp to come up to global standards. A third was to drive the business-to-business advantages of the Internet throughout the group—including, most interestingly, its ship-repair business (SembCorp has the world's biggest supertanker-repair operation). Wong aimed to eliminate dockyard downtime by linking every supertanker owner in the world to SembCorp's scheduling and pricing system via the Internet. To make sure his managers got the point. Wong made a fetish of financial targets like return on equity. Bonuses were even going to be tied to yearly or maybe half-yearly performance on economic-value-added measures.

Western businessmen in Asia began taking notice of Singapore's shift in attitude. In contrast to Hong Kong, which went into a severe recession in 1998 as the dollar peg cut economic activity without cutting costs sufficiently (see next section), Singapore let its currency float, cut wages by 5 percent and reduced employers' mandatory pension contributions by half, and began more aggressively lobbying multinationals to relocate. One of the attractions was the workforce's level of education. It helped that Singapore was in the process of setting up three business schools, one on its own (though advised by Pennsylvania's Wharton School) and two as branches of well-known foreign institutions: INSEAD of France and the University of Chicago. (Chicago reportedly had first offered to set up in Hong Kong but got no cooperation from the government.) Fund managers, at least those opening new offices, seemed to be choosing Singapore for their location in increasing numbers: assets under management there rose by more than a third in the first half of 1999. And by late 1999—thanks partly to disgruntlement with the high costs, low quality of life and general sense of drift in Hong Kong, and party to assiduous courtship by Singaporean officials dangling tax breaks and other inducements—Western multinationals began considering a move of their regional headquarters to Singapore (though few were actually taking the step). That fit nicely into Lee Kuan Yew's strategy. When asked why Hong Kong's response to the crisis—a seeming retreat from the global economy rather than an advance into it—looked like the opposite of Singapore's, he said:

> We have different destinies. We see our future as an independent international city, a cosmopolitan center. Hong King's future is totally different. They are a part of China.
>
> There are abiding long-term consequences from going cosmopolitan. We emphasize Confucian values more than Hong Kong because we are at greater risk of losing it. Their close links with the mainland will keep them Chinese and Confucians. Singapore can change its culture over two generations.
>
> Hong Kong can't help becoming a Chinese city rather than an international city. Hong Kong has got to decide what is its value-added to China. It has to maximize the value of its links with America, Europeans, and the rest of the world by using them to facilitate the mainland's growth.
>
> You do have excesses at the beginning [of the process of Hong Kong's absorption into China]. It's a rebound from many years of bowing to the British. Now that Hong Kong Chinese are in charge, they must behave differently. In Singapore, we got over that phase long ago. We need foreign players. We are either an international city where everybody's welcome or we'll fail.
>
> In the long run Hong Kong has no choice because it's written they will be Chinese in 50 years. As long as Beijing has a man like C. H. Tung whom they trust, they'll leave Hong Kong to look after itself. [But when Zhu Rongji went to North America in the spring of 1999, he said Shanghai] is China's New York and Hong Kong is their Toronto. I thought, why the downgrade? Fund managers, take note. Do you want to be in Toronto or do you want to be in New York?

Ouch! What is Hong Kong's retort?

THE KINGDOM BY THE SEA

The Singaporeans talk a good line, which sounds better still because Hong Kong's leaders are inept communicators, but it is important to recall how far ahead Hong Kong is at the start of this race for the future. Singapore's intentions make strategic sense but its small population of only 4 million could make them hard to execute. Hong Kong (population 7 million) has a much bigger commercial and financial mass than its rival. At the end of the 1990s Hong Kong was the world's tenth biggest exporter of goods and ninth biggest exporter of services. It was the eighth largest international banking center, with around 400 banks from 40 countries on hand. It was (after Tokyo) Asia's second biggest fund-management center, host to almost 100 fund-management firms. It was also (again after Tokyo) the second largest insurance center, with more than 200 insurance companies. And it had more venture-capital firms than anywhere else in Asia.

Hong Kong reached this position through strengths that are still unimpaired. For all Singapore's ambitions it is Hong Kong that remains by far Asia's most internationalized city. The Securities and Futures Commission, for instance, the territory's stock-market regulator, is chaired by a Malaysian Chinese. Of the six executive directors, only one is Hong Kong Chinese—and she has a Canadian passport. This broad-minded attitude to foreigners holding high positions in public bodies is hard to imagine anywhere else in the world. Moreover, with its unfettered flows of trade and capital, almost no welfare state, low taxes and excellent infrastructure, Hong Kong is better placed than anywhere else to respond to shifts in global demand. And that has always been its practice. From the 1960s onwards it ruthlessly shed the businesses of the past for those of the future. By 1999 85 percent of Hong Kong's economy was in services, the highest share on earth.

What used to be an export-driven manufacturing center, and then (after the factories moved to China) a re-export-driven processing center, has become a regional nerve center for finance, management and trade. Geography helps in this. However ambiguous the overall effects of Hong Kong now being part of China, Hong Kong sits at East Asia's center of economic gravity and has a basically friendly hinterland in China itself. Hong Kong is close to both Korea and Taiwan and not that far from the bulk of Southeast Asia (whose whole regional economy in any event is smaller than that of South Korea alone). Singapore, by contrast, though a fine place from which to conduct business in Southeast Asia, is far from the big action in East Asia; it is also a small Chinese city wedged between two Malay and mostly Muslim neighbors, a hinterland that has always kept (and always will keep) Singapore looking nervously over its shoulder every so often.

Hong Kong's own strides toward dominating the business of managing regional commercial networks have been so great that, by 1997, the value of the territory's "offshore trade"—meaning exports that never touch down in Hong Kong but are produced elsewhere by Hong Kong-owned firms—already amounted to five times the value of Hong Kong's own exports and 85 percent of the value of its re-exports. In other words, not only has Hong Kong's manufacturing moved offshore but even a large chunk of its physical trading activity is moving offshore. Some find it alarming that Shenzhen, a city of 4 million (same size as Singapore) just across the border in China, has in just 20 years risen so fast—its GDP has grown at a compound rate of 38 percent a year—that in all sorts of things from property to retail services to the running of a container port it can now challenge Hong Kong. It may not, in fact, be too many years before the port of Shenzhen, a city that did not even exist until 1979, handles more traffic than Hong Kong's.

Worries about this are misplaced because an important shift in Asia's economic structure is under way and Hong Kong is leading it. The physical activities that used to happen in Hong Kong are increasingly taking place elsewhere, but Hong Kong is masterminding them and is taking a growing stream of income from them. Hong Kong is well on the way to having a "virtual" economy in which high-value-added services provide most of the territory's output. William Fung, the CEO of Li & Fung, a longtime Hong Kong-based trading house that is in the forefront of moves to create networked Asian businesses that act as facilitators for worldwide manufacturing production but also develop local retailing and branding (see Chapter 14), thinks this process is much more advanced than most people realize. He points out that conventional statistics are not very good at painting an accurate picture of an economy founded more and more on "invisibles"—especially when much of the money is funneled through British Virgin Island or other offshore corporations, as it is in Hong Kong's case, a lot of offshore Taiwanese and mainland Chinese companies are involved, and Hong Kong does not even collect GNP figures (which, unlike GDP figures, take into account overseas activities). With China and America having agreed in late 1999 on China's admission into the WTO, Hong Kong's progress toward becoming a virtual economy should, if anything, be speeded up as greater efficiency in China expands the demand for ever more sophisticated services from Hong Kong (though over, say, 20 years the "Toronto factor" mentioned above could start to weigh on Hong Kong as Shanghai gains in economic depth and competence).

Yet, though the future beckons in such ways more strongly in Hong Kong than in Singapore, Hong Kong has some serious problems. The worst long-term problem is the standard of education. One element of this is that the standard of English in Hong Kong, which has never been good, is becoming dismal. But the problem goes well beyond basic competence: in an increasingly networked and information-driven age, Hong Kong's students at all levels are seemingly being left behind their counterparts in other high-income countries in terms both of attitude and of training. Richard Li, the head of Pacific Century CyberWorks, a multi-pronged Internet company based in Hong Kong, told me in 1999 that in the various Internet ventures he was trying to get up and running in Hong Kong he had found that graduates of American junior colleges were better than graduates of Hong Kong's most prestigious universities. The situation is now so bad that, if the government spent the money it is planning to lay out for high-tech gizmos (one of which, a subsidized "Cyberport," see below, ironically is a Richard Li project) on upgrading education instead, the money would deliver a vastly higher return.

Second, despite a 50 percent fall in property prices in 1997–99, real estate remains extremely pricey on a U.S. dollar basis—all the more so in relative terms regionally since all of Hong Kong's neighbors except China devalued their currencies substantially during the panic while Hong Kong did not. The land prices feed through to all other costs of doing business, making the territory far more expensive than almost anywhere else in Asia save Tokyo. Third, the deterioration of the environment—especially air quality—has been so noticeable in the past few years that it has hurt tourist arrivals and begun to affect multinationals' decisions about where to locate themselves. Singapore is physically a lot nicer. Lastly, scratch the surface and you find that Hong Kong is hardly the free-market paradise most people imagine.

The government is bigger and more intrusive than it looks. In 1999 Hong Kong had 185,000 civil servants, and another 160,000 worked for government-owned corporations. The government owns several businesses it need not, notably the profitable subway system, which (to be fair) it started selling off late in 2000. It has been slow to abolish private sector anti-competitive agreements. It has been running a vast public-sector housing establishment, which in 1998 alone absorbed $6 billion in government spending (20 percent of the capital budget) and received 62 acres of some of the most expensive land in the world at no cost. Worst of all, Hong Kong runs a harebrained land policy inherited from British colonial days. The policy coddles the territory's overmighty property developers, sharply restricts the supply of buildable sites, and makes the government beholden to the special interests that profit from the setup because 70 percent of Hong Kong's capital-spending revenue comes from land auctions (and, if you add in direct and indirect taxes on property transactions, 40 percent of total government revenue comes from real estate). Hong Kong's income taxes are wonderfully low and mercifully simple, but there is no free lunch and the cost in this case has been needlessly high land prices and several serious market distortions.

The government may be prepared to tackle some of these problems in interesting ways (see below) but, based on its record during the dark days of 1997–98, then again maybe not. To be fair, there can hardly be a newly formed government that has recently taken over under such unlucky circumstances. Hardly had the second set of fireworks in two days been shot off on the night of July 1, 1997 to celebrate Hong Kong's return to Chinese sovereignty when, next day, Thailand devalued the baht. Civil servants who, having been brought up under the protective carapace of British colonialism, had never been tested under fire were immediately thrown into the front lines; on their own they had to make decisions without the advice of seasoned people from, for example, the Bank of England. They were functioning, moreover, within a governmental setup that is simply preposterous. Post-colonial Hong Kong is run by an indirectly elected chief executive in whom vast powers are vested, only to be questioned in public by a partially directly-elected legislature which has practically no powers and whose surveillance of the administration is therefore almost always done irresponsibly and for grandstanding purposes.

The heart of Hong Kong's recent confusion, though, lies in the chief executive's office. Tung Chee-hwa, a former shipping tycoon, is a hard-working man of unquestioned probity who has the absolutely indispensable quality for someone in his position: China's trust. In private he is not only warm and personable but shows a sharp and deep intellect. Yet he disdains politics, feels little need to peer into the future in public as Singapore's leaders do and draw conclusions about what direction the ship of state needs to be steered in, and (worst of all) feels even less need to explain those conclusions to the citizens and persuade them that they make sense.

The trouble with this is that at the top of any system of government—including in one-party states like China and (effectively) Singapore—political leadership is essential. Civil servants are implementers. They cannot make strategic policy, still less can they lead ordinary people, and in the absence of the political role a lot of random policy shots can be fired.

They certainly were in Hong Kong in 1998–2000. In August 1998, after almost a year of intermittent harrying by hedge-fund speculators playing off interest-rate moves tied to the automatic defense of the Hong Kong dollar peg against corresponding moves in stock-market prices, the government's patience snapped. Using lurid language about "foreign speculators" and "manipulators" that could have come from Mahathir Mohamad's mouth, Donald Tsang, the financial secretary, mounted a huge government buying program of Hong Kong stocks. In less than two weeks $15 billion was spent on a quasi-nationalization of blue-chip Hong Kong, making the government the biggest single shareholder in many of the 33 companies that then made up the Hang Seng index. The excuse given at the time was that the Hong Kong dollar was in jeopardy. This is not credible. As explained before, if the peg's automatic mechanism is allowed to work it can never be successfully attacked by speculation. In any event, just one month later the government introduced technical changes in the operation of the peg that would very likely have removed any risk of destabilization.

Instead, this was a straightforward, albeit massive, stock-propping move intended to rebuild the confidence of man-in-the-street investors in the price levels of the financial markets. A year or so later Tung Chee-hwa, asked if he had any regrets about the intervention, admitted to a small gathering that "Hong Kong's whole financial system was under attack, it could eventually have threatened the fixed-link rate [the peg], and we were right to respond as we did." Defending price levels in free financial markets, though, is a pretty dubious proposition. Milton Friedman called the intervention "insane." Lee Kuan Yew put his finger on the real damage it did—to Hong Kong's reputation: "Are you a referee or are you a player? You cannot be both. Foreign market players may be apprehensive that in a future crisis the authorities may not play by the rules."

In one sense the intervention was a success. No thanks to the authorities, over the next year or so the value of the government's holdings rose some 70 percent as the stock market boomed. Late in 1999 the government successfully floated a little over $4 billion-worth of the stock in a widely-bought index-tracking mutual fund. But the long-term damage done to Hong Kong's reputation as an open and predictable financial center was, as Lee suggested, immense. There was besides, a direct impairment of the workings of what had traditionally been Asia's biggest and most liquid stock market outside Tokyo. In the year June 1998 to June 1999 (the intervention came in August) turnover on the Hong Kong market fell by half—partly because the government had removed so many shares from the market. And despite the late-1999 successful flotation of the index-tracking fund, the government still had the problem of holding some 5 percent of the whole stock market and not knowing what to do with it.

Other interventions followed, including plans to use government money to help build a Cyberport that bafflingly would subsidize billionaire-laden American Internet companies to come to Hong Kong, a Silicon Harbor for chip companies, and a large contribution of land and infrastructure to get Disney to build a Disneyland in Hong Kong. Unlike the stock-market intervention, none of this was devastating in itself, but altogether these plans raised nagging questions about how much more dabbling would be done in the future. It did not help that the seeming drift to interventionism was accompanied by efforts, apparently not at Beijing's behest, to involve the Chinese government in matters (particularly over immigration from the mainland) that the Hong Kong government should have been able to solve on its own. One of the most alarming side effects of all this is that it seems to have encouraged a greater sense among Hong Kong's people that the government should be solving more of their problems—a dismaying development in a place where self-reliance used to be taken for granted. Even Tsang, who a year earlier had become Hong Kong's chief stock-market investor in part to buck up the spirits of the man in the street, felt compelled to give warning in late 1999, "The government is not Santa Claus, to hand out gifts."

There is a cheerier view, held by some whose unconventional readings have often been right in the past, that even though the government is not bothering to explain itself it has actually embarked on a path of significant reform. The greatest optimist is Stephen Brown, a longtime Hong Kong resident who, unlike almost all expatriates, actually lives with his Cantonese in-laws in a deeply Chinese part of the city that foreigners rarely glimpse or think about. Brown, the research head of Kim Eng Securities, argues that behind the scene the government has become "hell-bent on a supply-side reform platform that opens up endless new opportunities." He foresees the civil service being cut by two-thirds over ten years. Partial privatization of the efficient subway is already under way, and more public bodies will follow suit. "Contracting-out" of all sorts of public services from hospitals to education is in the cards. Most important of all, in 1999 public-housing rents started being brought closer to market levels as a prelude, Brown argues, to gradual privatization. With privatization, the government would become less reliant on land auction revenues to fund its budget, and the batty land system could then be reformed. One delphic sign that the government's thinking may be tending this way was Tung Chee-hwa's announcement in late 1999 that an Urban Renewal Authority would be set up to redevelop nine large sites. It could order compulsory land purchases for which, crucially, it would pay the government no "land premium," a sort of tax that is the main ingredient of the land-auction system. It could be the beginning of the end for the worst legacy of British colonial rule. Such a structural revolution would not only open the way for new growth industries but also send the stock market soaring.

This is a radical and appealing vision; it may even be right, though given the way the Hong Kong government "communicates" its intentions that is anyone's guess. Overall, it seems inevitable that Singapore will be gaining some ground on Hong Kong because of the constraints on the Hong Kong government's policy-making abilities, some imposed by the territory's delicate relationship with its sovereign power in Beijing and some by the reticent and inexperienced nature of its own leadership (though that may change as the post-colonial transition ends). But nobody has ever made money for long by betting against Hong Kong. The strengths at the bottom still seem a lot deeper and more influential than the weaknesses at the top. What sticks in my mind is a conversation over dinner with some Hong Kong business people in 1999. After half an hour of general bemoaning of the sorry state of the Hong Kong government, one woman threw up her arms and exclaimed, "Who cares about this government anyway? No government ever made Hong Kong what it is. We did."

THE THAI ADVANTAGES

Suppose the conventional wisdom proves right (I think it won't, see Part Three) and, thanks to buoyant stock markets and renewed capital flows, the push for reform flags throughout Asia. Many people, particularly from the IMF, began warning in 1999 that this could set the stage for slower growth and another crisis in the future. Using John Greenwood's division of Asia's problems into the structural and the cyclical, the answer would probably vary from country to country, with the more structurally-impaired more at future risk from a retreat from reform. But matters are more complicated than that. Remaking whole societies and economies is a massive task connected with the whole process of modernization and development; it would not be surprising if it took a few tries at different intervals to get the job done. Besides, Russia's experience in the 1990s was hardly a testimonial to the virtues of reform at one whoosh. Greenwood guesses that even if only 20 percent of the reforms are accomplished in the first post-crisis round a real recovery will take hold in Southeast Asia. By mid-2000 it seemed the opposite, with Southeast Asia falling way behind China-centric Asia at reform and recovery. But who knows? A few things about Thailand show why.

Most of the following story is taken from David Scott, a long-time expert on Thailand and the research head of W.I. Carr in Hong Kong, who thought as early as September 1997 that the Thai economy's flexibility and openness to market signals were so strong that a recovery was likely to be more complete than the worriers about crony capitalism believed. His conclusion was that "this is basically a sound economy working off the effects of a ten-year credit binge, even though you don't work that off very quickly."

First, apart from mismanagement of the exchange-rate regime and of bank supervision, Thailand's economic management has been surprisingly good for a country at its income level. The government takes less than 20 percent out of GDP in the form of taxes and, until it began spending countercyclically to ease the pain of the crisis, consistently ran budget surpluses. Even pre-crisis, the government had gone far down the road to deregulation—licensing requirements for industries like steel and cement were abolished—and privatization. Measures taken since the crisis have pushed this ahead. In beer, for example, Singha (the biggest brewer) saw its market share fall in a few months from 90 percent to 50 percent when licensing deregulation led Surathip Group, Thailand's largest whiskey maker, to enter the beer market and compete with Singha.

Moreover, the government is not keen on prestige projects of the sort that more authoritarian regimes often use to boost their control or fill their private purses: "we don't have herds of national white elephants in the making; there's no national car, no national steel mill, no national plane, no state-owned-tallest-building-in-the-world." Lastly, the Thai economy has been one of the most open in the region to the outside world, with tariffs lowered faster than elsewhere in Southeast Asia and, at least since the crisis, a receptiveness to foreign takeovers of domestic banks, firms and property that has been unexcelled. Thailand already has one of the most competitive retail and consumer markets in the world, with European firms like Carrefour, Tesco and Marks & Spencer in strong positions. And as Southeast Asia's free-trade area takes shape over the next few years, the foreign influence will rise further: the foreign-owned car plants on the country's eastern seaboard will be selling their wares throughout the region.

The easiest way to gauge the lack of distortions in an economy is to compare prices there with world market prices. Scott looked at Portland cement prices in Southeast Asia, which are a pretty good proxy for prices generally because cement is a commodity with few variations and the ratio of value to bulk and weight is extremely low, so even if tariffs are low imports can offer relatively little discipline in local markets. Even before the crisis, cement prices in Thailand were the lowest in Southeast Asia—little more than half those in the Philippines, for instance. This is not so surprising: the industry was deregulated in 1989 and competition is fierce. Post-devaluation, prices of all sorts of things in Thailand seemed to adjust faster than they did elsewhere in Asia. By early 1999, for example, in cost surveys for multinationals Bangkok was one of the cheapest capitals in the world for doing business—even though pre-1997 it had had horrendously expensive real estate. The years 2000–2001 will likely spread the efficiencies much more widely as recapitalized and reorganized banks (many of them with foreign ownership or participation) at last begin to liquidate their debtors' assets.

Then there is the quality of the Thai workforce. By most conventional measures Thailand has done a poor job of raising educational levels to where they should be for a country with its income. Yet Scott argues that education reforms introduced in the early 1990s will make themselves felt in significant ways over the next ten years. Spending on education quadrupled in dollar terms between 1987 and 1997, and sensibly the policy was to target government spending on poor rural areas while leaving the well-off in the cities to educate their children in private schools at their own expense (and the private schools, interestingly, are more and more often run by foreigners). Enrollment rates are rising steadily at all levels—a 50 percent increase in university enrollment is expected in the five years to 2002—and while Thailand is no Korea in terms of worker quality it is also no Indonesia. Bill Heinecke (see Chapter 7) sees this at a micro level. One of his divisions sells Time-Life books house to house and does extremely well. He has also found that health insurance is a good business to own because Thais tend not to take advantage of it: in many of his factories it is routine for workers to go five years without taking any sick leave.

There is another human element, too little mentioned in analysis of the recuperative powers of Southeast Asian economies, in which Thailand has unrecognized advantages: indeed it is top of the heap. In Northeast Asia—Japan, Korea, Greater China—the countries are mostly homogeneous in their ethnic makeup. Southeast Asia is uneasily fractured between what can broadly be described as ethnic Malays (often Muslim) and ethnic Chinese, who outside Singapore are in the minority but dominate commercial throughout Southeast Asia far more than the Jews did in pre-war Europe. The ethnic tensions in Southeast Asia are nowhere near the level that led to such catastrophe in Europe in the 1930s, but they still weigh heavily in the economic balance.

At the dismal end of the scale is Indonesia, where repeated pogroms against the Chinese minority were a blot on the post-Suharto months; apart from anything else, they caused capital flight possibly in the scores of billions just when Indonesia most needed the money. There are also problems in Malaysia, the Philippines and Vietnam (and of course between Singapore and its neighbors). But in Thailand the ethnic Chinese are woven seamlessly into Thai life.

Behind the stark contrast between Jakarta's burned and smashed Chinatown in 1999 and its bustling and peaceful counterpart in Bangkok lies a radically different historical experience. Everywhere in Southeast Asia, waves of immigrants from coastal China over the past few centuries peopled and then overwhelmingly dominated the commercial and financial classes in the countries where they landed. Yet although they amassed often stupendous wealth, the Chinese usually remained isolated, politically weak and prey to attack. Thailand was different. The Chinese began coming in the thirteenth century; in the peak years, from 1892 to 1930, more than a million settled there. The early immigrants were often laborers who built the railways, but they included shopkeepers, traders and moneylenders. By the 1940s they had begun to establish and run industrial and financial conglomerates (many of which the upheavals of 1997–99 have begun radically reshaping).

There were occasional bursts of anti-Chinese sentiment—the king himself wrote a vituperative tract in 1911 denouncing the Chinese as "the

Jews of the Orient"—but for the most part they were left in peace. Like America, Thailand has had strong assimilative powers. Since early in the 1900s, anyone born in Thailand of whatever parentage has automatically become a Thai citizen (and long-resident whites like Bill Heinecke are also naturalized, an uncommon liberality in Asia which suggests that the resistance to foreign involvement in the economy may be more apparent than real). Every Chinese coming to the country took a Thai name, often chosen for him, Ellis Island-like, by the official registrar. The welcoming spirit endures: more than 500,000 tourists from mainland China visited in 1998, and Thailand is the only country in the world that doesn't require citizens of the People's Republic to get a visa before coming in. Many who come also stay. The publisher of a Chinese-language newspaper in Bangkok, whose business increasingly depends on her publications being bought by mainland Chinese, guessed that by late 1998 there might be as many as a million mainlanders indefinitely resident in Thailand and doing business there.

What has made Thailand so tolerant? A common religion helps: the Chinese, like the Thais, are almost all Buddhist, so the tensions between the Muslim Malays and the Christian or Buddhist Chinese in Malaysia or Indonesia are absent. As in America with English, the children of Chinese immigrants in Thailand grow up speaking and reading Thai, not their parents' native tongue. Thailand's famously relaxed attitude to sex also counts: intermarriage between Chinese and Thais has long been the norm. Most important of all, Thailand was never colonized by a western power, and the Chinese were never seen—as they were elsewhere in Southeast Asia—as the business henchmen of the colonialists. Moreover, they have successfully moved beyond the usual Overseas Chinese confines of business and finance. Chuan Leekpai, the prime minister in the aftermath of the crisis, is part Chinese, as are several members of parliament. The result was that Thailand weathered its economic troubles with a complete absence of ethnic strife or disruption to the normal patterns of business life. It is not that Chinese businessmen sailed serenely through the crisis. As noted before, whole fortunes built up during the giddy years 1985–96, often by incautious financiers who got started as moneylenders in Bangkok's Chinatown, were wiped out. But this will produce a shift in power among the Chinese, not wrench business away from them.

All this is why even a partial purging of excesses and partial overhaul of the way business is done in Thailand could well produce another burst of growth in the next decade. For similar (albeit more general) reasons, that is also true of Asia as a whole.

TOUGH AND YOUNG

In 1997–99 it became easy for people in the West to forget what Asia had going for it. America was enjoying its biggest and longest economic boom in at least 50 years; Europe seemed to be following the American structural-reform model at least tentatively and was in the midst of a cyclical upswing anyway. Yet, as has happened so often before, the next ten years may well bring a reversal of the fortunes of the previous ten, with problems cropping up in the Untied States and Europe while Asia recovers its verve of 1985–95. If you try peering ten years into Asia's future you find three optimistic trends staring you in the face.

The first is a collection of patterns that point to success if they are properly deployed. It is impossible to repeat too often what a difference it makes if a country saves 40 percent of its income a year instead of 15 percent (even if a lot of the higher figure is wasted due to various inefficiencies), and most of Asia tends toward the former rather than the latter. Nobody disputes the value of education, and Asians value it more than anyone else once income differences are taken into account (and often sometimes more even when income differences are not taken into account, e.g., in China today). All the evidence is that Asians, particularly the ethnic Chinese and the Koreans, have lost not an ounce of their willingness to work hard (due in part, no doubt, to the continued absence of a welfare-state mentality in Asia, see below). Last, as Thai prices suggest, Asian countries tend to be pretty open to world standards and that helps drive them toward efficiency. All of this impresses world financial markets. Few would suggest that markets always price risk correctly even over a fairly long period, but they do not price it incorrectly over a very long period. Despite fluctuations over the past decade, world bond markets have consistently demanded to be paid 12 to 15 percentages points more to hold long-term debt issued by Latin American governments than equivalent debt issued by Asian ones—meaning that Asia in the long run is seen as much less risky by international investors.

Second, the main reason why the markets discount Asian risk so much compared with that of other emerging economies is the quality of

Asian governments. Despite their frequent institutional weaknesses, like corruption and feeble regulatory powers, Asian governments tend to perform well at nurturing a pro-market environment. They tax and spend little and, with notable exceptions, do not interfere too much with the transmission of market signals. In particular, they almost uniformly shrink from the welfare-state mentality that leads all European governments, and to some extent the American government, to use public services to try to redistribute income. One seemingly offbeat example illustrates the point perfectly: mass-transit railways (MTRs).

In 1996 A.T. Kearney, a consulting firm, did a study for Hong Kong's Kowloon-Canton Railway Corporation (KCRC) of 37 MTRs around the world. It found that the eight most efficient were all in Asia: five in Japan, two in Hong Kong and one in Singapore. The study made adjustments for variables such as differing wage rates and population densities, and still found that the Asian MTRs easily outstripped their western counterparts in operating and financial efficiency. American and European MTRs received taxpayer subsidies that accounted for some 50 percent to 70 percent of their total revenues; the Asian MTRs received virtually nothing from the taxpayer. For example, since the early 1980s, when the KCRC received some $400 million in equipment-purchase and start-up money from the government for new commuter lines (and repaid the start-up money within two years), it has financed capital spending and operations entirely from its own resources—not a penny of taxpayer money has gone into it for 20 years. And, unlike in Europe or America, service on the Asian MTRs is good and their customers are satisfied rather than enraged.

Why the difference? Part of the reason is that the Asian lines are much newer and thus could avoid mistakes made by the older European and American systems (though this isn't much of the reason since San Francisco's BART system, which came into existence around the same time as the Asian MTRs, is still subsidized to the tune of 48 percent of its revenues). Also, it costs a lot more in Asia than in Europe, not to mention America, to buy and run a car, making an MTR ride a more appealing option. But the overwhelming explanation is in the fare-setting process. In Europe and America this is highly politicized, with unions, special-interest groups and politicians on the make all lobbying for their own sake and forgetting the system's customers. The result is usually a downward spiral of inadequate cash-flow, inadequate investment, deteriorating services, resistance to fare increases and ever greater government subsidies. In Asia fares are set on the basis of what is needed to make an MTR profitable. The KCRC, for instance, is required by its charter to be commercially viable, raising its own capital in the markets and achieving a target return on assets of 12 percent to 15 percent. Fare increases are subject to public discussion, but given these financial constraints they are rarely a matter of controversy. The result of dispensing with extraneous objectives like pandering to unions or politicians or providing jobs is that the taxpayer's money stays in his pocket, service is good, capital investment is adequate and fares are not noticeably higher than in the West. The attitude in Asia that even public services should be services rather than cash cows for special interests is deeply ingrained, and it puts an immense constraint on the ability of governments to follow their instincts for self-aggrandizement.

Yet however important it is to get savings, education and so on right, and for governments' and lobbyists' hands to be strictly tied when they are anywhere near the cookie jar, there is a third thing that is most important of all. The chances that Asian economic growth over the next generation will resemble that of the miracle years 1970–95 will be decided above all else by the age profile of Asia's population—by demography.

Shifts in demographics—especially those that affect the size of the working-age population—are of enormous importance everywhere. Indeed, they account for a bigger share of economic behavior and performance than any other single thing. In America, for instance, the movement of the baby-boom bulge through the population profile has successively shaken up the markets for police services (too many teenage boys on hormones), higher education, entertainment, housing and then in the late 1990s—because baby-boomers have been the least thrifty American generation ever—do-it-yourself pension planning through the stock market. In Asia the impact of demography has been far more profound than that.

The reason is that in the two generations after 1950 East Asia went through the fastest-ever shift in the age structure of any big population anywhere. All modern societies follow the same pattern as they begin their economic take-offs. First comes a rise in life expectancy and a drop in infant mortality; only with a lag of many years do birth rates come down to restore some balance. Meanwhile there is a population explosion. For a time these baby-boomers are a drag on economic growth and savings rates. Then, as they enter the workforce much more quickly than new babies arrive and old people stop working, they boost the whole economy a lot. In America the process took a century.

In post-1945 East Asia it happened two or three times as fast, partly because mortality-reducing drugs came in with a bang. For two decades economic growth was dragged down as the baby-boomers grew up. Then, in 1965–90, the economies exploded. The relatively fast growth in the workforce gave a kick to economic growth in many ways, the most important of which were, first, the simple relative increase in the ranks of the able-bodied and, second, higher savings and capital investment which in turn made the expanded workforce more productive. David Bloom and Jeffrey Williamson, two Harvard professors, have calculated that between a third and a half of East Asia's growth in the miracle years came one way or another from this "dynamic" shift in the age structure of the population.

What happens next in Asia depends on two things: how much more demographic dynamism is left—how long the workforce can grow faster than those too old or too young to work—and how productive the workforce is. For most of East Asia the years of a disproportionately fast increase in the workforce are almost over: Hong Kong, Singapore, Taiwan and South Korea are just about peaking now; China's and Thailand's acceleration will be over by 2005. But the Philippines, Indonesia and Malaysia, as well as the whole of the Indian subcontinent, have a good 25 years more to run. Those are the places to which Asia's fastest-growth potential, other things permitting, will now be shifting.

But Asia has a second source of potential advantage. Once the workforce as a share of population has peaked, it maintains that share for at least 20 years—so nowhere in Asia save Japan will the relative size of the workforce be shrinking before 2015–2020. This means that all of Asia will enjoy at least a constant high ratio of workers to non-workers for a couple of decades during which that ratio will be declining in America, Europe and Japan. In a world where the importance of educated labor relative to natural resources or capital is inexorably rising—this is the information age after all—the advantage of a high ratio of educated workers to non-workers can only increase. As a rough guide to how well-educated East Asian labor is across the board, recall not only that secondary-school students in half a dozen Asian countries consistently rank among the top ten in the world in standard math and science tests, but also that the bottom quarter of South Korean students outperform the bottom quarter of same-age American students.

Population is not destiny. Much of Latin America went through a demographic transition similar to East Asia's without reaping nearly as much benefit. Sensible economic policies are needed too. But there is nothing, in the financial crisis or otherwise, to suggest that Asian policies are so cockeyed they could squander much of the demographic advantage the continent will enjoy for the next generation. In fact, this advantage gives Asia a lot of room for policy error.

Spread across 60 percent of the world's population, even modest rises in, e.g., consumption of fast food have a big impact on the world's fast-food market; and the idea that increasingly well-educated twenty-something Asians are going to be a less dynamic force in the world economy than forty-something Europeans and thirty-something Americans defies everything we know about what happens as people age. Besides, my guess is that despite the messiness of the process during 1997–2000 much of significance has already changed for the better in the structure of Asian business and finance that will give these demographic shifts fuller scope for making themselves felt. And much more is about to change as market movements based on globalization and technology reinforce the institutional reforms that the Asian crisis of 1997–99 ushered in.

PART THREE

MAKING
MARKETS

CHAPTER

10

Technology and the
New Asia

The investment lesson of the 1990s has been that investors
should have paid more attention to emerging industries than
emerging markets—

Michael Hughes, Director
Baring Asset Management, London 1999

L ooking back on what most lifted America up in the 15 years following
its late-1970s trough, three changes were at the top of the list: the establishment of a stable, non-inflationary macroeconomic framework
combined with deregulation and lower taxes; swift technological change,
especially in communications and telecommunications; and the development, thanks mainly to new financial instruments, of a much freer market
for corporate control (see Chapter 1). The list for Asia today looks pretty
similar. The first two parts of this book were about how the big forces unleashed by the crisis of 1997–99 are changing the economic and regulatory
framework in which Asian companies function; part IV will deal with the
possibly destabilizing influence of politics, which still counts in Asia although it has become almost an irrelevance in the United States and the
countries of the European Union. Part Three is about the titanic forces of
globalization—technology, finance and the global market for corporate
control—and how they will be brought to bear on markets and companies
in Asia. It wouldn't be a surprise if the greatest of these forces, in Asia's case,
turned out to be technology.

203

The reason is not that Asians have previously been latter-day Luddites, figuratively smashing the West's machines to preserve an old way of life (except for India until a heartening turnaround in economic policy this decade, see the next chapter). Ever since the Meiji Restoration in the 1860s, first the Japanese and then other Asians have had an insatiable appetite for western technology to help in their modernization. In the past two generations, moreover, Japan has become not just a major producer of high-tech hardware but Asia's only world-quality source of R&D, South Korea has become a significant producer of memory chips, Taiwan has begun producing more personal-computer components—including screens and certain kinds of chips—than almost anyplace else, India has become one of the world's biggest software-writing establishments, and factories throughout Asia have been set up to turn out components of all kinds for assembly elsewhere into completed electronic devices.

The difference just now is that the greatest global technology wave of, say, 1995–2010—the Internet—could not have been better designed had it been done on purpose to destroy the methods, structures and assumptions that guided Asian governments and businesses during their spectacular rise of 1970–95. When combined with the sharp dislodging of comfortable old habits that events described elsewhere in this book have provoked, the Internet has the potential to remake corporate Asia beyond recognition by 2010. You do not have to believe that the Internet is a century-churning event like the invention of electricity or penicillin to realize that for Asia it comes at a crucial turning point. The Internet stands for almost everything Asia's old order was against.

The Internet stands first for the consumer against the producer. The costs of buying goods and services over the Internet are considerably lower than through usual channels, the choice is wider and the process is more transparent (meaning the consumer has more information). Second, it puts a squeeze on the pricing power that allows market inefficiencies such as overstaffing and excess inventory to exist. Third, it makes good personal connections in business a less powerful advantage because information about finance and market conditions is so much more readily and widely available. Lastly, it forces firms and countries everywhere to conform to best business practices because money will flow elsewhere if they aren't followed.

All this contributes to the most significant effect of the Internet for Asia: its ability to make the absorption of knowledge, technology and ideas from the most advanced economies considerably easier. Almost every

Asian government (and every other government, for that matter) is deeply confused about what makes technology important. Governments tend to focus exclusively on the production of technology, whereas it is the consumption of it that has the greater impact. A study by the OECD of the relative contribution to economic growth of R&D spending and spending on the acquisition of technology in rich countries found that acquiring technology was at least as important as creating it, and in many industries the productivity gains were greater and the return on investment higher from buying rather than producing technology. In poor countries the advantages of buying technology rather than trying to produce it are even more striking. Paul Romer, the Stanford economist mentioned earlier (see Chapter 3), clearly explained why this is so many years before most people had heard of the Internet. Here I will just plagiarize from my previous book:

> Ideas are the world's pool of existing knowledge—the most efficient sequence, in an example of Paul Romer's, for sewing twenty pieces of cloth together to make a shirt—and of new knowledge that people tinkering with the processes on an assembly line or with a string of symbols like this sentence come up with.
>
> The main reason the rich world is rich—and why half or more of its economic growth comes from productivity increases—is not because it has physical and human capital in abundance (though that helps) but because it is rich in ideas it knows how to apply. In the world described by Romer, "ideas are the critical input in the production of more valuable human and non-human capital." If so, for a poor country ideas have a spectacular virtue. Once they exist anywhere, anybody can acquire and use them—and, just as important, use them at the same time as everybody else without doing any harm to anyone else (which is not the case with, for example, an office building). These days you not only do not have to reinvent the wheel, you can find out how to make the car and then improve on the car-making process yourself. That is why countries starting out very far behind the rich would have the chance—if they get things right—to make up ground so fast.
>
> Getting things right means, above all, making an economy as open as possible to foreign influences. In Romer's view, by far the most common mistake made by poor-country governments is to practice a sort of "neo-mercantilism" of ideas: the belief that a country must "own" some ideas of its own and reap monopoly profits (and technological advancement) from them even if this means restricting the entry of ideas from the rest of the world via trade and foreign investment. This sort of approach—which is

what advocates of industrial policy usually have in mind when they argue for active government intervention to support "strategic industries"—is almost invariably disastrous. It makes an economy poorer than it otherwise would be and retards rather than accelerates the acquisition of ideas and their dispersion through the economy. Thus, the surest good policy for a poor country to follow is to do nothing—that is, to open its doors as wide as possible to foreign goods and foreign investment and then sit back and watch nature takes its course.

By 1999 Romer was pointing out that the spread of the Internet made this argument even stronger than it had been before. The speed and unlimited geographical reach with which ideas about almost everything can now be diffused make the absorption of ideas vastly easier than it was even five years ago. Moreover, the cost of acquiring the available ideas is falling rapidly. The huge bulk of information of all kinds on the Internet is free (which is leading industry professionals to do some serious rethinking about whether intellectual property can be charged for any longer, see Chapter 11). Getting access is also getting cheaper: telecoms charges are being slashed worldwide, and in China's big coastal cities by the end of the century consumers could walk into grocery stores and buy $500 personal computers. There may still be a case, within strict limits, for governments to promote moves up the technological ladder with research parks and the like—after all, in Romer's words, ideas can be used or they can be produced and as an economy becomes more sophisticated it will find itself producing more ideas than before. But the Internet clearly makes the production function less important than earlier. And, in addition to the crucial need for governments to make the flow of foreign ideas to their people and businesses even more unimpeded than before if they are to get their full economic advantage, governments might want to reflect that these changed circumstances also argue that Cyberports or Cyberjayas bring less benefit than better education.

Yet, as noted above, much more than economics is going to be changed in Asia by the new technologies. One of the first Asians to understand how revolutionary and wide the effects are likely to be was Jimmy Lai, a grade-school dropout immigrant from mainland China who came to Hong Kong in 1960. After factory stints and unimpressive jobs, he successfully set up in several Asian countries a cheap and cheerful chain of clothes stores called Giordano, then moved into publishing in Hong Kong with Chinese-language magazines and a lurid but highly popular newspaper called *Apple Daily* and then, in 1999, started an Internet-modeled grocery delivery business in Hong Kong. Along the way he became persona non grata in China by delivering blunt public views on Li Peng, the dour hardliner most associated with the Tiananmen Square killings in 1989 ("the son of a turtle's egg with zero IQ," Lai called him, and that's even more insulting in Chinese) and on the imminent death of the Communist Party ("it will last less than ten years," he now says). Visiting American liberals warmly receptive to his anti-China views are discomfited to hear lectures from him over lunch about how the welfare states in the West need to be ended and Asian family values preserved. In the mid-1990s, sensing what was coming out of California, Lai tried to set up a business in Silicon Valley but found it impossible to do from a distance. Yet he still thinks technology is what is going to matter most:

> It's not just a crisis, it's a fundamental change here. The international investor was looking at the Asian balance sheet to invest before, now they're looking at competitiveness and once they do that they know Asia doesn't have the competitive advantage they assumed. Asia has to come out of the closet and be open to the global market to be competitive. Before they do that they have to change the regulations and laws, which is easy, but they also have to change the value systems the business community holds, the attitudes of the people and their aspirations. Investors used to think Asia is like a high-growth company so they put a very high P/E on it; now they know it is not. The high-growth places are going to be where knowledge and technology are the most highly intensive, which is the States now, a little bit of Japan, and Europe. This element is going to dominate the market for the next few decades.
>
> Once the regulations and the rules of the game are made compatible with those of the Americans, that will make knowledge and technology much easier to transfer. It will make us more receptive to the knowledge and technology. The transfer has to have a parallel, it needs a compatible value and order. We don't have that yet. The problem is not just the financial infrastructure, it's also the cultural infrastructure, the value infrastructure, the attitude of the people: these are the greatest problems to be solved in Asia. The attitude that makes personal relationships more important than the market has to change. The market is becoming a lot more impersonal

now, more transparent and objective. In Asia the personal relationship is still very strong, and until that is changed we won't be compatible with today's objective and transparent market.

This gets to the heart of what Asian economies, societies and businesses are going to look like by 2010. Gordian Gaeta, a Hong Kong-based business consultant, points out that the varying forms of capitalism in the world can be sorted into three broad categories (leaving out the unstable looting-sort that existed throughout the 1990s in Russia among other places). First is the American individualistic sort, largely shared by the Anglo-Saxon world, in which the driving force is the maximization of returns. Second is the continental European variety. Gaeta describes this as essentially conservative socialism, a collective market economy in which the government's role is prominent, high unemployment is made tolerable through large welfare programs, there is little initiative or significant movement up or down the economic and social scale but a lot of leisure and a high quality of life, and the big winners are not allowed to sweep the chips off the table as they can in America but the big losers in the game of life do not suffer as much deprivation as they do in America. The keenness of Europeans to preserve this conservative existence was, as noted in Chapter 1, one of the main motivations behind the creation of the euro—though, despite Europe's accumulated wealth, it remains an open question whether even that can hold back the tide of dollarization.

Then there is Asia. Gaeta describes this model as an odd blend of maximizing returns but not at the expense of others. Asia has not enforced this do-not-harm rule through government-guided income transfers via taxation and other public programs as its European counterparts have done—which is why profit maximization is still potentially a more potent force in Asia than in Europe—but more through social and family systems that allowed the weak to be supported through institutions like the corporation (in Japan) or the overseas Chinese business network. The question is how much of this can survive the global onslaught from America's awesome business model.

Jimmy Lai has no doubts about which way the world is moving:

> The transmission of American standards all around the world is not going to stop, it's only going to be increased because the whole of Asia is changing the American way. It's the model for the world, not just for Asia but for Europe also. Europe has the euro and all that bullshit; they think it's going to

work. I don't know why they think just having a unified currency is going to work a miracle.

They're crazy, those guys. I talk to the French, they bang on, they say you're American swine and all that. I had dinner with a French cabinet minister and said what Europe needs now is flexibility, because you guys have to restructure your social system, your social infrastructure. Now you have only one currency, your currency is the wheel of the economy and you want to have a wheel that you lock. You know, you're crazy, when you need flexibility now you have a euro which is total rigidity. I mean, those guys, I don't know why they think this way. I don't understand them, but they will fool around with that idea until the idea fails.

Eventually they will come to their senses; they will realize what's right, it will only take them longer. America's going to be very dominant in the next century. You Americans will be a lot more dominant just because American technology is going to pry open all the countries of the world, and make all those countries open up because American technology, American ideas, American values, all that as a package will be prying open, will be invading all the world, will be making changes everywhere.

In Asia it is a most difficult thing to overcome, to keep the Chinese audacity and risk-taking but combine it with modern managerial methods that do involve much more objectivity and transparency. Some will be able to change, some will just be out of the game. The younger generation, the generation who are educated in the States, will come back, get into trouble and they will have to rethink the way of doing things. That's the great hope, that some of them will come to their senses and no longer rely on their fathers' way of doing things.

Is he right? Technology, both in the sense of ripping the existing order to ribbons and in offering the best business opportunities, should tell first.

MEN OF IRON

"Who cares about the Asian financial crisis?" I was told in mid-1999 by Frank Huang, a Taiwanese high-tech entrepreneur. "We care about what happens in America and Europe." For the Asian companies that make the hardware on which the world's software runs and information is transmitted, the sentiment is understandable. During the 20 years after 1980, in many lines of manufacturing Asia became the world's workshop. That is where much of its comparative advantage in trade will continue to lie, although because of the spread of the Internet and changes in the business organization of multinationals it is going to have to be fitted into a different world of global production than it has known before (see Chapter 13).

The dangers for Asia in that new world are acute. As the twenty-first century dawned, it was clear that making things, even very sophisticated ones, was not yielding profit margins as good as those generated by providing services connected with those physical objects. Under Jack Welch, who is to retire in the spring of 2001, America's phenomenally successful General Electric explicitly turned itself from a manufacturer to a "solutions provider" that did continue to sell physical machines of various kinds but did so packaged with a wide variety of services to support them and the customers that used them. The most financially successful Japanese company of 1998–99 was based on a business model under which the firm gave away mobile phones for free and made all of its (considerable) profits from a percentage of the service revenues generated when the customers used the phones (see next chapter). Walter Russell Mead of America's Council on Foreign Relations has gone so far as to argue that profitability in manufacturing alone has entered a long-run decline of the sort that farming suffered in the late nineteenth and early twentieth centuries, with a similar future consequence of falling employment and wealth for manufacturing-based economies. If true, this is not good news for the workshop of the world.

If it does not upgrade itself, that is. Even though farm employment fell to near zero in the rich world toward the end of the twentieth century (except where, in Japan and parts of Europe, it was with ridiculous extravagance financed by taxpayer subsidies), in places like America, Australia and the wheat-producing region of France global comparative advantage was strong enough to keep profitability high. If Asia keeps its wits about it, there is no reason that the world's natural manufacturing workshop cannot, over the next generation, become not only the market that everyone must sell into because of its size but also the place where everyone has to manufacture because of its skills.

And among lines of manufacturing it is in information-technology hardware that Asia has enjoyed—and will continue to enjoy—some of its fastest and highest value-added growth. By 1999 Asian countries including Japan accounted for five of the top ten slots in the world's production of personal-computer hardware. Japan, Taiwan, Singapore, China and

South Korea together produced $110 billion-worth, compared with America's $95 billion-worth. Asia's collective output, moreover, is growing significantly faster than America's—8 percent versus 5 percent between 1998 and 1999, an exceptionally robust year for American production—and the gap will widen as American firms shift more hardware production offshore. There are several surprising twists in the tale of East Asia's relentless rise as a hardware producer. One is the spread of the industry to the Philippines, long thought to be the sick man of Southeast Asia. In fact, in the five years after 1994 foreign high-tech firms like Intel and Motorola invested more than $7 billion in factories in the Philippines to assemble chips and other computer components. The result was that between 1988 and 1999, years when the value of the country's exports almost quintupled to some $34 billion, the value of its electronics exports rose from $1.4 billion (20 percent of total exports) to more than $20 billion (more than 60 percent of total exports). If the Philippines, with its reputation as a low-value-added agricultural-commodity exporter, could make such a change this fast, imagine what is going to happen in Asia as a whole over the next decade.

A second turnaround with global implications came between 1997 and 1999 at Korea's Samsung Electronics. One high-level Samsung executive told me in 1998 that, if only Samsung Electronics didn't have to support "weak brothers," its chip-making unit would be fantastically efficient—more so than any other memory-chip maker on earth. Yet, in common with long-standing *chaebol* practice, even at relatively forward-looking Samsung the profitable electronics units were required to give financial support to several other companies in the group, including the woefully unprofitable new car division. All that changed after mid-1998, when Yun Jong Yong, the new president of Samsung Electronics, was given a free hand to restructure the company. Out went cross-guarantees for other units. Inventories were slashed ($3 billion in costs were saved in less than two years through better inventory and accounts-receivable management), the company sold almost 60 businesses (some to their employees), staffing was cut in 18 months from 84,000 to 54,000, and debt was cut over the same period from $18 billion (three times equity) to $7 billion, making Samsung Electronics one of Korea's least leveraged *chaebol* firms.

Not only did profits jump on a 25 percent increase in sales in 1998–99, but Samsung Electronics also began moving up the global technology ladder. It expanded its memory-chip capacity at exactly the right time to take advantage of the global 1999 turnaround from glut to deficit in the supply of memory chips, and also undertook plans to design and produce high-margin logic chips for PCs. It also reinforced its strengths in consumer electronics, where in many digital "appliances" (like palm-held computers) it could compete on even terms with other global producers, and dominated production of the most advanced (thin-film transistor) computer displays. Samsung also became the world's sixth-biggest producer of mobile phones, with a head-start on technology and production for the next-generation sets based on the CDMA standard (it already had 20 percent of the American market for CDMA mobile phones in 1999). The turnaround of Samsung Electronics not only belied the general view that Asian companies were not restructuring in the aftermath of the financial turmoil—in fact those in the industries of tomorrow were remaking themselves with alacrity—but also showed that the West and Japan do not have world markets for the next generation of electronics hardware locked up.

For several reasons, however, Taiwan will be the place in Asia to watch most closely. For its economic size, it is by far the world's biggest producer of personal-computer hardware (and for many components it is the biggest in absolute terms as well). It is facing the most pressure from the global profit-margin squeeze in IT hardware and from the shift away from PCs and toward network and other devices. And it is the most prominent example of the transpacific ties between Asia's emerging technology industry and Silicon Valley, ties that are going to have a deep influence on how high-tech industry on both sides of the Pacific evolves.

By the end of the 1990s, Taiwan's industrial economy was dominated by the production of computer hardware and this economy in turn dominated the world's output of several computer components. As noted in Chapter 6, high-tech hardware accounted for some 40 percent of the country's manufacturing output of $230 billion in 1998, figures expected to rise to 50 percent and $300 billion by 2003. Some three-quarters of Taiwan's exports are already accounted for by high-tech hardware. This is not a big-fish, small-pond phenomenon. In 1999 Taiwan made 20 percent of the world's desktop PCs, half the world's notebook PCs, 60 percent of monitors, two-thirds of motherboards and keyboards, and 90 percent of scanners. Taiwan also dominates the provision of certain kinds of hardware services, notably the chip-foundry business (which manufactures chips to order for other companies so they do not have to run their own highly expensive chip factories).

Nor is Taiwan's gobbling up of the world's hardware market slowing down. In 1999 Taiwan made a minuscule 3 percent of the world's liquid-crystal displays (LCDs) for notebook computers. By 2001 that share will probably zoom to some 20 percent, much of it taken from Korean and Japanese firms. The scope for expansion across the board seems almost limitless for the next few years. More and more American high-tech companies are subcontracting more and more of the business of actually making the stuff to other firms such as chip foundries: as one observer put it, "manufacturing in-house is going the way of the dinosaur." By 1998 America's Dell Computer had subcontracted 95 percent of its notebook-computer making to Taiwanese firms. Many Japanese firms—notably Toshiba, Sony and Fujitsu—had barely begun to hand off production to others by 2000 (Toshiba took its first step, with a Taiwanese firm, in 1999), and as they begin to succumb to the American urge to outsource they will add to a trend that is expected to triple the revenues from high-tech subcontracting to $300 billion in the five years after 1999. Taiwan is the world's best-positioned place to grab a lot of that growth, with other parts of Asia not far behind.

Yet if you wandered into many high-tech Taiwanese firms at the turn of the millennium and talked to their chiefs you would have found a sense of disquiet. Part of the reason was that—except for the chip-foundry business, which during an up-cycle in the world chip market (as occurred in 1999–2000) enjoys profit margins well into double digits—profits in most of Taiwan's high-tech industries were meager and shrinking. Morris Chang, the head of Taiwan Semiconductor Manufacturing Corporation (TSMC), the world's biggest chip foundry, guessed in 1999 that making PCs earned a firm 5 percent to 6 percent returns, monitors 2 percent to 3 percent, memory chips zero. He blamed "competitive convergence" for Taiwan's plight. By this he meant that, unlike their American counterparts, Taiwanese entrepreneurs try to wrest competitive advantage not from innovation, strategy or branding (any of which can give at least a bit of sustained pricing power) but instead from superb operational efficiency. They are excellent at this—which is why so much high-tech manufacturing has been migrating to them—but except in somewhat sheltered high-growth businesses like chip foundries it is a form of competition that creates a "degenerative cycle" of too many new entrants into a market, fierce price competition and disappearing profits. If the danger described earlier of a structural decline in manufacturing margins worldwide is realized, Taiwan's habits will make it even more vulnerable than before.

The second thing gnawing at Taiwan's high-tech firms in 1999–2000 was their acute realization that the era of the high-end personal computer, of which they had become the manufacturing master, was quickly giving way to a new age of "appliances" like personal digital assistants, ultra-cheap stripped-down PCs and products based on networks. Taiwan was not the only placed besieged by this shift—Singapore, the world's disk-drive capital, was also discomfited by the move to network-based servers, which unlike PCs do not use hard drives for memory—but it stood to lose the most because of its concentration on the PC world.

Taiwan started responding in two ways. The first was to seek out cheaper places to make things whose prices were falling precipitously— and that mostly meant moving their factories to mainland China. Since the 1980s that has been the reflexive response of Taiwanese manufacturers in all lines of business—from shoes to plastics—when things got too expensive at home. In the decade after 1987, according to Yang Shih-Chien, a science-and-technology cabinet minister, a total of 30,000 Taiwanese factories were transferred to the mainland, with another 10,000 going to Southeast Asia, investments in all worth some $40 billion. Already by 1999 the $21 billion-worth of IT hardware that Taiwanese firms were producing in Taiwan itself was almost matched by another $19 billion-worth that Taiwanese firms were producing elsewhere—70 percent of it in mainland China. It is quite likely that in 2000 China will surpass Taiwan to become the world's third biggest producer of IT hardware. With some 60 percent of China's IT hardware output already accounted for by Taiwanese-owned firms in 1999, and the transfer of production from the island to the mainland accelerating, it is easy to see where a lot of the growth is coming from (an economic intertwining that also raises some interesting questions about cross-strait politics, see Chapter 16).

Taiwan is also groping its way up-market. To some extent the government is taking a hand in this. Taiwan has long had one of Asia's (and probably the world's) most astute systems for giving incentives and guidance to fledgling high-tech companies without muffling the market signals that ultimately tell them what they ought to be doing. TSMC's Chang, for instance, notes that his foundry got started with half its original funding from the government. The decision to back his idea was made single-handedly by Lee Kuo-ting, the legendary godfather of Taiwanese industrial policy from the 1960s through the 1980s, who saw the market potential when no one else did and supported Chang ("others wanted to call in western business consultants to evaluate the idea, and if consultants had been called in it would have been killed"). More systematically, the government has cultivated R&D through direct grants, especially for process technology, and tax credits, and has helped funnel students into engineering programs through scholarships and tax credits for "manpower development." The government-funded Hsinchu Industrial Park in northern Taiwan, now home to most of Taiwan's successful high-tech firms, provided facilities for basic research for everyone's use. And the government's Industrial Development Bureau has taken a role in telling firms how much longer it thinks a business can remain profitable given Taiwan's cost base, without trying to tell the firms what to do. The government is continuing to push this policy mix. In 1999 it began sponsoring research at Hsinchu into futuristic nanotechnology for computers—the use of molecules, or even subatomic particles, instead of transistors etched in silicon to store and process information. This is computer research as advanced as anything going on in America.

Some move out, others move up. Stan Shih, the head of Acer Group, Taiwan's biggest PC firm, has been trying since the mid-1990s to build a brand name for his products (a first for Taiwanese high tech), realizing this was one of the few shelters against the commoditization of the business. In late 1999 Biotechnology, a Taiwanese chip maker (your guess about the name is as good as mine), bought the chip-design unit of America's National Semiconductor as a step away from pure manufacturing and toward design innovation. Aiding such steps is one of Asia's biggest venture capital industries: by the turn of the century Taiwan boasted some 125 venture-capital firms, which had invested a total of $3 billion in around 1500 Taiwanese companies. If Taiwan seemed hesitant in 1999–2000 about migrating from the PC world that had served it so well to newer sorts of hardware (and, more problematically, software, in which it had never shown much aptitude), the hesitation was likely to be brief as the financial and other markets began beaming their signals about the future more strongly.

Perhaps the most important, and least appreciated, reason why Taiwan will probably upgrade successfully is that no other place in the world has its finger so firmly on Silicon Valley's pulse. From the 1980s until well into the 1990s Taiwanese made up the largest single pool of foreign graduate students in American universities (a distinction that has been held for the past few years by students from China, which if Taiwan's experience is anything to go by has interesting future implications of its own, see below). Almost all were in engineering or science and, although beginning in the late 1980s an increasing number returned to Taiwan to work or start up high-tech companies there, an increasing number of those who stayed in the United States opted not for the older choice of joining a big firm like IBM but instead for starting up firms of their own in Silicon Valley. Frank Huang, the head of a Taiwanese firm called Umax that in the late 1990s was the world's biggest producer of computer scanners, guesses there were 10,000–20,000 Taiwanese working in Silicon Valley in 1999. Yang Shih-Chien, the cabinet minister, counts 60 Taiwanese venture-capital firms with operations in Silicon Valley and a total of 300–400 investments there. Nor is Silicon Valley all: the Overseas Chinese Biotechnology Engineering Society had 2000 U.S.-based members in 1999.

But the Valley is where Taiwanese have most made their mark. A survey by AnnaLee Saxenian, a Berkeley professor who specializes in analyzing Silicon Valley, showed that in 1990 20 percent of Silicon Valley's engineers were immigrant Asians. The Taiwanese are not alone in this—there is a saying that "Silicon Valley is built on ICs," meaning not integrated circuits but Indians and Chinese—but they are disproportionately represented, especially at the highest levels. By Saxenian's reckoning, in 1998 a quarter of Silicon Valley high-tech firms had an Indian (see next chapter) or Chinese CEO, with Chinese accounting for almost 80 percent of them—in other words, for almost 20 percent of all Silicon Valley firms albeit "only" 13 percent or so of Silicon Valley's sales. Almost all the "Chinese"-run firms were Taiwanese, though that will change sharply over the next decade since, to take one pointer, between the late 1980s and the late 1990s the proportion of science and engineering degrees granted to immigrant Chinese by Berkeley flipped from being two-thirds Taiwanese versus one-third mainland Chinese to almost the reverse.

The Asian immigrant presence at the Valley's upper reaches rose as the 1990s wore on—they ran 13 percent of the firms in 1980–84 but 29 percent of those started between 1995 and 1998—and so did the links between Taiwanese in the Valley and those in Taiwan's Hsinchu region (where the industrial park is located). The traffic between the two in investment money, in people ("astronauts" are regular Taiwanese commuters between the Valley and Hsinchu) and, probably most significantly, in ideas is heavy. In these circumstances it beggars belief that Taiwan's high-tech industry will not figure out which way the world market is headed and adapt to it.

Which in turn raises another intriguing thought. If, as seems likely, American firms continue to subcontract more and more of their manufacturing to Taiwanese and Koreans (among other Asians), the Americans may well find themselves creating competitors instead of biddable servants. Asia's competitiveness will also be sharpened as it closes in on America's greatest single advantage inherited from the 1980s, telecoms deregulation.

THE PIPELINES

By the end of the 1990s, however, it seemed that Asia had done little to make up for the roughly ten-year head start America had in the race for a free market in telecommunications services. As noted in Chapter 1, a free-wheeling and innovative telecoms industry is less important in its own right than as an essential enabling technology for the rapid growth of a networked computer-based economy—which, for reasons explained in Chapter 11 on the Internet, changes all businesses not just high-tech ones. As the 1990s wore on, there was no sign that America's breakneck pace of telecoms reform was being slowed. Indeed, partly thanks to the Telecommunications Act of 1996, the door was opened to practically unrestricted competition in the United States for every kind of telecoms service (the equipment market had long been free). The result at the end of the 1990s was a breathless scramble for market position as companies of all stripes—long-distance, local and cable TV—began to fight each other for customers, and huge takeovers and mergers (many of them international) reshaped the competitive landscape first in America and then in Europe.

Meanwhile, Asia seemed stuck in an eddy. One of the difficulties was that deregulation, which had proceeded confusingly enough even in America in the 1980s, had by the end of the 1990s in most of Asia produced a bewildering tangle of industrial structures and regulatory methods and motives. In a mistake common in Asia in many industries—this is what caused so much trouble in Indonesian banking, for instance, between the late 1980s and late 1990s—liberal licensing regimes were paired with weak regulatory ones, leading to both too much competition and too little. The Philippines, with one of the world's smaller telecoms markets, by 1999 had licensed two local carriers, five mobile-phone operators and (unbelievably) ten long-distance carriers. Malaysia, with only 20m people of very modest means on average, had five carriers in each of those categories. Indonesia set up seven regional operating zones only to find by 2000 that the outfits running the five in which private joint-venture partners were allowed to team up with government-owned PT Telekom were bankrupt and had to be restructured. On the other hand, the original fixed-line carrier in almost every country retained its overwhelming advantage in the provision of local services. Before 2000, there seemed to be scant evidence anywhere in Asia of the competitive ferment that had so transformed the American scene for the better in 1985–2000.

Yet, beneath the surface, changes were taking place that have a reasonable chance of allowing Asia to leapfrog the more advanced American market in two important respects: the provision of broadband access and the spread of mobile telephony. Part of the reason for this is that, despite the messy regulatory environment, the simple but powerful forces of supply, demand and pricing have been making for a welcome revolution in Asian telecoms. First, it would take a collapse much longer-lasting and more comprehensive than the financial crisis of 1997–98 to prevent explosive growth in Asian telecoms over the next 20 years. China, India, Vietnam, the Philippines and Thailand among them have 40 percent of the world's people but at the end of the 1990s had fixed-line penetration of less than 4 percent, compared with a rich-world average of 50 percent; even modest Asian economic growth over the next generation will push up penetration rates significantly, and with them the already substantial absolute numbers of telephone subscribers in Asia. Despite comparatively low penetration rates, China in 1999 already had more than 100 million fixed-line subscribers, 80 million pager users (already the world's biggest market) and 40 million mobile phone subscribers. And since the mid-1990s China has been adding more fixed-line carrying capacity to its network than any other country, rich or poor, in the world. But it is not just subscriber growth that will drive Asian telecoms markets up. The growth in data traffic will vastly outstrip that in voice traffic. This is partly because capacity of all kinds is being added at phenomenal rates. Between 1999 and 2003, for example, the capacity of fixed-line circuits between America and Asia is due to grow 50-fold, leading inevitably to sharply falling prices for access in Asia to still-dominant America-based Internet content.

Then, too, competition within Asian countries has been growing despite regulatory and other obstacles such as the entrenched status of existing telecoms networks. Pressure for restructuring came in part from sharp falls in the market capitalization of many telecoms companies: by mid-October 1998 the companies in Korea, Thailand, Indonesia, Malaysia and the Philippines were worth on average only 40 percent what they had been in mid-1997 (though in Japan, Hong Kong, Singapore and Taiwan the drop had been a mere 13 percent). Restrictions or bans on foreign ownership were relaxed or were about to be almost everywhere. Ceilings on foreign holdings in traditional telecoms service firms, which in many cases had been zero before, were raised to an average of 49 percent; even China committed itself in its 1999 WTO deal with America (see Chapter 13) to allow 49 percent foreign ownership of telecoms service and Internet firms, rising to 50 percent (and full management control) in 2002. Alarmed at the ferment in Hong Kong's telecoms market that promised to give it a lead in the contest to be Asia's communications and information hub, Singapore in April 2000 abruptly and with immediate effect introduced complete deregulation of all its telecoms markets two years ahead of schedule. American carriers, too absorbed in restructuring and other battle at home, paid little attention to the opportunities opening up in Asia. In addition to Singapore Telecom, Japan's Nippon Telegraph and Telephone (NTT) did some shopping in the neighborhood, but the company that took by far the biggest plunge into Asia as the 1990s closed was British Telecom. In the 18 months after mid-1997 BT invested more than $3 billion buying stakes in companies (some mobile, some full-service) from India to Malaysia, Singapore, Hong Kong, Japan and Korea.

Competitive pressure was being applied in other, more innovative ways as well, thanks to deregulation and the falling price of equipment and services due to technological change. In Hong Kong, for example, the dominant local carrier, Cable and Wireless HKT had over the years built a local network worth $4 billion in fixed assets in 1999. Yet it faced a serious challenge to its dominance of the "local loop"—the last half-mile or so between the branch network and the retail customer—from an upstart called City Telecom. Using a new technology called LMDS, City Telecom was able to mount a territory-wide challenge to HKT by investing a paltry $300 million. Or consider NTT which, with its stranglehold over local telecoms service in Japan, had long been criticized for time-metered charges that meant Internet access cost Japanese users as much as five times as much as users in the West paid. But by 2000 several firms were beginning to challenge NTT's pre-eminence in the local loop. A joint venture called SpeedNet, set up by Tokyo Electric Power (Tepco), Microsoft and Japan's Softbank, uses fiber-optic cables strung along Tepco's power lines and wireless transmitters to carry signals between the cables and homes or offices. Sony is setting up its own high-speed wireless network to bypass NTT; and another consortium, headed by a trading firm called Mitsui, was given regulatory approval to hook up to NTT's network in a way that allows it to avoid NTT's metering system and thus to offer flat-fee Internet access.

The most significant result of all this activity is big reductions in costs to the consumer. NTT's new competitors were expected to charge about half of what NTT did when it grudgingly introduced a geographically limited flat-rate Internet-access service at the end of 1999; that competitive threat alone was enough to cause NTT to announce early in 2000 that during the course of the year it would cut its own interconnection fees by half. By late 1999 Internet-telephone providers in China, though with a minuscule market share, were offering calls to America at one-third the rate China Telecom charged and to Hong Kong at one-half the rate—and that was after the government, recognizing that high phone charges were suppressing both phone and Internet use, had ordered China Telecom in March 1999 to slash international call rates by as much as 38 percent and connection charges for mobile services by 70 percent. Overall, prices for telecoms hardware and services dropped throughout Asia in 1999 by some 15 percent, with the biggest falls coming in wireless telephony and international calls. Bigger declines are in store, especially in international rates. Because of the massive expansion in transpacific carrying capacity mentioned above, in the nine months after June 1998 the average price of wholesale bandwidth between America and Asia dropped by more than 30 percent. At that rate of decline over four years, nominal prices at the end of the period would be not much more than one-twentieth of their level at the beginning.

Price reductions and capacity increases, the two most important trends that boost telecoms innovation and usage everywhere, will quickly drive Asia into an era of broadband and mobile-telephone growth. Broadband—meaning high-capacity telecoms links that allow extremely fast two-way handling of all kinds of data all the way up to and including movie-quality video—may actually expand faster in Asia than in America. The reason is that, because most of Asia is substantially less wired than America, it is easier to install new technologies without worrying about what to do with existing plant, equipment and subscribers. Fixed-line broadband connections to American homes, for example, are proving troublesome to adapt to new demands. Most of America was cabled in the stone-age days of coaxial lines in the 1980s, and upgrading these to accommodate high-speed data through cable modems is hard and expensive; the same sort of problem afflicts local phone lines.

In Asia, by contrast, most cable TV networks were built in the 1990s and have enough of a fiber-optic component to allow easy upgrade to cable modem. Likewise, a higher share of the fixed-line telecoms network in Asia than in America has already been built to handle ADSL ("asymmetric digital subscriber line") traffic, which is likely to prove the dominant broadband technology in the early days. Asia's much higher population densities also make it more economical to install new lines or upgrade old ones. True, PC penetration rates in Asia average only half America's 50 percent, but with the price of PCs continuing to plunge and the availability of Internet-specific machines or Internet-adapted TVs continuing to grow, that should serve as only a minor obstacle to the advance of Asian broadband links in the next few years. Jardine Fleming, a Hong Kong investment bank, has reckoned that by 2002 broadband penetration rates in the rich countries of East Asia will range from 10 percent (Taiwan) to 14 percent (Japan) of households, compared with a modest 8 percent in America.

Waking up late to the Internet should also give Asia an advantage over the next few years in riding a second technological wave that could cause America some trouble: the explosive growth in mobile telecoms, especially services linked to the Internet. In the rich countries of East Asia in 2000, mobile-phone penetration rates are 40 percent (Korea) to 60 percent (Hong Kong), compared with less than 30 percent in America—just about the reverse of penetration rates of PCs. America has badly lagged both Europe and East Asia in mobile telephony, with costly handsets and calls and a patchwork of providers, many offering incompatible standards. America's peculiar aversion to mobile phones at times seems almost inveterate rather than just the product of unstandardized services and high costs: it is hard to imagine American 20-somethings following growing numbers of their Hong Kong counterparts and not even bothering to have a home phone because the mobile serves for both.

Americans in the Internet business, especially its consumer e-commerce branch, have tended to underestimate the dangers this indifference poses. Asian firms, especially Japanese and Koreans, are like their European counterparts far advanced in development of mobile phones that use the next-generation "wideband CDMA" (WCDMA) standard, which will allow faster Internet access than most Americans now can get on their home PCs. Already by the end of 1999, Japanese users could get color-screen mobile phones and were using mobile phones in simple Internet transactions like buying movie tickets.

One of the most spectacular consumer successes of the 1990s anywhere was the growth of i-mode, the mobile Internet service provided by NTT DoCoMo, Japan's dominant mobile-phone carrier. Started only in February 1999, by early 2001 i-mode was expected to have 17 million users in Japan alone, with DoCoMo already busy on efforts to expand its reach into the rest of Asia, Europe and America. Missing out on what will probably be an increasing slice of the consumer e-commerce pie would be bad enough in itself but could also be hard for American firms to correct because their cash-flow is a dwindling stream. In America, telecoms industry profits on each mobile subscriber declined throughout the late 1990s by about 17 percent a year. Margins on mobile data traffic, however, which is growing considerably faster in Asia, are much fatter and are holding up better.

The result is that the telecoms revolution that served America so well in the 1990s looks like it is about to arrive in Asia just when it may be taking a breather in America. It will be just in time for Asia to partake belatedly of another revolution whose implications are, if anything, even deeper on the western side of the Pacific than on the eastern: the Internet.

11

Asia Online

I f any one symbol had to be chosen for the worldwide Internet bubble at its most distended, it may have come in Hong Kong on New Millennium's Eve 1999 rather than in the bubble's birthplace in America. That December 31, Richard Li, the 33-year-old son of Hong Kong's richest man and himself a fast-rising Internet and high-tech entrepreneur, threw a dinner party on behalf of the Hong Kong Cancer Fund for 1000 people in the Hong Kong Convention Center. The party was called Utopia and the guests, asked to come in "Cyber Couture or Black Tie/ Shimmer and Shine/Glitter and Glow," were treated to endless food and drinks, a laser light show, various Asian and Western entertainers, an all-night disco and Western and Asian breakfasts in the morning hours; the centerpiece was a live performance by Whitney Houston, flown in from America with an entourage of 55, to usher in the new year. The assumption is that Li spent $4 million on this, of which Whitney Houston's share came to $2 million (she was worth it, by the way). How much more was spent by sponsors, like the provider of the champagne or other companies hosting tables, is anybody's guess. During the course of the evening Li slipped out to a bare plot of land a couple of miles away on Hong Kong island's northern shore. He presided over a spectacular outdoor laser light show, introduced through video by Professor Stephen ("A Brief History of Time") Hawking and intended as a sort of modern ground-breaking ceremony for the Cyberport Li was starting to build to house Internet and other high-tech companies. After years of mostly ignoring high technology except when it came in boxes and could be exported Asia had, by 1999, come down with a raging case of Internet fever.

For at least two years the valuation of high-tech companies in America—especially Internet ones—had been a topic of intense controversy. In 1999 Asian high-tech stocks began to make up for lost ground. During 1999 one Asian Internet-stock index rose more than half again as fast as an American counterpart (which itself was up more than two-fold). Korea's Kosdaq index more than quadrupled in 1999, and Kosdaq's turnover as a percentage of the turnover of Korea's stuffy Korea Stock Exchange rose from near zero in early January to more than 40 percent in December. By the end of 1999 high-tech stocks in Taiwan accounted for 80 percent of market turnover, up from 30 percent a year earlier. No market in Asia was exempt from this radical split between investors' perceptions of high-tech stocks and of all the others. Internet indexes throughout Asia outperformed general indexes by about four-to-one. Some individual companies did even better. China Telecom (Hong Kong), the arm of a mainland mobile-telephone operator (see Chapter 10), rose about two-and-a-half-fold in a year when the Hang Seng Index was up by about a third—in other words eight times higher, in a year when the overall market's performance was excellent in itself. By February 2000, China Telecom (HK)—later renamed China Mobile—had the biggest market cap in Hong Kong, surpassing HSBC, the world's most profitable bank. And on December 23, 1999, the day Nasdaq broke through the 4,000 level for the first time, Pacific Century CyberWorks (PCCW), the Hong Kong-listed vehicle for Richard Li's high-tech operations, went up 41 percent. That extravagant New Millennium's Eve party could have been paid for with less than one one-thousandth of the *increase* in PCCW's market capitalization on that single day.

Asia's sudden high-tech infatuation poses all sorts of questions. For instance, many investors had assumed that, if there was a serious correction in American high-tech stocks during 2000–2001, a reasonable amount of money that lost interest in Nasdaq would find its way to Asia, whose Internet businesses are years behind America's and therefore presumably have much more room to grow. Yet by the end of 1999, thanks to the new weightiness of high-tech shares in Asia, Asian markets looked highly correlated with Nasdaq—not a comforting thought in the event of a Nasdaq crash. And sure enough, when Nasdaq briefly fell by 30 percent in the spring of 2000, a lot of Asian Internet stocks fell by even more. But more broadly, there is the fundamental question whether in America, Asia or anywhere else, the level of high-tech stocks is evidence of a true asset bubble—a situation where valuations vastly outstrip the long-term ability of the underlying business to support them—or of a historic shift in the structure of the economy and in the proper way to value stocks compared with other assets like bonds.

That argument can and probably will run for years. Here it is worth recalling some observations made by Warren Buffett in 1999 on the level of stocks in America. Buffett, who rarely comments on the stock market as a whole, argued that it was highly improbable stocks would do as well in 1999–2016 as they had done in 1982–99. He showed considerable skepticism about the ability of "the New Economy" to continue generating fabulous returns for investors, and pointed to the examples of cars and the aviation industry to explain why. These industries, he noted, had enormously changed the economic, business and social landscape of the twentieth century, yet for investors they had overall been a huge disappointment. During the century more than 2000 companies had been formed in America to make cars; by the 1990s three were left, "themselves no lollapaloozas for investors." The case of aviation is even more cautionary. Between 1919 and 1939 America had 300 aircraft makers, of which only a handful have survived. Between 1980 and 1999, 129 American airlines filed for bankruptcy. By 1992, Buffett said, the cumulative profit of American airlines for the entire century was "zero. Absolutely zero. . . . I mean, Karl Marx couldn't have done as much damage to capitalists as Orville Wright did." Buffett went on to conclude:

> I won't dwell on other glamorous businesses that dramatically changed our lives but concurrently failed to deliver rewards to U.S. investors: the manufacture of radios and televisions, for example. But I will draw a lesson from these businesses: The key to investing is not assessing how much an industry is going to affect society, or how much it will grow, but rather determining the competitive advantage of any given company and, above all, the durability of that advantage. The products or services that have wide, sustainable moats around them are the ones that deliver rewards to investors.

It is quite possible, in other words, for Asian Internet stocks (like those elsewhere in the world) to be in a big bubble whose bursting will leave only a few very lucky or very perceptive investors unscathed by the flying shrapnel, but also—to turn Buffett's syllogism on its head—for the

Internet to have deep and wide-ranging effects on almost everything. Especially in Asia.

NODES AND NETS

Three months before Richard Li's party, and a seeming world away, Jerry Yang was sitting in a luxury hotel lounge in Shanghai quietly telling me over coffee about the Internet. Yang, who co-founded Yahoo! in 1995 with David Filo, then a fellow graduate student at Stanford, was 30 when I met him in Shanghai and had a net worth of $3 billion-$4 billion depending on Yahoo's share price from one day to the next (those rough figures had tripled 90 days later only to be halved from that elevated level six months after that). He wore his billions lightly. No one recalled ever seeing him wear a necktie, let alone a suit, in those days at least his only car was a used BMW, and he traveled on commercial flights rather than a private jet. Those curiosities—in addition to personal wealth and age, of course—were enough to mark him off from the overwhelming majority of American corporate titans attending that week's *Fortune* conference in Shanghai (see Chapter 8). More important, whereas all too many of the chairmen or CEOs from big companies in more traditional industries had advanced cases of self-importance and platoons of aides, Yang had good manners, behaved modestly and naturally and made his own phone calls. Perhaps calm self-assurance comes from making a fabulous fortune that early and quickly—or perhaps it's the other way around. In any event, his interest was not that of most American investors who had become obsessed with the Internet—they thought about where share prices were going in the next month or minute—but rather what was going to happen over "the next couple of decades" during which the Internet would continue to increase people's productivity and efficiency. His thoughts were mostly his own: he had not, he said, read a book in ten years.

Yang's view of the power of the Internet begins with a well-known idea about increasing returns in a networked system. The value of a network increases with the number of people using it. The usual example is the telephone. If you are the only one in the world with a telephone, it is a useless instrument. If one other person gets a phone, yours suddenly becomes worth something; the more people who get one, the more you get out of the network. There is even a simple statistical formula for this, based on combinatorial theory, which shows that the value of the network increases faster than the number of additions to it (the exact return varies, depending on how many people are already on the network and how big the addition is). Here's the formula, if you want it: $n(n-1)$, where n is the number of people on the network, so that, e.g., going from 9 to 10 raises the connections from 72 to 90, but going from 90 to 91 raises them from 8010 to 8190. Unlike the case in many economic activities—making steel, for instance—there never comes a point when the addition of new capacity adds no extra value at all or even reduces it. Yang pointed out that, with the Internet, two kinds of value enhancement are in fact at work. There is the network effect, just mentioned, which raises productivity through increased communication among people; but in addition, the power of each "node" (person) in the network to work on its own is enhanced by being plugged into the network—each becomes "more informed, knowledgeable and productive."

This model of an information economy is very different from what Yang called the "client stuff" of the personal-computer era—when a single "node" operated more or less on its own, with information running vertically between it and an authority above it. The horizontal and integrated character of the Internet arose from its origins. Created in the late 1960s by America's Department of Defense (and sure to be remembered as one of that institution's greatest, albeit accidental, contributions to human welfare), DARPANET was designed as a national security communications infrastructure that would keep working even after a nuclear attack. Normal communications systems, then based on centrally controlled networks with rigidly specified pathways, certainly could not cope: an attack that knocked out a crucial part or two would knock out everything. So the creators of DARPANET at the Defense Advanced Research Projects Agency made their network completely decentralized—the rules built into the system would allow any part of it to make decisions on its own about how traffic would be routed—and also organic: like a neural network in the brain, if some parts were damaged or busy, new links would automatically be made to route signals through pathways that were intact.

As its military origins faded and it evolved first into a data communications network for academics in the 1980s and then into commercial uses in the 1990s, what came to be known as the Internet preserved its decentralized and organic character. This had several consequences. One, as Yang pointed out, is a fluidity of roles in the marketplace: each person in the network can move rapidly between being a producer and being a consumer. Another often remarked upon result is the speeding up of information transfers and thus the growing disutility of hierarchical forms of organization: centralized decision-making just takes too long now. The rabid destruction of the role of the middleman is obvious from a simple comparison of the costs of almost any transaction on-line versus off-line: on average, on-line costs are about a tenth of off-line costs (see Table 11.1). With cost savings of this order, it is inevitable that most transactions will eventually migrate to the Internet. Firms that do not use it heavily will be uncompetitive because their costs will be too high.

Paradox after paradox unfolds from such changes. One of the most arresting is going to be the death, or at least the radical transformation, of copyright and patents. At first glance, it would seem that protection of intellectual property ought to come even more into its own because so much more wealth will be created through ideas and their manipulation. Yet the opposite will probably happen: It will become increasingly difficult either to establish or to enforce intellectual-property rights. This is partly because ideas—which, in the formulation of Paul Romer (see Chapter 10), are the bedrock of modern wealth—can be spread more easily and quickly on the Internet and are less subject to being policed, whether for the purpose of protecting copyright or of collecting taxes. "Internet time" shortens not just product cycles but also the durability of an innovation. The nature of the Internet itself also breaks down walls put up around ideas. The cooperative interchange of thoughts is at the core of what makes the Internet valuable. If you go to almost any Web site, you will find on-line conversations among users asking questions and getting answers to problems that are puzzling them. Norman Macrae, a former deputy editor of *The Economist* and probably the best financial journalist of the past fifty years, has pointed

Table 11.1
Distribution Costs

Category	Traditional System (US$)	Internet (US$)	Savings (%)
Airline tickets	8.00	1.00	87
Banking	1.08	0.13	89
Bill payment	2.22–3.32	0.65–1.10	67–71
Term life insurance	400–700	200–350	50
Software	15.00	0.20–0.50	97–99

Source: OECD study.

out that this cooperative spirit is nothing new in the computer world but is about to become much more important:

> I do heretically doubt if present copyright restrictive practices can last during an age when we should all be advancing mankind through contributing our brightest ideas collaboratively via the Internet. An American dictionary said I had invented the word "privatization" because in some 1975 *Economist* articles I had used it and had proceeded with ideas on how to do it. I later apologized to Peter Drucker who had printed the word in 1969, but he said it had probably been used orally earlier. If you publish a book in America, you now have to guarantee against "piracy," which means if you report something in the best already available words you have to use something less than the best recorded ones (which would eventually destroy all good literature).
>
> The copyright on pop stars' disks turns a few teenagers from millionaires into billionaires, even when only slightly better than their peers. I cannot believe the consequent high price of disks adds to human happiness, or is tenable when we can all record anything. In medicine any entry on the Internet, saying some drug may help some sorts of AIDS or asthma, brings huge pressure on taxpayers to give this free to all sufferers and every grandma. When somebody really discovers a cure for AIDS, the world will not tolerate a high-price monopoly for the patent holder. This is behind [Harvard economics professor] Jeffrey Sachs' points about how the patent system is stopping research into tropical diseases.
>
> The greatest advances in the new century will be sequential ones. Every expert can nowadays call up all new ideas in his subject on the Internet, and contribute suggestions for improvements in them. This process of sequential improvement helped explain technical advances in wartime, when patents were not to the fore. John von Neumann, who probably made the main inventions in the development of both the modern computer (which still has what is called von Neumann architecture) and the Nagasaki atom bomb, was against computer patents because he had been paid by the government at the time and wanted everybody who could understand this great development to publish sequential ideas about the next steps. An able engineer (Eckert) and useless academic (Maudsley), who had been in von Neumann's wartime computer project, set up the Eckert-Maudsley company. They claimed that all patents connected to the computer were now registered as their property. They went bust because an American court wrongly ruled that Maudsley had pinched all his initial knowledge about

the computer from another professor who had suggested in the 1930s a different computer project that could not conceivably work. I think this happy innumeracy by a Minnesota court has contributed to the marvelous advance of computers, surprisingly free of patents, peopled by brilliant sequential improvers like Bill Gates.

I now think we will eventually need some sort of international royal commission to make patent and copyright law chime with market forces, but it will be necessary to keep most lawyers off it.

Not everyone in the Internet world sees things this way—in 1999, for instance, Amazon.com took to the American courts to try to enforce patents on various aspects of its website—but Jerry Yang does. He said Yahoo had made a decision not to try to use copyright or patents as a tool to gain competitive advantage "because they are harder and harder to prove and defend"; his view was that in the new world TM (trademark) was going to prove more important. Again, this does not seem obvious at first. After all, the transparency and low entry costs of the Internet should level the playing field for newcomers. Yet the same shifts that are reducing the usefulness of patents are increasing the influence of brands, which is why American Internet companies (Yahoo included) have been spending fortunes on brand-building. Brands matter so much on the Internet because, with the almost limitless ease of access to the new medium, they are the best way of assuring on-line consumers, who have few resources for verifying anything, that they can trust what they are buying and how they are buying it. By definition, brands bring loyalty and that in turn attracts advertising dollars, still the Internet's main source of revenue. This is why, over time, off-line companies with good names should be some of the best-equipped competitors on-line too.

Another big paradox lies in what Yang described as the local character of the Internet. Because it can provide nearly instantaneous broadband communication around the world, the Internet might seem a force for homogenization. Hardware and software (not to mention Disneyland and movies) are global, the same everywhere and dominated by powerful American companies. Some firms are betting that this will still be the case, at least in a single market like the United States. The logic of the merger between AOL and Time-Warner, announced in January 2000 and due for completion by the end of 2000, depended crucially on the idea that size and financial clout—and hence economies of scale in the production of content—will shape the converging communications, media and Internet businesses.

Yang looked at it differently. Content for the Internet, he said, will mostly be generated locally; far from being stamped out by this globe-spanning medium, national and even local variations will be enhanced. As with all advances in computing, only much more so in this case, the Internet allows for what might be described as mass customization: because costs are so low and speed is so high, it is possible profitably to create something for a very precisely defined audience. China's movie theaters, Yang noted, will probably still show mostly American films because they have such rich and sophisticated production and distribution systems behind them. But it will also be possible for an aspiring Chinese director to shoot an Internet movie in Beijing on a shoestring and then show it on-line throughout China, whether its audience is watching on a PC or on a TV equipped with a set-top Internet receiver. For its part, Yahoo treats each of the 20 or so countries where it does business as an entirely separate market with content produced locally in the local language. There is no pan-European content on Yahoo's European portals, nor will there be any cross-border content in Asia.

Asia is better placed than almost any other region to profit from the spread of the Internet over the next decade. This is so partly because of what Asia has been good at: the manufacture and sale of export-oriented goods. The American experience has shown that business-to-business commerce is transformed first, and quickest, by the movement of transactions to the Internet. Unlike the case with business-to-consumer e-commerce, transactions between businesses tend to be, well, more business-like: both parties know a lot about what they are doing, the transactions are larger and the benefits of cost-savings and speed hence greater, branding is relatively unimportant and the usefulness of middlemen is low. America's General Electric, for instance, moved swiftly in the late 1990s to put all of its massive procurement on-line and easily saved hundreds of millions of dollars within a couple of years (see last section of Chapter 13). The improvements in efficiency, moreover, are greater the longer the supply chain in a transaction—both geographically and in terms of the number of intermediaries. With their heavy weightings in export-oriented manufacturing for markets around the world, Asia's economies stand to reap enormous gains from more frictionless international commerce. And however slow off the mark Asia has generally been in adapting to the Internet, big business users have been quick to recognize its potential. By 1999 Evergreen Marine, a Taiwanese company that runs one of the world's biggest seaborne cargo operations, had for two years already had a website that, in the words of one analyst, allowed

> a customer in Europe wishing to ship U.S.-made components to his factory in China for manufacture and re-export to South America to identify the type of container available to him, the ships plying the necessary routes, the length of time for sea transportation, and track each shipment's location and movement through every port of call. Information is both detailed and useful, providing full specifications on all equipment, allowing the customer to select the precise container type and ship suitable for his needs, as well as select the most appropriate travel time, delivery date, and individual vessel for his shipment.

In 2000–2001 not only would Evergreen's customers be able simply to log on to the Internet and, through a GPS satellite transmission, find out as much about where their own cargo was (including on trucks or trains to or from the port) as the Federal Express system told it about where its billions of packages were at any given moment, but also to book containers and space for particular ships on particular routes without going through booking agents. How much value this sort of thing will add to the output of the region that will continue to be the world's manufactory is anybody's guess, but it would be surprising if it were not immense.

Paradoxically (here we go again), Asia will also be well-placed to profit from the Internet because of what it has been bad at: services and distribution. With the sole exceptions of Hong Kong and Singapore, every place in Asia has followed Japan's lead and emphasized usually efficient export-oriented manufacturing while making distribution and service trades a sort of quasi-welfare system serving as the dumping ground for the unproductive. With a tangle of regulatory restrictions, from Japan's decades-old (though now mostly rescinded) tight controls on shops above a certain size to China's outright ban on foreign participation in any aspect of distribution, Asia managed to create one of the world's most expensive and least productive service sectors. Markets were fragmented (in China and India there are enormous discrepancies in the prices of identical goods from one region to another), choice was limited and prices were high by world standards. Japan provides as good an example as any of how relatively stunted and unproductive Asia's service industries had become. In America employment in services surpassed that in manufacturing in 1984, and by the late 1990s twice as many Americans worked in services as in manufacturing (30 percent of the workforce to 15 percent); in Japan it was only in 1995 that service-sector employment inched past that in manufacturing and by the turn of the century the respective figures were still a close 25 percent and 20 percent. Conversely, whereas in America in the late 1990s revenues for the wholesale trade equaled just 30 percent of GDP, in Japan it was 90 percent.

Yet from telecoms to wholesale and retail distribution, that situation has begun changing throughout the region as technology, competition, deregulation and (in China's case) entry into the World Trade Organization are razing the old barriers to lower prices and higher productivity. It is in distribution and services where the Internet should have its most beneficial effects in Asia. It is hard to overestimate the good that will probably come of this. Before the Internet revolution started, America had (and still has) the world's most efficient service sector; even so, the Internet has already wrought an appreciable improvement in efficiency there. Imagine, then, what a boost to Asian productivity and economic growth the Internet will give if it is allowed the scope to work its magic and Asian levels of efficiency begin their steep climb to American standards. (Just how steep a climb it will be, and how much more productive Asia has been in manufacturing than in services, is shown in Table 11.2. This will also help contribute to another important shift. As services and distribution improve, domestic consumer markets that have long been artificially suppressed will flourish, adding more to Asia's economic growth than they have in the past.

Table 11.2
The Output Gap

Country	Output per Worker Relative to Annual Employment Costs[1]		Output per Unit of Labor and Capital Employed[1]
	Manufacturing	Services	
U.S.[2]	2.46	3.31	74.5%
Japan	1.93	1.52	15.6
Taiwan	2.22	2.55	37.0
Hong Kong	2.90	2.56	38.2
Singapore	2.36	2.13	16.5
South Korea	1.94	1.00	−19.1

[1] 1995–99.
[2] 1995–98.

Source: Dismal Science Group.

The most significant result of all this will be to help force Asian companies to organize themselves and behave in ways that raise their returns on equity. The erosion of pricing power might pinch profits, but the transparency and freer information flows brought about by the Internet will accelerate the (already begun) process by which providers of finance differentiate among Asian companies, increasing the flow of money to the more efficient and squeezing it to those who fail to perform. In the past, Yang notes, "in socialist countries like China or France the lowest-common denominator [the urge to protect the losers] drove every decision." Because the imperatives of commerce are becoming so strong, that will have to change. There may be fewer companies—there certainly will be a raft of different ones—but they will all have to deliver higher returns.

One of the most telling market judgments of late 1999 confirmed all this. It became apparent in South Korea as summer drew to a close that Daewoo, the second-biggest *chaebol* and one of the most inefficient, in effect was bankrupt with debts amounting to at least $70 billion, much of it held by the country's investment trust companies (ITCs). In the past the very thought of one of the biggest conglomerates going bust would have devastated the Korea Stock Exchange. Instead, once it became clear the government would protect the liquidity of the ITCs and not allow a systemic financial crisis to develop, the market completely shrugged off the symbolic death of the old Korea Inc, with Kosdaq rising by half during the last three months of the year and the Korea Stock Exchange more than holding its own. A massive transfer of wealth to technology and shareholder-oriented companies was taking place.

Hardly any corner of Asia is likely to remain untouched by the spread of the Internet. Projections of the number of Internet users is an inexact "science," but conservative guesses are that by 2003 there will be 60 million in Japan, 35 million in China, 15 million in Korea, 10 million in Taiwan and another 15 million elsewhere in Asia—some 135 million in all, compared with 100 million in America in 1999. Already in Korea by the end of 1999, more than 40 percent of stock-market turnover by value, and more than that by volume, was accounted for by on-line trading. Not even China was immune. Early in 2000 a Beijing-based computer company called Legend started to sell TV set-top boxes equipped with Microsoft software that allow instantaneous on-line trading of stocks; with 320 million televisions in China, and the initial price of the boxes about half that of a personal computer, the potential market is enormous.

These developments suggest that the spread of Internet culture throughout Asia is likely to be rapid. It will be helped by a flood of capital through Internet funds, venture capital and M&A deals that will inundate Asian start-ups in the early years of the century. Japan's Softbank, Hikari Tsushin and Trans Cosmos (see next section) and Richard Li's Pacific Century CyberWorks, which aims to do in Asia what the Internet investment firm CGMI began doing in America in the late 1990s by taking stakes in a wide range of Internet firms and giving secondary investors a piece of the action through its own stock-market listing, are early prominent examples of the swift fanning out of money and technology that will now happen in Asia.

All this will affect the "old" economy as much as the new. Like Softbank, which by 2000 was going into banking through the takeover of a bust Japanese bank, PCCW—at that point a 10-month old firm with no real business apart from investing—astonished the markets in early 2000 by beating out solid Singapore Telecom in a bidding war for the controlling share of Cable & Wireless in Hong Kong Telecom. Even more astonishing, C&W—a traditionally unadventurous British telecoms firm—accepted a big slice of PCCW's madly price-gyrating shares in part payment.

As the Internet spreads throughout Asia, the star performers will be found in Northeast Asia—Korea, China and greater China (Taiwan and Hong Kong)—with Southeast Asia (conspicuously save for Singapore) playing a modest supporting role. Yet the two places where the impact will be the strongest make quite an odd couple: rich orderly Japan and poor chaotic India.

LAND OF THE RISING NET

Always before, when I visited Japan on business, I would have a few meetings where the people were interesting or innovative, but in most of the big companies I called on the formality and tedium of my interlocutors almost put me to sleep. In late 1999 I spent a week in Tokyo visiting only Internet companies. The difference was staggering. The new firms had far more in common with their Silicon Valley counterparts than they did with their old-line business compatriots at home. Japan's Internet firms are full of outsiders, mostly very young (the staff's average age tends to be in the mid-20s and that of board members in the mid-30s, respectively versus mid-40s and early 60s at traditional firms) and rich (share options are almost universal). The Internet entrepreneurs have immense contempt for the views of their business and government elders about how things should be run. The feeling is mutual since, as one old-timer put it after a no-nonsense speech by one Internet founder at the ultra-respectable business association Keidanren in Tokyo, the establishment finds the upstarts "so rude." Yet they can change Japan vastly for the better. The potential for the Internet in Japan, in terms both of the returns the industry can earn and its overall impact on the economy, is probably the highest in the world. The reason is simple. Japan is the rich world's most middleman-laden economy, and as discussed above if there is anything the Internet is great at it's killing off middlemen.

The upstarts have the financial wherewithal to carry out this revolution. The Nikkei index of the Tokyo Stock Exchange (TSE) rose a respectable but not stunning 52 percent in dollar terms in 1999. As in America, though, all of the action came in high-tech stocks, which quadrupled their share of the market's capitalization. The TSE's second section, which lists younger and smaller companies, was up 145 percent, and Jasdaq, the over-the-counter market, rose almost 250 percent. With specific stocks the picture became starker. Whereas the shares of construction and utilities firms actually fell in 1999, and those of insurance, real estate and iron and steel companies barely rose, Japan's big four Internet stocks outperformed the shares of all but a handful of Silicon Valley firms. Stock in NTT DoCoMo, which has half the country's mobile-phone market and is leading the charge into mobile Internet services (see below), went up by more than 300 percent in 1999, raising the firm's market capitalization to some $340 billion. Softbank (by early 2000 Japan's fifth biggest company by market cap) was up more than 1,250 percent, Hikari Tsushin (a four-year-old mobile phone and Internet-investment firm that by early 2000 was bigger than Honda or Matsushita) up almost 2,900 percent. Yahoo! Japan was up more than 4,200 percent, presumably the steepest rise in history for any serious company anywhere, giving it a share price of $1 million in early 2000 and a p/e ratio of more than 1,000.

To some extent, of course, Japan was simply sharing in worldwide Internet mania, and by mid-2000 Japan's Internet stocks had been slaughtered even more comprehensively than America's had in their springtime bloodbath: Softbank's shares were off by 70 percent and at one point Hikari Tsushin's shares were down 98 percent from their peak. Even so, the long-term impact of the price declines may be less pronounced than the raw figures make it sound. Unlike their American counterparts, many

Japanese Internet firms are highly profitable, and the earlier stock-market gains were driven in part by the imminent removal of obstacles to Internet growth posed by Japan's telecoms and financial systems. The telecoms reforms (see Chapter 10) were the bedrock, but new sources of finance were also essential. Japan's stodgy banks would never have backed the young entrepreneurs building the Internet there, but they were simply bypassed. Billions in private-equity capital have been mobilized by Japanese firms like Softbank, Hikari Tsushin and Trans Cosmos for Internet investments, and not just in Japan: Softbank and Hikari Tsushin invest widely in America and Asia, particularly through vehicles and partners in Hong Kong, notably including Richard Li's Pacific Century CyberWorks. Foreign money began to pour into Japan as well. Taiwan's Hambrecht & Quist (Asia) started investing in Japan, and J.H. Whitney & Co., the leading American private-equity firm in Japanese Internet investment, had already put in $120 million by the end of 1999. Once beyond the start-up stage, moreover, equity financing is increasingly easy to come by. In addition to Jasdaq, fast-growth firms can turn for nurture to a TSE section coyly called Mothers (sort of standing for "Market of the High Growth and Emerging Stocks") and in 2000 Nasdaq Japan, a joint venture between the American exchange and Softbank, is set to be up and running.

To see what might happen take banking, which by global standards has been one of Japan's most pathetic industries. Not only are outsiders like Sony and Ito-Yokado, a retail chain that is the parent of Seven-Eleven Japan, getting into the finance business and threatening to shake it up partly by providing Internet services, but several banks both regional and national are setting up on-line services of their own. Sakura Bank, a middling national bank that intended to merge with Sumitomo Bank, founded a new company called Japan Net Bank that began operations in 2000. It is bringing in strategic equity partners such as Fujitsu, which runs Nifty, the biggest fixed-line Internet service provider (ISP) with 3.5 million subscribers, Nippon Life, Tepco and Mitsui and Company, one of the biggest trading houses. Transactions over the Internet will cost 2–3 percent as much as those processed by humans at teller windows and 10 percent as much as those handled over the phone. Collecting deposits is also cheaper. Sakura expects Japan Net Bank to have about $10 billion in deposits by 2003, which would make it the size of a second-tier local bank in 1999. The conventional version of such a bank, however, would have maybe 50 branches and a staff of 2,000–3,000; Japan Net Bank will have no branches and a staff of 100, including part-timers, of whom 60 will be manning a call center. The sharp reduction in costs will allow Sakura and other banks to offer customers not only lower interest rates and fees and commissions but also a different structure of rates, with finer targeting of credit and other risks.

Spread across the whole economy, such improvements will make a huge difference. The Tokyo office of McKinsey & Co. in a joint study with MITI estimated that the Internet would produce cost savings in Japanese industry of about $600 billion a year every year from 2003 to 2008—an amount equal each year to 13 percent of Japan's GDP in 1995 (not much different in size from its GDP in 1999). The biggest gains will come in domestic manufacturing, professional services like health care, and in retailing and other distribution trades; the smallest (no surprise) in already-efficient export-oriented manufacturing.

As in America, business-to-business e-commerce (B2B) will financially dominate Japan's Internet development in the early years. B2B in Japan was worth a modest $110 billion in 1999, a figure Morgan Stanley Dean Witter expects to rise to $650 billion–$700 billion in 2003 (depending on exchange rates), maybe 10 percent of Japan's GDP then, compared to about $1.6 trillion in America (around 15 percent of GDP). MITI predicts that these B2B transactions will spread rapidly from the car and electronics industries that now account for the lion's share of them to businesses like food processing. As a by-product of the improved efficiency the growth of B2B should bring, it will radically transform the country's industrial system. For obvious reasons, the trading companies that have long dominated Japan's—and in some respects Asia's—commerce for decades as the region's great middlemen are finding their traditional position undercut (which is one reason why Mitsui has been branching out into various Internet joint ventures so urgently). More significantly, the massive rise of B2B is going to cripple the customary relationship-based and cross-ownership-based methods of doing business. The transparency and cost-consciousness of Internet transactions will break the back of keiretsu [family-company]-centered procurement, pricing and loyalty. The head of Fujitsu's global software and services businesses said in a newspaper interview, "In e-commerce the keiretsu does not matter. The concern is not how to stay in the keiretsu but how to win in the international marketplace. Companies concerned with the keiretsu will be wiped out."

By the raw numbers, business-to-consumer e-commerce (B2C) in Japan is a minor appendix to B2B. It was worth less than $2 billion in

1999 (2 percent of B2B), and MITI projects it rising fast but to a still modest $30 billion in 2003 (5 percent of Japan's B2B transactions and about 15 percent of America's B2C transactions then). But the raw numbers may be misleading. Retail trading and distribution in Japan has been at least as distorted as the business-to-business market. The Internet promises to force the pace of restructuring in retail distribution, helping to boost domestic consumption in a country where this has been chronically weak by international standards. And Japan is already on the leading edge of what will be one of the biggest Internet surges worldwide—consumer access through mobile phones—in which it has a good chance of becoming the dominant player.

The fixed-line (or PC-based) consumer Internet market has a familiar look. Yahoo Japan, 51 percent owned by Softbank and 34 percent by America's Yahoo, dominates the portal business with 9 million customers among the 18 million in Japan who used the Internet in 1999, and by early 2000 more than a billion page-views a month, up 90-fold in just over two years and still about four times higher than its nearest competitor. Yahoo itself has ten times as many page-views as Yahoo Japan, but the Japanese offshoot is already the most heavily trafficked site among Yahoo's 20 non-U.S. operations. Masahiro Inoue, a former Softbank executive who is Yahoo Japan's president, says that the firm simply copied Yahoo America's business strategy and even website design—partly to meet his deadline of getting it up and running in just two months early in 1996. He still finds that the American model works just fine in Japan, though some tweaks are needed because of the wider variety of access devices there. But, like America's Yahoo, Yahoo Japan is choosy about which companies it lets handle on-line shopping, issuing invitations rather than accepting applications and opting for established brands people can trust.

One difference between the American and Japanese cousins is that, although Yahoo itself was modestly profitable (still quite an accomplishment in the US Internet market), Yahoo Japan is extremely profitable. In the first half of the 1999 fiscal year, which ended in March 2000, Yahoo Japan had operating income of almost 40 percent on sales of about $20 million, and a post-tax profit margin of 20 percent. It even makes profits on its marketing spending: its main monthly magazine, designed solely to drum up interest in going on-line with Yahoo, has 200,000 paid subscribers; more than half of each issue's pages consist of paid ads. On-line advertising, though, accounts for 85 percent of Yahoo Japan's revenues.

Not all on-line retailers rely heavily on advertising. Rakuten is an on-line shopping mall that in late 1999 had about 2,000 "stores" and was adding new ones at a rate of 200 a month. Founded in 1997 and 70 percent-owned by Hiroshi Mikitani, a 34-year-old Harvard Business School graduate who took it public in April 2000 with a listing on Jasdaq, Rakuten in late 1999 had only 60 employees, who worked out of spartan offices in a modest Tokyo suburb (most looked barely into their twenties and all of course will get stock options). Mikitani thinks the Internet is going to take off exceptionally fast in Japan because the society is so homogeneous and the "community"—the pool of like-minded users—therefore exceptionally large. This is part of his reason for thinking that an on-line shopping mall, an Internet concept that never really took root in America, will work well in Japan, where the bazaar is a familiar notion. Unlike Yahoo Japan, Rakuten is quite unchoosy about its tenants; any company, whether it is peddling Seiko watches or used junk, is welcome once it shows it is solvent and can deliver what it promises. Rakuten collects a monthly fee of $500 upwards depending on the prominence of the "store" in the cyber mall plus fees for whatever ads a store wants to post. Rakuten aims to distinguish itself by giving courses to store-owners in how to market on-line and by providing sophisticated processing of transactions through its special servers. It seems to be working: posh department stores like Seibu have Rakuten stores and in 1999 the company turned a profit of $2.4 million on sales of $5.7 million.

Rakuten is also quietly doing something else: collecting information on every transaction, and especially details on every buyer, processed through its servers. Internet firms worldwide are devoting furious efforts to amassing the best customer databases. An especially interesting data-collector is a company called Recruit, Japan's biggest publisher, with annual revenues of almost $3 billion—about 60 times Yahoo's—derived overwhelmingly from a stable of 54 publications selling a total of 80 million copies a year. The publications consist almost entirely of classified ads for everything from jobs to schools to housing to wedding venues to cars to holidays, and are sold mostly through street news kiosks. The firm was reluctant to resort to the Internet for fear of cannibalizing its profitable paper operations and losing their distribution channels—or was reluctant until a bit of market research showed that while it would lose 2 percent of the 20 percent of potential readers it already had if it went on-line, it would gain 40 percent of the 80 percent it did not have, for a net gain of more than 30 percent. What really tipped the balance, however, was the realization that Recruit could use the Internet to build up an in-depth database for one of the best classes of consumers in Japan. Each year Japan turns out some 380,000 university graduates looking for jobs. Of these, about 350,000 register within one month of graduation with Recruit's job-search website, which they supply with some 200 pieces of information about themselves. Recruit is assembling a long-term detailed database on users as they migrate from original job search to cars, vacations, houses and weddings.

The Internet is also quickly being adapted to some peculiarities of the Japanese market. Because on-line payment systems are ill-developed and transportation and distribution such a headache, innovative delivery methods are being developed. On-line orders can be placed one day and the goods picked up the next at one of the ubiquitous local convenience stores or even a gas station; this allows the use of cash for payment, still preferred by many Japanese, and a delivery time to suit the buyer's schedule. An obvious beneficiary of this is Seven-Eleven Japan, with 8,000 outlets the country's biggest convenience-store chain. In January 2000 it formed a joint venture called 7dream.com with seven partners including Sony, Mitsui, NEC and Japan Travel Bureau. The idea is to use multimedia stations in the stores or Internet mobile phones as vehicles for ordering various goods and services, including music downloads and settlement-only banking services, for delivery at the stores. Within two weeks another joint venture involving other convenience chains was set up to do the same thing.

With fixed-line telecoms charges and PC costs coming down, the use of PCs will expand, but they are never likely to bulk as large on Japan's Internet scene as they do on America's. For a lot of reasons the Japanese have always warmed more to consumer-electronic gadgets, and this heritage is leading Japan to a somewhat different model of Internet use. In Japan the general-purpose PC will probably yield pride of place to "appliances" that do only one or two things and are totally reliant for their power on the network (no wonder Oracle's Gates-ophobic Larry Ellison has a Japanese motif to his Silicon Valley house). These appliances run the gamut from car navigation systems to palm-held devices to toys like Sony's PlayStation 2 and Sega's Dreamcast to micro-TVs. This may sound like a blueprint for chaos but probably isn't. Toru Arakawa, a bespectacled engineer who runs a Tokyo software firm called Access, says his ambition is to be "the Microsoft of the non-PC world." He is much of the way there. His NetFront software, which is designed to give Internet access to appliances running on any sort of operating system, already has 80 percent of the Internet-browser appliance market in Japan.

The appliance that will matter most, and not just in Japan, is the mobile phone. For now this is a mere curiosity in America, where the broadband future of the Internet seems defined almost in its entirety by fixed-line competition between cable and telephone providers (with a dash of satellite access added for spice). It is different in Europe, and especially in Asia. Even in Japan, of course, some kinds of content, such as full-action video, will have to be delivered over PCs or TV-like devices. But mobile phone penetration rates in Japan, at 50 percent, are almost twice those in America, and mobile broadband services are not only just around the corner but make commercial sense, particularly for B2C e-commerce. The two Japanese companies that will count the most as the mobile Internet evolves are NTT DoCoMo and, if it survives a mid-2000 share-price and business crisis, Hikari Tsushin.

DoCoMo is a huge company, with the world's biggest mobile-phone subscriber base in any one country (more than 30 million), 1999 revenues of some $36 billion, and net income of more than $3 billion. In February 1999 it began offering a mobile-phone Internet service called i-mode, which from the start enjoyed phenomenal growth and celebrated its first anniversary with 5 million subscribers signed up. Keiichi Enoki, who runs DoCoMo's i-Mode business, says that by March 2001 the service may boast 17 million subscribers; other mobile-phone companies, not yet in the market but egged on by Hikari Tsushin (see below), may contribute another 5–10 million by sometime in 2001. Already, the overwhelming majority of new mobile phones sold in Japan are Internet-ready, and some enthusiasts predict that by 2003 half of mobile-phone service revenues will come from Internet services. Astonishingly, DoCoMo may over take America Online sometime in the next couple of years as the world's biggest Internet service provider, with all its services coming through mobile devices.

The early i-mode services were elementary: e-mail, news, stock quotes, games. The most popular use at first was to download daily horoscopes. But that did not blunt i-mode's appeal, in part because it already had an important advantage over other forms of Internet access: the user is continuously hooked up to the Internet so there is no need to dial up an ISP to go on-line. Moreover, advances are coming so quickly that demand seems sure to accelerate. In December 1999 i-mode phones with color screens went on sale. New mobile phones also had small cameras in them to record and then transmit images; sometime in 2000 it will become feasible to download color graphics files. In the spring of 2001 so-called third-generation broadband services under

WCDMA, offering download speeds of 364 kilobits per second, will become available. That access is three to five times faster than millions of American PC users now enjoy, and by 2003 Japanese mobile phones will be capable of operating at download speeds of 2 megabits per second—fast enough to put color video clips on mobile-phone screens. Enoki reckons that WCDMA could lower mobile-phone Internet costs in Japan fifty-fold to seventy-fold.

All these developments will stoke a boom in demand. Web pages are already being designed in two formats: one to suit PC or TV screens, and the other for mobile-phone screens. Nobody is going to watch a movie on a mobile phone, but a lot of other Internet uses will be just as convenient on the move—or more so. Neighborhood guides to shops, restaurants and movies (with preview clips) will be hard to beat, and various kinds of purchases—say, spur-of-the-moment or previously intended but forgotten ones—will more likely be made over mobile phones than any other devices. By 2000 Japan's biggest mobile-Internet content provider, Mobilephone Communications International, run by (what else?) a 34-year-old, offered 200 services ranging from auctions to racing results to personal ads to chat groups, used mostly by people under 30; the number of users, 1.5 million as of April 2000, was then growing by more than 300 percent a year. For those with somewhat more mature tastes, mobile phones are also well-suited for some financial transactions, such as share trading, where speed is an advantage. Several banks have been in talks with DoCoMo about mobile banking; faster to the punch than most, Sakura Bank had 125,000 i-mode clients by March 1999. And that is just in Japan. DoCoMo is already making alliances to extend the i-mode formula to the rest of Asia and Europe—a market grab it is hard to imagine any American competitor even attempting, although some European telecoms firms will probably be snapping at its heels.

Another Japanese firm that probably still bears watching is Hikari Tsushin, though in mid-2000 it ran into financial troubles so serious that they threatened to undermine its basic business strengths. Hikari Tsushin (the name roughly means "light-speed communications") was one of the hottest start-ups in global Internet lore, even though it did not begin as an Internet company at all. Yasumitsu Shigeta, its 34-year-old president, founded the company as a telecoms-equipment leasing and long-distance firm in 1988 after he dropped out of a university after three months. But the company did not take off until 1995, when deregulation of the mobile-phone market allowed newcomers to challenge NTT's previous monopoly.

The newcomers had no marketing strategy, so Shigeta created one for them. Tumbling to one of those simple but brilliant business ideas that so often create billionaires, Shigeta realized that it was not sales of the phones themselves that generated significant cash flow but rather the services delivered over them. Through franchising, he swiftly set up a series of "Hit Shops," of which there were more than a thousand in mid-2000, to sell the new companies' phones. In Japan, unlike America or Europe, the handset and service are sold as an indivisible package. Rather than rely on markups on the handsets, Shigeta made his money by receiving a hefty commission (about $375) for each customer he signed up, plus a 5–10 percent cut of the monthly phone bill indefinitely. In fact, realizing that the price of the handsets was almost irrelevant, he began giving most of them away to get his share of the service revenues.

It seemed an almost-risk-free high-return business model. As the newcomers built up their share of the mobile-phone market to 40 percent over the next five years, the market itself was exploding from 1.5 million to 50 million users and generating torrential cash flow for Hikari Tsushin. Revenues rose by an average of 80 percent a year and grew to about $2.5 billion in 1999; operating income rose by almost 90 percent a year, reaching $160 million. The stock market responded with abandon, especially in 1999, when it understood how much Shigeta intended to tie Hikari Tsushin's future to the Internet. At various points in 1999–2000 the company's market cap approached $50 billion. Shigeta, who still owns 62 percent of the company, was sometimes worth $31 billion or more. All seemed to end in tears with the stock-market collapse of mid-2000, but the firm should not be written off.

Shigeta, who in meetings with English-speakers uses (and even travels with) two simultaneous translators because he "hates to waste time," tells a clear story about how Hikari Tsushin will maximize shareholder value—which it is doing pretty well, since ROE was 27 percent in 1999 and ROA 21 percent. The strategy, Shigeta explains, is to generate half of income from commissions and half from products and services. In addition to mobile phones, the shops are starting to generate commissions from selling satellite TV dishes, Web TV boxes, and PCs (and Shigeta is thinking of giving some of those away too). Hikari Tsushin also became a major investor in Internet firms in Japan (where it launched a $300 million venture capital fund in 1999) as well as in America and the rest of Asia. Shigeta admits that 90 percent of the firm's business was still in mobile phones at the end of 1999, but the number of mobile phone users in Japan will level off at

70–80 million in the next few years. The Internet is where the firm's future growth will come. For Hikari Tsushin, that will not necessarily be such a business leap. Shigeta is sure that the mobile Internet, and the e-commerce over it, will have a central role during the next five years. He says that, within a few years, Japan alone will have 50 million Internet-capable mobile phones, and although DoCoMo looks dominant now it may not remain so as the market matures.

Whether Japan is or is not positioning itself to bestride a great new global industry, however, is less significant than what the Internet in all its ramifications has the potential for doing to Japanese business and he Japanese economy. By undermining the cozy relationships and pro-manufacturing bias of the old Japan Inc., the Internet promises to do more than any other single trend to force the wholesale restructuring of Japanese industry. And the whole world, having grown too comfortably accustomed to the sorry state of the place during the 1990s, should realize that a restructured Japan is going to be an immensely powerful competitor in all sorts of businesses both old and new. If you thought Japan in the 1980s was mighty, wait till you see the post-Internet version.

Then consider Asia's most improbable rising Internet star.

Elephant.com

Of the world's eight most populous countries, India is the poorest—more wretched even than Pakistan or post-crisis Indonesia. It is fairly easy to see how Japan, with its industrial sophistication and wealth of educated people, could absorb the Internet and profit mightily from it, if only politicians would allow the institutional and industrial debris of the past to be promptly cleared away. But India? The country's 1 billion people have only about 60 million TVs, 4 million PCs, a 2 percent telephone penetration rate and, as the new century opened, only 500,000 Internet connections (though that may quintuple in just two years). It has nothing like China's rates of literacy, relatively well-shared prosperity and a broad-based export-attuned economy. Yet it is precisely "socialist" India's appalling inequalities and prior insulation from the outside world that have created the fodder for an Internet revolution there, one that might benefit not just the super-educated engineers who are driving it but the whole economy.

Compared to India's first 40 years of independence—when economic policy was long on leftist and "anti-colonial" development theory but short on common sense—the country had a great decade in the 1990s. During the previous two generations, it relied on a systematically imposed isolation from global economic currents and a pointillistically detailed edifice of government regulation (and often ownership) of the domestic economy that together did more harm to its people's prospects than any other major post-war regime except the Soviet Union's. In the accurate summing-up by the American writer P.J. O'Rourke, India in 1947–91 was "the smartest country in the stupidest way." It paid the price with 40 years of economic growth that kept only marginally ahead of the growth of the population, leading to real incomes doubling only once during a period when in many parts of East Asia they were octupling. By every measure of material welfare, even totalitarian and certainly post-Mao authoritarian China did better by its citizens than formally democratic India. This shame began to be rectified after a balance-of-payments crisis—foreign-exchange reserves had basically run out—brought a pro-reform government under IMF tutelage to power in 1991.

In the nine years that followed, successive governments made fitful but cumulative progress toward dismantling the "license *raj*" of industrial regulation which had so thickly swathed Indian industry in red tape that companies could not make new and improved products without first getting a bureaucrat's approval. Similarly, though more tortuously, barriers to imports—especially of hitherto banned consumer goods—and to foreign direct investment were lowered to the point where trade had crept up to almost 20 percent of GDP in 1999 (a 50 percent rise) and FDI to a projected $3 billion in 2000, a 30-fold increase in a decade. By East Asian standards these figures are still shockingly low—for the whole of the 1990s China's FDI, for instance, ran at 10–30 times the Indian level—but by earlier standards India had indeed opened up and had begun moving itself toward the East Asian model of development. It had also begun reaping the rewards, with GDP growth in the range of 6 percent to 7 percent and growth of GDP per capita 4 percent to 5 percent in 1991–99, compared with 4 percent and 2 percent respectively in 1965–90.

Because of its isolation and its being at a different stage in its economic cycle, India was largely untouched by the East Asian financial crisis of 1997–98. Even so, many of the lessons driven home in East Asia by force of capital flows were also driven home in India by force of example. The pace of economic reform, although painstaking, was not noticeably slowed. And in the autumn of 1999 a welcome point of no return in the progress of reform seemed to have been passed. In the general election the Hindu-nationalist Bharatiya Janata Party won another term, with an apparently stable majority, over the demoralized main opposition Congress Party, which had ruled India with only brief breaks from independence until 1996. More significantly, after years of zigzagging, both the majority and the opposition had reached a consensus that continued reform was inevitable and had substantially cut back on the political posturing over it. An insurance liberalization law (including permission for foreign firms to take minority stakes in Indian insurers), which would have been unthinkable a few years earlier, was passed without much fuss in late 1999. A speed-up in privatization followed in 2000.

By East Asian standards this was too little and much too late; it also promised little of the broad-based farming reforms and mass industrialization that did so much in East Asia (on a huge scale in China) to lift incomes and crush poverty. But even if the reform path in India is not as wide as it should be, the Internet promises to push the country down this path a lot faster than anyone would have dreamed possible a few years ago. If in general the Internet is a technology that—like electricity, cars, telephones and airplanes—transforms and improves all businesses, in India's rare case it has the potential to work this broad transforming effect across an entire society and economy, demolishing the barriers to wholesale change that made India an Asian laggard for the second half of the twentieth century.

Like Taiwan (see Chapter 10), India has succeeded both in building an internationally competitive high-tech industry and in forging close ties with Silicon Valley. In a way, however, this being the early years of the Internet era, India has an advantage over even Taiwan: India's strength is in software rather than hardware. The origin of the industry can be found in India's exceptionally deep pool of scientific and engineering talent. Some 40 percent of Indians are still illiterate, but those at the top can take advantage of some of the world's best opportunities for technological education. Advanced computer-science courses are taught at more than 350 universities and engineering colleges and at 700 private colleges and technical institutes. In 1998 India produced 65,000 engineers at college degree level or higher, contributing to a pool of engineering manpower that in size is now second only to America's. Nor is it just a matter of quantity. Some Indian universities—most conspicuously the several campuses of the Indian Institutes of Technology and the Indian Institutes of Science—are just as good as any of their counterparts in America. Partly because India's misguided economic policies left the country with a narrow and weak manufacturing base whether high-tech or low, and partly because the English-language skills of educated Indians are very high, India's engineers and the companies that hired them gravitated to software and computer services rather than hardware. By the end of the 1990s India had about 1000 software companies employing some 280,000 engineers.

Although software companies can be found in several locations, they are concentrated in the south and particularly in three cities: Bangalore, Hyderabad and Madras. They sprang up there in part because of good engineering schools in the vicinity (and in Hyderabad's case defense-based research facilities). But, also, business enterprise found a more favorable climate for its growth far from the overweening bureaucrats of Delhi and the political shenanigans in the financial capital of Mumbai (Bombay). The attitudes of state governments came to matter even more as the 1990s wore on and the loosening of central control allowed the states more freedom to compete with each other for FDI and domestic investment through deregulation and other pro-business policies. Chandrababu Naidu, the chief minister of Andhra Pradesh, of which Hyderabad is the capital, has been the country's most outspoken pro-reform politician. He espouses openly East Asian ambitions and methods, aiming to eliminate poverty in his state through 10 percent GDP growth a year for the next 20 years (it grew 11 percent in the fiscal year ending in March 1999). To build up infrastructure, whose inadequacy has always been a crippling handicap for business in India, he has raised water tariffs, privatized the ports and been courting private investment in utilities. He promises a first-class international airport by 2003 and fiber-optic links for every village in the state by 2005. Just before the 1999 election, he took what many thought would be the politically suicidal (albeit economically impeccable) step of slashing rice and power subsidies in the teeth of a populist campaign by the opposition Congress Party calling for free electricity and debt forgiveness for farmers. Naidu told the voters that the Congress proposal was pro-rich and anti-poor—he was of course right since only the top 5 percent of farmers would have benefited from it—and the voters, by giving Naidu a landslide victory, proved to Congress that it is possible after all to go broke underestimating the intelligence of the Andhra Pradesh public. After the election he began pressing the central government to pass more taxing and spending powers to the states and to let them borrow directly and without restriction on international capital markets—we'll see through competition for funds, he argued, whose policies are best.

Yet in the case of the software industry even national policies have encouraged growth. In 1991 the central government set up an independent agency with the authority to establish separate zones called Software Technology Parks (STPs), of which 13 were up and running as the century turned and more were under construction. The STPs are intended to provide a business-friendly environment in which both Indian and foreign firms can operate with as few as possible of the myriad frustrations that doing business anywhere else in India entails. The communications infrastructure is first-rate (uniquely in India, the STPs were allowed to use their own satellite networks to by-pass VSNL, the government-owned international carrier, even before its monopoly was abolished late in 2000), imports are duty-free, a corporate-tax holiday of 10 years is given, and red tape involving customs and other regulations is in theory minimized by "single-window" clearance of approvals (though in practice some places, like Hyderabad, are much better than others because of differences in the attitudes of the state and local authorities). Ideally, of course, a nationwide program of red-tape burning and lower taxes for all industries would be preferable, but this ignores the reality of the reform process in large poor countries. It also underestimates how much good can be done by a targeted opening-up that allows practical experimentation to be done and lessons to be absorbed before they are extended to other parts of the country. Although industry-specific, the STPs are strongly reminiscent of the special economic zones China set up in the late 1970s and early 1980s as its reforms were just building up steam. These turned out to be superbly successful tools for introducing the basics of capitalism into a society where such ideas had long been suppressed. More important still, they offered a way of beginning to dip China into the currents of the wider world—an initiation that reflexively xenophobic India needs every bit as much as China did.

Maybe more. At least China had its overseas Chinese, an ethnic diaspora that stood ready to pour money and management expertise into the mainland as soon as the door was opened a crack. Indian has its own overseas sojourners, called the non-resident Indians (NRIs). They number 10 million, located mostly in America but with big contingents in Britain and Southeast Asia too. Money they certainly have—with average incomes of $30,000 a head, their collective "GDP" equals 75 percent of that of the 990,000,000 Indians who made the mistake of staying at home—and if the Indian government had been more hospitable the NRIs would have invested some of their wealth in the motherland with more enthusiasm. But whereas the overseas Chinese were overwhelmingly traders and businessmen, and thus brought business savvy to

China when they started investing there in the 1980s, the NRIs are mostly professionals: doctors, scientists, mathematicians, engineers. They seemed to have little business expertise to offer India—until software came along.

In addition to the advantages conferred by the STPs and a large number of well-educated English-speaking software engineers, a simple equation of economic gravity explains why the Indian software industry boomed in the 1990s. As the 1990s ended, a software engineer with three years' experience in India made two-three times what a similarly skilled person would make in other lines of work in India—so everybody wanted to write software—but only a sixth to an eighth as much as someone comparable would be paid in America. The pay discrepancy ran all the way up the management chain—and unlike in China, for instance, there actually was a management chain. India has a relative abundance of high-level English-speaking managers who are pretty much up to international snuff. A former head of Hindustan Lever said at a conference in Mumbai in 1999 that, whereas until a few years ago Unilever in China had 80 senior expatriate managers costing the company on average $400,000 a year, Hindustan Lever had had an Indian CEO since 1961 and now almost no expat managers at all. Multinationals setting up in the STPs have found they need almost no high-level expatriate managers. Once proprietary satellite communications were allowed and their price fell during the 1990s, there was little reason for an American software firm not to set up shop in an STP: Hewlett-Packard, Novell, Texas Instruments and Oracle have significant operations in Bangalore, and in Hyderabad Microsoft (where it put its second ex-America research center) and GE Capital (though only for call-center operations) have nestled in. And in the fall of 2000, General Electric itself was due to open only its second full-blown R&D center ever (after Schenectady, New York, in an industrial park on the outskirts of Bangalore).

Unsurprisingly, India had to start on the bottom rung of the global software business. Call-centers and some other back-office operations were physically relocated from America to southern India (so successfully that in many instances the young women answered the phones in flawlessly emulated Kansas or Texas accents). But most of the real software-export work in the early years—90 percent in 1990—was done "on-site" in America or Europe through what came to be known as "body-shopping": teams of Indian engineers were sent for weeks at a time to customer premises to do coding, testing and other low-grade programming work where their ample cost advantage over Americans proved decisive.

As international telecommunications improved and became cheaper, and the competence of the Indian industry rose, the proportions shifted: by 1997 around 40 percent of India's software exports were generated in India itself rather than on-site in the West, and by now more than half are. It is no wonder. By December 2000 more than 90 percent of India's 300 top software firms will have received internationally recognized quality certifications. Already, four Indian firms—Motorola India, WIPRO, Satyam Computers and ICIL—have received the highest possible level of certification, WIPRO distinguishing itself by being the first software-services company in the world to snare one. A breakthrough in India's struggle to move into more sophisticated businesses came as 1999 drew to a close. Much of the industry's super-fast growth in the late 1990s came from a large volume of fairly mundane Y2K debugging work thrown India's way, and there was speculation of a slowdown once that nonproblem was out of the way. Instead, the best Indian firms made a smooth transition to doing more and more e-commerce and other Internet work for customers both at home and in the West. Satyam, for instance, had for two years relied on Y2K projects for almost 30 percent of its revenues and they helped fuel an annual doubling of sales. By the summer of 1999 only 5 percent of sales were Y2K-related but Satyam still enjoyed sales growth of 60 percent in the fiscal year that ended in March 2000—almost all of it driven by Internet work such as setting up India's second-largest ISP and selling Internet services to American customers. The example is not isolated. As early as the first half of 1999 some 16 percent of the whole industry's software export revenues came from Internet projects, generally selling customized e-commerce "solutions."

India's drive up-market had been substantially helped by its Silicon Valley ties. AnnaLee Saxenian's study of the Valley's immigrant entrepreneurs (see Chapter 10) found that 5 percent of the engineers there in 1990 were Indians (about half as many as were ethnic Chinese from the mainland itself, Taiwan and Hong Kong), a share that undoubtedly rose sharply during the 1990s thanks to higher immigration rates. Indians, 55 percent of whom had advanced degrees, were more highly educated even than the Chinese, 40 percent of whom had them (fewer than 20 percent of whites did). Between 1990 and 1996 the number of doctorates in science and engineering granted to Indians by American universities doubled to almost 700 and, since California graduates Asian engineering students at more than twice the rate of the rest of America and most California engineering graduates go to Silicon Valley, the share of top-level

Indian talent in the Valley must have risen substantially during the 1990s. Moreover, Indians have been starting their own Valley companies at an accelerating rate. Saxenian reckons that by 1998 almost 800 high-tech firms in Silicon Valley had an Indian CEO, nearly 7 percent of the total (Chinese CEOs, most of them Taiwanese, ran 17 percent of the Valley's companies). As the Valley's Internet boom widened, moreover, the reputation of Indian engineers soared. One of their greatest fans was Jim Clark—the founder of Silicon Graphics then Netscape then Healtheon—who said that "as a concentrated group, they were the most talented engineers in the Valley . . . and they work their butts off!" When Clark raided Silicon Graphics by proxy in early 1996 to get the Valley's very best engineers to come and build Healtheon, he picked an Indian as his chief engineer; six of the first ten on his team were also Indians.

Even so, in the case of India there has been relatively little of the proliferation of contacts or the two-way flow of people and ideas that has enriched ties between Taiwan and the Valley. But that is changing. In 1999 the Indian government set up a committee on venture capital to which it appointed several Indians who had made it big in the Valley: among them Kanwal Rekhi, who sold his software firm to Novell for $200 million, Sabeer Bhatia, who founded Hotmail and later sold it to Microsoft for $400 million, Suhas Patil, who founded Cirrus Logic, and K.B. Chandrasekhar, who set up Exodus Communications. These Valley NRIs have been raising venture capital for investment in India and lobbying the government to remove restrictions on venture-capital investments, including those barring pension funds and insurance companies from investing in venture funds and limiting venture holdings in unlisted companies to 40 percent of the capital. In the five years after 1995 on average only $100 million a year of venture money went into Indian start-ups. The goal of the NRIs is to get that up to $3 billion a year in short order.

American capital began to sit up and take notice. Not only was there an appreciable rise in investment by high-tech multinationals in the STPs and in exploratory forays by American venture capitalists, but in 1999 two Indian software firms—Satyam Infoway (the ISP subsidiary of Satyam Computers) and Bangalore-based Infosys Technologies—listed on Nasdaq. The usual triple-digit rises followed, with Infosys up 840 percent in the nine months after its listing. That gave it a market capitalization of $19 billion, only a little short of Amazon.com's, and equal to about 5 percent of India's entire GDP. Industry specialists in India think another 30 may be on Nasdaq by 2002. The process has already generated capital flows in reverse, as

Indian firms dream of using their Internet "currency" (their own shares) to make acquisitions in America.

The Indian stock market too started putting a lot of daylight between high-tech shares and the rest of the listings during 1999. The main index of the Bombay Stock Exchange went up about one-and-a half times, but the computer software index was up more than four times. By early December 1999, software stocks accounted for 60 percent of total turnover and were the biggest single industrial component in terms of both market capitalization and index composition. The wealth effects were predictable: By 1999 three of the five richest men in India were founders of software firms. Yet India's strengths in information-based industries extended well beyond software. For similar reasons—well-educated scientists and trained managers who command often as little as one-tenth of their counterparts' salaries in the West—the drugs business is beginning to show global promise.

But it is in the interaction of media and the Internet that India is showing the most uncanny parallels to the evolution of the information industry in the West. Shares in Zee Telefilms, the only media stock with much liquidity, went up ten times in 1999. Set up in 1992 by Subhash Chandra after the state TV monopoly was abolished, it quickly established itself as the dominant satellite-TV broadcaster and programmer in India. It branched out into Internet-ready cable TV (with 3 million subscribers), publishing, housing developments wired with optical cables, and a chain of cinema and entertainment multiplexes. But Chandra's big ambition—which he funded in part by issuing $500 million in American Depository receipts in the middle of 2000, one of the biggest international equity issues ever by an Indian company—is to start a satellite-phone service in 2002 that not only will provide reasonably priced Internet-ready service through handsets about as small as today's cell phones, but also will carry Zee's programs and other entertainment both to TVs (which can also be used as Internet terminals) and eventually mobile phones. One of the main attractions of this is that in less than a decade since TV deregulation India has become Asia's richest and most diverse source of digital-entertainment content, with an audience whose appetite for it is voracious.

Yet however dynamic, these are minuscule pockets of success in a vast and still mostly dilapidated economy. How can they make much difference? In the first place, they are in some important ways a lot bigger and more influential than they look. Fast-growing industries add disproportionately to economic growth. Between 1995 and 1998, for instance, information technology accounted for 35 percent of America's total economic growth even though it represented only 8 percent of America's GDP in those years. This could happen because IT was growing more than four times as fast as the rest of the economy. During most of the 1990s India's software industry grew at 40 percent to 50 percent a year, about ten times as fast as the rest of the economy, so by the end of the decade it was contributing some 20 percent to economic growth even though it accounted for only 2 percent of GDP. It has become by far India's single most powerful sectoral engine for growth.

Second, the software-becoming-Internet business has been crucial for plugging India into the outside world. The simplest effect has been through software exports. These reached almost $4 billion in 1999 and continue to grow at 50 percent a year. Unextravagant projections are that India will export $50 billion in software in 2008. Put in perspective, India's total exports in 1999 were (an admittedly derisory) $35 billion or so. Software—three-fifths of which now goes to America with another fifth to Europe—is going to be India's most important export business. Investment flows both ways, especially FDI, will help transform the Indian business landscape. Yet it is changes in attitude that will matter most of all. Of all the handicaps which successive Indian governments loaded on to their poor country, none was more crippling than the policy of cutting it off as much as possible from the outside world. The software industry has exactly the opposite philosophy—whether it is in welcoming FDI with open arms or trying to plunge into the global economy itself—and as India's most obviously successful industry its attitude is being noticed by the rest of Indian business.

After decades of resistance the change of attitude is also soaking in at a political and social level. The Internet may not yet be bringing India the cost savings that it is already producing elsewhere in the world, but it is rescuing something much more significant for India just now: the idea that free commerce will produce much more good for society than government dictates will. Not only at the state level are politicians like Andhra Pradesh's pro-market Naidu beating populists in elections, but policy-makers in Delhi are noticing that the software industry left to itself has outperformed every industry that has been hindered or "helped" by government intervention. When the central government upgraded the Information Technology Department to a ministry in November 1999, it took pains to assure the software industry that the government was going to keep its hands off; the new minister's first proposal was to lower state sales tax on IT products to 2 percent from 8 percent. This produces a much more hospitable climate than has ever existed for deregulation and privatization generally. But there is more. When Deng Xiaoping told the Chinese in the 1980s that "to get rich is glorious," it made people think they were living in a different China. The Indian equivalent is the success of the southern software entrepreneurs and the proliferation of satellite TV, which have made Indians think the future lies with this new world of possibilities rather than with the old one of stagnation.

An article in *Business Week* in late 1999 on India's young people featured a photo of a 16-year-old girl in rural Uttar Pradesh, a northern state that is one of India's poorest. In the photo she is smiling broadly and holding a mobile phone. To stimulate phone usage, the local mobile-phone operator lent the handset to the girl which she rents out to villagers to make their phone calls. She pockets as much as $8 a day, a fortune by local standards that she plans to use to attend computer classes. It is the most heartening picture to have come out of India in its 50-plus years since independence.

CHAPTER

12

What's the Asian
for Milken?

O f the three trends that gave America such a boost beginning in the
late 1970s—macroeconomic good sense, technological flexibility
and a free market for corporate control—Asia today looks like it has
a reasonable grip on the first two. Its governments may not be the world's
cleanest or most efficient, but at least they tend to be small and keep their
borrowing requirements down. Asia's ability to absorb and profit from
technological change, especially the Internet, is large. But the market for
corporate control still looks anemic. It apparently remains hard for insurgents to get rid of entrenched managers and for newcomers to get funding. Will that change? It needs to: after all, destruction is as much a part
of creative destruction as creation is. Globalization will help this to happen (see Chapter 13), but it requires the lubricant of a financial system
that is allowed to be commercially objective in its judgments.

As explained in Part One, it's no accident that Asia's latest transformation began with a financial crisis: finance has been one of Asia's most backward sectors. Banks overwhelmingly dominated the formal provision of
finance, and far more often than not their standards were slipshod and
their lending was dictated by considerations of public policy. Just how
much of a deepening and widening lies ahead of Asia's financial systems is
shown by the state of affairs in America, which has the world's most advanced finances (see Table 12.1). In 1999 bank assets (loans) in the United
States accounted for only 16 percent of total financial assets, with bonds
representing 41 percent and stocks 43 percent. The assets of mutual funds
alone exceed those of the entire banking system. The "disintermediation"

Table 12.1
Distribution of Assets by Major Classes (Billions of Dollars, 1999)

	Stocks	Bank Assets	Bonds Total
United States	15,300 (43%)	5,600.0 (16%)	14,607.0 (41%)
Japan	3,300 (25%)	4,857.2 (36%)	5,228.1 (39%)
Germany	1,200 (14%)	5,547.2 (65%)	1,842.0 (21%)
UK	2,600 (36%)	3,820.5 (52%)	849.5 (12%)
France	1,200 (20%)	3,564.6 (61%)	1,110.5 (19%)
Italy	570 (17%)	1,255.8 (39%)	1,435.5 (44%)
Canada	700 (40%)	568.0 (32%)	505.0 (28%)
Hong Kong	530 (37%)	871.0 (61%)	30.5 (2%)
Australia	580 (49%)	290.0 (24%)	323.7 (27%)
Sweden	450 (46%)	285.0 (30%)	236.7 (24%)
Finland	300 (68%)	60.0 (14%)	76.8 (18%)
Singapore	260 (60%)	170.0 (39%)	2.0 (1%)
Mexico	120 (58%)	39.0 (19%)	46.9 (23%)

Source: Zurich Financial Services

of banks means that the capital markets—through stocks, bonds and more exotic instruments like derivatives and asset securitizations—are doing more and more of the job of channeling savings (whether they are generated by households or by institutions like insurance companies and pension funds) into investment.

The judgments made by the highly dispersed decisions of the capital markets are not what you would expect of the average bank loan officer—or at least not in such volume. In the 1990s investors in the United States made a collective judgment about the stock market that in essence kept America's traditional industries on a fairly tight financial leash while allowing new high-growth businesses almost unlimited access to cheap capital (which is an excellent reason for thinking that the new businesses will sooner or later suffer an almighty crash since, like Asia in its cheap-capital 1980s and 1990s, they will have invested far too much to offer a decent rate of return). David Hale, the Chicago-based global chief economist for Zurich Financial Services, has pointed out that the market capitalization of high-tech companies went up 15-fold in the 1990s, from $300 billion to $4.5 trillion (about the size of Japan's whole economy). By the end of this process technology stocks accounted for 30 percent of America's market capitalization, compared with 15 percent in Japan, 10 percent in France and 5 percent each in Britain and Germany. New companies and new ideas were getting unprecedented opportunities to prove themselves. By the end of 1999 American venture-capital funds commanded $100 billion in assets; $25 billion of that was raised in the first half of 1999 alone, two-thirds of which went into information-technology (IT) companies. By comparison, all of Europe raised less than $7 billion in venture capital in all of 1998 and Japan's total venture-capital assets at the end of 1999 were also about $7 billion, only 7 percent of the American level in an economy that is 60 percent as big as America's. The access of fast-growing firms to capital was lavish beyond the start-up stage as well: in 1999 initial public offerings of stock (IPOs) raised $69 billion, equal to 20 percent of the total for the whole of the 1990s.

Precisely how overdone this vast expansion of one sector was (i.e., how big a bubble American tech stocks are in) will eventually come to light. Even if there is a nasty crash—even nastier, that is, than the correction in the spring of 2000—however, it is clear that the massive investment in this up-and-coming industry has given the United States a big lead in the transformation of its economy to an information-based one. Research and development spending as a share of GDP went up by about 10 percent between 1995 and 1999, and the record 140,000 patents granted in 1999 were more than half again as many as had been granted in 1990. Capital investment, the biggest single share of it in IT, accounted for a third of American economic growth during the 1990s, twice the proportion for the years 1950–99. And IT's share of America's total output doubled in the 1990s to 6 percent.

The question in Asia is in what way and how fast finance will move toward a structure that judges risks and rewards according to more market-based standards, and in the process promotes the rise of profitable new industries and the shrinkage of unprofitable old ones. In the formal financial sector this will inevitably involve a curtailing of the traditional role of banks in favor of capital markets and—through private equity, venture capital and merger and acquisition (M&A) activity—the creation of more of a market for corporate control. But to get an idea of what might happen at the tip of the iceberg, first consider the part of finance in Asia that has consistently worked efficiently to allocate capital: the informal financial system that has mostly been hidden beneath the surface.

UNFUNNY MONEY

For several hundred years, village families in rural China would pool their savings and lend the money to one of their own when it was needed to pay for a wedding or build a house—or to start a small business. It may seem that these *hui,* or credit clubs, with their humble origins in the medieval Chinese countryside, have nothing to do with the high-tech businesses in Taiwan's Hsinchu Industrial Park. But they do. Many of the gleaming businesses in Hsinchu got their first seed money not from banks or venture capitalists but from informal sources like relatives of the founders or from Taiwanese *hui.* The *hui* have also funded copra traders in the Philippines, seed merchants in northern Thailand and shopkeepers in Jakarta. Indeed, this informal financing system has sustained the remarkable success of the Overseas Chinese business empire for generations. The system is, of course, being displaced as modern technology and standards of transparency and financial disclosure make themselves felt in Asia, but its methods are likely to furnish the basics for much small-business financing in Asia for a long time to come.

The reason is that, unlike Asia's banks and (until recently) investors in Asia's stock markets, the *hui* system has been deadly serious about how it prices and allocates capital. The system became most highly evolved among the Overseas Chinese, but it also flourished in South Korea until the government stamped it out in the 1970s. In fact, finance in non-Japanese East and Southeast Asia (Japan was simply bank-dominated) was two-tiered. Toby Brown, head of General Oriental Investments in Hong Kong (see Chapter 1), points out that at the formal level the big Asian conglomerates devoured the lion's share of bank credit, often (especially in South Korea) at the behest of the government and almost never based on an objective assessment of creditworthiness. The negative results for profitability, culminating in the financial crisis of 1997–98, are well known.

At the other end of the scale are the millions of anonymous small businesses that produce the clothing, housewares and other goods that fill Wal-Mart's shelves. Such companies, says Brown, "millions of which are formed and die every day," are the real drivers of the Asian economic engine, "funded by a highly disciplined capital-allocation system that allows Asia to be as effervescent as it is." They get their money through informal tax-evading mechanisms that include black-market currency transactions, the *hui* and (in India) channels of offshore credit based in the Persian Gulf that use gold and silver as currency.

The *hui* themselves work as clubs in which pooled savings are periodically auctioned to the member-bidder offering the highest rate of return for an agreed term. When the loan falls due, often after strictly monitored monthly installment payments, the capital is auctioned again.

But whatever the exact mechanism, the money is borrowed from people who are intensely interested in how their investment is performing and the cost of capital tends to be very high—often in the range of 20 percent in real terms. That forces the borrower to be highly efficient. His incentive to perform is further sharpened by the fact that he is usually tied socially to the lenders through family, neighborhood or the workplace, and thus feels that his personal as well as financial reputation is at stake. And when a *hui* borrower fails to repay, these lenders don't shrink from muscular enforcement techniques. The system has worked wonders in East Asia: where it is strongest (preeminently Taiwan) it has produced Asia's most balanced and competitive industrial structures. But it also accounts for such far-flung successes as the small Korean grocery stores in America's inner cities.

In the age of globalization and the Internet, all this may seem merely quaint. It is not. Brown reckons, for instance, that in Taiwan the *hui* still intermediate 30 percent of household savings. Several things explain the continued importance of informal finance. First, in Asia (as in America and in the thriving parts of Europe like northern Italy) small businesses employing fewer than 200 people remain the backbone of the economy. McKinsey has estimated that of the 45 million or so companies that existed in Asia in 1996, fully 99.8 percent of them were small businesses. They predominate in Asia even more than elsewhere, both because the world-workshop duties tend to be contracted out to a multitude of small suppliers and because the rising domestic service industries are even more prone than light manufacturing to an atomized industrial structure. This sort of business, small individually but mighty collectively, rarely looks to conventional sources of finance until relatively late in its development (even in VC-happy America a large number of businesses get going with the wherewithal provided by their founders' personal credit cards). In Asia such finance will continue for some time to be provided by methods based on traditions like the *hui*.

Second, the businesses financed in this way are extremely interesting to private-equity investors since they are so disciplined about the high returns they have to generate and are utterly outside any government's grip—if only the investors could find a way to tap into them. "The trouble," as Brown points out, "is that goods produced by companies you have ever heard of are the exception rather than the rule." Third, the old methods sit better with Confucian cultural traditions; more on this in Chapter 14, about how Asian companies are now likely to evolve. Just note here that the decisions of "impartial" loan officers in banks and sufficiently numerous and impartial bankruptcy judges are ideals that are far from being realized for workaday business transactions except in the richest places in Asia which also, like Hong Kong and Singapore, have been implanted with western legal institutions. Lastly, in the poorest and therefore usually fastest-growing parts of Asia a patchwork of financing mechanisms, most of them informal, is the only way to keep pace with explosive economic growth in an environment where the political and legal framework is weak.

Consider China, which is already Asia's light-manufacturing powerhouse yet has one of its most underdeveloped financial systems. In the late 1990s China was reckoned to have 30 million family firms and 450,000 private businesses that employed seven or more workers. They generated about 75 percent of industrial output yet got only 20 percent of bank credit, the other four-fifths of which went to the lumbering state-owned enterprises (SOEs). How then was China financing the bulk of its output?

Part of the explanation is that the bank lending figures were not all they seemed. Policy changes meant that new lending was increasingly being directed away from unproductive SOEs and toward businesses that made profits—almost 40 percent of new bank lending in 1999, by one informed estimate, went to non-state firms. A bigger share is likely to. Reform-minded Zhejiang province, for instance, on China's eastern seaboard near Shanghai, set up a government-backed loan-guarantee outfit in 1999 to insure up to 80 percent of the value of bank loans made to small businesses. Anyway, in commercial China's characteristically happy-go-lucky way a lot of the money lent to SOEs is not coming to rest there. Intercompany loans are illegal, but that does not stop them from being made in large numbers. The procedure is sometimes flagrant, as when an SOE simply sells a government credit quota to a private firm, which then takes it to a bank and gets the loan directly. Some SOE managers also take their firms' loan proceeds and lend them on to private companies or even make equity investments in them. The managers are well aware that they can earn higher returns on investments in well-run private firms than from spending the money on their own businesses.

But banks are only half the story—literally. Only half of China's total household and corporate savings, in all worth some $2 trillion in 1999, are on deposit with banks. How does the half of China's savings outside the banking system get invested? Investment choices are extremely limited in China. Domestic stock markets are small, the bond market is nothing to talk about and modern insurance is still in its infancy. So instead many people invest their savings directly. Start-ups, most of which are initially family affairs, usually demand no more than $10,000 to $50,000 in financing. Millions of urban families can muster an investment pool that big. The larger non-state companies often finance themselves—not hard when their savings (retained earnings) are 30 percent to 40 percent. Beyond all this, China does have a big informal finance industry, especially in the coastal areas, where non-state businesses predominate. There is a lot of loose money in China (*yue zhi,* or free-floating capital, is a familiar term), some generated through smuggling and the like, all of it uncounted in the formal economy.

Some of the informal lending practices are singular, to put it mildly. The township and village enterprises (TVEs), semiprivate businesses that grew spectacularly in the early 1990s, finance many public services, from road building to garbage collecting. Levies from farmers or villagers (as well as contributions from local governments) go into the TVEs' capital base; they pay few if any dividends but provide some job opportunities. Workers often must make a capital contribution or loan to the TVE to be employed. Local government officials are also big investors in both TVEs and truly private firms. Local taxes are supposed to amount to 5 percent of incomes but often run as high as 8 percent to 12 percent—a subject of much bitter complaint—with the extra take invested by functionaries in creditworthy businesses, sometimes on the local government's behalf and sometimes on their own. *Huis,* banned in China when the Communists came to power, nonetheless exist in profusion, especially in the coastal regions where Taiwanese businessmen are active. A variation is the thousands of small credit co-operatives scattered around rural China. The government clamped down on them in the mid-1990s, but five years later they were making a comeback as the central government began realizing that they filled a financing gap for small business in the countryside. The informal channels follow the Taiwanese pattern, with real interest rates in the neighborhood of 20 percent, and disciplined credit allocation. Even uneducated rural people commonly use some basic forecasting techniques to judge whether a project is worthy.

Then of course China gets financing from foreigners—in unusually large amounts for a poor country. By the end of 1999 cumulative FDI amounted to $300 billion. There are some 300,000 foreign-funded enterprises in China, and the foreign partner is required to put up at least 50 percent to 60 percent of the capital. In all, foreign-funded businesses account for about 15 percent of investment in China each year. Plenty of portfolio investment also arrives, usually via the Hong Kong and New York stock markets, and Chinese companies have also borrowed about $15 billion from western banks. American venture capital money, through firms like Intel, is also making a modest appearance. Some of the routes by which foreign capital arrives are convoluted. Much mainland money has been brought out and recycled back through Hong Kong to take advantage of tax breaks and other privileges that would be unavailable if the money were invested directly. Smuggling has also played a prominent role. Until a partly effective crackdown on the army's business interests in 1998–99, it was civic-mindedly using much of the proceeds not just to line its officers' pockets but to invest in mainland businesses too.

China offers just one snapshot, albeit the biggest, of the range of financial intermediation that takes place at the broad base of economic life throughout Asia. The picture is inevitably fuzzy but, whereas even at the informal level political ties and favoritism are often present, many of the signs for the future are good: even rapacious officials and army officers in China, for instance, tend to make sharp judgments about the companies they invest in because they think of the money as their own. Shareholder returns in Asia's informal sector—which means in the bulk of the Asian economy—are in fact quite high. This may be the main reason why Asian economies continue to thrive, and bounce back quickly, even when the visible corporate sector is performing poorly. Can Asia's formal financiers learn to focus on returns the way their informal counterparts have so successfully done?

SHRINKING BANKS . . .

The recapitalization and restructuring of banks described in Chapter 7 have been leading to an Asia in which three things will happen to the banking system in the next few years. There will be a lot fewer banks. Many more will be under the control of foreigners or of local firms without a banking background. And banks will be shrinking their lending overall while redividing the reduced pie by extending fewer loans to big corporate borrowers and many more to consumers. A foretaste of how big the shake-up will be was given by Latin America's experience after the banking crisis there set off by the Mexican devaluation of 1994. In just three years the number of financial institutions in Latin America shrank by anywhere from a sixth to a third and the amount of bank assets controlled by foreigners rose between threefold and fivefold; by 1997 more than half of Argentina's bank assets were in foreign hands. Three foreign firms—Britain's HSBC and Spain's Banco Santander and Banco Bilbao Vizcaya—which had earlier had a negligible presence in the region almost overnight came to dominate it through a judicious snapping-up of local bank assets that were forced onto the block by the crisis. It will be a surprise if Asia does not now relive this history.

Change is being forced foremost because most Asian banks—the "most" is not sloppy usage—are basically bankrupt. (For a snapshot, see Table 12.2.) Peak nonperforming loans (NPLs) in many countries were equal to 300 percent to 500 percent of bank equity. Relative even to plunging stock markets, bank shares collapsed everywhere. The final bank recapitalization bill for Asia (including Japan) may run to $400 billion. Governments (i.e., hapless taxpayers) will have to provide most of this, and they have already begun to do so: money spent on nationalizations rose from zero in 1996 to more than $12 billion in 1998. But new equity from

Table 12.2
**Financial Sector Restructuring (End-March 1999 or
Latest Available Data—Percent Unless Otherwise Indicated)**

	Indonesia	Korea	Malaysia	Thailand
Capitalization				
NPLs/total loans[1]	55	16	24	52
NPLs/GDP	22	23	35	53
Provisions/NPLs[2]	22	13	43	25
System capitalization[2]	−29	29	12	15
Financial Restructuring				
NPLs sold to AMC/total NPLs	51	42	23	—
Average discount of NPL purchase[3]	100	55/97	40	—
System recapitalization/GDP	35	8	2	14
Of which: Public funds	33	8	2	7
System recapitalization/estimated				
recap requirement[4]	—	31	40	51
Number of merged institutions[5]	5	4	12	18
Number of intervened institutions[6]	93	59	9	17
Number of closed institutions[7]	66	44	—	57
Merged institutions/system assets[8,9]	30	15	>20	16
Intervened institutions/system assets[9]	75	14	>20	12
Closed institutions/system assets	14	7	—	13

Source: International Monetary Fund

private sources—whether direct investors or through stock-market flotations—will be a crucial element as well. That is where the big changes in Asian banking are beginning.

First comes consolidation. Almost everywhere banks are uneconomically small. As noted in Chapter 2, even Japan's banks have meager revenues despite (or rather because of) their massive asset base. The situation is being rectified faster than it seems. In the mid-1990s Japan had 25 major banks and trust banks. Three went bust; of these, one (Hokkaido Takushoku) was taken over by a trust bank and the other two (Long Term Credit Bank and Nippon Credit Bank) were nationalized. LTCB was then sold to a consortium led by Ripplewood, an American private-equity firm. The government also made a deal to sell NCB to a Japanese group led by Softbank and including Orix, a leasing firm that is aggressively expanding into other lines of finance. In late 1999 three of the country's biggest banks—Industrial Bank of Japan, Dai-Ichi Kangyo Bank and Fuji Bank—agreed to merge with full effect in 2002. Based on actual and announced consolidations by mid-2000, the twenty-five banks of 1995 are now down to eight. The process is being widely replicated. Malaysia's fifty-five-odd banks are becoming ten, and the 230 or so of pre-crisis Indonesia's banks will end up as no more than two or three dozen. Consolidation does not in itself guarantee efficiency, but it is a necessary first step.

More modern banks also demand better management. Often, this is provided by foreigners. In Thailand, where banks used to be predominantly family affairs, only three banks remain in the control of their original family owners and in the biggest of the three—Bangkok Bank—the family has brought in professional managers, including foreigners, to tighten the managerial grip, especially over credit and risk analysis. Even in Indonesia, where a union-inspired nationalist backlash in 1999 sank plans by Standard Chartered to take over the bust Bank Bali, two other big failed banks were being run by Western CEOs by mid-1999.

Majority takeovers by foreign banks have not advanced as far in most of Asia as they did in Latin America during 1994–97, but progress has not been negligible either. Some foreign banks, like America's Citigroup, had long ago chosen to expand in Asia by building up their own operations rather than by making acquisitions and during the financial crisis simply continued doing so—succeeding handsomely at least in the case of Citigroup, which now gets more than $1 billion in earnings from Asia. Even in the most xenophobic markets like Japan (where LTCB was sold to a foreign consortium that then appointed a Citigroup-trained Japanese to run it) and South Korea (where Korea First Bank was sold to an American-led investment group in late 1999), foreign takeovers were no longer considered scandalous.

Yet probably the greatest strategic windfall from the crisis for a Western bank belonged to Holland's ABN-Amro. Rather ambitiously for a relative tiddler (with $500 billion in assets, it is only the world's sixth biggest bank), it is trying to follow the example of Citigroup and HSBC and be a bank with a global reach. When the crisis broke it had already decided on an aggressive expansion in Asia, largely because it was keen to raise its profitability (which as a share of revenues was only about half that of HSBC, the world's most profitable bank) and slow-growth markets in the West could not do the trick. In part, and in common with other western banks already established in Asia, ABN-Amro just passively benefited from general public disgust with the corruption and incompetence of local banks: in Indonesia, for instance, in the 18 months after the crisis hit, ABN-Amro's customer base rose sixfold as deposits effortlessly flowed out of mistrusted local accounts and into those of bank multinationals. But in the same 18 months the Dutch bank also spent $500 million buying distressed local banks in Thailand, Taiwan, the Philippines and India. Just what a difference this could make not only for ABN-Amro but for the local banking system was shown by the spectacular performance of Bank of Asia, a Thai bank that the Dutch firm took over in 1998. The family owners, say ABN-Amro executives who now run Bank of Asia, saw reality early in the crisis and sold out for about $190 million. The exact price was at first indeterminate, to be calculated later by a clever amalgam that allowed the buyer to hedge its exposure to then unfathomable bad loans and the selling family to benefit from future good performance. Performance proved to be very good indeed. Even a dollop of western management methods allowed the bank to run rings around the local competition; within a year and a half the $190 million ABN-Amro had paid for its share of Bank of Asia was valued by the Bangkok stock market at $750 million.

Lastly, Asian banks are not what they used to be. They used to be fonts of cash for corporate borrowers; now they think about retail consumers much more. There is an obvious reason for this, which is that corporate loans are a lot less profitable: loan spreads in Japan, for instance, were only 1.6 percent in 1999, compared to 4.7 percent at Chase

Manhattan, mostly because Japanese banks had a much higher share of corporate loans on their books. One way around this is to "securitize" corporate loans, the process of packaging loans as tradable securities and selling them on capital markets; but that will require the cozy nexus between companies and banks to be broken. Meanwhile, consumer loan books are expanding as economic growth shifts more toward consumption and away from capital investment, and instruments like credit cards come more into use.

For more than a decade, for instance, Japan's Suruga Bank, which used to be a minor regional player, has been building up its consumer business through new computer systems and a different product line-up and sales culture. Suruga's chairman, Okano Mitsuyoshi, who with his fancy razor haircut, trim suits and lavender shirts looks like nobody's idea of a Japanese banker, aims to increase the bank's consumer assets to half the total by 2003, up from 40 percent in 1999. Suruga has also been whittling the number of branches (down 15 percent in three years) and prodding its customers to do more telephone and Internet banking. It also started making deals with Softbank and others to build up its consumer business further. When he talks about the competition Mitsuyoshi does not even mention established banks: the firms he thinks about are Orix, Softbank, Ito-Yokado, Sony and Hikari Tsushin (see Chapter 11). That points the way to the future for Japanese and other Asian banks: the Tokyo stock market, having taken on board Suruga's profit-oriented consumer and remote-banking strategy, tripled the bank's share price in mid-1999 while other bank stocks remained basically unchanged.

. . . AND THEIR SWELLING ALTERNATIVES

Getting money from Asia's savers to its borrowers is one of the financial world's biggest businesses. The reason is that, by one estimate, Asia has half the world's stock of household savings: a pool worth some $14 trillion at the end of 1999, 85 percent of it in Japan. As bank loans shrink in relative importance and incomes rise, all the other transmission belts will be bolstered. And because finance is, along with technology, one of the most globalized industries, western investment bankers, fund mangers, pension-fund managers and insurers have already started swarming over Asia seeking to establish or entrench themselves.

The shift away from banking as a funding source for companies has already become clear. Throughout the crisis-hit Asia of 1997–98 the growth of bank loans was negative and loan-to-deposit ratios shrinking. According to Citigroup, syndicated loans in Asia peaked at $142 billion in 1997. They fell to $72 billion in 1998, the trough of Asia's brief descent, but in the strong economic recovery of 1999 recaptured ground only modestly, rising to about $100 billion—still 15 percent below their level in 1996. Meanwhile, issues of stocks and bonds were rising sharply.

Almost all of Asia's stock markets performed well in 1999, especially the "new economy" stocks (see Chapter 11). But what counts in terms of capital-raising by companies is new issues; these were up often spectacularly. After falling to $69 billion in 1998, Asia's new issues drew in some $105 billion in 1999, the highest figure ever, and the first time companies raised more from the stock markets than from banks. On Tokyo's various stock markets, around seventy firms raised about $70 billion in 1999. In South Korea 100 companies were listed on Kosdaq; at one point, optimistic investment bankers expected as many as 300 to be listed in 2000, but the market's poor performance beginning in the spring will dash that hope. Still, new Korean issues amounted to more than $12 billion in 1999, five times as much as the year before. But it was not just new firms driving the Korean boom. Because of government requirements that the *chaebol* reduce their debt–equity ratios, and new restrictions on their ability to issue bonds to replace bank loans, the conglomerates reluctantly turned to the stock market in 1999 (reluctantly because this dilutes the control of their family owners). Rights issues on the Seoul stock market in June 1999 alone amounted to almost $6 billion (more than the annual totals in 1990–97) and for 1999 as a whole were four times the previous high of about $11 billion in 1998. The upward sweep seems to be continuing. At the outset of 2000, companies in Asia outside Japan were expected to raise as much as $70 billion that year; if Japan chipped in another $90 billion or so, the overall Asian total would be half again as large as the 1999 record, and triple the rate in the mid-1990s.

What matters as much as the overall figures—which will be lower than bankers had hoped—is where the money is coming from. Institutional buyers like pension funds have been increasing their exposure, of course, but more significantly the mutual-fund culture that blossomed in America in the 1970s and 1980s and then began to make its way to continental

Europe in the mid-1990s seems to be arriving in Asia at last. In just three months in mid-1999, the Buy Korea Fund raised about $5.3 billion from small investors shifting their money out of low-interest bank and bond accounts. In Japan monthly sales of equity mutual-funds rose constantly from about $1 billion in December 1998 to nearly $20 billion a year later. Even more Japanese money is likely to be footloose in the years 2000–2002 as $1 trillion in postal savings accounts falls due and people start comparing the modest returns available there with what mutual-funds can offer. Elsewhere in Asia—notably Singapore, where the government-mandated provident fund is allowing the beneficiaries more choice about where their pension money is invested, and Hong Kong, which early in 2000 set up its own scheme—retail investors are also being given greater opportunity to scrutinize the performance of their savings. This matters so much because it should reinforce a trend that already became pronounced in 1999: the sharp distinction the market began drawing between firms delivering good returns (which money was flocking to) and those delivering poor ones (which investors were increasingly cashing out of).

Asian bond markets too are changing, although they may be less effective than stock markets at prodding companies to deliver better returns. Bond markets, like equities, bounced back in 1999, increasing the value of their new issues by 40 percent to $100 billion (about 10 percent ahead of syndicated loans). One feature of Asian bonds has not yet had much impact though it will gain in importance in the next few years. A large chunk of the money used by governments in most Asian countries to help recapitalize their wounded banks came in the form of government bonds that went on to the banks' books as capital. At the moment this debt is mostly inert, sitting quietly on bank balance sheets, but as the banks get back on their feet at least some of it could come onto Asia's ill-developed secondary markets for government-bond trading. This might complicate government efforts to run a steady monetary and currency policy, but it would have the advantage of creating a fairly large and liquid market that would allow all bonds to be priced more accurately and traded more smoothly.

Yet it is the corporate-bond market that in theory could provoke the most intriguing shake-up in the market for corporate control in Asia. Already by 1998–99 in Japan (by far the biggest corporate-bond market in Asia, with Korea a distant second), both domestic issues and offshore yen-denominated ones had reached record highs. These were conventional issues by well-thought-of borrowers, but even so they were helping to force a loosening of *keiretsu* ties and increased attention to capital-market demands. Similarly, in Thailand firms began resorting far more to the local-currency bond market, a move that allowed them to reduce their borrowing costs, pay down syndicated-loan debt and also sharply prune the number of their bankers (excessive numbers had been a big headache when restructuring efforts were undertaken in 1997–98). Yet these are all examples of companies already on their feet: the effect of more bond finance on the not-so-well managed could be deeper.

Recall that in America junk bonds filled two useful roles: allowing new companies to get financing that would otherwise have been out of their reach, and allowing insurgents to oust management that was not delivering adequate returns. At the moment, anyway, Asian start-ups have little trouble getting the money they need to grow because stock markets have been so liquid and the combination of venture capital, private equity and M&A (see next section) gives new sectors plenty of buoyancy. The same cannot be said for the needed function of tearing old and badly run companies limb from limb. Hostile takeovers are no longer unthinkable, even in Japan. In 1999 Britain's Cable & Wireless won a contested bid against a Japanese firm for control of IDC, a telecoms firm, and early in 2000 Boehringer Ingelheim, a German drugs company, took a controlling stake in SSP, a Japanese drugs group, in an unsolicited bid. More arrestingly, a young Japanese renegade (ex-MITI), backed by Orix, the leasing firm, launched a bid early in 2000 for a miserably performing mini-conglomerate called Shoei in what was the first postwar hostile bid for one Japanese company by another. But far more than this is needed. Goldman Sachs guessed in late 1998 that more than 40 percent of the companies on the main board of the Tokyo Stock Exchange had book values higher than their market capitalization—in other words, close to half of Japan's blue-chip companies would be worth more broken up and sold off than intact. By early 2000, the situation was not quite so dire, but it was not as much better as the overall stock-market rise since then might have suggested since that rise was concentrated very heavily in well-managed and new-era companies. There remains a crying need for methods and people prepared to unlock the immense asset values still lying immobilized in corporate Japan and the rest of Asia.

Can some Asian version of junk bonds help with the unlocking? There are one or two examples in Asia of them doing just what they are supposed to. Thailand's Nakornthai Strip Mill (NSM), a minimill steel producer whose $1.1 billion mill (the world's most expensive minimill) was still far from completion when the financial crisis hit Asia. To save NSM from collapse, advisers put together a deal that raised $650 million from American investors, $450 million of that in junk bonds. As part of the deal, the characteristically Thai tangle of interlocking companies and interests in NSM was cleaned up, and the company's founder agreed to let outside investors onto the board and give up majority control. Refreshingly, he said, "Whenever I have a choice between dignity and money, I choose money."

Carson Cole is dubious that there will be many such tales. Cole is one of Asia's longest-time debt specialists. In late 1999 he set up his own boutique firm, DebTraders (the capitalization could give the wrong impression of what the firm does), in Hong Kong to try to interest international investors in Asian junk bonds, but he thinks the institutional framework for the sort of revolutionary transformation that was accomplished in America in the 1970s and 1980s is lacking almost everywhere in Asia. For one thing, the market is just too small. Cole reckons that the face value of all Asian dollar-denominated junk bonds was a mere $50 billion in 1999, hardly enough to restructure a single big company. Second, securities regulation for high-yield bonds is utterly inadequate everywhere except Singapore. Third, the market participants that proved instrumental in supporting the American market—pension funds, insurance companies, financial institutions like S&Ls—have no counterparts in Asia: local institutions have been deeply averse to holding debt. Lastly, distribution is rudimentary. No firms in Asia have the capital base or powers of placement that Milken's team at Drexel Burnham did in the 1980s, or the clients with the appetite and depth of resources needed to support big issues. Asia shows no sign of being ready for a big breakthrough.

All that can and will change, perhaps quickly and especially in Japan, which commands almost 90 percent of Asia's pension-fund assets and more than 80 percent of life-insurance premiums. With a frighteningly large share of Japanese pensions unfunded and an insurance industry whose balance sheets are so weak they make those of Japan's banks look downright strapping, the pressure for improving yields is intense. Still, the embryonic development of bonds generally and junk bonds in particular makes it likely that the lion's share of pro-shareholder restructuring will come through the equity markets, which offer an exit strategy for and are backed by plentiful start-up money for newcomers, and through M&A takeovers.

VC, PE AND M&A

The distinctions between venture-capital, private-equity and merger-and-acquisition investments are not always sharp, but one thing for sure is that in Asia there have been very few of any of them until just recently. The early thinking, after it became clear in 1998 how severe a collapse Asia had suffered, was that a "fire sale" of Asian corporate assets would follow, allowing both local and international investors to lay their hands on promising companies and handsome market shares without paying much for them. That has in fact happened to a greater extent than anybody pre-crisis would have predicted (though not at prices that were as great a steal as anybody post-crisis had hoped), but purely in volume terms it shows less promise of shaking up Asian business than the disruptive effects of Asian Internet firms deploying their vast financial reserves do. That is not really any surprise when you think about how much the rise of the Internet in America changed a much deeper and more sophisticated financial system in the second half of the 1990s. Giving a certain number of listed firms almost unlimited free money in the form of a purchasing currency consisting of their own shares does allow them pretty much to call the shots. But it does raise the question what will happen to the remaking of the Asian corporate scene once Asia's own Internet bubble bursts.

Still, the accomplishments of the more traditional methods of transferring corporate control should not be underestimated. The least significant remains venture capital, which differs from private equity mostly in that venture capital buys into a business at an earlier stage. There has just not been much of this in Asia and only two places that even register: $7 billion in Japan (as noted above, 7 percent of the American level), with perhaps $3 billion more in Taiwan thanks to its strong technology base, its bias toward small companies and its familiarity with the ways of Silicon Valley. Part of the reason for the stunted state of VC in Asia is that the usual way for venture capitalists to cash out—through a stock-market listing of the company—has been widely obstructed. In Japan, for instance, "venture" capitalists would often come into a company only ten or even twenty years after it was founded, when (amazingly) it had still not met listing criteria. New stock markets all over Asia for "emerging" or "growth" companies will change that equation, and some foreign VC funds have already started exploratory work, especially in Japan. Second, says Hsu Ta-lin, the head of Taiwan-based Hambrecht & Quist Asia Pacific, in the past the Silicon Valley approach hasn't worked in Asia "because in the Valley high-tech start-ups are a home-run game, but since Asian start-ups aren't innovators they didn't hit home runs." So H&Q Asia concentrated on buying into firms just two or three years before they went public, when venture-stage financing had already been done by other means (see first section of this chapter). Yet, Hsu notes, this too is changing as some Asian firms actually do start to innovate and—surely more important—Internet stocks in Asia have proven they can smash home runs as powerful as any in America, even if using valuation yardsticks that are even more exaggerated.

Private-equity firms, which usually take minority stakes in already established but mostly unlisted companies, have been prowling Asia with bags-full of money. One Hong Kong-based financial consultant guessed in mid-1999 that as much as $10 billion-worth of international private equity was looking for investment deals in Asia. H&Q Asia's Hsu, whose firm had $1.5 billion in invested or investible funds in Asia by the end of 1999, says that whereas before he would buy only into firms that were on the way up, the pressures of the 1997–98 collapse opened the way to majority acquisitions of distressed companies. H&Q Asia's approach with these was to mount a fairly quick restructuring and then resell the firm to an international company in the same industry looking to expand in Asia.

M&A is hard to distinguish, especially in the statistics, from private-equity deals, but it tends to involve bigger deals and more often ones with listed companies; the acquiring company also—almost by definition—gets a high degree of managerial control. Overall, Asian M&A in 1999 expanded enormously, especially in Japan, where $78 billion-worth of deals were done, almost a 350 percent increase from the year before (see Chapter 5). The total for the rest of Asia was $82 billion, with South Korea on top with $19 billion (almost three times the level of 1998), Hong Kong next at $13 billion, China at $12.5 billion and Singapore at $9 billion. Throughout Asia, the two biggest lines of business for

M&A were telecommunications first and finance second (same as most of the rest of the world).

The numbers, especially for Japan, may look impressive at first glance but they need to be kept in perspective. In global terms the deal-making in Asia is still peanuts. America in 1999 had deals worth $1.7 trillion and Europe deals worth $1.2 trillion. A single acquisition in Europe launched in 1999 (though admittedly the biggest M&A deal in history), Vodafone AirTouch's takeover of Germany's Mannesmann, was by February 2000 worth $180 to $190 billion—20 percent to 25 percent again as much as all the deal-making in Asia in 1999. Australia, with an economy less than a tenth the size of Japan's, nonetheless had total M&A activity of $40 billion, half as big as Japan's. In fact, taking account of economic size does not give any more of an impression of vigorous M&A activity in Asia than the absolute numbers do. America's M&A deals equaled about 17 percent of its GDP, Japan's less than 2 percent of GDP. Even South Korea, which boasted Asia's most feverish M&A market, mustered deals worth less than 5 percent of GDP. Lastly, from a longer-term view, the M&A market in Asia outside Japan is not even growing very fast. The value of the deals in Asia ex-Japan was up 41 percent on the year before. But it was up only about $13 billion—or a bit more than 20 percent—on 1997, two years after a financial earthquake that was supposed to create a wealth of corporate shake-ups and consolidation. What is going on here?

First of all, the numbers for "pure" M&A in Asia understate matters considerably. Because of the financial turmoil of 1997–99, Asia's less sophisticated capital markets, the need to structure deals differently because of various corporate peculiarities (see next chapter), and the fact that privatization is just beginning in most of Asia, pure M&A represents far less of total restructuring there than in the West. If you add in items like asset sales, liquidations, privatizations, and various kinds of share swaps and debt conversions, the true total of M&A, broadly defined, is probably closer to $300 to $400 billion than $150 billion. Second, in relative terms too Asian M&A is understated. M&A always goes up when a stock market and economy are near peaks, as they certainly are in America and possibly also in Europe, so with Asia at the opposite point in its economic cycle in 1999 its share was bound to look artificially small. Third, this is just the beginning. M&A has been almost unheard-of in Asia before now, but it is spreading fast. If, to take the most extreme example, you could find anyone who at the end of 1996 predicted that Korea could have clocked up almost $19 billion of pure M&A in 1999 (a third of it from foreigners), you would be making him up. And, outside Japan at least (where in the first half of 2000 the value of deals was up only 6 percent on a year earlier), the pace of Asian M&A is accelerating: Asia ex-Japan deals in the first half were worth $87 billion, practically the same as in the whole of 1999. Fourth, the effect on the running of companies can be greater than the size of the deals alone would indicate. China's dismemberment of some of its SOEs through state-directed M&A (see Chapter 8) is having as deep an influence on corporate behavior in China as the specter of Milken did on American managers in the 1980s. Similarly, some Asian industries with strong leverage over their economies like the cement business (see next chapter), have been completely remade through a handful of M&A deals whose influence will spread far wider than the headline figures might suggest.

In the end, and provided the flood of money into Asian Internet companies outlasts the probable stemming of that flow to their American counterparts, the most influential shake-up will likely come from the investment funds deployed by the Internet firms. They are, after all, looking for everything old blue-chip Asia was not in terms of corporate management and financial returns. The big mistake for outsiders, however, would be to forget that the two-score million small businesses that really made modern Asia have been subject to severe financial disciplines all along, and that these are now beginning to percolate up to industries and companies foreigners can actually get their hands on. And, helping in Asia's makeover, the foreigners are getting their hands on them more and more.

CHAPTER

13

White Hunters

We have never valued ingenious articles, nor do we have the slightest need for your country's manufactures—
—*Qianlong, 1793*

Things have improved a lot in Asia, though not uniformly, since the Chinese Emperor Qianlong's famously contemptuous dismissal of King George III's offer of British technology in exchange for open trade. That came a couple of hundred years after China shut the doors, thinking it had no more to learn from anybody else, and thereupon entered almost a half-millennium of decline that was the most disastrous in its long history. Cutting off trade was a mistake that export-oriented post-1945 East Asia never made, but there has been much ambivalence about other contacts with foreign business. Almost every place except Hong Kong and Singapore had severe restrictions on foreigners buying significant stakes in local companies, and in Japan and Korea FDI was virtually unknown. Flows of portfolio capital and currency trading have often been sore points (remember the rants of Malaysia's Prime Minister Mahathir in 1997–98). Over the next decade, however, the forces of technology and globalization are likely to ensure that all of Asia will be more open to foreign business influence of all kinds than in the past. Western businessmen are going to find the interaction much more complex and reciprocal than they might think at first. True, they have world-class methods and technologies that locals mostly cannot match. But they will be operating in environments where a lot more needs to be mastered than objective skills, and where the local talent is quick to learn and ferocious at competing.

After the panic of 1998, when foreign private capital flows to Asia's emerging economies ebbed to less than $6 billion (compared to an all-time high of $176 billion in 1996), the money began to return in 1999 and should have done so much more strongly in 2000 (see Table 13.1, which importantly does not include Japan, Hong Kong and Singapore). In fact, one kind of money never left: foreign direct investment, which broadly reflects foreign firms' long-term view of prospects in the place where the money is going, actually rose for the developing countries of Southeast Asia even in 1998, and in Northeast Asia it boomed. Japan took in about $14 billion in 1999, almost five times as much as the year before. Korea absorbed some $12 billion in 1999, compared with $3 billion in 1996 and an average of $1 billion a year in the decade before that. The composition of capital flows also began changing. Presumably to everyone's relief, net foreign-bank lending has been shrinking, by a massive $60 billion in 1998 but also by appreciable amounts in 1999 and 2000, as borrowers pay off their loans. FDI is mostly holding steady overall but

Table 13.1
Asia/Pacific External Financing (Billions of Dollars)

	1996	1997	1998	1999[1]	2000[2]
Current account balance	−51.8	−2.8	95.2	64.7	51.2
External financing net	181.4	104.6	37.0	43.6	67.7
Private flows, net	176.3	67.9	5.8	39.3	59.4
Equity investments, net	62.7	57.9	60.2	69.5	72.0
Direct investment, net	45.4	51.9	55.2	54.6	53.6
Portfolio investment, net	17.2	6.0	4.9	14.9	18.4
Private creditors, net	113.7	10.0	−54.3	−30.2	12.6
Commercial banks, net	80.2	−13.3	−58.5	−30.7	−14.2
Nonbanks, net	33.4	23.4	4.2	0.5	1.6
Official flows, net	5.0	36.7	31.2	4.3	8.3
International Financial Institutions	0.3	24.7	22.1	−3.2	5.0
Bilateral creditors	4.8	12.0	9.1	7.6	3.3
Resident lending ≠ other, net[3]	−74.9	−92.8	−80.7	−53.5	−70.1
Reserves (= increase)	−54.6	−8.9	−51.5	−54.7	−48.7

[1] = estimate
[2] = forecast
[3] Including net lending, monetary gold, and errors and omissions.
Source: International Monetary Fund

portfolio investment—remember all those new IPOs—is shooting up, having tripled between 1998 and 1999. As for the geographic source of all this, in the case of FDI and international M&A (which overlap more and more) America tends to pour about half into Japan, with Europe accounting for most of the rest. America provides 35 percent or so elsewhere in Asia, Continental Europe another 20 percent, and Japan and Britain 15 percent each.

Why does all this foreign money think it is going to get what it wants out of Asia—i.e., good returns? In the case of much of the new portfolio investment and all of the FDI—which is what this chapter is mostly about and why the FDI figures didn't even flicker during the financial crisis—the explanation is that unless something goes catastrophically wrong over the next 10 to 20 years Asia is going to outperform the West economically twofold to threefold. The reasons for this were set out in the last section of Chapter 9. To Asia's basic strengths is now added something missing before: a partial reform of corporate and financial systems that will allow superior economic performance to be translated more fully into corporate returns. If you believe that is true, and a lot of western companies clearly do (a survey by the Boston Consulting Group showed that by 1999 not a single one of the 100 top Western multinationals in Asia had left), then the arithmetic is overwhelming. Asia has 60 percent of the world's population but only about a quarter of gross world product, with twice the economic growth rate of the West and an age profile that (except in Japan) is a maximum of half as old as the West's. It should therefore be in a position to generate market growth and increases in cash-flow substantially greater than in the West. Take your pick of businesses—infrastructure, capital goods, financial services, consumer markets most of all—and you find penetration levels that are vastly below those in rich countries but which should now rise breathtakingly. Car-makers, for instance, think that fully 70 percent of the growth in the world car market in the years 2000 to 2005 will come in Asia. Provided Asia can generate the economic growth (though not even that necessarily, see next section), and the transmission between that growth and corporate profits is now engaged, it would be mad to stay away.

One example from the crisis days shows how much can be at stake (and belies some of the grumbles about how few opportunities the crisis threw up for foreigners). Cement is a global industry dominated by six multinationals that nonetheless have to build up a strong local presence because the product can profitably be transported long distances only by

sea. For a long time the big six—five from Europe and one from Mexico—
have wanted to break into the Asian market. I got an inkling of how keen
they were in late 1996, when Lorenzo Zambrano, the head of Cemex (an
NYSE-listed firm that is now the world's third-biggest cement producer),
gathered his top executives in the Mexican resort of Cancun and among
other things had them listen to presentations about Asia from imported
specialists. The executives, whose experience was basically confined to
the Americas, were bemused by the exotic tales they heard, but Zambrano, a no-nonsense Stanford MBA, made it clear to them that expanding in Asia was now going to be Cemex's highest priority. The trouble
was how to do it. Asia was full of home-grown cement producers which,
at the height of the Asian construction boom, were adding capacity
hand-over-fist. In such a competitive market starting from scratch
seemed undesirable, but the cash-flush locals had no interest in selling
assets either. Cemex nonetheless started hunting for acquisitions but in
the next year came up with little more than potential alliances and minority stakes.

The financial typhoon hit Asia. Perhaps because they are in an
unglamorous and highly competitive industry that governments have
never been greatly interested in, or perhaps because their foreign debts
were enormous, cement companies in Southeast Asia mounted few of the
delaying tactics to foreign takeovers that their counterparts in many other
businesses did. In 1998, the year of the cement deal in Southeast Asia,
about fifteen takeovers of local independents by Western multinationals
were completed, with a total value of more than $1 billion. Switzerland's
Holderbank led the way with six deals, and Cemex completed three.

The window of opportunity was narrow. Within a year most of the attractive local partners had been nabbed, and the price for taking over
enough existing capacity to produce a metric ton of cement a year had
risen from $70 to $150, close to the cost of building a new plant with the
same capacity. The industry was already being restructured to come up to
international norms, in part because of the new multinational bosses
brought into many of the operations, but importantly also because even
those that remained independent, like Siam Cement, began ruthlessly
slimming themselves to compete with near neighbors that had been taken
over, like Siam City Cement (now under Holderbank's control, with a
Swiss managing director), and had then begun showing how much efficiency could be introduced. The multinationals raised their stake in Asian

cement capacity from less than 20 percent to 60 percent in less than two years. One global competitive benefit of this for the multinationals was the ability to export cement by sea to their rivals' Western markets, off a cost base that even including transportation was as much as 30 percent lower. Far more important for the long term is that cement's big six have more or less overnight dominantly entrenched themselves in a region that, because of its construction needs, is almost sure to be the fastest-growing cement market in the world over the next generation—and they have done so from what seemed, before 1997, to be a precariously marginal position.

Unless Asia crashes again, the chances of a jackpot of that size and scope in another industry are slim. Yet even if less dramatically, almost all multinationals have taken advantage of the crisis to try to figure out how to expand their Asian operations and improve their profitability, and those efforts are now being redoubled. But there are a lot of choices to be made about how to do it.

CRISIS AND RECOVERY

Even for businesses that are in Asia for the long haul there were some mind-boggling crisis-management issues, see next paragraph, but in a strategic sense the crisis was just the blip it was optimistically advertised to be when it started. It nonetheless opened some important questions, whose answers differed depending on where a business stood in a useful descriptive scheme developed by the Boston Consulting Group (BCG). There has always been a dual character to foreign investment in Asia: whether to try to use the place as an export platform to launch products and services into the rich world, or as a way to position yourself for an attack on what should prove one day to be amazingly big local markets. BCG found that both in responses to the crisis and in rebuilding for its aftermath there were two kinds of multinationals active on the local-market front—those that already had a significant presence and made money and those that didn't have either presence or much in the way of profit. On the export front there was pre-crisis only one sort of company: the kind that used Asia as a significant link in its global supply chain. All three, the two local types and the one export-led, were affected differently by the crisis itself. Now all are reacting similarly: deciding how, as the world's cement giants did, to reorganize their operations and grow their Asian business the most profitably.

However, in any discussion with people who were on the front lines at the time, do not open by telling them there was no crisis. No multinationals faced worse problems than those in Indonesia. A telling case was that of Novartis Indonesia (NI), the Indonesian operation of a big Swiss "life-sciences" company that deals in prescription and generic drugs, agribusiness and nutrition. Formed by a 1996 merger between two other Swiss firms, Ciba-Geigy and Sandoz, Novartis had a minor presence in Asia (which contributed only 4 percent of the group's worldwide drug sales in 1997) but an ambition "to be the leading healthcare company in Asia and grow each year at least 2 percent faster than the market." That was ambitious enough, but first NI's new country head, a Swede named Jan Eriksson, had to execute a merger of the Indonesian subsidiaries of the global merger partners, a task that not only took great effort internally (both had wayward local partners that had to be brought around) but also brought Eriksson face-to-face with the reality of dealing with the Indonesian bureaucracy, a task that was about to become a lot harder thanks to the financial crisis and political turmoil. Government approval was needed for the local merger, which Eriksson said

> on the surface looked very easy. We submitted the name change to the Ministry of Justice in May. We heard nothing. In November they told us they were not satisfied with our articles of association. We discussed it with Basel [the Swiss capital, Novartis's world headquarters] and local shareholders and resubmitted them in one day. They said okay and nothing happened. When we get the name, it is not the end. The articles are published in a state newspaper. You get a certificate. You go to different ministries—the Ministry of Manpower and down the list—to inform them that you are going to change the name. It is unbelievable. You have a lot of meetings and fill out many forms and submit everything in five copies. Business is not done on the phone. You have to see people. We have 15 binders on this merger.

In all, a merger that should have taken two months to carry out took two years. Meanwhile, the financial crisis broke. NI's 1998 budget had been agreed to in September 1997 on the assumption of an average exchange rate of 3,000 rupiah to the dollar. Four months later the rupiah was at 15,000 to 17,000 and fluctuating violently. Just when Eriksson had planned to get started in earnest on an ambitious five-year growth plan, he had to cope with financial chaos combined with food shortages and street riots. The one unambiguously positive thing was that, unlike a lot of companies doing business in Indonesia (and almost all Indonesian ones), NI began hedging its foreign-currency exposure in early 1997, a move that a year later had forestalled losses of about $40 million.

But Eriksson also faced other problems: retaining his workforce when operating costs in hard-currency terms were soaring well beyond budget, and handling both emergency and long-term strategy for product lines in very different situations. His decision was to concentrate on preserving or better yet increasing market share in lines where NI had a relatively weak position (patented drugs and generics) by investing in marketing and increasing output without raising prices as much as costs. This strategy was designed to take advantage of competitors that were in even worse shape than NI. Eriksson also hoped to take advantage of industrial distress by acquiring a local over-the-counter drug maker (a line NI had not before been in) while the price was good. This expansionary part of the strategy was to be paid for, Eriksson hoped, first of all by a budget increase but also by maintaining profitability in a business (selling raw materials for the local manufacturing of antibiotics) where NI had a lot of market share and hence some pricing power. The reasoning behind this combination of strategies was that Indonesia would bounce back in a year or two and, if so, NI should keep its losses meanwhile to a minimum while still expanding its operations as much as possible during the downturn to take advantage of the eventual comeback.

Convincing headquarters of this was another matter. Eriksson came up with his plan in January 1998, and regional headquarters said it could arrange a meeting on the subject in about 90 days. Given the pace of events in the financial markets and in Jakarta's riot-torn streets, that would have been about 89 days too late. So Eriksson got the two bosses to whom he reported—one in Singapore, the other in Austria—to do rolling monthly plans that ignored the budget ("the first time I have ever seen this in a multinational," Eriksson laughs). It mostly worked. Profitability in the raw materials business was largely maintained in 1998, and in drugs NI at last started gaining instead of losing market share (though by 2000 it had still not become number one). Eriksson did not have to lay off anyone for economic reasons and by 2000 NI had more employees than just before the crisis. Also by 2000 NI's revenues had returned to their 1997 level (not bad in an economy that was 15 percent smaller), vindicating Eriksson's mid-crisis view of Indonesia's potential for a comeback and leading him to think business in Indonesia was going to be good for the next several years.

Not every multinational in crisis-hit Asia faced a nightmare as har-rowing as that, but all had to decide just what the balance was between crisis and opportunity and act accordingly. The multinationals that at first had the roughest time were, seemingly oddly, those in BCG's first cate-gory: ones that had already established substantial profitable local opera-tions in Asia and were looking to grow them vigorously. Examples from this category include Coke, Gillette, Unilever, Avon and Nestle. Their problem—which for many, notably Coke and Gillette, was still nagging at their share price even in 2000—was that they really were global com-panies, with significant streams of revenues and profits from Asia and other emerging markets. In fact, in pre-crisis days some of the cleverer analysts came up with the sales angle that, although you couldn't buy Asian exposure through Asian companies without sacrificing corporate transparency and shareholder rights, you could do so through companies like Coke while still enjoying spic-and-span corporate governance.

The sales patter seems to have worked too well. When Asia started being seen by investors as at best volatile and possibly worse, the shares of Coke and the like began underperforming. Although by 2000 the global firms were tinkering with branding and the like to spruce up their perfor-mance, none had recoiled from a strategy of expansion in Asia. Coke, Gillette and Nestle, for example, all made significant acquisitions in Asia during the crisis. The globals will probably have the last laugh, especially once the American stock markets rebalance themselves after the pro-tech excesses of the late 1990s. BCG's analysis of Coke's position in Asia, for in-stance, showed that in the decade after 1988 almost 80 percent of growth in per capita consumption of Coke came from population growth (8 per-cent) and increased market penetration (70 percent), with only the minor remaining share from GDP growth in the decade when Asia's economies were booming most. This implies that, even in the extremely unlikely event that Asia's economic growth falters year after year, the overall market-growth opportunities remain at least three-quarters intact.

The second sort of multinational did not have much of a local Asian position, profitable or otherwise, before the crisis so the immediate im-pact of it on these firms' global performance was lighter and the open-ings it created for bigger market share in Asia more tempting. At least one of these companies, General Electric, took advantage of the crisis to increase the size of its Asian operations dramatically (see the last section of this chapter). One whole industry in which foreigners were able to grab market share easily was non-luxury retailing. In 1998 Wal-Mart, which has still not found the translation of its ultra-American culture into foreign markets all that smooth, nonetheless bought four super-stores in Korea and six sites for future development, at the same time beginning an expansion program in China to bring the number of its stores there up to nine by 2001. In 1997–99 Carrefour, a French hypermarket operator, more than doubled the number of its stores in Asia. And, after years of study, Carrefour decided in 1999 that the Japanese market was at last cracking open. It plans to open its first Japanese store in 2001, with the idea of expanding eventually to at least 65 stores. Even in seemingly dismal Indonesia Carrefour and Promodès, another French retailer whose 1999 merger with Carrefour created the world's second-biggest retailer (after Wal-Mart), put up five stores in the depth of the downturn and did so well that by the end of 1999 the merged firm were planning three more. The opportunities kept coming: in late 1999 the Philippines changed the law to allow 100 percent foreign ownership of retail outlets for a two-year period, and in mid-2000 Metro, a German group that is Europe's second-biggest retailer, announced that it would expand its existing Asian operations from China into Vietnam and Japan.

As an industry, though, it was western carmakers that made the widest bids to build up a significant presence in Asia. It is not surprising when you think that Asian car sales should amount to about $60 billion in 2000 and the market is growing at 8 percent to 10 percent a year, compared with almost no growth in North America or Western Europe. The highest-profile push into Asia as the century ended was Renault's purchase of a 37 percent stake in Japan's Nissan in the spring of 1999 and the installation of one of the French car company's managers, a Brazilian-born Frenchman named Carlos Ghosn, as Nissan's chief operating officer. The outcome will matter as much for the fate of corporate restructuring in Japan (see Chapter 5) as it does for Renault's global ambitions.

While he was at Renault itself, Ghosn earned the nickname he hates, *le cost-killer,* for his role in a $4.8 billion restructuring in 1996 that put Renault back in the black. Less than six months into his new job at Nissan, Ghosn announced a restructuring so radical that it would have been inconceivable before at any big Japanese firm. He proposed cutting costs by almost $10 billion (20 percent) over three years through staff reductions of 21,000 (14 percent of the workforce), by shutting five plants and reducing capacity by 30 percent, by cutting overheads 20 percent (mainly through fewer dealerships in Japan) and by chopping the number of parts suppliers to Nissan by half and requiring the survivors to cut their prices by 20 percent. He wants to use the savings in part to raise capital investment by a third, to 5 percent of sales, and aims to get Nissan to break-even point by March 2001. Astonishingly for Japan (though with flawless logic for a global company) the lion's share of the cuts will come in Japan rather than overseas. It is a huge gamble (Renault invested $6 billion in Nissan for its controlling 37 percent stake), especially in Japan's business culture, but Renault felt it had no choice. Even in Europe it is a middling carmaker, and at the time of the Nissan foray it was selling 85 percent of its cars there. Renault had no presence to speak of in America or Asia, and in both places Nissan has a foothold however poorly maintained. After a couple of other failed acquisition attempts, it was an Asian firm that offered Renault its only realistic hope, however much of a long shot, to go global (and, with luck, survive). The Asian theme seemed to appeal to Renault even beyond Nissan: in April 2000 it also bought Korea's Samsung Motors for $550 million.

Renault was not the only one thinking along these lines. In the spring of 2000 DaimlerChrysler made a bid for a third of Japan's Mitsubishi Motors, a deal that would make it the third biggest carmaker in the world. And General Motors and Ford, which as recently as the 1970s had dominated foreign car sales in Asia until the Japanese practically wiped them off the map, have also leapt on the chance that the crisis and Japan's decade-long woes have given them to push their way back into contention. GM has been particularly intent on regaining market share in Asia; it has a publicly announced target of 10 percent by 2004, up from 4 percent in 2000. GM has done this in part by building its own factories—two joint-venture plants in China and one of its own in Thailand—but it is pinning most of its hopes on a complicated set of alliances in Japan and on a big acquisition in Korea. GM has technology-sharing agreements with Toyota and Honda. More important, its Japanese equity alliances, with Isuzu, Suzuki and (as of early 2000) Fuji Heavy Industries (which makes Subaru cars), are based on minority stakes that GM hopes will give it not just an entree to the Japanese market but also models and distribution channels for Southeast Asia.

GM also mounted a vigorous attempt to take over Korea's bankrupt Daewoo Motors. It is easy to see why. In all, Korean-owned capacity for making two million cars a year was for sale in early 2000 (including the Samsung unit eventually captured by Renault), but Daewoo was by far the juiciest item on the menu. Taking it over would give immediate access to 25 percent of the Korean car market, Asia's second biggest. More significantly, it would give a big boost to any carmaker's global ambitions. Daewoo's cars have begun selling well in America, its Polish plant gives access to Eastern Europe, and Korea itself is an excellent launch pad for an export push into the rest of Asia, especially China. So it is not surprising that GM—whose share of the world car market has fallen below 16 percent while that of Ford (number two in the world) has been rising toward that level—made a generous $6 billion offer to Daewoo's creditors in late 1999. But the Korean government decided to throw the bidding open, and five companies (four of them foreign) entered the contest: GM in concert with Italy's Fiat, its new global partner; DaimlerChrysler, together with Hyundai Motors in which it had taken a 10 percent stake; and Ford on its own. In June 2000, Ford won exclusive negotiation rights for the Daewoo purchase. Having seen the books and the opeations, Ford backed out of the talks in September, reviving GM's hopes that it might land Daewoo Motors after all.

The third type of company in BCG's taxonomy comes at this from the opposite direction; these are the exporters from Asian production sites that are now using their Asian resources to exploit local markets as well. The obvious examples are chip and computer makers, and consumer-goods producers like Nike and Reebok. Companies in this position are interesting because if they were already on hand in Asia when the crisis struck, they were actually able to strengthen their cash flow from the region as exports boomed in 1998–99. On top of that, they could use the disarray to go shopping for local assets or distribution chains that would allow them to expand Asian sales once the storm blew over. Such a dual-function view of Asia was behind many of the deals that global multinationals enthusiastically closed during 1998–99. The cement takeovers and some of the car deals mentioned above are the biggest examples, but there were plenty of others. BASF, a German chemicals company, was particularly attuned to this opportunity and made several acquisitions, notably the takeover of Daesang's lysine business in South Korea, which was useful for sales to customers worldwide but also ideal for sales into neighboring China (see Chapter 9). Likewise, Volvo's acquisition of Samsung Heavy Industries' construction-equipment division not only gave it access to North Asia's booming markets but also fit perfectly into its global strategy by filling a big hole in its product line.

With foreign expansion sure to continue in Asia, one way some will go about it is to go it alone, as Carrefour and Citibank have done (though Citibank, for one, is no purist about this if it can find the right acquisition). Yet the preferred route is likely to remain acquisitions. The distressed-sales opportunities seemed to be almost over as 1999 drew to a close, but that was probably wrong. In Thailand and Indonesia particularly, but also in South Korea (witness Daewoo Motors), the bite of bankruptcy laws and the disposal of industrial properties following on the clean-up of bank balance sheets may just be starting to put companies and their assets up for sale. In any event, a lot more Asian companies than before, having learned some lessons from 1997–98, will prove willing to sell stakes to foreigners. That will raise the same questions over the next few years that crisis-years deals did: what is the best way for a western company to do them?

MATING RITUALS

In more innocent days, when possibilities in Asia seemed boundless and risks trivial, decisions about foreign investment were simpler. And since the nuts and bolts of FDI can seem a rather dry subject, it may be best to begin with the human angle—or "the Tanamur factor," as a direct-investor friend of mine in Hong Kong describes it. The Tanamur is an extremely successful nightclub in Jakarta. It is a centrally located but fairly down-at-heel disco on two levels that is packed late almost every night with a mixture of foreigners and, on the lower level, slim Indonesian girls and, on the upper, somewhat fay Indonesian boys. Most of the youngsters are happy to go home with foreigners for the night for a fee. They are professionals in a way but freelancers, and the place is also full of couples, both foreign and local. No visitor feels guilty or sordid that he (or she, for there are plenty of them too) is on hand. The Tanamur factor, in my friend's lexicon, is the feeling of being comfortable with the place you're investing in, the instinct that you can sort of relax there. It is one reason why Thailand, for instance, got as much FDI as it did. When they are being honest, not many westerners disagree that the Tanamur factor had quite a bit to do with the pattern of pre-crisis foreign investment in Southeast Asia.

The story is a bit mischievous (albeit entirely accurate, ask any investment banker who travels in the region), but gets at a lingering truth—no, not that one—about investing in Asia. For all the coming improvements in corporate disclosure and governance, this is still a region whose cultural and other complexities make its reality almost unfathomable to the vast majority of western companies. This puts a premium, in all but the biggest deals, on a certain level of instinctive comfort and trust in a relationship. For some time to come, such rapport will mainly drive deals even after the due-diligence corps has had its say.

Or tried to. Accounting and disclosure standards in most of Asia remain so low that it takes Herculean efforts for a would-be buyer to have any confidence at all that he is buying what he thinks he is. Documentation of loans is haphazard, and few Asian firms yet keep their books according to internationally recognized standards. In 1997–98 Citibank was looking at a takeover of First Bangkok City Bank (FBCB) in Thailand. For three to four months Citibank had 100 professionals combing FBCB's books and at the end of the process still had no clear idea what FBCB's liabilities added up to, let alone exactly to whom they were owed. Citibank gave up on the deal. Even when the accounting is not sloppy it can be opaque. For example, until new laws come into effect in the next couple of years, in both Japan and Korea industrial groups are not required to consolidate their accounts to reflect the financial performance of subsidiaries they control. That is even more worrying than it sounds. Korea's entire *chaebol* structure has rested on cross-shareholdings among companies in a related group and on cross-guarantees of related firms' debts; to a lesser extent the same has been true in Japan as well.

Nor is it always easy for a buyer to figure out who has the legal power to dispose of a firm or its assets. In pre-crisis days it was common in Thailand, for instance, for a company to have upwards of 30 creditors, each likely (unbeknownst to the others) to have a lien against the same collateral. And, in the murky world of Asian business, control is not a simple matter of ownership of shares. Koh Boon Hwee, head of Wuthelam Holdings, a Singapore investment firm, notes that in the Chinese family-owned companies of Southeast Asia the founding entrepreneur or his children are often able to call the shots even with ownership shares below 30 percent.

All these hazards explain a couple of peculiarities in the Asian M&A world that are likely to outlast crisis-era deals by at least a few years. The first is that most acquirers have had a long-standing relationship with the target company. That way it's a lot easier to know what you're getting into, which is where the Tanamur factor comes into its own. This is why so many deals involved a western joint-venture partner buying out its local partner's interest (as BASF did with two of its Korean partners, Hanwha and Hyosung) or buying down its partner's interest (as Procter & Gamble did in late 1997 by purchasing a further 11 percent stake in its China joint venture and taking management control of it from its Hong Kong conglomerate partner). Other investors, notably Coke in the case of a Korean and a Thai bottler, expanded by increasing stakes in companies they have long had relations with. Even divorces have not altogether ruptured ties. One reason GM was so keen on Daewoo is that, until it sold its stake in frustration in 1992 over its inability to control the Korean carmaker, it owned half of it; getting reacquainted would have taken less time and presented less risk than getting acquainted would. The second peculiarity is that sales of going concerns or whole companies have been rare. The reason is that cross-shareholdings and cross-guarantees make it much safer for an acquiring company to take over only specific assets from which the liabilities have been stripped. Practically every deal in the early years of Asia's restructuring era has been done this way, and the method will prove indispensable until laws on accounts consolidation and the unwinding of cross-guarantees actually take effect.

A thorny question, especially during the market turbulence of 1998, has always been valuation. Potential acquirers have tended to divide into two camps—understandably, in view of their different purposes and payback horizons. Purely financial investors—buyers, say, of corporate debt in Southeast Asia—find that price is a big issue, since a good price is all that makes a high-risk financial investment worthwhile. "Strategic" investors, companies that are in the same line of business as the target and that therefore in effect are entering into a long-term business-development partnership, are looking ahead five to ten years for their returns and are therefore willing to pay more.

Even so, and even in the better times that began in 1999, the perceptions of both classes of buyers are more at odds with those of sellers than they are in deal-making in the West. Part of the reason for this is that because of the opacity of company accounts the usual valuation measures produce vague answers. This uncertainty is why many deals have involved contingent payments so that the ultimate purchase price would depend in part on the performance of the company in the year or two after the sale was made.

But there are fundamental differences in thinking as well. Recall that most lending in Asia has been based on assessments, however inaccurate, of the value of collateral rather than on guesses about future earnings discounted at an appropriate interest rate. Because owners of companies have been inclined to think in the same way as their bankers, they have been very reluctant to sell assets at any sum below the value at which they were booked. Western buyers look at it from the other end of the telescope, worrying more about future cash-flow than about what was originally paid for an asset. The older Asian way of thinking is being overtaken, especially in younger industries, by new events, but for many acquisitions of older concerns the difference in perception will continue to matter for a long time.

The biggest issue in an acquisition, however, is how to manage it afterward. Should an acquiring firm take majority control or not? Should it bring in its own managers? Should traditional (i.e., seniority lockstep) methods of compensation be changed? These are not technical questions. Outside Japan most Asian companies are really family firms (and even inside Japan the firm is often thought of as a family), so parting with a significant share of it can be a highly emotional matter. Rajiv Lall, who was involved in negotiations throughout Asia in the late 1990s for Warburg Pincus, a private-equity firm, says "the human dimension in these deals is extremely important." This is why the talks can be so protracted. It is a process, Lall explains, of establishing a dialogue so that the target can get to know the acquirers and see that they really have something to offer.

Hunters are sharply divided in their views about ownership and managerial control. Wuthelam's Koh, for example, thinks that, because of the penchant of Chinese family firms to keep a secretive grip on the business, an acquirer has little choice but to take majority control if he wants to protect his investment fully. A lot of American firms, under pressure from headquarters to maintain uniform standards around the globe, tend to agree. But many think otherwise. Trevor MacMurray, who until early 2000 was head of McKinsey & Company in Singapore, says that in his experience an insistence on majority control can lead to years of unproductive infighting in an acquired company; if you are buying a company for its unique strengths, he reasons, rather than simply to get a foothold in the market, then you want to bring existing management into the revamped operation as much as possible. It may seem perverse to keep on managers who are often responsible for having steered a company into the ditch, but Lall for one points out that a strong team of local managers is indispensable for a foreign owner in any event and that in operational terms—as distinct from financial ones—pre-crisis management in Asia was not at all bad. What he looks for is simply some way "to exercise a meaningful influence on local management," not to replace it.

Nelson Chang agrees. This Taiwanese businessman runs part of the direct-investment portfolio of Taiwan's billionaire Koo family, at least until he can retire in the next couple of years to his ranch in Montana and take care of his twelve horses and 200 head of cattle. Meanwhile, Chang sighs, getting back to business, corporate Asia in the late 1990s experienced "not so much a failure at the operating level as at the balance-sheet level." His approach to acquisitions is to focus on getting the balance sheet in good shape but in other respects to treat the existing owners and managers "not as adversaries but as partners." He points out:

> You need to give them some upside. Why should they sell if they get nothing? You can't say, I'm in, you're out. It won't work. You have to be multidomestic rather than multinational. You can't get rid of the managers. Even when you control the company, you don't outvote, you persuade.

Chang relies on the finance side for control. He usually engineers just one managerial change: his own man as CFO. The only supervisory reins he insists on keeping in his own hands are finance in general and risk control in particular, and the only operational policy he demands is complete transparency not just in the books "but in every internal document." Otherwise, technology sharing and other forms of cooperation among his various acquisitions are the norm, and local managers remain in charge of operations.

For most Western multinationals, says MacMurray, the first phase of their Asian adventure—getting established—is over, and the second phase—consolidating and rationalizing their operations—is beginning. Looking ahead, Philippe Lasserre, an Asian specialist at INSEAD, a French business school with a branch in Singapore, thinks that the next phase for Western multinationals in Asia will be shaped by the increasing openness of the regional economy to the rest of the world and (thanks to the lowering of tariffs and other barriers) within Asia itself. The global integration of Asia will lead foreign firms to think of the region more in terms of what makes sense for their worldwide operations than what Asia's own peculiarities might otherwise require (for a detailed example, see the last section of this chapter, on General Electric). And thanks to greater regional openness, Lasserre foresees more integrated management and cross-border activities for multinationals in ex-Japan Asia, and fewer independent country operations. There is, he says, one exception, for size and other reasons: China.

AS CHINA OPENS

After a spectacularly botched negotiation in Washington, DC, in April 1999—when President Clinton turned down a Chinese offer for terms of admission to the World Trade Organization (WTO) that even longtime friends of organized labor thought was fantastically favorable to the United States—America and China at last agreed in November 1999 on a deal under which China could get into the WTO. It took a terrific months-long fight to get the American Congress to approve "permanent normal trading relations" (i.e., nonreviewable by Congress and nondiscriminatory) for China in the fall of 2000, and a last-ditch negotiation with both America and the European Union to dot all the i's and cross all the t's, but at last China looked sure to be admitted by early 2001. This opening of the Chinese economy, the greatest since Deng Xiaoping got the ball rolling in 1978, will create the most significant long-term business opportunity for foreigners in Asia over the next generation. It will not, however, be an effortless opportunity to seize: China's opening is a good illustration of how the scope for doing business in Asia can increase dramatically but at the same time how tough competitive conditions can be even—or perhaps more—when the playing field is leveled.

But begin with the advantages. The first effects foreigners notice will undoubtedly be positive because operating conditions will improve. For example, lower tariffs and the gradual elimination of quotas will make a welcome difference, especially for American and Australian farmers. They are much more efficient than their Chinese counterparts; with the conversion of agricultural quotas to tariffs, they could easily double their exports to China. This will also matter significantly for car exporters. In 2000, cars and parts were subject to tariffs as high as 100 percent. By 2005 these are to fall to 25 percent and 10 percent respectively. China has also agreed to clean up the opaque quota and licensing system that imposes even more obstacles than tariffs do.

For multinationals on the ground in China even more is at stake. Despite their huge FDI commitment ($300 billion by the end of 1999) it was clear that foreign businessmen were feeling a sense of "China fatigue."

Multinationals coming in during the 1980s and early 1990s were promised fair market access in exchange for investments of money, people and technology. But the promised access was not forthcoming, leading foreign investors to be increasingly fed up with what one seasoned American in China described as "fueling an insiders' game that learns just enough from the West to set up a spoils system." The grumbling was never very convincing—at the height of the complaints, in 1999, FDI inflows into China were still $40 billion, much higher than the complainers had been predicting. In the words of INSEAD's Lasserre, even without near-term profits "the downside for a Western multinational of 'missing' China is just too frightening." But that is a negative reason. WTO membership is the jolt that is needed to give a strong positive push to the next decade of foreign investment.

Overall, guessed Goldman Sachs in a study published early in 2000, the openings WTO would produce both for China and for multinationals will be extremely wide. Goldman thought China's total annual foreign trade would rise to $600 billion by 2005. If so, and trade between European Union members were disregarded, China would probably then be the world's fourth biggest trading nation after America, Japan and Germany. The same year FDI inflows could reach $100 billion, more than any country including the United States had ever received up until the early 2000s. Goldman reckoned that by 2005 there would be 16 multinationals making more than $1 billion a year in revenues from China: eight American, five Japanese and three European. Another 14 would double their revenues to the hundreds of millions by 2003–2005.

The biggest expansion will come in services, where American firms in particular are at their most competitive globally. The range is wide. By the end of the century, Exxon already had 25 service stations in the Pearl River Delta just north of Hong Kong. Exxon guessed in 1999 that WTO membership would smooth the path for doubling that and getting enough economies of scale to make serious money. Foreign ownership of telecoms services, hitherto flatly prohibited, is to be opened in phases—a juicy concession in the world's fastest-growing telecoms market. Finance is not to be opened to the same degree, but that does not unduly fuss western bankers, who tend to think China is so far behind them that any improvement at all will amount to free extra market share.

But the entertainment business will have no reason to complain. Michael Primont, an American who came to China in the mid-1990s to set up the Beijing office of Cherry Lane Music, one of the biggest American music publishers, managed by the late 1990s to collect about $10 million in royalties in China for his clients. He guessed that sum would grow to hundreds of millions of dollars "when the doors to the outside world open—and the biggest door to the outside is the WTO." Hollywood agrees. Pre-WTO, just ten American films were allowed into China each year, but even then they dominated the screens. Not only will twice as many films be coming in, but foreigners will now be able to own and operate cinemas. Cineplexes in Xian would have sounded absurd a few years ago; now they are probable.

Western insurers stand to gain the most the fastest. By the end of 1999 thirteen insurance licenses had been handed out to western firms, but they were tightly hedged with geographic and other constraints. With those restrictions relaxed, China will become the world's biggest market opportunity for western insurers—and it is a real market rather than (as is so often the case in China) a potential one. The pool of personal savings in China is vast, with not many places to put it. Few Chinese have life insurance—in 1999 the penetration rates were one-twentieth those in Malaysia and one-ninetieth those in Hong Kong—and when the Chinese are offered the right products they snap them up. AIG, an American firm that is the world's most profitable insurer, was the first western insurance company allowed back into China. In the six years after it set up shop in Shanghai, the life-insurance market there grew by 60 percent a year, a rate that doubles the size of the market almost every year, and increased it about 30-fold over the six years. AIG's share of the market went from zero in 1993 to 20 percent two years later (for the rest of the story, though, see below).

For foreign firms in all lines of business, manufacturing as well as services, one issue stands out: distribution. China's system has been the most archaic part of a none-too-modern economy, and it was strictly off-limits to foreigners. Foreign firms had to go through a state-run foreign-trading company to import their goods. Multinationals could not distribute their goods wholesale or retail, or offer after-sales service. General Motors China, which with $1.5 billion in FDI in 1999 was the single biggest foreign investor in the country, was making cars and selling them in peculiar isolation. "We can't get anywhere near our customers," GM China's vice-chairman complained. "It greatly handicaps us." By 2003 most of those restrictions will be stripped away, along with related ones that require foreign factories to export part of their production and that dictate a cumbersome joint-venture form of organization for much FDI.

The way will be cleared for far deeper penetration by foreigners into the Chinese market. Qianlong, not to mention Mao, would be appalled.

In the long run, what will matter most for Western multinationals as well as everyone else is the impetus that WTO will give to Chinese economic reforms. The awesome scale of the needed changes, especially in the SOEs, is described in Chapter 8. WTO will give them a powerful boost—the Goldman study mentioned above reckons it will be big enough on its own to raise potential GDP growth by half a percentage point. The Development Research Center of the State Council (China's cabinet) reckoned in 1999 that in the seven years after China joins the WTO nearly 10 million jobs in farming will be lost, and another one million or so will be shed in car-making and the machinery and equipment industries. Offsetting those losses will be gains of 2.5 million jobs each in the textile, clothing and service industries (western insurance firms reckon that insurance alone will add one million jobs). This is exactly what you would expect from an opening of the economy. China will shift toward activities in which it has a comparative advantage, such as labor-intensive light manufacturing, and away from those in which it does not. Another change you would expect is a reduction in inefficiencies. Industrial rationalization and restructuring will be most pronounced in cars and petrochemicals. In 1995 China had 122 car companies scattered among 17 of the country's 30 provinces; the biggest company produced fewer than 300,000 vehicles a year, around one-twenty-fifth the global output of GM and one-fifteenth that of DaimlerChrysler. A sure result of China's entering the WTO will be a consolidation of this industry. The same will be true for refined oil products and petrochemicals.

Probably the greatest single benefit of the WTO will be to bring world-class management methods and technologies into China, substantially increasing the efficiency of local producers. Yet this is where foreigners will have to be on their toes. Up-and-coming private Chinese firms are extremely quick studies and ferocious competitors. Take the case of Michael Coorey, president of Bessemer Holdings Asia, who in the late 1990s ran a bottled-water company based in Shanghai. When the company started up, his main competitive worry was multinationals and SOEs in the water business. Both proved to be pushovers. The real competition was private Chinese firms under the control of youngish entrepreneurs who mercilessly drove down costs and prices in the free market for bottled water. Coorey wrote in 1999 that, driven by this competition, he had to drop his own prices by a third each year, vertically integrate his output ("we produce our own empty bottles, and our lowest-cost competitors even produce their own caps"), build up production scales ("in 1996 $30 million-worth of equipment meant a big water plant, now there are three companies that have $50 to $80 million"), and spend hugely on advertising and brand-building ("in 1996 $1 million was a big TV advertising budget, now $5 million is reasonable and $30 million raises few eyebrows"). Perhaps predictably for a relatively small foreign operator, Coorey thinks "all but the very best" multinationals are going to be wiped out in the Chinese "rush for brand domination on a massive scale."

Many multinationals have already been given food for thought about this. In the mid-1990s Compaq owned the Chinese personal-computer market. Then Legend Holdings, a Beijing-based Chinese firm, began competing aggressively on price, service and distribution. By the end of the decade Legend had far and away the biggest PC market share, Compaq having been shoved down to the number 5 slot. Similarly, during the two years AIG gobbled up 20 percent of the Shanghai life-insurance market, its local competitors figured out its methods and strategy (which largely involved the novelty, for China, of using a large team of salespeople to call on prospects in their offices and homes), and began successfully imitating it, in part by poaching many of the skilled AIG-trained salespeople. In another two years AIG's market share had fallen by two-thirds to just 7 percent. But this is not quite the sob story it seems for AIG. One of the beauties of a market with the potential of China's is that competition, even if painful, tends to expand the market very quickly for good domestic and foreign firms alike. The Shanghai insurance market grew so fast that AIG's 7 percent share of it in 1997 delivered the company higher revenues and profits than it had earned from its 20 percent share in 1995. But China alone is not the end of the matter. INSEAD's Lasserre points out that increased Chinese efficiency and scale will allow at least a handful of mainland firms to begin venturing out on their own—and even with their own brands—into the wider world. Haier, the appliance maker described in Chapter 8, is already on its way, having built a factory in South Carolina in 1999 to begin its push into America.

What all this suggests is that, even if life for a foreign firm in China will rarely be relaxed, most Western multinationals in the first decade of the new century are going to find that they have to be there doing business—in part to take advantage of the world's fastest-growing market but also because it is where so much of the world's manufacturing will be done. Lastly, it is where strategic attacks by Chinese firms on westerners' home markets will start to be launched from, and where they must be at least partially outflanked in: for that reason alone, westerners will dare not leave China entirely to the Chinese. All this is particularly true of Asia's biggest country, but it also applies to Asia as a whole. Yet how can any multinational hope to get a grip on the world's biggest and most populous region? Consider how one of the biggest and best multinationals started going about it in the late 1990s.

GE in Asia

Under the leadership of Jack Welch, who took over as CEO in 1980 and is due to retire at the end of 2001, America's General Electric became one of the most successful and admired companies in the world. It also expanded fast outside America and became one of the most global American multinationals. Welch's attitude was always that crisis equaled opportunity, and the firm's biggest bursts of expansion tended to come when there was blood in the streets: in America it stuffed its portfolio with real estate loans during the savings-and-loan crisis of the late 1980s and early 1990s; it pushed hard into Europe in roughly the same years, when much of Europe was in recession; and it began its Latin American drive after the Mexican collapse of 1995. So it was no surprise when, in the firm's 1997 annual report, Welch wrote that "the path to greatness in Asia is irreversible" and that this was where he saw some of GE's biggest opportunities for growth.

And, sure enough, GE did go on a buying spree in Asia in 1997–2000. GE Capital Services, the company's monster division with about half of group revenues before GE acquired Honeywell late in 2000, in the world's biggerst-ever industrial merger, had $1 billion-worth of assets in Japan in 1995; powered almost entirely by a series of big post-1997 acquisitions, GE will have grown that figure by the end of 2000 to $40 billion, 10 percent of Capital's global assets. That rate of growth was twice as fast as GE Capital achieved during its big push into Europe in the early 1990s. GE Plastics now sells more polycarbonate (a raw material for plastics manufacturing) in Asia than in Europe, and GE Medical Systems (which makes equipment like CAT scanners and MRI machines) already sells 50 percent more in Asia than in Europe. But that turned out to be less interesting than the interaction of GE's famously strong corporate culture with Asia's famously strong national ones. Perhaps the biggest surprise is that this presented a working model not just for the Asian operations of western multinationals but for a new sort of Asian corporation as well (see next chapter).

The best way to begin is at the individual level. Consider the meeting in a windowless conference room at GE's China headquarters on a hot morning in Beijing in the summer of 2000. The CEOs of General Electric's 20 or so business operations in China were there for one of their thrice-yearly internal reviews. Each gave a brief report on how business had been. They heard about the new R&D center that had just opened in Shanghai, about which parts of China were beginning to run short of electrical power and where new generating capacity would therefore be needed, about how many additional planes China's airlines would be ordering (and how many might be fitted with GE aircraft engines), about the stupendous 50 percent to 100 percent growth in sales by the plastics and medical-systems divisions, and about the large sums GE had saved in just a year—maybe a third overall—by putting procurement from its 1100-plus suppliers in China on-line. The main point of this particular meeting was to begin a systematic assessment of how China's entry into the World Trade Organization will affect each of GE's businesses. The discussion was focused and was peppered with GE lingo like "critical-to-quality" requirements. The attitude and discipline were so familiar that you felt you could be anywhere in GE's global empire—until you looked around the room and realized that only two of the business heads were non-Asians and all except one of the Asians (an Indian) were ethnic Chinese, some from China itself and some from Taiwan or Hong Kong.

The meeting said a lot about the advanced experiment GE has been running in Asia since 1997 on the interaction of the global and the local in world business. GE has done it by taking a universal and unbending corporate culture, transplanting it into a multitude of native soils and then, through the nurture of local talent, letting it grow to suit local conditions. That isn't the only way for a multinational to tackle Asia, but it has been working for GE. By 2000 its Asian revenues were growing about twice as fast as revenues elsewhere, and the Asian operations enjoyed appreciably higher margins.

Odd though it seems, perhaps the biggest secret of this success is that "Asia" is an almost meaningless term for GE. The firm's last overall head of Asian operations moved on in 1999 and wasn't replaced. Why have an Asia head anyway? Welch told me that GE doesn't even have an Asian strategy (see interview on pages 299–301). Almost every GE organizational arrangement in Asia is ad hoc. The plastics business in India reports to

WELCH ON ASIA

An interview with Jack Welch in Fairfield, Connecticut, on July 25, 2000.

Q: Given the way you run the company, is there an Asian strategy?

A: No, there's no Asian strategy. There's a strategy in Asia for each business. We're the sum of the business strategies in many ways. And the way we move forward is a business-by-business issue. We don't have a China strategy for GE. Medical has a China strategy, plastics has a China strategy, aircraft engine has a China strategy. We have directions and initiatives like globalization, our services, our Six Sigma quality program, e-business. We would drive that from here, to find opportunities in this vast area but in the end it's the ability of the teams to take it up and share best practices. So it's nothing more than how well they grab it.

The reason why we ended up not having an Asian leader is we've built capability in each country. And having somebody responsible for Asia is almost insane. I mean, how do you cover an area that size? All you do is have people on planes traveling all the time. So we needed to start to seed Asia, but once we seeded it, the country managers are the people who will cover the countries.

But you ask me what my role is. My role in this company is often vastly overstated. I'm responsible for the social architecture, for the personnel. And I'm responsible for the moves of people in Asia. And I have something to say about how much we're going to invest where. But they bring the investments forward.

Q: Can you spell out how much to invest where?

A: No, I can't. I can tell you they bring the investments forward and I look at the investments and then at the end of the year we add them up and I'll tell you where they went. But we're looking at them on a deal-by-deal basis. And we look at expansion of plastics, we look at expansion of Capital, we look at expansion of medical.

But I don't have a number that will tell you Asia's going to be X percent of GE or it's going to be Y percent of GE. Because those numbers don't mean anything. It's going to be whatever it is, based on the initiative of those people. We want to expand in Asia. We want to expand as fast as we can in Asia. But it will be the result of a lot of inputs. I'm not a believer in we're going to put 25 percent here and 30 percent here and 20 percent here in a multi-business like this.

Q: How does it work in practice?

A: The best story I have is about a fellow named Mark Norbom. He was in Thailand in the middle of the Thai crisis. And we get a book every night before the GE Capital board meeting, which is monthly, describing every deal. And I'm home with my wife, I've got the book on my lap and I'm flipping through it and I said, "Look at this deal here. This guy, this nut, wants us to invest a billion dollars," I think it was, "in autos." I said, "I'm going to blow him out of the water tomorrow. I mean, this guy's got no chance."

But Norbom comes in and he makes the most convincing case. No indigenous car manufacturers, why people would pay, why they would keep their car, why it would work, why it was a good deal. And in forty-five minutes he had taken a group of us across the other side of the table and flipped us over on our heads with a real passionate plea, and logic to it.

(continued)

So we bet on it. Now that was in the worst moment of this whole thing. So you know, what it was is this guy flying over from Bangkok and he was in there and he was making the case.

It's almost a perfect example of how it works. We were convinced. If you asked me five minutes before the meeting, I'd say, "Get out of here, what are you, nuts?" And yet he had good people making a great case and you bet on him, and you love him for doing it. You love him for knowing he's walking into the jaws of trouble to come and see you with the story. Now he's promoted to Japan.

Q: How do you mesh a very global set of standards, tools and principles with what necessarily are highly local conditions?

A: Through vast training programs, through constant education, integrity guidelines on line, constant conversations about environment health issues and safety, global training programs, an ever vigilant global standard on values, and local behavior but within those cultural standards. And through incredible amounts of training. We always pray that that training is working and that everything is being done according to our integrity booklet. We work on it constantly.

The local manager runs it within this global standard. And he or she knows that it's within that standard that they have to operate. But they run their own business. There is no central person controlling what somebody is doing in Thailand or what somebody is doing somewhere else. We trust local managers to instill those values into the local leadership. Those core values aren't negotiable.

When everyone asks me over and over again, how do you transfer GE values somewhere, they are really the most simple values of all. It's human dignity and voice. And if you think about it, if you talk to our people, what they try and do is give people dignity and voice. And by letting everybody raise their hand and say what they think. And if people have voice and they have a say in things, they respect it and they like it. Now that dignity and voice may be a little different in Beijing than Pittsburgh. But it's still trying to find what will give people dignity and voice.

That's why I think it works everywhere. You say what's this magic formula? It is nothing other than giving people the treatment that you would always want for yourself in that culture. And if you believe that to your toes and get people who manage businesses who believe that to their toes, you just end up getting it.

Q: What about bringing Asians into higher management jobs?

A: Obviously as we evolve in Asia and get bigger, that has to happen. We now have in Japan some great Japanese leaders and we've got an enormous drive to do two things. One is to globalize the company and secondly is to reduce the number of expats, who are a crutch and don't support a real global opportunity. And so I've just been going through a series of meetings here where all day people are showing me the local nationals who have been promoted to key jobs and the Americans who have come back. We've probably taken back, in twenty-four months, 50 percent of the Americans that we had overseas. And that's been an enormous benefit for globalization.

Q: Where do you feel you've missed opportunities or made mistakes?

A: Lighting has been a hundred times harder in China than I thought. I was right on appliances in China because I wouldn't run a factory. I figured we didn't have enough of a competitive advantage. So in appliances I saved a lot of money in China. What I was wrong on was that I thought lighting was based more on technology. Throughout the world, there are four, five, six players, high technology, sophisticated stuff. I didn't realize that every mayor in every town in China would fund a lighting player. The number may be several hundred lighting factories. Every province, every place. So I was wrong. And blew it.

Q: What do you think has been your best decision in Asia?

A: Best. I don't think there's any one. Again, it's the people that do it so I can't say I made a decision. I think one thing might be not losing a lot of money in China. You know, what you don't do is sometimes as good as what you do do.

Q: What's your view of Japan?

A: I've learned more in Japan probably than anywhere. I've learned a lot about management in Japan. I think a lot of the things we think about is part of Japanese training. I started going to Japan in '66. So I'm indebted to Japan for quality, for getting the workers involved in the decision-making; a lot of things, participative management and getting ideas from the factory floor, asset management, inventory turns. No one's as good as Toyota, you know, and we learned that. And we've learned their focus on quality.

I love the Japanese environment, I love the people, I like the business people. And I think with a little GE culture, it's a perfect match.

Japan has always been a fond place for me. We haven't always done as well as I would like to do there, but I've never felt for example some of the discrimination that was felt by some other companies. GE has always been treated very well there. I just like them and trust them. I've known the CEOs, all the CEOs of Toshiba, and I like them. I've always found it to be something that appealed to me.

Q: Do you feel the same way about China?

A: Look, what I know about China is this. I've been going there for twenty years, and every time I go there I laugh at how little I knew the time I came before. You know, every time I go I think I learn something. The next time I go there I learn how little I knew. It is so vast and so complicated and so hard to figure out. I don't know the answer. I truly don't. That's probably why I'm retiring. Somebody else is going to have to figure it out. Do you understand China?

Q: Of course not. It's got five times America's population with a five thousand year old culture and huge diversity. I don't think anybody really understands it. My instinct about it is that it's going to be spectacularly successful.

A: So is mine. So is mine.

the Netherlands; the medical-systems business in India reports to Tokyo. The head of all of GE Capital's Asian businesses outside Japan splits his time between Delhi (where he also runs the division's Indian operations) and Hong Kong. Some places—notably Japan and China—have a country head who has no responsibility for a line of business. In others (like India and Indonesia) the head of one of the business lines also wears the country-head hat.

A localized approach was dictated by the way GE runs itself worldwide. GE is in 20 or so major lines of business (GE Capital subdivides itself into a further 28). The firm is highly centralized about a handful of issues: what it calls its "core values" (its ethics); financial targets; one of the most rigorous and exhaustive procedures anywhere for personnel review, promotion and expulsion; and the occasional "initiatives" Welch came up with since 1985 for driving new strategic ideas throughout the organization—globalization in the 1980s, a move from products to products-plus-service in 1995, the Six Sigma quality program from 1996, and e-business since 1999. On these matters, everybody dances to the tune called by GE's headquarters in Fairfield, Connecticut, or else. Yet when it comes to operations, each business has enormous autonomy. Worldwide operational decisions—even big ones that in the end are formally taken at the top levels—are strongly under the control of the individual businesses. GE has grown fast in Asia not because it came to an Olympian conclusion at headquarters that this was the thing to do but instead because various of its businesses decided they had good opportunities there.

GE's structure therefore made it relatively easy for the firm to ride the natural tide of Asia's rise in the world. Catching that tide has depended both on some deep movements (like China's growing commercial power and Asia's global dominance in electronics manufacturing) and some fast breaks (like the opportunities shaken loose by the Asian financial crisis). The combination has pushed three lines of business to the forefront in Asia—GE Capital, Medical Systems, and Plastics—has made Japan and China the biggest markets, and has started to give Asia a greater role in the firm's worldwide drive for e-business and the internationalization of its intellectual capital.

For now, Japan dominates GE's Asian landscape, and the biggest figure in that landscape is GE Capital. The Capital unit is the GE division that changed the most in response to the Asian financial crisis. The problem for the unit in pre-crisis Asia was that, because of the region's generally closed financial systems, all foreign firms had trouble establishing a beachhead. Denis Nayden, who runs GE Capital from its headquarters in Stamford, Connecticut, says the firm's Asian strategy in the early 1990s was to "gear up" enough of a presence to understand what was happening in the markets and then wait and see how things would evolve. The firm had had a small operation in Thailand since 1993, specializing in car finance. When the Thai baht collapsed in mid-1997, the Capital unit immediately made plans to start buying distressed car loans. It took a lot of convincing back in Connecticut, but the Capital head in Thailand got the unit to increase its Thai workforce by 1200 people and its assets from almost nothing to about $1 billion.

Nayden says he felt "positive anxiety" about the Asian situation when these decisions were being made. Anxious or not, Capital didn't flinch from expanding (except in China, where it does little more than aircraft leasing and plans to lie low until the financial system loosens and deepens a lot). Pramod Bhasin, who from Delhi oversees Capital's Asian operations everywhere except Japan, grew the unit's Indian assets to $1 billion, split equally between commercial and consumer loans, and hopes for some good M&A opportunities in Indian insurance as the market liberalizes. The firm also bought modestly in South Korea when distressed assets there went on the block. The whole process may sound like bungee-jumping with frayed rubber, but it turned out not to be that scary. Pramod says that, astonishingly, after the crisis in Indonesia (Asia's worst-hit country) Capital had to write off only 1 percent of its consumer loans. Nayden says that the unit's growth prospects for Asia as a whole are much higher than anywhere else in the world: "15 percent to 20 percent a year at least."

The overwhelming bulk of GE Capital's Asian firepower is trained on Japan. For good reason: with $12 trillion in personal financial assets (80 to 85 percent of Asia's total), the world's biggest life insurance market by value, the world's fastest-aging population and a primitive financial system with weak domestic competitors, Japan is a dream market. Before 1997, Capital had been forced to build its businesses from scratch because acquisitions were pretty much out of the question. But, once banks and insurers began failing, it quickly made four big acquisitions—a life insurer, a consumer-finance firm and two leasing companies—and by mid-2000 was in the process of negotiating the purchase of a sales-finance company that would almost double the size of its Japanese consumer-finance business to more than a third of its worldwide total outside the United States.

The biggest single business is the life insurance company, called GE Edison Life. The name was chosen because General Electric has low brand recognition in Japan, but Thomas Edison (who founded GE) is well-known: the firm's market research says 98 percent of Japanese have heard of the man who invented the light bulb because its first filament came from a piece of bamboo from a town near Kyoto. GE acquired the life business in 1998 by buying the assets of Toho Mutual, a Japanese firm that went bust, and then put Rone Baldwin, an American who had been running GE Capital in Japan, in charge of incorporating the new firm into the GE system. Baldwin says that of the firm's 7000 employees only ten are expatriates and all (including him) are busy trying to work themselves out of their jobs. He says it has been surprisingly easy to bring GE's habits to bear in even an old-line Japanese firm. A good thing, since GE is still on the lookout for other acquisitions and expects to grow the Japanese business to about 25 percent of its worldwide life business.

The consumer finance business in Japan bulks even larger for GE: according to Dave Nissen, who runs the worldwide consumer finance business, profits in Japan are already almost equal to those in the whole of Europe. It is also an innovative market. Tak Yamakawa, who is in charge of the Japanese operation, says the firm runs 1000 "ACMs" (automated credit machines), which allow a customer to submit documentation and credit information to a kiosk-housed machine that scans them and within minutes can issue a card to allow the customer to withdraw cash from any of 15,000 ATMs that accept GE finance debit cards. In 1996 about 70 percent of GE's customers got credit through manned branches and only 30 percent from ACMs; today the figures are reversed, which is nice for GE since the machines can be run for half the cost of a manned branch. But this is just a start. In April 2000 the consumer finance unit started a mobile-phone Internet version that GE worldwide is studying as a model for future delivery of consumer credit.

GE has been in Japan for a century and in 2000 had 17,000 employees there (of whom only 100 were expatriates and only one of them CEO of a GE business). Japan accounts for about 6 percent of global revenues. Not nearly enough, says Jay Lapin, an American ex-lawyer who is the country head for Japan and, though he has no line responsibilities for any business, tries to advance all their causes with their bosses back in America. He is having some success. Since 1997 Japan has been GE's fastest-growing national market in terms of both revenues and profits. One way Lapin hopes to get that to continue is by working closely with Japanese manufacturing companies on product specifications so that things made by GE can be sold to them worldwide. It's worth it. According to Lapin, the overseas operations of Japanese firms have a bigger output than the whole of the South Korean economy.

This sort of "cross-border leveraging," as GE calls it, is central to the firm's worldwide strategy. It is especially important for the Asian operations because Asia consumes a lot and, in global manufacturing terms, produces even more. One of the businesses where this shows up most clearly is medical equipment. Medical Systems is headed by Jeff Immelt (who a lot of people were betting in late 2000 was the most likely of the three candidates to succeed Welch when he retires). Immelt, who made a habit of visiting Asia four or five times a year, says that the medical business has two aspects to it—global products and local markets—and that they need to be combined for it to work. GE handles the product side by making the machines in whichever place the right level of engineering talent and best cost base can be found—and that usually means the market where the demand for those machines is highest and the competition the toughest—and then selling them worldwide. The most sophisticated machines are made in America, which also has the biggest demand for top-end medical equipment. Japan is more mid-range, with a preference for small, high-quality machines, and China is the center for production of lower-tech CAT scanners. In all, GE Medical has eight factories in Asia, one each in Japan and Korea and three each in India and China. As for the marketing and service, Yoshiaki Fujimori, who runs the Asian operations of Medical Systems out of Tokyo, explains that you just "have to have a lot of popcorn stands"—that is, a lot of small local outlets with a good feel for the market.

The Asian medical business amounted to $1.5 billion in revenues in 2000 (about 20 percent of the world total), with Fujimori expecting $4 billion by 2005 (which would then be almost 30 percent of world sales). Around half of the Asian sales are in Japan, and Fujimori, an irrepressibly enthusiastic competitor, explains that GE went into Japan in the first place to take on Toshiba. Although GE lags Toshiba in sales and distribution, it has done well at concentrating on service, especially remote diagnostics. "Our competitors missed the boat on this," Fujimori says with satisfaction. That matters. Margins on services are about double those on products—which is one reason Welch launched his product-service push in the mid-1990s—and in Japan GE Medical still gets twice as much revenue from products as from services (in America it's one for one).

Yet although there is still room for improvement in Japan, the really fast growth in GE Medical's Asian business is coming elsewhere—especially in China. China alone is already the third biggest national market for medical systems (it is ahead of Germany) and, at present growth rates, could overtake Japan as number two in less than four years. Chih Chen, who as Welch puts it "would be as much at home in Pittsburgh as Beijing," is a mainlander who runs the China operations out of Beijing. China is a strong production base—in 1999 it made $300 million-worth of equipment and exported $100 million-worth of that—with, Chen says, the most economical low-end CAT manufacturing facilities in the world. It is also a surprisingly sophisticated and diverse market. Chen says there are 60,000 state-owned hospitals in China, most with budgets for the kind of low-end diagnostic equipment GE makes in China. But on top of that there are private hospitals and clinics in the big cities where two-thirds of GE's China sales are made, and they buy the higher end stuff that GE Medical produces in America and Japan. It is not only products that GE moves into and out of China with fluency. In 2000 Chen had 28 people directly reporting to him, of whom 15 were Chinese nationals and the rest overseas Chinese from Taiwan, Hong Kong, Singapore and Malaysia. All are occasionally rotated out of China for tours in America and elsewhere.

GE did not find China an easy market to penetrate (Welch admits to scratching his head about it, see interview), although it already contributes some $2 billion in revenues, a figure that could easily triple in the next four years. David Wang, a Taiwanese-born American who is GE's country head for China, looks forward to the changes WTO will bring because "the more local you are, the better able to cope with changes in the country," and a lot of opaque bureaucracy and "special deals" have made it hard for multinationals to settle down there and be locals. Sometimes this doesn't matter—businesses with a "concentrated technology content" like medical equipment, aircraft engines and plastics—escape the bureaucratic labyrinth, but GE has not had much luck with CNBC (media is poison in still propaganda-minded China), locomotives (the Chinese competition is good and cheap) or finance.

The line in which GE's China business is thriving most robustly is plastics, whose sales have been doubling every year. Gary Rogers, who runs the worldwide plastics business, reckons that within three years Asia will account for a bigger part of GE's plastics business than Europe, and the lion's share of the Asian market is China. The reason is simple. China is where most of the world's electronic gear is assembled, and you need a lot of plastic for all those computer housings and DVD players. In many ways, says Steve Schneider, who runs the China plastics business from Hong Kong, it makes things more manageable that the vast bulk of GE's clients in China are multinationals (apart from a few plastic water-bottle makers).

The China factories (there were two of them by the end of 2000) take raw material and turn it into the form that customers like Japan's Canon need for their production of cameras and other imaging equipment in China. The big innovation is an Internet system, started in January 2000, that in just six months put 15 percent of the business online. It saves money, of course, but Schneider says that the flexibility it gives to GE and its customers is far more important. Customers can put in specifications at the design stage and get several different recommended materials for what they want. If the design changes, the factory-line output at the GE plants can change in 24 hours; it used to take one-and-a-half to two weeks. The results in Korea have been even more impressive. In the six months since the opening of the Korean version of the plastics website at the end of 2000—GE Polyland—60 percent of the business moved online.

E-business was the last of Welch's "initiatives" and—as with the earlier ones—a mechanism was put in place to make sure that "best practices" were shared through this "boundaryless" organization. In Asia the guy who is supposed to make sure is Raymond Yang, who sits in Singapore and co-ordinates a staff of six who try to explain both to GE's own people and its customers in Asia why going online makes sense. The most staggering example of why it makes sense comes out of China. Because it is so global, GE tries to get the best deals by concentrating its procurement (of, say, machine tools) in one place. For mid-tech goods probably the world's biggest single source (and not just for GE) is China. David Wang in Beijing says that in just the year since the GE procurement outfit in China started getting its suppliers to resort to e-auctions in 1999, the quotes GE was getting from would-be suppliers dropped by 85 percent.

Raymond Yang's job is to get everybody in the organization, and persuade as many customers as possible, to understand what sort of savings this sort of "digitization" can generate for all the parties. One set of customers that needed little persuasion is the one that has seen how much easier life is when, for example, repair manuals for aircraft engines are online and instantly updated instead of in books that break your back to lift and are never up to date. Even so, Yang admits that Asia as a whole by 2000 was still a couple of years behind America in adapting to GE's e-world. The one exception, mentioned earlier, is the Asian enthusiasm for mobile-phone Internet use, which the firm started trying to export westwards in 2000.

The most important Asian export, however, may also be the most sensitive. Welch has been adamant that

> the real opportunity going forward is the globalization of intellect, whether it's software in India, engineering resources in China or Czechoslovakia. The real challenge is to globalize the mind of the organization. And at least in America, that's the most difficult part of the equation. Export was the easiest because it didn't threaten your jobs. When you start talking about globalizing the intellect and building massive laboratories in Bangalore and building foundries and other things in Czechoslovakia, you start really challenging the organization because moving intellect out of home base is a tremendously threatening thing. Until an organization truly sees itself as capturing the intellects of other areas, it really does have a problem. I think until you globalize intellect, you haven't really globalized the company.

This matters a lot for GE's business in Asia because the continent, albeit poor overall, has a disproportionate share of the world's engineering talent. GE has long shuffled overseas staff into American positions for awhile, especially tech-heavy ones. But the firm has begun a concentrated effort to cultivate Asian R&D resources. Lewis Edelheit, who retired in mid-2000 as the head of GE's corporate R&D unit (individual businesses like Medical Systems also have their own R&D teams), explains that, although there is a small R&D outfit in Shanghai, GE is making its biggest R&D bet in India. GE's only serious research center has, for a century, been in Schenectady, New York ("Not a lot of Asians in this cold place," chuckled Edelheit), where there are 1600 professional staff. A research center just getting started on a GE "campus" outside Bangalore may well, Edelheit says, end up with 1000. This development has not been entirely popular in Schenectady, but it is letting GE draw on world-class software talent (especially) and other engineering talent at bargain prices.

So what can other companies learn from what GE has done in Asia? Well, what can't you learn from GE? The main thing, though, is Welch's point about the globalization of the mind in a company: people from very different national cultures, with a huge amount of operational autonomy, but shaped by a few universal principles and disciplines growing out of a common corporate culture. Surprisingly, given their history of secrecy, personal control and dictatorial authority, that's the way Asian companies are beginning to head too.

14

The Anthill

Asian values may exist, but there is no such thing as Asian numbers—
Trevor MacMurray
McKinsey & Co., Singapore, 1999

Probably the hardest thing to foresee about business in Asia over the next few years—and not just in Asia—is just how the global will interact with the local to produce hybrids that never existed before. Technology and globalization are so dazzling in their power that they make it easy for people to think (or in many cases fear) that a mostly American-inspired uniformity is going to be stamped on businesses and even societies around the world. This is true in only a limited sense. The United States is almost unique in the world in being a country where the traditional social ties—race, religion, ethnic identity, even being born there—do not much matter. Of course, there are all sorts of racial tensions but they are pretty low-key compared to those in much of the rest of the world. By 2020 California's population will be more than half non-white (if you—technically inaccurately, but you get the idea—count Hispanics as non-white). But only nut cases will then dream of saying that mostly non-white California is therefore any less American than mostly white Nebraska.

Nor does the past count for much. Indeed, in Silicon Valley, the world's most creative place, strenuous efforts are made daily to destroy the past as fast as possible, and a lot of the entrepreneurs there would destroy the present too if they could (see *The New New Thing*, a 1999 book by Michael Lewis about a Valley businessman named Jim Clark who founded three multibillion dollar companies in the space of ten years, none of which had anything to do with the businesses of the others, and more or less as soon as he could restlessly got out of them to do something new). In many ways America is an objective place, defined by abstract ideas rather than by older human ties like race or by history, and it is ordered by impersonal and relatively transparent social institutions like the rule of law. As a result, a lot of the new things invented in this most advanced of human civilizations are not really "American" at all: it is just that in the case of these things America happens to be the first at discovering and incorporating the objective reality of all our futures. And only in that sense is the world's future really going to be "American."

Yet the common elements of mankind's future—the Internet, say, or returns on equity—also interact with far more parochial and slower-moving currents, which may as well be called culture. Lee Kuan Yew once described culture as "a map up here, in the mind," and said that "culture is destiny." He meant that whereas individuals might be able to change their mind-sets radically—e.g., by immigrating to America—it takes generations for whole societies to change their habits and ways of thinking. The bafflement and anger among older Japanese in 1999–2000 as the Internet firms came to power is one sign of this. And it is why the organization and behavior of Asian companies will be so contentious in the next few years. People tend to forget that businesses are as much social as they are economic organisms, and that their success depends on recognizing both sides of their character. The Asian firms that can best balance the forces of globalization and culture are the ones that will perform best. Lee put it this way to me in 1999:

> I do not believe that any business, whether it is Asian, German, African, Latin American, can ignore the basic factors that make for competitive advantage. So what you have to learn will be systems. What do I mean by systems?
>
> Eventually the system goes back to a certain mindset of a certain culture. How do you operate this system? That's where the difference comes in. If you want to put a satellite into space, you have to obey the laws of physics, never mind whether you meditate or you don't meditate. But the way you create that rocket, the team that you gather and the way they cooperate with each other to bring that final result, depends on the way human beings interrelate with each other. And I say the moment the Japanese have worked out what it is that does it, they will be a formidable team to beat because they have the capacity to fit with each other like Lego

bricks, which Americans are not so good at. So that's why the Japanese produce cars with zero defects, that where the culture part comes in.

And there's another difference: in the way you spread benefits and treat people. I don't know much about Americans but I know the British system. The bosses have keys for separate toilets and they eat separately. The Japanese all wear the gray uniform, all use the same toilets, all eat at the same canteen. So they create a sense of "We are together, we are part of a big family." And that increases productivity.

But the British cannot adopt that system. It's a change in culture so fundamental that it is difficult to change, and we have adopted some British practices. When we recruit, the engineer goes straight in as an engineer, a technician goes straight in as a technician, a skilled worker goes in as a skilled worker. The Japanese have told us that if you want to increase your productivity your engineer should start at the bottom. Maybe six months, one year, let him work his way up. Then when he gives orders, when he asks his workers to do that, he will know what he's asking them to do, what it means, and they will respect him and he will respect them. We can' change it. Our engineer says, "No, I've got a BSc, I've got an MBA. How can you make me?" So it's a problem. It's no lack of will on my part to change that. I can't change it. The bosses tell me, too much trouble, let's not try.

So that's where the difference comes in. We have to operate the same technical complements, but how we bring it about and the degree of excellence depends on your interrelationships. At the end of it all, the result depends on the human beings bringing it about.

But where will the balance between the global and the local be struck in Asia? Gordon Redding, a consultant and a specialist in the overseas Chinese business network who is now a professor at France's business school INSEAD, thinks the fulcrum of this balance will be a lot closer to the old model than many people think. It all goes back, he says, to the question of why the firm exists: in Japan it has existed to employ people, in Korea to advance national policy, in China to make the family rich, in Europe for the good of society and in America for the shareholders. Redding cites the "cultural predisposition" of different societies in their views of the proper place of authority, organization and rationality, with the Anglo-Saxon societies biased in favor of rationality and Asian ones in favor of authority. And in context the Asian choices made perfect sense. What the "value-laden and demeaning" term "crony capitalism" really referred to, Redding argues, was conditions of great uncertainty and volatility, both political and commercial, in which "political co-optation" was the logical way for a firm to manage risk. Despite distortions, this system did produce movement and growth—and "if they didn't do it this way, they couldn't have done it at all." Redding thinks that Asian markets will remain highly politicized, in part because with entirely free markets Asian firms "will be eaten alive by GE Capital and other efficient marauders." In Malaysia, partly because of the racial tensions there between Chinese and Malays, and to a lesser extent elsewhere in Asia, it would be downright "dangerous to disentangle business and politics" because the institutional structures for a transparent and objective business environment do not yet exist: "you can't take the bones out of the body, it will collapse."

Redding says change will come and, in particular, there will be a struggle over who has the power to allocate a firm's capital. America's devotion to shareholder value has meant in practice that it is the financial markets which have the last word on how capital gets allocated. In most of Asia, and especially Japan, it has been a firm's managers who decide what happens to the free cash-flow. The habit in a Japanese firm has been with, say, a 20 percent surplus, for the managers—under the supervision of a board of directors that entirely agrees with this approach—to give a 2 percent yield as a sop to the stock market and reinvest the rest in the firm. Overseas Chinese firms have been run in the same way. The owner-family's private companies capture the bulk of the cash flow, leaving a trickle for the group's publicly listed arms. Redding reckons that, over the past couple of generations in Asia, companies have thrown off as much yield as their American counterparts but it has gone to different uses: either to family owners or, more often, back into the business rather than to the stock market for redistribution across the economy. He thinks that, because opinions about the importance of shareholder value are shaped by both the availability of capital and the attitudes of the society in which the companies function, the likelihood of a higher cost of capital in Asia during the next decade compared with the past 15 years will help bring shareholder value more to the fore—but not by so much that it will eclipse Asia's deeply held social views, which favor other methods of capital allocation and decision-making.

My own guess is that Asian companies are going to change more radically than that. Asian firms are being pushed more toward the American model by various forces: a generational shift of leadership that is bringing overwhelmingly American-trained sons and daughters with

American attitudes to the top of family firms in Southeast Asia, Greater China, and South Korea; freer capital flows that are moving around the globe on the basis of shareholder returns; the move from banks to capital markets as the main source of corporate fund-raising; and the breakdown of social compacts, such as Japan's and Korea's lifetime employment guarantees or the "iron rice bowl" of China's SOEs, whose slow disappearance will favor the rise of firms and labor markets that are guided more by supply and demand than by public policy. The distinctive reason for expecting great change, however, is that Asian firms—like those everywhere—are starting to face a very different operating environment. This is why those who started worrying in 1999 that recovering stock markets and economies in Asia meant that the pressure for corporate restructuring would now be off will be proved wrong. Something much bigger than cyclical financial gyrations has become involved. Here we are, back to the Internet.

WHEN COSTS ARE CRUSHED

Almost twenty years ago, Steven Cheung, a professor at the University of Hong Kong who has since become more interested in being a businessman than an academic, wrote a paper called "The Contractual Nature of the Firm." This in turn was based on a famous article from the early 1930s by another economist, Ronald Coase, who tried to explain why firms exist. The answer to what may seem at first glance to be a stupid question (but isn't) was that people were willing to surrender their power to make their own bargains with buyers who wanted their services, because the information and transaction costs of functioning as individuals were too high. This is why, in labor markets, the "visible hand" of management in a company mostly displaced the invisible hand that reconciled supply and demand in markets for goods. Cheung took the reasoning a step farther by analyzing piece-rate contracts in Hong Kong. His conclusion was that different kinds of contracts—whether a "visible-hand" employment contract with a big firm or a spot-market bargain at an auction—exist because the transaction costs of different activities vary. The less information about consumer preferences is transmitted by prices in a raw market, the more corporate organization is needed to meet those preferences. Conversely, "the agency costs of a manager rise as the costs of discovering prices fall." In other words, if "the costs of discovering prices, including the costs of information, of measurement, and of negotiation," fall, then the value of management—and of the firm itself—also falls. "Contract substitution" takes place; the employment contract with a firm is displaced by a free-market contract between an individual worker and the customer.

This is an Internet subject because, first, as everyone is now aware, the most striking business fact about the Internet is that it decimates transaction costs. Recall Table 11.1, which shows that carrying out all sorts of transactions on the Internet, instead of using more traditional method, cuts costs by 90 percent or more. Second, the Internet makes markets far more efficient by providing sellers with much fuller and more transparent information about what buyers really want. The upshot, drawing on Cheung's observations, is that more and more business contracts will be driven out of "the firm" and onto the market because free-market contracts will be an increasingly better way to transmit information and organize production. Moreover, the pressure for a market-based solution grows even more intense because greater efficiency means more competition, and that in turn means a constantly worsening squeeze on companies' pricing power and profit margins. The experience so far (look at America) is that this does not reduce overall returns to capital—the reverse occurs, thanks to higher productivity—but it does make the struggle for corporate survival more savage and swift. Firms are not about to disappear. But, as a lot of American management gurus speculated in the 1990s, the nature of the firm is changing deeply. Authoritarian and hierarchical chains of command are becoming less and less productive, and flexibility and speed count for more and more—to the point where "virtual" firms, bringing together human and other resources for specific tasks and then disbanding, become a real possibility.

Now, with the Internet, there is a concrete reason for thinking the gurus were right. One of the clearest descriptions of how revolutionary the Internet is for business worldwide has come from David Roche, a flinty-eyed Hong Kong-based investment adviser who has seen it all in the financial markets and is no new-economy freak. In early 2000 he wrote:

> Far from being an add-on to the existing old economy, the cyber economy is much more like a genetic change that penetrates and alters all layers of the existing organism. Cyber is the dominant gene that will change every business and set its shape, strategy, failure or success. The cyber revolution will affect the macro economy by changing the structure of corporations,

governments and education into pure, hybrid and recessive entities in the way each adapts to the cyber gene. Choosing which to invest in is what investment today is all about. The old statistical certainties—based on history and sovereignty—won't work any more.

Not one to fear mixing his metaphors, Roche went on to say that

the change in corporate structure is from vertebrate to molecular (see Figure 14.1). In the cyber world, functions compete in an open-market configuration instead of being contained in a vertically-integrated structure. Competing molecules in the cyber system lower costs compared to non-competing "owned" supplier units in the vertebrate structure.

However, it is not just individual firms that face a revolution. It is the whole of the global economy:

Then the cyber economy busts the dam protecting national producers and national markets (with their high costs and limited competition) from the highly competitive global market. That forces price convergence and ends the cross-subsidization of exports by high-margin, low-competition domestic sales. All markets are now open to all comers. This signals the death of the national corporate model. To survive, corporations have to be competitive at

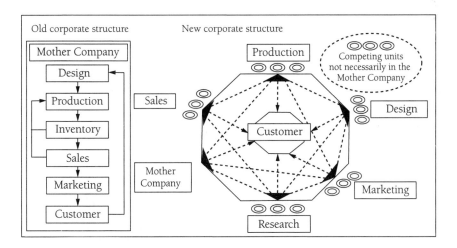

Figure 14.1   Impact of 'new' and 'old' economy vertebrates and molecules. (*Source: Independent Strategy*)

both ends of the production paradigm, not only at the output end. They must be competitive in human talent, capital, technology and share prices! That encourages a switch to a shareholder-friendly management principle. Toshiba either becomes like Dell or it won't be making computers for long. So globalization generates corporate convergence toward the Anglo-Saxon model.

In this way the new economy is super-charged by its three major elements: the cyber revolution, globalization and corporate rationalization. The elements are mutually reinforcing. The cyber economy is a deathblow to the national corporate model, the protected market and the profligacy of national governments with captive taxpayers. Then globalization forces corporations to be competitive in cost and structure on a world scale. This drives them to reduce business costs. In turn, this drives corporate restructuring. A global player could not cut business costs (think just of transaction costs in a multinational, for example) without heavy reliance upon the cyber economy to shorten the supply chain. The cyber revolution is not just an add-on to the existing business structure but the nerve system of the corporation itself.

The cyber economy puts government on the defensive. First, it introduces competition among governments to pursue business-friendly policies and to lower taxes. At the same time, it liberates the consumer and producer from the bounds of the national economy. So government has to attract them both back or risk losing its revenue base altogether. Government is also constrained by having to compete for capital with corporate bond and equity markets where returns on capital will be rising. That increases both the cost of capital and the costs of erroneous policies for politicians— no bad thing!

This worldwide phenomenon matters far more for Asia than it does for Europe, let alone America. In an economic sense, as Chapter 11 explained, it matters because the Internet sweeps away just the kinds of inefficiencies—e.g., of distribution—that Asia has been richest in, while delivering (because it shortens supply chains so drastically) its biggest benefits to the kind of dispersed manufacturing for global markets that Asia has been best at. But the Internet also implies an even bigger revolution in the way Asian companies will now be run. Stan Shih has thoughtfully explained why.

Shih is the 52-year-old head of Acer Computer, a personal-computer producer that is one of Taiwan's most successful high-tech firms. He is a rare intellectual among Chinese businessmen first in picturing what demands the future will place on Asian companies (since the early 1990s, and to much shoulder-shrugging among his fellow CEOs, he has been emphasizing the importance of brand-building if Asian companies are to move up-market); and, second, in thinking analytically about the subject (he even took a few months off from running his company to be a temporary business-school professor in Taiwan and reflect on what the Internet was doing to the world's business climate). The question he posed himself was, "How can you develop an Asian way to manage in the digital economy?" His conclusion was that Asian firms need an entirely different model of organization.

Shih's starting point is a familiar observation with global pertinence. The older, industrial-age model of a vertical and hierarchical business organization had already given way to the information-age model of a "disintegrated" organization and a "de-layered" and "empowered" management structure even before the Internet came along. In the new, knowledge-based model the rule is "super dis-integration" of decision-making through a "network" of operational units in a firm. The company headquarters practically ceases to exist (see previous chapter on GE's world-beating model of this), its only remaining function being to set a few rules, incentives and financial targets for the operational units, where the real work of the firm is done. This is what Shih calls the "Internet Organization Protocol" needed to put such a model successfully in practice.

So far, so universal. But Shih sees a big split between what American firms must do to adapt to this new world and what Asians must do. Echoing Jerry Yang of Yahoo! (see Chapter 11), Shih notes that the digital economy has both highly universal elements that reward economies of scale—products and technology—and highly particular ones that demand craftsmanlike attention: service and contents. A firm has to be big if not dominant in its market segment with its products (like Microsoft) but also appeal to a wide audience with its content. In America it is relatively easy to kill these two birds with one stone, because its vast single market with fairly uniform tastes allows a firm that focuses well on its product or technology to have a big audience for the "softer" parts of its offerings. Focus is enough for success: "A market in America is huge even if narrow, practically global on its own." In Asia, though, markets are too small and fragmented. Focus on a market segment has to be combined with diversification—of language, culture and content. American companies, Shih suggests, may actually have to be more centralized than

Asian ones because market power has such a premium in the United States. Asian ones must become radically decentralized.

This implies a complete overturning of all sorts of assumptions about business (and politics and society) in Asia. Firms will be facing smaller markets, more room for innovators, the rising significance of local advantage, and less room for "me, too" methods and products and hence a shift in weight from anonymous manufacturing prowess to branding and marketing skills. More deeply, democracy, the rule of law, and dispersed power and wealth and decision-making will all become important. This smells of a market-dictated revolution, because the institutional weaknesses and opacities that have plagued Asia all these years despite great economic success have put a premium on the "visible-hand" functions of the firm in mediating between production and consumer preferences, between governments and the private sector, and between society and markets. Whether it is Japan's and Korea's firm-as-family, the Chinese diaspora's family-as-firm, India's firm-as-government-lobbyist, or everybody's private network of information-gathering and political and other contacts—all those skills based on prominent imperfections and discontinuities in Asian markets are being savagely devalued by the globe-spanning transparency of prices and information that the Internet produces, and the managerial disruptions it imposes. Too much of the old Asia Inc. depended on what economists call "rent-seeking": instead of competing in the marketplace, firms exploited imperfections through devices such as *guanxi,* or connections, to capture a stream of income without doing any economically useful work for it. As Shih's analysis implies, the invisible hand is about to get the whip hand, and in a big way. Rent-seeking in Asia is facing, if not yet extinction, then a sharp curtailment of its role. Like all animals whose ecological niche is suddenly destroyed, the old-style Asian firm must remake itself or perish. The animals who have been around for awhile refuse to believe this. The younger ones are embracing it.

GENERATION UNTO GENERATION

As corporate Asia adjusts to this new world, four transitions will shape the future of the Asian firm:

1. The move from an old generation of owner/managers to a new one.

2. The move from old lines of business to new ones, and from diffuse ones to focused ones with a clear strategy.
3. The move from politics to the market as the main source of business power.
4. The move from trading assets to managing businesses as the source of big rewards.

The generational change is a matter more for family-owned firms than for institutionalized bureaucracies. So it does not bulk large in the shaping of Japanese, mainland Chinese or some Indian enterprises: they face serious issues of managerial succession but, like those faced by big western firms, these involve the selection of the next generation of professional managers not the more emotional choice of who is going to have the family's wealth and destiny in his hands and how that power is going to be exercised. In other words, generational change is mainly a question for some big Indian firms, for Korea's *chaebol*, which in essence are family firms grown to monstrous proportions on a diet of cheap-capital steroids, and most of all for the firms of the Chinese diaspora in Taiwan, Hong Kong and Southeast Asia.

A striking fact, for which I have no statistical evidence but a lot of convincing stories, is that in general the Asian family firms which best weathered the financial and technological storms of the late 1990s were those where the old man had gone and leadership had been passed to the second or third generation. In South Korea, the two big *chaebol* that fared the worst were Daewoo—which in effect went bankrupt in 1999—and Hyundai, where the founders still called the shots until mid-2000 and unfortunately tended to call them in accordance with conditions that existed ten or 20 years before. By contrast, the SK Group and Samsung had already passed the torch (in the case of SK to American-educated sons in their forties) and these groups moved faster to shed businesses and move into new industries—and got their due rewards in the stock market. In Thailand the obdurate founder of Thai Petrochemical Industries pushed his firm into the arms of the bankruptcy court rather than let his traditional power and ways of doing things be taken away (see Chapter 7), but Banthoon Lamsam, the 50-ish president of Thai Farmers Bank (Harvard MBA), forced his 70-ish uncle, the bank's chairman, more or less over his dead body to accept management changes and a two-thirds cut in the family's shareholding (to 6 percent) as the price of an $800 million recapitalization. Banthoon's analysis: "The older generation simply cannot accommodate these new ideas. Frankly, it's beyond them."

The stories go on, from Taiwan to Hong Kong to India to the Philippines to Indonesia. In Taiwan the Koo family, which owns one of Taiwan's biggest fortunes (see Chapter 12), in 1999 handed over the reins of Chinatrust Commercial Bank to 35-year-old Jeffrey Koo Jr, who is pushing the stolid firm into Internet and mobile-phone banking and aiming for a merger with the family's investment bank and securities house (run by his then 34-year old brother) to go into e-commerce. "It's because of e-commerce that I'm president," Koo told a journalist in 2000. In Hong Kong, Sun Hung Kai Properties, whose founder died in 1990, was then run by three sons in their 40s who ten years later were successfully moving into high-tech businesses. Ditto for Henderson Land, whose 70-ish founder announced at the end of 1999 that his 36-year old son would be in charge of the firm's shift into the electronic age, commenting that "High tech is best managed by younger people."

There is a complex of reasons for the importance of a generational shift in preparing Asian firms for the new world. The background is explained well by Margie Yang, a Hong Kong Chinese who was born in 1952, was educated at MIT (in pure mathematics) and Harvard Business School, and then put in a one-year stint at the First Boston investment bank in New York before returning to Hong Kong in 1978 to join the Esquel Group, a firm 100 percent-owned by her family. Yang began running Esquel, the world's biggest maker of high-end men's shirts, in the 1980s when her father's health faltered. Yang, appointed to Gillette's board of directors in 1998 and an apostle of American-like transparency and corporate governance in Asia, has spent more than a decade trying to haul Esquel up the global technology and management ladder. There will be more on Esquel itself later in this chapter. For now, note Yang's ready admission that, had her father (who founded Esquel) not been too ill to intervene, she could not have done much to transform the firm. On the difficulty and slowness of introducing modern corporate governance into Asian firms, Margie Yang says, "the old guys just won't have it."

> They don't want creative dissent. Look, these guys are used to being the smartest guys in the firm. Why should they listen to anybody else? And the best ones, the ones who built billion-dollar empires when Asia was nothing—Li Ka-shing, Robert Kuok—are legendary. They have minds as powerful as Lee Kuan Yew's with egos to match. They're brilliant, they're

convincing, but they're one-man shows. And of course the old man happens to hold the money.

The significance of the personal element in this can't be overstated. Simon Murray, a Brit who joined the Legion (French Foreign Legion to Americans) when he dropped out of school and eventually emigrated to Hong Kong, worked his way up in the construction business and rose to became the head of Hong Kong's Hutchison Whampoa, the first British trading house there to be taken over by a Hong Kong Chinese (Li Ka-shing). Murray gives a wonderful thumbnail sketch of the 1970s and 1980s patriarchal Chinese firm:

> Every night they sit around the dinner table, not much TV, the old man holds forth, for recreation they play poker and golf and then it's back to the office. But, despite the power of money, it's based on charm and deep-down humility because of the poor origins.

The next generation is different, in terms of both work—unlike their elders they do not think of work as their whole life—and recreation. In a shocking admission for an Asian businessman, Hong Kong's Dickson Poon, who runs up-market retail operations in Asia that he successfully expanded to London (by buying the Harvey Nichols department store) and aims to expand to America, flatly tells would-be partners: "I don't play golf." Deeper change will come, in Simon Murray's words, because of the "battery of returnees from America who will do business more in the market." This battery is astonishingly large. From Harvard, MIT, Columbia and Wharton Business School in the East to Chicago in the Midwest and Stanford and Berkeley in the West, not to mention a Canadian university or two and some regional American schools, second-generation Asians are emerging, like Margie Yang, and coming back home to their family firms with attitudes and interests that cannot help but be vastly different from those of their fathers.

The precise concoction that results from this intergenerational mix, however, is not always obvious. Banthoon of Thai Farmers Bank, for instance, thoroughly reorganized the bank but proceeded with extreme care so that he didn't directly undermine Thai traditions about a firm's loyalty to its employees—i.e., the firm didn't sack them, it transferred them after decent training to entirely new jobs within the organization to give them the chance to cope. Less dramatically—because never in trouble—

Robert Kuok, an ethnic-Chinese Malaysian who operates his extensive businesses out of Hong Kong, began bringing his two sons and other professional managers into the operations in the 1990s. Kuok, by then in his seventies, had built one of Asia's most intricate, widespread and secretive business empires. His early trading in commodities like sugar and palm oil expanded later into property, hotels and the Coke bottling operation in China. By 2000, and approaching the age of 80, he still exercised ultimate control but had passed on management responsibilities (and considerable chunks of the family's shares) to sons, nephews and a dozen or so professional western managers. Still, probably the most interesting example of the complexity—and potential—of the mix of old and new generations comes from Hong Kong's preeminent business family, that of Li Ka-shing.

Li's legendary rise from being a penniless immigrant making and selling plastic flowers in the 1950s to being the territory's richest man 30 years later is Hong Kong's favorite business story. As soon as Li had broken into the ranks of serious business, he focused on lines where speed of decision-making and the ability of one man to keep a grip on the big decisions were paramount: notably property development and investment and infrastructure (especially ports) around the world. He did expand in the 1980s into unrelated businesses—pretty unsuccessfully in the case of oil production in Canada but very successfully in the case of telecoms in Hong Kong and Britain (where he set up and then handsomely sold a mobile phone service called Orange). Yet even telecoms in the 1980s, in Hong Kong at any rate, was a highly restricted business in which good government contacts were essential to obtain a license (another specialty of the old Asian model), and Li had these in spades. Moreover, although Li gave his listed companies—Cheung Kong Holdings and its subsidiary Hutchison Whampoa—a veneer of professional (even western) management, nobody had any doubt about who was in charge. Phil Elvis, a Hong Kong academic who has done an extensive study of overseas Chinese firms, says flatly, "In the end Simon [Murray] did what he was told."

During the 1990s Li's two sons came home from their years of North American tutelage. Simon Murray was eased out as the head of Hutchison, and now runs a private investment firm in Hong Kong that Li took a stake in (in Asia loyalty is always well rewarded). Li's elder son, Victor (Stanford engineering), was first slotted into top understudy roles at Hutchison and (especially) Cheung Kong, which is where the family's power and interests are most heavily concentrated. Richard (Stanford computer science) took a path of his own, first setting up a pan-Asian satellite service called Star TV and then selling it to Rupert Murdoch in 1993. Using the $800 million he got out of that excellent deal, he tried various lines of business—property, finance and vaguely defined technology—under one corporate umbrella. He seemed to be doing all right but no more until, in 1998, he foresaw the Internet's imminent arrival in Asia and having quickly set up his vehicle, Pacific Century CyberWorld (PCCW), he never looked back. With his company's spectacular stock-market rise in 1999–2000, his daring seizure of Hong Kong Telecom in a bidding war in 2000, and his strengthening ties with powerful Internet investment firms in America and Japan, Richard looked to be on his way to building an empire every bit as big as his father's (from whose businesses he severed all formal links after the HKT acquisition) and doing so in about one-thirtieth the time.

With the HKT acquisition, PCCW was instantly catapulted into the top rank of the world's Internet firms: in July 2000 it was behind only AOL and Yahoo! by market capitalization. By the time the deal was completed in August, Richard had plans to use HKT's nice cash flow and PCCW's technological and stock-market dynamics to double the combined firm's market cap through an array of ventures, including the provision of broadband content worldwide. A lot could go wrong with these plans—the broadband venture is especially audacious—but with the HKT anchor Li has a reasonable chance of building something big and enduring.

There are many ironies here. After his years at Stanford and imbued with the Valley Guy spirit, Richard is an ardent admirer of Yahoo!'s Jerry Yang and Intel's Andy Grove and no public fan of any previously known Asian way of doing business. And Margie Yang, for one, gives him more than full marks for being "about the only" prominent Asian scion to break with the "family" way of doing things and set up his own business model. On the other hand, the breathtaking rise of PCCW on the back of the HKT acquisition was based on a piece of flawlessly timed deal-making that could have been stamped with Li Ka-shing's own peerless hallmark. Because of the temporarily fantastic prices of Internet stocks in late 1999 and early 2000, said one investment banker, "There were only three months in history you could have pulled off a deal like that."

Meanwhile, Li Ka-shing himself, seeing the trading potentials in Asia's dot.com madness, set up his own Internet firms and poured money to spectacular deal-making effect into his telecoms interests; and Victor, named managing director of Cheung Kong in 1999, continued his gradual ascent to full control of the family's flagships.

It looked like the Lis had all bets for the future of Asian business covered. But how it turns out will depend on how well they, and other Asian firms, now manage their empires.

CONCENTRATING THE MIND

The shift in Asia from old businesses to new has been mentioned several times in this book and needs little more comment. The old sources of growth will dwindle, sometimes in absolute terms (property, banking) sometimes only in relative terms (exports to the West), to be replaced by businesses like intra-Asian exports, non-bank finance, retailing, education, health care and of course media. The stock markets already started making their forecasts as they recovered after 1998, with, e.g., property stocks in Hong Kong by early 2000 accounting for less than half as much of the market's capitalization as they had three years earlier—a decline which (along with understandably unbridled greed) quickly drove property firms to start dot-comming themselves. Once the Internet mania fades, however, neither in Asia nor anywhere else is it likely to be so much New Economy companies that thrive but instead all sorts of companies that incorporate New Economy methods. A major sign of which in Asia those might be is how much the crisis concentrated companies' minds: both on sound management strategies in general and on the businesses that actually make them profitable in particular.

A couple of studies have confirmed this in general terms. The Boston Consulting Group found a sharp split between companies that had good stock-market performance in 1995–96 and those that did well in 1997–98. In a premonitory echo of the global Internet boom a few years later, the companies that did best in the last days of the Asian bull markets were those seen to have some special short-term advantage—the classic being Hong Kong's "red chips," mainland firms with a Hong Kong listing that were assumed to have good political ties with the mainland. It was only in the crash which followed that companies with a good long-term strategy were rewarded and the fashionable short-term stocks deserted. Some, like exporters with local-currency costs but dollar revenues, were bound to be in a privileged position. But others just thought hard. Singapore Airlines, which had one of the region's strongest balance sheets (always nice in a cash crunch), also quickly shifted capacity out of Asia and onto global routes as traffic fell in Asia and costs rose in Singapore dollar terms.

Indonesia's Indosat, recognizing that international voice-traffic revenues were in a sharp decline for global reasons (and also being lucky enough to have dollar revenues), used the crisis as a chance to expand its mobile-phone business. Malaysia's Sime UEP Properties, in one of the worst businesses you could be in during 1997–98, nonetheless suffered little damage because it had managed its balance sheet prudently and had focused on the fairly nonspeculative residential property market instead of the headier options of commercial or office space.

Focus also figured strongly in another study of the firms that did best coming out of the crisis. An analysis done in 1999 for the *Asian Wall Street Journal* by Chicago-based Holt Value Associates, which tracks cash-flow returns of companies around the world, separated the Asian wheat from the chaff by asking who if anybody produced double-digit cash returns over the previous three years. The answer was about 180 firms, pretty depressing compared to some 370 in Europe and 800 in America—though remember that these included fantastically awful years for Asia, excellent ones for America and okay ones for Europe. Still, it is even more depressing a result when you realize that a huge proportion of "Asia's" impressive performers were in Australia and New Zealand which, despite geography, are culturally as western as America or Europe. The stock markets noticed the star pupils in Asia, though, awarding the good performers with a 465 percent return over three years, compared with a rise of 7.6 percent for Morgan Stanley's broad Pacific stock-price index. Unsurprisingly, the truly Asian successes were those with the least conglomeratized structure and the most westernized management; firms with the best-expected future performance were the innovative young ones, like Legend, the biggest personal-computer maker in China.

As the studies suggest, the concentration of Asian business minds has been sharpened over the past few years more than many people assume. In South Korea, for instance, Rhee Namuh, the research head of Samsung Securities, guesses that some 300 businesses had been spun off by the top *chaebol* in 1999 alone. Sometimes minds have been concentrated in the time-honored way: by knowing you are about to be hanged in the morning.

A good example is Indonesia's Salim Group. It was set up in the 1950s by Liem Sioe Liong, an ethnic-Chinese peanut-oil trader in central Java who had the good luck to strike up a friendship in those days with an unknown young army officer named Suharto. By the time of President Suharto's fall in 1998, Salim (Liem changed the family name because the variation sounded more indigenous) had grouped 500 companies in a vast range of businesses that had $20 billion in assets and 200,000 employees. The president's fall threatened to drag the whole group down: $6 billion-worth of market capitalization was sliced off its valuation, and the group's captive bank, Bank Central Asia (BCA), and its $10 billion or so in bad loans (most of them to Salim companies) were taken over in 1998 by the new government's financial-restructuring agency. In exchange for immunity from a criminal rap (banks in Indonesia were prohibited from lending more than 20 percent to affiliated companies though almost all flouted this law), Anthony Salim, the 50-ish son of the firm's founder and now its head, got the chance to keep the group going if he paid off the $5 billion BCA had lent to Salim companies.

He raised the money by handing stakes in some 150 companies to the restructuring agency, which in turn began selling them to private buyers, often foreigners. Not all the sales went smoothly. The biggest single asset, BCA, was still in limbo in 2000, but sales of minority stakes in the cement business and in commodity-based interests like plywood and palm oil raised reasonable amounts of cash; and in mid-1999 Salim pulled off something of a coup by selling 40 percent of Indofood, the world's biggest maker of instant noodles (8 billion packs a year, with enough installed capacity in 1999 to produce 13 billion) as well as a flour miller and producer of edible oils. Indofood seemed headed for disaster in 1997, when it suffered some $200 million in foreign-exchange losses. But the basic business is excellent—Indofood has 90 percent of the Indonesian market for packaged noodles and state-of-the-art satellite-linked sales monitoring systems—and even in grim 1998, when the economy shrank 13 percent, sales were down only 9 percent and the firm turned a profit. In addition to getting cash to pay down its debt, the Salim Group was able via that sale to move control of Indofood offshore in a politically perilous time and still keep indirect control through its own stake in First Pacific, a Hong Kong-listed firm that bought the 40 percent share of Indofood. It was a classic piece of Asian deal-making—financially rewarding, politically astute and managerially well-structured—and, when combined with the myriad other sales Salim carried out in 1999–2000, it left a group that had been bloated and sprawling and apparently near its end two years before in a position to use its newly trim structure and financial fitness to start growing again in 2000. Not a bad response to adversity.

In that respect, First Pacific is a story in itself. Anthony Salim set this group up in Hong Kong in 1981 and hired Manuel Pangilinan, a Philippine investment banker, to run it. For a start, that was unusual: overseas Chinese families are not known for giving professional managers a free hand to run significant outposts of their business empires, not to mention giving them a significant share of the equity as well. Why the Salims took a hands-off approach to this one venture is not entirely clear. Pangilinan (Wharton MBA followed by a stint at American Express in Hong Kong) says the model was driven in part by geography—Hong Kong was too far away from Jakarta for micromanagement—and in part by the need to compete on their own turf with Hong Kong's relatively professional conglomerates. First Pacific itself adopted the conglomerate approach, dabbling in interests as diverse as mobile phones and property development in the Philippines, potato processing in China and running a Dutch trading operation, Hagemeyer, that by 1998 had become the world's second-biggest trading house.

When disaster struck Asia in 1997, First Pacific was mostly unprepared, though it had had the good sense to hedge its foreign-currency exposure. But with a debt-to-equity ratio of 2.3:1, it was cash-poor in an environment where cash was king. Moreover, it was majority-owned by paragons of "crony capitalism" whose own existence in their homeland was under threat and who might have been expected in these awful circumstances to milk their subsidiary's assets with impunity. Pangilinan reacted with breathtaking aggressiveness and non-herd thinking. To lower debt and raise cash, he sold some $2.7 billion-worth of the group's best-performing assets—and the ones most sheltered from the Asian storm—notably Hagemeyer (sold at the top of the market for $1.7 billion), a Hong Kong mobile-phone company, an Australian computer company and a small Californian bank. His reasoning was that in a combined liquidity crunch and panic he needed to pay off debt furiously (group-wide, including subsidiaries, it was slashed from about 250 percent to 20 percent more or less overnight) and get cash to buy distressed Asian assets cheaply. If crony capitalism actually had been at work, Pangilinan points out, the Salims would have drained the cash generated from the sale of Hagemeyer and other conglomerate bits and pieces into their own pockets through extraordinary dividends. Whether or not that temptation ever crossed their minds, they did nothing about it. Against the tide, Pangilinan used the cash he had acquired to buy in Asia—notably paying $750 million at the depth of the crisis for a controlling share in Philippine Long Distance Telephone (PLDT), the country's onetime telecoms monopoly and still the dominant telecoms company there.

He also focused. He says the stock markets (rightly) don't understand conglomerates, and his aim is to be in fewer and larger businesses—basically telecoms-plus-Internet (mostly in the Philippines), property (heavily in the Philippines with a project called Fort Bonifacio that is intended to create an alternative financial center for Manila), and retail and distribution (especially Indofood). "Holding companies don't make sense," Pangilinan argues: "it is better to be an operating company that has some other assets under its wing." Despite the appearance of collusion in the Indofood purchase, Pangilinan says the deal made perfect business sense not only because Indofood undeniably is a good business but also because it helped First Pacific to diversify out of the Philippines, where two-thirds of its assets were then located.

The returns from this bold strategy did not come quickly. PLDT has been a nightmare to try to turn around (its telephone lines per employee are about half those in America), Fort Bonifacio will take at least as long as London's Canary Wharf did to become a success (though Canary Wharf then did become a spectacular one), and Indofood generates cash like a utility rather than a growth company. Even though the stock market remained completely unimpressed, Pangilinan's refocusing campaign produced almost a doubling of profits from core business operations between 1998 and 1999. Sooner or later even the stock market will notice. And it is not a lone story in Asia: Siam Cement in Thailand and Lion Group in Malaysia did similar things. More Asian companies—and I bet the ones that will still be around in 2005—have done this than most people think.

MARKET AND STATE

Asians have no patent on crony capitalism—think of Latin America, France or the American Congress. But because of the weakness of fairly neutral institutions like transparent capital markets and the rule of law, Asian governments have been in the paradoxical position of being small (almost universally, they tax and spend a percentage of national income no more than half that in the West) but at the same time deeply involved in business. Many examples like Malaysia are well-known, but the most arresting case is that of Taiwan.

Taiwan is interesting because, as explained in Chapter 6, it arguably has Asia's freest private domestic economy (Hong Kong has fewer restraints on international finance and commerce), with little industrial concentration and free movement of people and capital in response to market signals. Yet, until the spring of 2000, it also had the ruling Kuomintang (Nationalist Party) and its mighty business empire. The Kuomintang (KMT) and the Communist Party of China, while not exactly twins, were extremely close cousins, sharing a Leninist organizational structure, an authoritarian bent, a penchant for corruption and a thirst for wealth and for control of the sources of wealth. Even after 15 years of democratization had softened other aspects of KMT rule in Taiwan, by the time of the presidential election in March 2000 the ruling party owned business assets worth anywhere from $2 billion to $20 billion—nobody on the outside really knew—with income in 1999 of some $250 million. What is sure is that through its Business Management Committee the KMT held majority stakes in 30 big companies and significant stakes in 300 more firms, in virtually every line of business but most notably in banking, construction, chemicals and media. This not only generated income, patronage and influence but also the wherewithal to dominate politics. When combined with the strong sway over political life held by organized crime, the KMT's business empire offered one of the most extreme examples of the politicization (and indeed criminalization) of business in Asia. No wonder the foreign investors who best understand the ways of business in China itself are the Taiwanese.

One lesson of this, disappointing for idealists, is that a shocking amount of corrupt political involvement in business can happily co-exist for decades with a strongly market-oriented culture and practically the best economic performance the world has ever known. The more forward-looking lesson came in Taiwan's presidential election of March 2000, when the KMT was ousted from power by an opposition candidate who won not on the headline-grabbing (and eventually abandoned) policy of his party in favor of formal independence from China, but instead on a popular revulsion with money-politics and corruption. And, fairly soon after the transfer of power in Taiwan, the state-owned banks that had been KMT milk cows began refusing to roll over some of the worst loans to KMT units.

The disentangling of politics and business will go only so far in Asia (as elsewhere) but it is a strengthening Asia-wide trend that is not going to be reversed. In addition to Taiwan, by 2000 Korea, China, Indonesia, Thailand, Singapore and India had taken positive steps toward reducing the role of politics in business. Japan's retrograde government was holding the line in some respects (support for its core backers in the construction industry) but giving way in others (deregulation). The Philippines was backsliding, but in a characteristically haphazard way. Only Malaysia, under a refreshed Prime Minister Mahathir, seemed to stand foursquare behind the old model. A shift like this is necessarily a matter of degree and time, but the Asian business needle has already swung through a significant arc between the political and market poles.

STIR-FRY AND SLOW-BAKE

Anybody who has ever visited a Chinese restaurant and seen the kitchen has watched a wok-chef stir-fry: whatever meat or vegetables are being cooked in the sizzling wok are quickly flipped again and again with a flat ladle and are done in seconds, burning hot and delicious to eat. In Hong Kong just before the crash of 1997, trading in mainland Chinese stocks was called stir-frying: you kept the stocks only long enough to turn them over—or better yet turn them over a few times—and munch on the fast profits. America's day-traders of the late 1990s may have known their Chinese food only from cardboard take-away boxes, but they certainly understood stir-fry. Even so, it is in modern Asia where the trading of assets has amassed fortunes that builders of longer-lasting businesses could only envy. It might seem, given stock-market behavior worldwide in the early years of the Internet, that stir-frying has become all the more attractive, but in the medium and long term the opposite may be true because of the premium the Internet puts on efficiency and productivity.

This is a dichotomy that has its greatest implications for the businesses of the Overseas Chinese, which is what the rest of this chapter is about, but it will challenge every company. In a heady stock market all companies are tempted to raise profits through financial speculation as well as their own operations. It is easy for this to get out of hand, as it did in Japan during the 1980s, when *zaitech* (financial engineering) accounted for more and more of company profits, and in America in the late 1990s. The difference in much of Asia in the 1980s and 1990s is that a disproportionate share of business was in lines like property and banking that naturally lent themselves to a trading mentality as their guiding purpose rather than just a tempting sideshow. If the argument made elsewhere in this book is right and such industries prove to be declining ones in Asia, while the rising industries are in variants of technology and consumer services, then the implications for the way Asian companies run are wide-ranging. Ownership structures, management methods and business attitudes in these sorts of companies are very different from those in companies whose main skill is to trade assets.

That had become obvious in Hong Kong—where asset-trading is the civic religion—well before the upheavals of the late 1990s, in the contrast between the famed property and trading firms and little-known technology-based firms like Johnson Electric (micro-motors), Varitronix (liquid crystal displays) and VTech. Take VTech. Founded in 1977, the firm makes cordless telephones and electronic educational toys, most of the toys now Internet-enabled. Alan Wong, its chairman and CEO, is a 50-something bespectacled engineer educated in Hong Kong and at the University of Wisconsin. His company began exporting "from day one," has 13 subsidiary branches outside Hong Kong employing 600 people (not including R&D), 400 engineers in Hong Kong itself, 400 in China and 200 elsewhere (including Canada) and a board of directors that is half foreign. By the end of the 1990s the firm was making 10 million cordless phones and 15 million toys a year in a single factory in China's Guangdong province next door to Hong Kong and servicing them from a center in Guadalajara, Mexico. The firm, which spends 5 percent of sales on R&D ("low for a technology firm but we get more out of it because R&D in China is so cheap"), has worked hard for 15 years to build its own brand around the world, especially in the United States. Although publicly listed, VTech remains 40 percent-owned by Wong himself with another 5 percent held by board members. Yet, Wong says, "this is not a family business"—in fact, family members are discriminated against in employment there—and could never be one because "in technology, unlike property, you can't run at your own pace" and family firms lack the "necessary aggressiveness because the family must move as one." Nonetheless, Wong thinks, within the framework of its global disciplines VTech is better off with its concentrated ownership since it does not have to worry about quarterly financial targets and the "alignment of managerial aims and shareholder value" is precise. The firm has a clearly stated five-year goal for revenues and margins "that every member of the staff understands."

If this sort of firm represents Hong Kong's—and Asia's—future, then the past two generations'-worth of thinking about the nature of the Asian company is going to have to give way to something more global. In Japan,

Korea and India the likely result won't be too surprising because in those places a fairly objective institutional structure is in place that will sort out modern companies—like Japan's great exporters—from soon-to-be-extinct dinosaurs, with the modern ones looking pretty indistinguishable from their western counterparts. It is different with the Overseas Chinese.

RAINDROPS ON A POND

The Overseas Chinese firm—meaning firms in the majority Chinese places of Hong Kong, Taiwan and Singapore plus those run by ethnic Chinese in the rest of Southeast Asia—was shaped by some peculiar historical circumstances that placed a premium on trust in a time of great volatility and insecurity, and on inside information in an opaque business environment. The firms that succeeded tended to be run by an autocratic family founder who called the shots and kept knowledge about the firm's detailed inner workings confined to select family members. What these firms lacked in organizational depth they made up for in extreme nimbleness of decision-making and execution: at their best, Overseas Chinese firms made Silicon Valley start-ups look plodding and bureaucratic. Yet the circumstances in which these firms rose to prominence have already changed a lot and, thanks to the Internet and globalization, are about to change even more. How will the Overseas Chinese respond?

Begin with a fundamental fact about the Chinese world: even more than the rest of Asia, China and its offshoots have been mostly devoid of the objective institutions of a modern society. There are exceptions, like the common-law heritage bequeathed to Hong Kong and Singapore by their British colonial masters, but for the most part Chinese society is bound by what Toby Brown of General Oriental Investments in Hong Kong (see Chapter 1) calls "intersecting orbs of Confucian responsibility, like the pattern created by raindrops on a pond." The orbs have different origins—such as family, province of origin in China, same schooling, same company—but all are guided by the same principle of personal and extended-family responsibility. Bargains struck within these orbs, say to borrow capital, are secured by the collateral of the borrower's Confucian relationship to the lender—an obligation it would create a huge loss of face not to meet. Such bargains tend to fall outside of government control, and especially outside a government's tax-collection system, and have nothing to do with "the web of laws that regulate interactions in a western society." Brown argues that the idea of an impartial lending officer in a Chinese society is "absurd," but that the Confucian rules allocate capital just as efficiently as the West's "spreadsheet credit." There is a structural problem with this: because no objective authority outside the orb is recognized, Confucian societies are "incapable of refereeing themselves" and any impartial authority has to come from outside. Brown recounts the story of a girlie-bar owner in Hong Kong's Wan Chai (Suzie Wong territory) who hired only western bouncers not because Chinese were physically not up to the job, but because Chinese patrons would not obey them. They were, however, grudgingly willing to accept the word of an outsider in a dispute. Yet when the Confucian orbs are functioning—when personal and family ties are at stake—it works "as well for them as the Uniform Commercial Code does for us."

This kind of setup makes the family want to have control not just of a company's income stream but of the running of the company as well. It also rewards quick asset-trading more than it does company-building: raise the capital, make the return, move on. Anthony Ko, a business professor at City University of Hong Kong, did a big study of family firms in Hong Kong and unsurprisingly found that whereas family management is highly unsuitable for businesses where a wide variety of management decisions need to be made each day, it works fine for businesses like property, shipbuilding, commodity-trading, hotels and franchises (like ports and public utilities) that depend on political connections. The reason is that for non-managerial businesses success comes from investment timing and financial strategy; a large group of professional managers is unimportant, what counts instead is "acumen, *guanxi* [connections] and credit." Echoing Brown, Ko points out that "these elements relate to a person rather than a company," and that the interpersonal style is "very much part of the culture" because "Chinese culture is not very trusting, even of your own children." The managerial weakness is not reflected in poor financial performance: Ko found ROEs among such companies in the range of a respectable 15 percent. But asset-trading dominated. From the mid-1970s to the mid-1990s nonoperating income—i.e., extraordinary profits from asset sales—accounted for 30 to 45 percent of total profits, an extremely high percentage over such a long period.

Old habits persist. In Hong Kong early in 2000 Li Ka-shing's preposterous dot-com listing (a "Chinese" portal mysteriously called Tom.com whose website wasn't even finished at the time the stock was listed) was 700 times oversubscribed and led to minor street riots by retail investors who couldn't get their hands on listing applications; and even his tech-savvy son Richard (along with the Softbanks and Hikari Tsushins), despite his belief that "success at the Internet depends on cultivating people," seemed mightily tempted by the trading gains his company was making before it did much real business at all. And, at first glance, the future of Chinese trading firms looks doubtful. As long ago as 1996, pre-Internet days in Asia, Ronnie Chan, an American-educated (of course) Hong Kong property developer and international networker, gave a biting speech in Los Angeles about "Overseas Chinese businessmen and the global century." While praising the past successes of the Overseas Chinese model—with with its "short-term view of doing business," its "minority syndrome and refugee mentality," its "patriarchy" and its ability to make "convictions easily translated into risk-taking"—he went on to say that "the inherent weaknesses of these organizations are not easily surmountable." Chan explained that "the commercial environment in much of East Asia in the past decades was very unregulated and the market highly inefficient. Factors for success are not so much knowledge and expertise but connections and nimbleness."

And now that was all changing. Chan noted that not only was management—or lack of it—a growing impediment to the success of the Overseas Chinese, but the favorable external environment of unregulated and uncompetitive markets was giving way to a more globalized and transparent environment:

> To survive therein, interpersonal relationships alone will not do; other capabilities are necessary. Intuition must be complemented with analyses and one will have to work not only harder but smarter as well. In fact, the new environment calls for a new set of skills which at times runs contrary to previous success factors. And to simultaneously deal with changes in the family, within the company, in the local environment, as well as in the international marketplace is tough indeed. Failure to cope with any one of them may well be detrimental.
>
> To put it another way: the success of the Overseas Chinese businessmen could to a good extent be attributed to the fact that they were in the right place at the right time. They contributed to the prosperity of their economies which in turn rewarded them with tremendous asset inflation—be it in real estate or in the stock markets. As a result, multibillionaires abound in East Asia. It is not too much to say that compared to corporate captains of the

West, the knowledge and management skill of these Overseas Chinese are not commensurate with the wealth they command. In terms of the necessary factors for success in this new age, what they have is at best second-class.

As one mentally scans the commercial landscape of East Asia (again outside of Japan and Korea) one can hardly find a sizable enterprise which is a major force in any significant global industry. There is not a single company of size which has globally defensible expertise—be it technology, proprietary processes, control of distribution or international brand names. Put it another way, there is not one important global industry in which the Overseas Chinese are dominant players. Nothing even comes close! Without competitive companies and powerful industries, no country or region can claim to be a dominant economic force in the world. As such, the so-called Asian Century is nothing more than wishful thinking.

Only with much better corporate management and improvements in the institutional environment—such as greater democracy (though combined with an avoidance of western-style welfare states) and less corruption—did Chan see any hope of second-generation family firms getting "East Asia to play a significant role in the increasingly globalized world."

In this sense the rise of the Internet only compounds the difficulties facing the firms of the Chinese diaspora. Companies that thrived on segmented markets with many imperfections, especially of information flows, are not obviously suited to a business environment where borders are increasingly irrelevant and transparency of prices and information the norm. Nor do patriarchal, autocratic and hierarchical organizations in which owners jealously guard their equity stakes look like winners in a world of flat management structures, abundant stock options and CEOs in their 20s. The response of governments to this challenge, notably Hong Kong's, has (probably fruitlessly) been to try to encourage a sudden flourishing of high-tech companies where hardly any existed before. Yet, although the occasional VTech may be found in Southeast Asia, the more promising future for Overseas Chinese commerce—and the likely way it will shift from opportunistic trading to a more stable management model—lies in the grafting of technology onto the kind of non-property and non-banking businesses the Chinese have traditionally been good at. Three Hong Kong firms give a glimpse of what this future might look like.

REGION'S SHOPS, WEST'S FACTORY, WORLD'S CO-ORDINATOR

Trading assets is not the only kind of trading the Chinese are good at—and the other kinds can be extremely productive indeed. A retail firm, a clothing manufacturer and a supply-chain manager show what can be accomplished in a region that is both manufacturer to the world and the source of what is likely to be the biggest regional rise in consumer spending over the coming decade.

Giordano is a moderately priced Hong Kong-based clothing retailer founded by Jimmy Lai, who eventually sold out to build a media empire instead (see Chapter 10). Peter Lau, who took over as chairman and CEO in 1994, faced not just the effects of the Asian crisis but a crisis of Giordano's own in mid-1997. The T-shirts—sold mostly to tourists and Philippine maids in Hong Kong—that had been the firm's staple earner fell out of favor when tourism dried up. The first thing he did when sales started dropping was to stop expanding, even shutting down a factory Giordano ran in China, and conserve cash. Next was to shift to "smart casual" clothes that had bigger margins and appealed more to local Chinese. By early 1999 sales had bounced back by 20 percent even in Hong Kong, which was in general a retail disaster land at that point, and for the year as a whole profits more than doubled.

Giordano had always had sophisticated sales-tracking systems but Lau relentlessly upgraded them. The firm found it was possible to teach even staff who lacked a high school diploma to use computers, and Lau insists on e-mail as the main form of communication within the firm; he even toyed with the idea of banning fax machines within the firm so that everyone would go on-line. By 2000 it was possible to make daily morning Internet broadcasts to all of the company's retail outlets explaining how yesterday's performance had been and what the goals should be for today. Lau is fanatical about making the firm leaner. "When the business gets bigger," he says, "the company should get smaller." He ensures this in part through outsourcing as much production as possible (more on this global phenomenon below) but also by refusing to provide more resources when he thinks the job can be done with fewer. Computers are used much more intensively than ever in Giordano, but the actual number of computers has been cut in half. The accounting staff has not grown since 1987 even though revenues are 20 to 40 times bigger. When Lau finds that sales per employee or gross margins per employee or inventory levels are not on target, he does something to force a change. With inventories soaring in 1997, he simply eliminated one of the two floors of warehouse space the firm kept in Hong Kong. The staff figured out how to make do, and the inventories dropped.

Lau's financial ferocity (he was trained as an accountant in Canada) does not extend to personnel matters. Lau says, "People are the biggest asset. They're not like stationery, they're sacred, and if you can't afford to groom and develop them then don't hire them." Giordano has a training program in Hong Kong for a rotating group of 150 university graduates from all over Asia, including China, Singapore and Taiwan. They get a year's experience working in the retail outlets, and then work their way through the managerial ranks. He expects the training to pay off in 3 to 5 years, with the trainees becoming mature managers in 5 to 10 years. The attrition rate is 70 percent to 80 percent, "but that's okay"—it is worth it to have even a relative handful of the excellent managers the program produces. The program has convinced Lau that Hong Kong has the potential for staying on top as a "managerial regional resource" for Asia.

If Lau runs as tight—albeit not as big—a ship as any of his western counterparts, Margie Yang, whom you met a few pages back, presides over a smoothly integrated high-end clothing manufacturer that is one of the world's biggest. Esquel has a family firm with revenues in 2000 of probably $500 million and contracts to provide such top brands as Abercrombie & Fitch and Tommy Hilfiger with some of the 48 million shirts and 5 million pairs of pants the firm's 43,000 employees turn out each year from factories in six countries around the world. Yang's American experience convinced her of the importance of technology in a big manufacturing operation. Some of the technology is hardware, and a visit to the firm's main factory in Guangdong province reveals a spotless set of operations (even though clothes-making with its dyes and so on is a very dirty business) with equipment as up-to-date as any.

Yang points out that there is a close relationship between good management, high-quality products and information flows. Before, she says, textile and apparel companies in Asia competed on the basis of cheap labor. Quality was of little concern and waste—of materials, time and information about the market—was common. Because her products are high-end, quality control is crucial. This is why Esquel runs every part of its production chain, from the cotton it grows on a huge farm in Xinjiang province in China's northwest ("as good as Egyptian cotton") all the way through spinning, weaving and clothes-making (the firm even makes its own buttons and labels). But quality also demands sophisticated management, and for that communications and information management are crucial. Esquel has an intranet to link its operations worldwide and also is linked to the information systems of many of its big customers. Yang says that, like American firms, Esquel has been introducing information-technology systems for 20 years and is only now beginning to see a big jump in productivity. This in turn complements, in fact makes possible, a decentralized "cell-like" management structure that takes advantage of the skills of professional managers. Many of Esquel's staff at the Gaoming plant are graduates of Qinghua, one of China's best engineering universities, and even at the Xinjiang plant she has 12 or 15 university graduates managing the place.

Yang's ambitions go much further, though. An admirer of the minimalist management philosophies—"they've gotten rid of the fancy footwork"—of Jack Welch and Warren Buffett (she sits with Buffett on Gillette's board), Yang requires all her managers to limit their goals to three. Hers are, first, to build the organization through the right personnel appointments (like Welch, though to much more tut-tutting among her managers, she has ennobled the human-resources function, appointing a high-powered director whom she pays at CFO rates and whose office is next to hers); second, to direct corporate marketing (logo, image); third, to form the company's vision and make long-term strategic decisions. That's it:

> My goal is to work myself out of my job. I don't want to be the smartest guy in the company [see above section, about Asian patriarchs]. I don't want to make operational decisions. If my managers can explain things to me and convince me and I'm an idiot, then they'll be able to explain them to the professionals who are working for them and convince them. I want to be the idiot who has tea every afternoon at 5 in the Peninsula [Hotel]. I don't want it to matter to the company when I finally go.

So much for the old-style family firm.

The third Hong Kong firm is a trading outfit poised to take global advantage of one of the strongest currents in manufacturing: the outsourcing of actual production from the company designing and selling the product to specialty manufacturers around the world, and the management of the long "supply chain" that this dispersal of manufacturing creates. Dell Computer, which as early as 1998 outsourced 95 percent of its production, was in the avant-garde of this trend, but almost every western manufacturer will follow suit—and few firms are better able to profit from this than Li & Fung.

Founded almost a century ago, Li & Fung was originally a simple middleman between production in China and consumption in the West. Today it is run by two roly-poly brothers in their early 50s who between them own about half the firm. Victor Fung, the chairman, has two engineering degrees from MIT and a PhD in business economics from Harvard; indefatigable, he also chairs Prudential Asia, a private-equity investment firm, when he is not busy chairing the Hong Kong Trade Development Council (a job he at last shed, after eight years, in 2000) and the territory's Airport Authority. William, his kid brother, has an engineering degree from Princeton and a Harvard MBA, and is in charge of Li & Fung's day-to-day operations. When asked for broad thoughts, William modestly says Victor is "the visionary," but there is nothing wrong with his own clairvoyance. Li & Fung's business now is the complicated knitting together of a western buyer's need for a product made to its specifications and the manufacture and putting together of the various components—often from several different sources. Li & Fung does business with 2,000 factories spread around 31 countries, mostly in East Asia but also in the Middle East, Africa, the Mediterranean and the Americas.

By now most western companies know all the big Asian manufacturers, but for a modest commission Li & Fung can present a full package to its customers that will include production planning, supervision of manufacturing, and logistics. Now Li & Fung wants to control the other end of the pipeline: logistics and distribution of western products in Asian markets. To that end it is trying to build up brands in Asia (it even has a venture-capital unit to acquire good ones), along with distribution channels and logistical and warehouse facilities to serve Asian markets. Isn't the Internet a threat to all this? The Fungs think not, because putting together buyer and seller at the right price, which the Internet is superb at, represents only a tiny fraction of the value the firm adds as the overall manager of the supply chain.

In fact they think that, far from being a threat, the Internet is going to allow them to expand their business substantially because they will now be able to serve small and medium customers with revenues of less than $100 million a year—a class that simply cost too much to handle before. In announcing a $250 million share placement in the spring of 2000 to fund Li & Fung's new Internet strategy, William Fung predicted that by 2004 the firm's Internet revenues alone could reach $2 billion, as much as its total sales in 1999.

In financial terms, Li & Fung is one of the best-run firms in Asia. Since part of it was listed on the Hong Kong Stock Exchange in 1992, that arm's earnings have grown by an average of 26 percent a year. Its ROE in 1999 approached an amazing 50 percent. William expresses admiration for American financial disciplines and planning methods but disapproves of American "short-termism" (not that Li & Fung appears to have any returns problems of its own in the short term). The firm sets a rigid three-year strategic plan for itself and then doesn't change it. The goals of the 1998–2001 plan were to double earnings again, as the firm has done every three years since 1992, and to become global.

Part of its globalization involves intelligent pieces of non-conformism, like staffing its entire Korean operation with women because Korean companies tend to be so beastly to them (so they're delighted to move) and Li & Fung has found them far more entrepreneurial than the men. It also involves the use of Western managers acquired through purchases of trading units of Inchcape, a British firm with strong Asian connections. William says with satisfaction that these expatriate managers, unlike Hong Kong colleagues, will fan out anywhere in the world as "a mobile strike force" to get business for the firm. Like everybody else among Li & Fung's top 100 managers, the expats and the Korean women negotiate individual employment contracts with the firm under which their compensation consists mostly of bonuses tied without limit to the profits they generate. If they do well, they can do very well: William says that in 1998 under this system five managers got paid more than he did.

If that sounds even more American than the Americans, Li & Fung nonetheless shows a very Asian attitude to employee relations. William says that when he and Victor returned from America to Hong Kong in the 1970s they found that they couldn't use many of the things they had learned. Whereas the American methods are better at planning the structure of the business, he feels that the Chinese model is better for handling the human behavior of the organization:

> You can't be at loggerheads with local culture; we have a lot of longtime employees and we have to take care of them. Businessess here are very socially based. Your staff will treat the company the same way the company treats them. We Chinese have a saying: "At some point the mountain meets the

stream," meaning you don't destroy relations with people you are bound to run across again. People go through cycles. They can't be at peak efficiency all the time. You must have some tolerance, and then the staff will see the company through troughs too.

William finds that explaining the firm's human-resources policy to investors takes a lot of time, "but we stick to our guns." The devotion to long-term profits is easier because few retail investors go for Li & Fung stock: it is held mostly by institutional investors, who have the 3 to 5 year returns horizon that the brothers Fung consider about right.

These three Hong Kong models probably give as good a guide as any to the nature of the next-generation Asian firm: strongly influenced by America and by the power of technology and finance, but also embodying a culture that puts a higher premium on personal and group loyalty than individualistic Americans do. To revise the quote with which this chapter opened, it looks as though in the new Asian firm the watchwords will be Asian values but American numbers. Which may well be what Asian societies as a whole also come to look like.

PART FOUR

POLITICS
AND SOCIETY

CHAPTER

15

Participation and Democracy

It is the bourgeois spirit, more than a particular system, that
provides for stability and civil society—
Robert Kaplan, quoted in The New York Times, *June 30, 1998*

One of the most surprising features of the Asian crisis of 1997–98
was that, except in Indonesia, there was so little political upheaval
or social unrest. It is surprising because the natural assumption
would be that precipitous falls in income would breed disorder—especially in places that had enjoyed a generation or two of almost constantly rising standards of living and had little or no welfare net to
cushion the fall. But with that one big exception (Indonesia's 210 million people make it the world's fourth most populous country), it simply
did not happen. In a dramatic way, this equipoise amid turbulence
raises again the always vexed question of authoritarianism and democracy in Asia.

The suffering was real enough. At the relatively mild end of the scale
unemployment rates doubled or worse. At the more severe end people
started going hungry. Taking Thailand as a convenient example—it's a
middle-income country where the crisis started, after all—surveys reveal a dismal picture. The prison population, already at full capacity at
the end of 1997, doubled in the following two years, with almost all the

increase due to drug offenses. Suicides went up by 40 percent between 1996 and 1998, the number of children sent to orphanages rose by a fifth and the divorce rate sharply increased. Chris Baker, an economist and consultant in Bangkok, guesses that at the height of the problems as much as 20 percent of the capital's migrant-heavy population moved back to the countryside.

Yet all this is somewhat deceptive. The worsening trends in social indicators like divorce were in place well before the crisis. Moreover, except in already rich countries like Japan and Taiwan, modernizing Asia's great progress has been concentrated in a few cities like Bangkok; the countryside, where most Asians still live, has benefited mostly from money sent back by daughters who became bar girls and sons who became construction workers in the big cities. Baker and his wife Pasuk Phongpaichit, an expert on the Thai underground economy, point out that the "crisis" barely changed the lives of the vast majority of Thais who are outside Bangkok. They benefited marginally from the boom and were hurt marginally by the bust. A lot of them had to move out of Bangkok—and when things got better they moved right back in—but they knew how tough life was before they moved to Bangkok in the first place, and were not overly fazed by a downturn that was based on electronic zeros and ones moved around the world on satellites and fiber-optic cables by banks with assets six times as big as their whole country's annual GDP. Anyway, being young—as almost all Asian countries are—means being resilient.

Lastly, the urban middle class that you would expect to have been battered by these tides of globalization mostly wasn't. The huge savings generated in the good years nicely tided the well-off over. ACNielsen, an American market research company, found that the number of city-dwelling Asians with above-average incomes and ownership of a car, a computer or a credit card rose by 10 percent in the "crisis" years of 1997–99, to reach 10 percent to 20 percent of the whole population in Hong Kong, Kuala Lumpur, Singapore and Taipei, and around 5 percent in Bangkok, Manila and Jakarta. Even in worst-hit Indonesia, Nielsen found that 20 million people during the depths of the downturn were still spending no less than $100 a month on rent and food, which is why so many western retailers busily went on putting up new hyperstores in the place (see Chapter 13). What, if anything, did governments have to do with this ability of societies and economies to bounce back?

OH NO, NOT ASIAN VALUES AGAIN

In the mid-1990s an extremely tiresome debate about something called "Asian values" was conducted over and over again in articles, columns and speeches by people in both the West and Asia who care about such things. Maybe they just got tired, but most of the people who used to offer an opinion shut up about it once the Asian financial crisis broke. The main reason a stop was put to it is that, as in the case of the furious arguments in the mid-1980s about whether Japanese capitalism was superior to America's version, events in the real world seemed to have made even the premise of the argument silly. Once much of East Asia had collapsed in 1997–98, the triumphalism of some Asians about the virtues of their social and political methods seemed to have no place, and the worries of some westerners that maybe their values were not self-evidently universal seemed groundless.

This is too simple, because the debate was about a difference of attitude that remains both real and interesting. The West's unquestioning devotion to electoral democracy for everybody everywhere immediately, and its belief in the primacy of individual rights (usually called human rights, which wearing that emotive label are also universally supported in the West), does suggest a common view about some fundamental issues. Yet there is plenty of evidence that an equally deeply held—and significantly different—view about many of these same issues is shared by Asians of all sorts of ethnic, religious and even political stripes. Consider the opinions of two antagonistic Asian celebrities, one from Singapore and the other from Hong Kong, about social policy.

Lee Kuan Yew's views about the importance of order, authority and discipline are well-known (though his total willingness, extremely rare in western politicians among others, to engage in a no-holds-barred intellectual debate is not much appreciated, probably because his detractors are justifiably scared of getting beaten up—see a telling 1999 interview with William Safire of *The New York Times*, www.nytimes.com/library/opinion/safire/022299safi-text.html). But Lee's conviction about something else is even more arresting. It is the biological one that the "building brick of society" is not the individual but the family. And if there is a dominant strain in modern Singapore's social policy it is the effort to make the family paramount. As he once said, "Governments will come, governments will go, but this endures." Or, more specifically:

Whatever you do, however remarkable your technology, you are not going to change the way children have to be brought up. You can't program a child like a computer. A child grows up with inborn instincts, but the moral values have to be inculcated. That is done by interaction between mother and child, father and child, between siblings and friends—the social environment. If you destroy that incubator what have you got left? You've got Columbine [Columbine is a high school in suburban Denver, Colorado, where just before I interviewed Lee a couple of misfit students had mowed down several of their fellow students and a teacher with automatic weapons]. There you have liberty and freedom carried to extremes. Parents had gone to the police [about threats at Columbine] to ask for action and were told to go away. You've got to interfere with the rights of an individual when he becomes a menace to other people's rights. However you improve technology, the way to bring up a child does not change. If you want your child to be a decent, moral, self-respecting, filial son or daughter and a good citizen, you've got to provide him with examples and precepts.

The public-policy implications of this conviction may not seem immediately obvious, but the road to them is in fact pretty straight. You emphasize education, you keep taxes low, you do not provide public welfare for broken families, and you force people to save for their old age (or make their families do it) rather than putting the burden on the taxpayer. You probably also—Singapore makes a point of it—shame not just some teenager hauled into court but his whole family for what he's done.

Now consider Hong Kong's Jimmy Lai (see Chapter 10), one of Asia's born rebels. Entirely self-made (in case you don't remember, he is a junior-high-school dropout who fled from China to Hong Kong and had no further formal education), he is a serially successful businessman in the retail trade, print media and now (he hopes) Internet retailing. He despises political authority of all kinds, especially that of China's Communists, whom he gives no more than another decade in power. He also cannot stomach Lee Kuan Yew. When I asked him in 1998 about Singapore's future, Lai said the city-state was "no different from a big conglomerate that has to change," and when asked when he thought things would change there he exploded: "I really don't know. I hope Lee Kuan Yew dies tomorrow so that the change comes quickly. As long as he's there, you know, he's definitely a deterrent to change." Nonetheless, a few years earlier I was at a small lunch in Hong Kong where Lai lectured a visiting *New York Times* editor about the importance of not allowing welfare states to develop and in fact of America demolishing the welfare system it already had. When the shocked Manhattan liberal asked how the poor would then get by, Lai shot back: "They'll do what humans have naturally done for millions of years. They'll form families."

Despite the broad Asian consensus in favor of what in America has sometimes been called "family values," the grip of the region's governments on social behavior and cultural expression is noticeably weakening. The Singapore government is usually the best indicator of what is happening on this score because it is so explicit in its aims and reasoning and has been among the strictest in curbing public expressions of sentiments it thinks may harm society. True to form, I thought, when in the spring of 2000 Singapore's government-owned television banned an episode of "Ally McBeal" because it contained a brief lesbian kissing scene. Yet at just about the same time Singapore's *Straits Times,* the main English-language daily that is no government mouthpiece but certainly is sensitive to strong government disapproval, prominently ran a notice on its entertainment page of a new play "based on what a group of women say about their vaginas." The play ("Vaginalogues") was even being put on in Mandarin instead of English. Just a couple of years before, it would have been inconceivable for the government to have allowed a public theater to perform something like this—especially in Chinese—let alone for *The Straits Times* to run such an explicit notice of it.

The truth is that Singapore has long been surprisingly tolerant of aberrant behavior so long as it was kept entirely private. I was surprised many years ago, for example, to discover that in Singapore known homosexuals and even homosexual clubs suffered no official harassment if they did not flaunt themselves. Singapore's leaders are no fools about the run of human behavior, but the distinction between public and private spheres is important to them. Said George Yeo, the trade minister (and before that a longtime culture minister), when asked by a journalist why censorship should exist when society was becoming more open and free, or even whether censorship was any longer possible:

> Well, censorship is part of education. We are not trying to prevent young children physically from accessing pornography. They will always be able to find it in college or from their peers. It is on the Net. You can't stop it. But do you condone it? There is always a certain amount of hypocrisy involved in all of this. But then, as they say, hypocrisy is the compliment which vice pays to virtue.

Through symbolic censorship, you establish in young minds that certain standards of right and wrong exist. We will always fall short of those standards, but we must have them. If you access a porn site on the Internet in front of your teacher, you will be rebuked and punished. Now, is that censorship? It is a form of censorship. The teacher is completely aware that when the child is on his own he is going to access the same site. But not in front of me, please, and not blatantly and not in school and not in the public library. Because if you do it in school or in the public library, there will be a negative reaction. In this way, the norms of a culture are established in the tribe or the community—which is necessary. In the end, you must still have a sense of what is right and wrong.

Yet the government has recognized that many kinds of public behavior it used to find intolerable must now be allowed. The hard-to-tame Internet is only part of this conversion. By 2000 Singapore was a solidly middle-class city—incomes even in dollar terms were higher than America's—and the tolerance of Singaporeans for government bossiness was lower than it used to be. Lee Hsien Loong, Lee Kuan Yew's elder son and Singapore's prime-minister presumptive, points out that since 85 percent of Singaporeans now get some higher education compared to 20 percent in his generation (he turned 49 in 2000), they have to be given more leeway: "If we respond with a sledgehammer and demolish or humiliate people every time they disagree with us, then nobody is going to speak up."

And one of the crucial reasons for allowing people to speak up and read and see what they like is the rapid globalization of the market for the world's best-educated and most talented people. This works both ways. First, Singapore has long had a brain-drain problem with its own citizens, many of whom have preferred less constricted places to live, and the problem is becoming more acute as options for the best of them widen geographically. As George Yeo says:

You still have powers of monopoly, you still have powers of legal violence over your own citizens. You can do nasty things to them. You can make life miserable for them. You can hound them for taxes and so on. But eventually the smart ones say, "Why must I put up with all this hassle? I can be just as comfortable in Hong Kong as I am in new York or Sydney." Governments are being forced by external competitive pressure to change and reform.

Second, there is the matter of attracting foreign talent. One of the most interesting questions of social change everywhere in the next couple of decades is going to be the ability of a country to absorb immigrants. America's strength in this respect is unparalleled, and it is going to be one of the major questions hanging over Europe's ability to become a real counterweight to the United States in the next generation (see next chapter). A Europe that does not get better at bringing in and integrating much larger numbers of young people from places to its east and south is increasingly going to resemble an old folks' home for whites. Japan, whose society has about as much absorptive capacity as oil-cloth, faces the greatest challenge because it has the rich world's fastest-aging and fastest-shrinking population. In the late 1990s there were about 1.4 million foreigners living (legally and illegally) in Japan, the lowest percentage of immigrants and expatriate workers in the rich world; but the UN has estimated that given the speed at which the country's working-age population is shrinking Japan needs to take in at least 600,000 foreigners a year indefinitely (i.e., the whole of the present stock every two years) merely to maintain the present size of its workforce. The social resistance to any such thing is so embedded that it is fair to say Japan's antipathy to immigration, especially the immigration of other Asians who are the logical candidates to go there in numbers, is the biggest threat to its future prosperity.

Singapore, by contrast, has made the internationalization of its population a central plank of policy (see Chapter 9). This is in fact one of the things behind the government's recent moves to loosen its cultural grip. As Yeo puts it:

> We know that to attract scientists, scholars and entrepreneurs to Singapore, we must provide cultural facilities and nurture the arts. They provide brain food. Why have they become brain food? One day we will find out. But provide the food and the brains will come. Starve them of this food and they will leave for somewhere else. Because we brought tens of thousands of talented foreigners into Singapore in the past ten years, we're seeing a wonderful efflorescence. Cross-fertilization is an essential part of the creative process.
>
> Diversity breeds creativity when the combination is right. It can also lead to conflict and friction. If you have a culture that enables you to absorb talented individuals and fit them into the community, and allow them to knock against each other in a creative way, then you succeed. If you can't accommodate the tensions, then the diversity is destructive.

"Fitting them into the community," however, is the trick, especially when the community is led by people who have so clear an idea of what values it should harbor. On the issue of Singapore opening itself up more, Lee Kuan Yew says simply, "We have no choice," but when challenged as to how Singapore can preserve Asian values when half the population is not Asian, he replies:

> Well, I'm not so sure that it cannot be done. You've got to start off with a core group, right? If you don't allow that core group which holds those values to weaken, then newcomers will adjust to that core culture. You take the Americans here. We have 25,000 Americans and their children. You just impose those values and say you will comply and after awhile . . . well, I'm told many Americans now who are taking refuge from the troubles in Indonesia are very pleased that their children are free from all those stresses. We get them to change. They comply with our values. I'm not saying you won't change. I mean, you cannot *not* change. Culture that doesn't change is a dead culture. The culture has got to change, but with the parts which are valuable for survival, which have proven to be necessary to transmit survival instincts from generation to generation, being retained.

It is hard to escape the conclusion that social and cultural liberalism will be gradually insinuating itself in Asia over the next decade but that—thanks to the widespread antagonism of most Asians to welfare-state attitudes and policies—Asians at all levels of income are going to remain more family-bound than their western counterparts. A strong case can be made that a fair amount of freedom combined with strong family-based societies is what has made Asia quite stable in the face of the economic ups and downs of the past few years. Most Europeans would find the idea odd, but it may be that government's absence as an income stabilizer made things better than they would otherwise have been. But then perhaps the spread of democracy will make Asian governments rather different, and rather more like their western counterparts, than they have been before.

SUBSTANCE AND PROCEDURE

Most businessmen (and in fact most ordinary people) wish politics would just go away. The sentiment is perfectly understandable but, like most emotions, it isn't clear-headed. The Asian proof that the quality of government matters is simple, and is found on the Korean peninsula. The distinction between North Koreans and South Koreans is negligible—Korea may be even more homogeneous than Japan—and before the war of 1950–53 split the country the North was the richer part. Since then, South Korea has increased real incomes at least twenty-fold, bringing them to between a third and a half of American levels and making the country a member of the OECD. Meanwhile, real incomes in the North have grown little if at all, and in the late 1990s hunger loomed so large that mass deaths from famine were feared and the Chinese were shoving back desperate North Koreans trying to get across the border into the promised land of Manchuria. There is no explanation for these almost quantum-mechanically different levels of performance except that for 40 years South Korea has had a very good government and North Korea has had one of the world's worst.

What has made for good government in Asia is a subject of fierce debate, but one thing that became clear during the crisis and its aftermath is that the recipe for success is undergoing a significant change. To understand how the change is happening, begin with this thumbnail sketch of Asian politics given to me in 1998 by Robert Scalapino, a retired professor at the University of California at Berkeley who is one of the wisest men on the subject:

> I would hazard one generalization about Asian politics. I am very wary of cultural generalizations and I think most of them are fallacious. First of all, there is no one Asia; there are enormous differences. And secondly, most of these cultural distinctions are more complex than some of the journalists make out. But I do think that, in very broad terms, politics in the West is based on legalism, despite our transgressions from time to time, whereas politics in Asia has been based very heavily on reciprocity—if you do this for me, I will do that for you. It has been highly personalized, with institutions very secondary to personal relationships and personal power. Hopefully, this crisis may not only improve transparency in terms of financial and banking institutions, in terms of the actions of government and the bureaucracy, but it may also induce a greater honesty, a greater openness in leadership, and strengthen institutions. That is the voice of the optimist. Again, I am sure the scene will vary from one country to another.

In Malaysia the bitter struggle between Prime Minister Mahathir Mohamad and his one-time deputy, Anwar Ibrahim (see Chapter 6), bore all the marks of a time-honored feud typical of the personalization of politics in Asia. The affair resulted in Anwar staying firmly behind bars (having at one point been beaten black-eyed by the Malaysian chief of national police himself, no less) and Mahathir going on to cement his power first in a general election in 1999 and then—despite his coalition's disappointing performance among the core Malay electorate—by facing down an intra-party challenge in early 2000 so effectively that it never even got off the ground. There were a few other examples of this sort of thing—notably the vendetta-like conviction and imprisonment of two former Korean presidents on corruption charges during the presidency of their successor (and Kim Dae Jung's predecessor), Kim Young Sam, in 1996—but it is likely that Mahathir's move against Anwar will prove the last example of rich-country Asian leaders thinking that a spell in prison is a perfectly normal way of dealing with a political foe. (To this day I remain taken aback by Mahathir's cool response at a breakfast meeting in his London hotel penthouse in the mid-1980s to a question about the recent jailing of one of his opponents: "I spent time in prison. It's part of politics.") The cat-fights at the top, after all, are only the most visible sign of how personalized a country's politics are, and the same forces that are changing the way the Asian corporation is run (see Chapter 14) are changing the way governments work as well—and along the same lines. This was Scalapino's guess in 1998 about how it will turn out:

> If one takes an optimistic view, as I tend to, and say that after a couple of years we're going to see a rehabilitated East Asia with more attractive economic policies and structures, then I think we will probably see an effort to strengthen the rule of law, the judicial aspect of the system. It's interesting that even in China this is going on rather significantly.
>
> I think that we will also probably see an effort to shore up parliamentary systems, and here much will depend upon the reforms and effectiveness of political parties and of their leaders. In a sense this is not just an Asian problem. If you look at present trends in the United States, I think there is a very great disillusionment with politics, with Congress, with the presidency. If you asked the average American, are politicians honest, are they worthy of respect, you know the answers, the polls have shown this, and I think there is a general crisis of democracy today. Asia's problem may be more acute in the sense that it doesn't have an institutional base that's really strong, its institutions are very recent, whereas ours are a couple of

hundred years old. But as I said earlier, this personalization is so powerful in Asian societies that it's very difficult to implant impersonal institutions and give them priority. But there is some evidence in the acceptance of the legitimacy of elections that we've seen very considerable progress in Korea and Taiwan, less so in Southeast Asia except Thailand; I wish we had better candidates in the Philippines . . .

But in my view, for the foreseeable future Asia will not have a single political system. Some societies will continue with what I've called authoritarian pluralism [tough centralized political rule combined with a diverse civil society] for the indefinite future, for various reasons—size, geographical factors, tradition, whatever. But I think that in general this effort to strengthen the rule of law, the role of the judiciary and the accountability of leaders is going to be a broad trend. Now perhaps the question is, with these institutional developments, can a more open political system avoid stasis, immobility. This is a real threat because if a political system can't act because it's just frozen in conflict, as we wonder today about India or even Japan, then I think a retreat of some sort from democracy is quite possible.

As these remarks suggest, there is a complicated and not at all obvious interaction in Asia between, first, good government; second, democracy; and third, public accountability, transparency and openness. The instinctive assumption of westerners is that these three good things must be more or less co-terminous. In modern Asia they have overlapped surprisingly little.

There are many examples. Singapore's Kishore Mahbubani describes democracy as merely one of "the processes by which governments come into being" and suggests the following qualities as characteristic of good government: "(1) political stability, (2) sound bureaucracies based on meritocracy, (3) economic growth with equity, (4) fiscal prudence and (5) relative lack of corruption." He adds separately that "there should be no torture, no slavery, no arbitrary killings, no disappearances in the middle of the night, no shooting down of innocent demonstrators, no imprisonment without careful review." Singapore itself is the best-known example of good government and accountability though not much democracy (even that is debatable, however, since its elections are clean and devoid of money politics). Hong Kong is a starker example, with good government and practically no effective democracy. India has had democracy but, until recently at least, really bad government. China fails on almost all counts, though its problems are on a scale of their own (see last paragraphs of this section). At the richer end of the scale, Japan has undoubtedly been a democracy, and in the past had many elements of good government though in the 1990s it began faltering badly in producing sensible policies. In South Korea the quality of government policy-making took a dramatic turn for the better with the election of President Kim Dae Jung. The irony there, of course, is that a big reason he was so effective at reforming the economy is that he used to the full the considerable authoritarian powers still vested in the Korean presidency as a legacy of dictatorial rule.

Peering ahead, the only clear trend, as Scalapino pointed out, is likely to be a growth in accountability, openness, rule of law and so on—in other words, the civil institutions of a bourgeois society. One simple thing pushing this is that very few places in Asia have governments that have shone on this score, so the scope for improvement is wide. More broadly, as Singapore's leaders have explicitly recognized, the demands of globalization are so imperative that it is not only companies and societies that are being remade: the strict controls that a government may have been able to exercise when the walls between a single country and the rest of the world were of a given height are not only futile but actually counterproductive when the height of the walls is cut in half. As usual, the impact of the Internet is hard to overestimate. A minor example came in Korea's parliamentary election in April 2000, when candidates' records (including criminal ones) were mercilessly scrutinized on unofficial websites devoted to unmasking the politicians, and those most harshly criticized overwhelmingly lost. More significantly, with the Internet driving a revolution in efficiency and transparency through the corporate sector in the next few years, it will be impossible for governments to keep delivering their services in quite the inefficient and opaque way they have in the past. This will change governments everywhere, but in relative terms probably nowhere as much as in Asia.

It is also likely that democratization will spread in Asia, though more haltingly than those other bourgeois institutions. In Taiwan in 2000, as in South Korea a couple of years earlier, the formal transition to full ballot-box democracy was completed with the election of an opposition candidate to the presidency—though in both places it will be a very long haul toward building up the supporting political institutions of a fully democratic regime. Indonesia likewise became something of a democracy in

1999, but there too a democratic superstructure exists without much if any of the infrastructure (see next section). All in all, though, the democratization of Asia is likely to be a slow process.

Does that matter? A strong theoretical argument for the superiority of a democratic system was put forward by Mancur Olson, an American economist, in a book called *Power and Prosperity* that he finished just before he died in 1998. Olson asks why governments are formed in the first place, and proposes a schematic sequence of historical events that gradually led to rulers identifying more and more with the broadest interests of society and hence pursuing policies that maximized society's long-term capacity to produce wealth. In the beginning, organized force was monopolized by nomadic raiders whose only interest was to pillage as much and as fast as possible: the long-term health of the communities they raided was of no concern to them whatever. The next stage was the creation of strong governments ruling more or less fixed pieces of territory. Even tyrannical versions of these governments had an interest in limiting their exactions of their subjects' wealth because, unlike the raiders, the tyrants did not move on after snatching private property and so had an incentive to keep the goose healthy enough to lay golden eggs year after year. The subjects, too, were happier with this state of affairs. At least the tyrant could protect them from the raiders, and that was a lot better than what had gone before.

The last stage of this process involves the creation and gradual extension of private-property protections and other curbs on the power of rulers until, with full democracy and the entrenchment of affiliated institutions like the rule of law, the government identifies as much as possible with the long-term interests of the population at large and limits its take—now in the form of taxes—to an amount consistent with promoting those interests. Olson was not starry-eyed about democracy. He first made his name with a devastating explanation of why democracies were almost inevitably prone to be captured by special-interest groups that twisted policy to suit themselves rather than the people at large, and which kept increasing the amount of private income that government helped itself to. But he still thought that democracy offered the best curb on the predatory powers of the state.

Yet his argument has many holes, especially in the Asian context. On the negative side, it would take quite a democratic idealist to argue that the brigandage, instability and economic drift that masquerade as "democracy" in Russia form a superior system to China's authoritarianism. More important, there is just no evidence that in Asia good government and democracy have gone hand in hand as the continent enjoyed its spectacular economic rise. There is plenty of support for the common sense proposition that democracy, openness and so on have been a gradually unfolding consequence of the material enrichment fostered by good government. But more often than not in developing Asia, it has been authoritarian regimes rather than prematurely democratic ones that have delivered good government. The reason, which fits with Olson's thinking about what makes for good government though not his views on how you produce it, is that the successful Asian authoritarians had the power to squash special interests in favor of the country's development as a whole and were actually willing to do so (on both counts unlike democratic counterparts in, e.g., the Philippines and India). It is likely, for example, that no Japanese government reflecting the popular will could have done what General MacArthur's dictatorial procuratorship after 1945 did to break the back of Japan's past and prepare it so well for the future. But home-grown authoritarians in East Asia, especially in South Korea and Taiwan up through the 1980s, took the same tack to equally spectacular effect. The mystery is what peculiar mix of history and culture allowed this to happen in Asian autocracies when the opposite seems to have occurred elsewhere (notably save General Pinochet's Chile in the 1970s and 1980s), but happen it did.

This is why a more subtle and convincing argument than Olson's about the importance of democracy has been delivered by another economist, this one a Nobel prize-winner, Amartya Sen, who (perhaps not coincidentally) is himself an Asian though one with a strong liberal democratic bent. In a lecture he gave in Singapore in 1999, Sen supported the undeniable though often denied proposition that for the long-run economic development of poor countries what counts is the pursuit of a few crucial policies, and that if those policies are pursued the nature of the political system is irrelevant—the country will haul itself out of poverty. Conversely, if they are not pursued the nature of the political system is also irrelevant—the country will stay poor. The policies which matter are those that "go early for human development, focusing on the basic enhancement of human capabilities." The specific policies— universal education (especially of girls, because of the effect it has on population growth), basic health care, land reform, the availability of credit—not only in themselves improve people's lives but give them "broadened *access* to the opportunities of the market economy," which not only helps them but helps the economy to grow.

Sen contrasts the modern experience of quasi-democratic India and quasi-totalitarian China. By all measures of human welfare and economic progress, China trounced India in 1950–99. The explanation is pretty clear-cut. Prompted by feel-good European socialist ideals, India spent its scarce bureaucratic and financial resources on grandiose schemes like a vast and detailed program to regulate and direct industry and next to nothing on basic human development in a country where 80 percent of the people still lived on the land. Prompted by its peasant origins and egalitarian ideals, Maoism in China poured its even scarcer resources into land reform (too bad about the landlords), basic education and health care. India's "democracy" became a vehicle for serving the elite, to the point where by end-century almost half the population was still illiterate, compared with a single-figure share in China, even though six times as many Indians as Chinese have university education. Of course it matters that China turned to the market economy as early as 1979, while India started only in 1991, but the important thing is that the mass of Chinese had been prepared to take advantage of the benefits of the market well before that. Sen's most devastating point is that, for all of the Maoist regime's vileness in so many other respects (my phrase, not his), even *before* China started going to market it was outperforming India despite the Great Leap Forward, the Cultural Revolution and other Chinese disruptions, because China consistently invested in human development and India did not.

The second half of Sen's story, however, is even more intriguing. As the saying goes, "in the long run we're all dead," and the fact that authoritarian regimes seem just as capable as looser ones—if not more so—at putting the right long-term policies in place does not end the discussion. Sen notes that it is "absolutely obligatory to see *security* as a central part of development. A view of development that judges progress by long-run growth averages and by the strength of upward trends misses out something truly central to the process of development, viz. protection against downside risk at a given moment of time." In other words, "the challenge of development includes *both* the elimination of persistent and endemic deprivation, and the prevention of sudden and severe destitution." And "in ensuring security in the form of avoidance of disaster—whether originating in natural calamities or in policy blunders—democracy and participatory politics have important roles to play."

The reason is that downturns and crises are "very divisive," with each group tending to adopt an attitude of every-man-for-himself and certain groups therefore bearing a disproportionate share of the burden (see first section of this chapter). Sen won his Nobel prize for his work on the causes of famine, which he found were always the product of a failure of government rather than of the crops. He argues:

> The instrumental role of democracy (including elections, multi-party politics, a free media, etc.) in making sure that the government does respond to people's needs and predicament can be of great practical significance. In analyzing this connection, we have to consider the political incentives that operate on governments and on the persons and groups who are in office. The rulers have the incentive to listen to what people want if they have to face their criticism and seek their support in elections.
>
> It is, thus, not astonishing at all that no substantial famine has ever occurred in any independent country with a democratic form of government and a relatively free press. They have occurred in ancient kingdoms and contemporary authoritarian societies, in primitive tribal communities and in modern technocratic dictatorships, in colonial economies run by imperialists from the North and in newly independent countries of the South run by despotic national leaders or by intolerant single parties. But they have never materialized in any country that is independent, that goes to elections regularly, that has opposition parties to voice criticisms, and that permits newspapers to report freely and question the wisdom of government policies without excessive censorship.

Sen says that this analysis applies not just to the extreme case of famines but to any significant economic disruption—like the one that hit Asia in 1997–98:

> Even though a fall of 5 or 10 percent of national income is comparatively moderate, it can decimate lives and create misery for millions, if the burden of contraction is not shared together but allowed to be heaped on those, the unemployed or newly made economically redundant, who can least bear it. The victims in Indonesia may not have taken very great interest in democracy when things went up and up. But when things came tumbling down for some parts of the population, the lack of democratic institutions kept their voices muffled and ineffective. The protective umbrella of democracy is strongly missed exactly when it is most needed. Not

surprisingly, democracy became a major issue precisely at a time of crisis, when the economically dispossessed felt strongly the need for a political voice.

This great weakness of authoritarian systems—their instability when things start to go wrong—naturally brings to mind the place in Asia where the risk of a social and political breakdown over the next decade seems highest and, if it happened, could lead to disaster throughout East Asia. Because of the weakness of its public institutions, modern (including pre-Communist) China has always been prone to sudden lurches both of leadership and of policies and political behavior. Outsiders probably make too much of this. The Chinese have grown accustomed to a degree of disorder that would alarm anyone coming from a more even-keeled place, and it bears repeating that although China's institutions are weak Chinese society—and especially the extended family—are extremely strong. As Scalapino points out, even the horror of the Cultural Revolution "demonstrated anew the fact that Chinese society can live with a high degree of tension and chaos, perhaps in part because its nuclear units remain so cohesive." Indeed, an argument can be made (as Hong Kong's Toby Brown does) that over the next decade the best recipe for China would be not democratization but an iron-fisted government capable of keeping order and stomping on corruption while simultaneously withdrawing completely from the SOEs and letting the country's still robust Confucian society operate unhindered by party or state.

The trouble with this recipe is that the time pressure for some institutional improvements—regularizing the relationships between different provinces or regions and the central government, and shoring up the rule of law—is beginning to grow. China's leaders are as aware as anyone of the danger Sen describes: that if economic growth seriously faltered the rigidity of the political system could generate considerable instability, which is why the leadership was so determined not to let growth fall too much during the Asian downturn of 1997–98. It is also why, with communism a dead letter ideologically, the government has been pushing Chinese nationalism—of which there is naturally plenty anyway—as a source of "values" for the country.

The worrying thing is not that China remains illiberal—a gradual evolution through Scalapino's "authoritarian pluralism" offers a good prospect for the country while fast democratization would offer disaster—but that its leaders seem to have no inclination to plan any political evolution at all. By 1999–2000 they appeared determined, if anything, to tighten the screws on any sort of political pluralism, including seemingly apolitical spiritual movements that for some reason they nonetheless found a menace to their grip on power, and freeish speech in the media and on the Internet. This is understandable in light of the tough hand that is going to be needed to deal with unemployment and the other dislocations that will arise from the dismantling of state enterprises (see Chapter 8), but on its own it is not a sustainable policy for the long run. In Shanghai in September 1999, Lee Kuan Yew gave a speech in which he tactfully but publicly reminded China's leaders that they needed somehow to move to "a more participatory system of governance." The reason is that the growth of a middle class in China and the political methods of close neighbors as Japan, South Korea and Taiwan "will have a profound influence on the Chinese people's aspirations for reforms in the governance of China. Unless the system can adjust itself to meet the increasing demand for good government, its legitimacy will be questioned." In other words, things may be all right for the moment but China's leaders need to envision a more pluralist political future and start taking a series of small but targeted steps for getting there. No place has better illustrated the dangers of not preparing for the future than Indonesia.

SUHARTO INTESTATE

Let us begin by throwing one popular misconception overboard. This is that President Suharto, who ruled Indonesia for 32 years before his forced ouster in May 1998, was a despot, and that his time in office was a catastrophe for the country. True, he gradually gathered almost all political power into his own hands, his regime became increasingly corrupt after time as his business cronies and greedy children were given freer and freer rein to make money from their connections to the president, and the institutions of state—particularly the civil service and the courts—were weak and usually corrupt. But, although there were a few political prisoners, Indonesia was no police state. Opposition politicians were hampered in their activities (especially Megawati Sukarnoputri, daughter of the populist President Sukarno whom Suharto had overthrown) but were not silenced or jailed, the press had a fair amount of leeway despite the occasional shutdown of bolder publications, and many of the institutions of civil society functioned without much restriction—particularly various Muslim associations, including the one headed by Suharto's eventual elected successor, Abdurrahman Wahid.

When Suharto took over in the mid-1960s, Indonesia was on the brink of disintegration. An attempted Communist coup and subsequent purge and score-settling had left hundreds of thousands dead, many of them members of the ethnic Chinese minority, and the economy was in a shambles. By the mid-1990s the vast and diverse archipelago was mostly united and stable, with its majority Muslim and minority Chinese communities living in tolerance if not exactly friendship. Most important, Indonesia had enjoyed a great improvement in material welfare. I'll quote from my earlier book again:

> In the late 1960s almost two-thirds of Indonesians were living in absolute poverty; life expectancy was the lowest in East or Southeast Asia, infant mortality among the highest in the world, primary-school enrollment and adult literacy almost as low as India's, and secondary-school enrollment much lower than India's. After a quarter-century of the usual East Asian tonic, when Indonesia's economy grew at an annual rate of more than 6 percent a year, the incidence of terrible poverty had fallen by three-quarters, life expectancy had risen by 20 years, primary schooling was universal, the rate of secondary schooling had almost quintupled, and adult illiteracy had fallen by two-thirds. Savings and investment rates both tripled to roughly 25 percent, and more than half of Indonesia's exports were manufactured goods, compared with the 97 percent that had been oil and primary products only 25 years before.

In some ways, considering how late Indonesia embarked on economic development and reform and how far back it was at the start, this is one of the best records in Southeast Asia—certainly so in the case of education when you compare Indonesia with, e.g., Thailand. Far from being a monstrous regime Suharto's was, at least in economic terms, almost an exemplary one: so much so that as one western investor naughtily put it to me in 1997, assuming the Suharto family stole, say, $5 billion–$10 billion (a plausible figure), if you compare that to the addition to national wealth over those decades then Indonesia did not get a bad deal at all, certainly no worse than shareholders in some American companies who happily shell out $100 million-plus in annual compensation to CEOs who add proportionally less to their company's market cap than Suharto did to Indonesia's wealth and its ability to grow in the future.

The trouble lay instead with the second of Amartya Sen's points about the usefulness of democracy. As Suharto's time in office wore on, he created more and more of a power vacuum around himself so that no political rival could be established. What that meant, of course, is that there was no remotely plausible successor—personal or institutional—in place when disaster struck in 1997–98. The crucial element of security in a downturn was completely absent. It is no accident, harking back to Sen, that only in Indonesia in 1997–98 did famine threaten anywhere as a result of the Asian financial crisis.

The comprehensiveness of Indonesia's collapse—especially contrasted with its neighbors' resilience—nonetheless remains a puzzle. On the financial front, a persuasive explanation for the depth of the rupiah's plunge in a country with an open capital account is still lacking (see Chapter 6). But the same is true of society and politics: Indonesia seemed fairly steady, but when things started going wrong it looked at risk of descending into anarchy and even civil war. By the spring of 1998 rioting was rampant in Jakarta and other big cities, with ethnic Chinese the main targets. A lot of fake atrocity photos were posted on the Internet during this breakdown of law and order, but I think the following e-mail, sent to me from Medan, was authentic:

> You see the scale of the riot was so big that the authority just couldn't cope with it for the first few days and on top of that, having to adhere to the "principles" of Human Rights they couldn't do any harm to the rioters which were in fact out not to demonstrate with the students but to rob and loot—they could only fire warning shots in the air. So the rioters went on their rampage as if no police and army were present, by first breaking down locked doors of shophouses and then started looting and in some cases after looting they set fire to us poor Chinese's houses!! In almost all areas the youths of 12–14 year olds would started to stone and then forced open doors with crowbars and what-not and when they succeeded, women (grandmothers too) and children as young as 5–6 years old will come for the spoil (these are confirmed, I don't make them up for dramatization). There were many gruesome facts of gross abuses of Human Rights on us Chinese which the western media are trying to cover up so as not to mar the glorification of the so-called student movement, 99 percent of property

destroyed belong to Chinese and in some cases the mob stood outside houses banging away at doors to demand the owners came out and when the owners didn't they started the burning and that resulted in one 13-year old Chinese girl being burnt to death but of course you'll never hear about it from the media here or otherwise.

Many western media portray these bastards as the poor and hungry ones but I don't see any shortage of food or anything in this natural-resource rich North Sumatra province and don't you know that many sold the goods in the side streets afterwards—sacks of rice as cheap as half the original price and televisions for a fraction of the listed price! Have you ever seen the hungry in any part of this world loot and rob shophouses and sold the loot afterwards? As a result of these enormous pressures on us who have been abandoned by our own protectors we paid tax to, we were forced to form groups of vigilantes patrolling our own neighborhood and in some cases there were clashes with these bastards resulting in bloody casualties on both sides but as a result of these vigilant acts, we Medan Chinese had prevented worse violence on us. You see, in Medan every Chinese stood up regardless of how much savings you had before in the banks—from the poorest to some conglomerate-quality ones and you know what, it actually made us proud to be able to stick together and in a sense it lessen the fear each of us have inside us!! Never have this phenomena happened before for us overseas Chinese here who I'm sure you know pretty well we're always the target of their fury at any problems. WE WERE THE TRADITIONAL SCAPEGOATS since the beginning of the formation of this republic!

A couple of months later, when I was in Jakarta, I went to Chinatown and found block after block of burnt buildings with smashed windows. The Balkanization of Southeast Asia along Malay–vs.–Chinese racial lines is everyone's nightmare, and in Indonesia in the spring of 1998 it started happening. Rich Chinese fled the country, taking scores of billions of dollars with them. After soldiers fired on student demonstrators in Jakarta, killing a handful of them in circumstances that still have not been adequately explained (Was it a mistake? A disguised coup attempt by Suharto's son-in-law, the general in charge?), Suharto threw in the towel in May. As pointed out in Chapter 6, Lee Kuan Yew blames misplaced American idealism for the collapse: "reform or perish," the Americans told Suharto, and a lot more than his presidency perished.

Suharto was succeeded by his vice-president, a weird jumpy little bug-eyed man named B. J. Habibie who—Jakarta rumor had it at the time of the presidential election early in 1998—had been named as the president's running mate because Suharto figured nobody would try to shove him out of office if they knew Habibie was waiting in the wings. There ensued almost 18 months of paralysis, as an extraordinarily cumbersome constitutional process was set in motion to choose the next president. Indonesia's economy shrank 14 percent in 1998 and inflation exceeded 80 percent; there were shortages of rice and cooking oil. Public order of a sort returned, but in 1998–99 outbursts of ethnic and separatist violence flared in scattered places in the huge archipelago, notably in East Timor which eventually voted for independence in 1999 in a referendum that was followed by an army-inspired pogrom that displaced at least half the population.

After mind-bogglingly complex maneuvering, in late 1999 a new president was chosen by an electoral assembly. Abdurrahman Wahid, better known by his Javanese nickname Gus Dur (roughly "older brother"), took office at age 59 half-blind and frail from a stroke a couple of years earlier, and tried to create a workable government by selecting as his vice president the sloth-like Megawati Sukarnoputri, who impresses no one except the voters: they had given her party a plurality in the election for the assembly. Wahid spent almost all his time during his first six months in office traveling to get diplomatic support (successful), outflanking his army opponents and bringing the often restive military under civilian control (apparently successful), and trying to defuse separatist agitations in places like oil-rich Aceh in the west and Irian Jaya in the east (jury still out). He also went some way toward soothing the ethnic tensions that had threatened to rip the country apart: in February 2000, for the first time since the 1960s, Indonesia's Chinese were officially allowed to celebrate the Lunar New Year—the biggest event on the Chinese calendar—in public. There was no violence in response.

Wahid's early political skill, however, was utterly unmatched by even a shred of competence on the part of his government at governing. On its own steam the economy began recovering, with growth of 4 percent projected for 2000. But Wahid's economics team, obviously wet behind the ears, was incapable of forming and executing badly needed clean-up programs. Corruption remained unchecked. A high executive of a supermarket chain told me in 1999 that each store his company opened required 48 permits, which took six months of time and $50,000 in bribes to obtain. When the company complained to government officials that "this is the era of *reformasi*," the protest was met with a shrug: "That's for politicians. We need the money and we don't have any." Bank recapitalization had been accomplished in 1999 by the government issuing recap bonds, but a year later the bonds remained frozen in the banks' vaults rather than trading on the secondary market—meaning the banks still had no cash to resume lending to the credit-starved economy. What's more, by mid-2000 corporate restructuring was also stalled. The government did manage in the spring of 2000 to sell off its interest in one company, Astra International (see Chapter 7), but did so in acrimonious and suspicious circumstances that suggested cronyism was no less strong in the new Indonesia than it had been in the old. Worst of all, it seemed impossible to bring stubborn corporate debtors to heel since the new bankruptcy courts—whether through incompetence or corruption (most bet heavily on the second)—repeatedly refused to throw anybody into insolvency. In the spring of 2000 the IMF threatened to withhold a loan disbursement to Indonesia unless it made some progress toward meeting reform targets. Under Wahid's prodding, the cabinet eventually did enough to get a reprieve but that was all it was. Moreover, during the summer things went from bad to worse as the president appeared to lose his political touch and his behavior became more erratic. A photo of Wahid from August 2000 showing him sound asleep on the parliamentary dais while an aide read the president's own speech said it all. Parliament eventually forced him into a power-sharing arrangement with Megawati that gave every sign it would only worsen the government's muddle.

The lessons from this sad tale are not yet clear, but Indonesia has every chance of chronically suffering from the "stasis and immobility" that Robert Scalapino feared unprepared-for democracy can bring. Indonesia today is depressingly reminiscent of the Philippines after the "People Power" revolution of the mid-1980s threw out a dictator (Ferdinand Marcos) who had been far more rapacious and done far less for his country than Suharto. It took eight years of politicking before the Philippines at last started focusing on policy rather than politics and putting in a decent economic performance. It might take just as long in Indonesia. You can reasonably argue either way whether it was lack of democracy or lack of good government that was to blame for this. What does seem clear is that a smooth succession strategy is crucial—perhaps democracy's strongest point—and on that score Malaysia was by mid-2000 the riskiest place in Asia, more so even than China, which is why Mahathir was so spooked by what befell Suharto. But not every risk in Asia is domestic. The international scene could prove much scarier.

CHAPTER

16

Asia, America and Europe

If we don't understand Italy, and vice versa, it's no big deal. If the U.S. doesn't understand East Asia, we're in trouble.

Washington CySip
Philippine tycoon, 1999

Since the 1980s East Asia has been the most peaceful part of the planet. There were no Iraqs, no Afghanistans, no Chechnyas, no Middle Easts, no Bosnias or Kosovos. "Civilized" Europe killed scores of times more people through state-sponsored violence in the last couple of years of the 1990s than Chinese troops did in the streets around Tiananmen Square in 1989, not that that subtracted an ounce from the self-righteous western indignation constantly vented about Asian disrespect for human rights. Even so, Asia is a region of potentially great geopolitical instability. Unlike in Europe, there is next to nothing keeping a semblance of international order in Asia except the United States—and America is an increasingly fickle policeman.

Bill Perry, a thoughtful man who was Bill Clinton's first defense secretary, points out that Asia has nothing like NATO. The Asian regional defense organization, ARF—Asean Regional Forum, how perfect an acronym is that for a talking shop?—is, as he says, just a forum. Geopolitical stability in Asia, he says, depends on three things: America's bilateral defense treaties with Japan, Australia and several others, and the presence of 100,000 American servicemen in East Asia backing up those commitments; America's always vexed but for 30 years always constant policy of trying to engage China rather than confront it as America did the Soviet

368

Union in the four decades after 1950; and a policy of preventing the spread of nuclear weapons in Asia. A couple of these pillars may be starting to split.

Everybody should be hoping this does not happen, because what Asia needs most over the next couple of decades is a continuation of the status quo as it continues to rise economically. The most important elements of the status quo remain in place even though, as Singapore's Kishore Mahbubani has pointed out, there are several paradoxes about them. The stability of the vital triangular relationship among America, Japan and China, for instance, depends no less on America's defense treaty with Japan than on its engagement with China. Despite their grumbling, the Chinese are aware that without America's sheltering umbrella—which was strengthened in 1998 by a revised security agreement between Japan and the United States—Japan would feel compelled to build up its armed forces significantly and probably arm them with nuclear weapons. Moreover, despite a common cultural background, both China and Japan are more at ease with America as a regional power broker than either would be with the other. Similarly, America's navy offers an implicit guarantee that the sea lanes through Southeast Asian straits and through the South China Sea will remain open for the oil lifeline that runs from the Middle East to Northeast Asia. If America can continue to act for another 20 years as a balance wheel for Asia, and as China is brought fully into organizations like the WTO that tie it more closely to the global system, the odd informal status quo that has kept Asia at peace since the Vietnam war could continue to work indefinitely. Yet the chances are that it may get harder to preserve. In ascending order of the damage they can wreak on the region, there are three main threats.

THE HERMIT COUSINS

Until June 2000, when North Korea abruptly agreed to a summit meeting between its president and his South Korean counterpart, the North Korean regime was apparently crazed and completely impenetrable. This always fed anxieties about the North's intentions, fears that rose all the higher when the North was found in 1994 to be developing a nuclear-weapons program in town called Yongbyon. An agreement was eventually reached to put a stop to that in exchange for billions of dollars in bribes from America, Japan and South Korea, but the doubts were never laid to rest, especially after the discovery of a new nuclear facility under construction in 1998 about 30 miles from Yongbyon. The provocation increased when the North conducted a series of ballistic-missile tests apparently aimed at Japan, as did the uncertainty about the regime's erratic potential when famine threatened the North in 1997–98. The possible dangers of a big war remain high. Bill Perry headed a study which concluded that, by the end of the 1990s, America and South Korea were in a much stronger military position on the peninsula than they had been five years earlier but that, even without a nuclear exchange, allied forces would suffer 100,000 casualties before beating the North.

Yet when in June 2000 the South's president, Kim Dae Jung, traveled to the North Korean capital, Pyongyang, for his summit with the North's number one, Kim Jong Il, the southern Kim—who later in 2000 was awarded the Nobel peace prize in part for his breakthrough to the North—and the televisually on-looking world were pleasantly surprised to discover in the northern Kim an intelligent, civilized, even affable host instead of the nut case of legend (though he could still have used some work on his hair style). Nothing much of substance changed in the few months after this breakthrough, although a visit to Pyongyang in October by the American Secretary of State, Madeleine Albright, seemed likely to pave the way for President Clinton himself to go to the North before he left office, a visit that would rank alongside Sadat's trip to Israel in the 1970s as one of the most dramatic breakthroughs in the annals of diplomatic travel. Meanwhile, a hundred people each from North and South Korea were allowed to go for a few days to the other's capital for emotional reunions with relatives they had not seen in decades, the absurd propaganda barrages ceased, high-level official contacts between the Koreas resumed, and a start was made on restoring a rail link between the two sides. But on the big issues—the North's missile-exporting program and America's deployment of troops in the South—it was business as usual. Most importantly, the matter of the American soldiers, both the United States and South Korea were firm that they would stay put for the foreseeable future, a position the North did not challenge. Nonetheless, the surprise opening did palpably reduce the risks of war.

I personally don't think they were ever that high. For all their absurdly inflammatory rhetoric, the North's leaders have always made pretty clear-headed decisions about what would keep them in power. Even the invasion that launched the Korean war in 1950 was taken after the North figured the withdrawal of American troops from the South meant that

America would not fight—especially after ambiguous statements from the American government about whether it had a national security interest in the peninsula—and after the North had received assurances of backing from the Soviet Union and China. In a strategic sense the North's position is now extremely weak, and even though because of the South's militarily precarious geography the North could inflict horrible damage it would eventually be not only beaten but destroyed. By all accounts, the bunch at the top in Pyongyang are not zealots but instead corrupt and comfortable, well able on the almost broken backs of the population at large to indulge their tastes for fast cars and even faster film actresses and probably with plenty of bulging Swiss bank accounts. Hedonists don't start wars that would personally destroy them—it takes a teetotal vegetarian like Hitler to do that. Perry's study concluded there was little chance the North's regime will collapse in the next decade. But, provided the North's ballistic missile and nuclear programs can be kept at bay and the country is gradually pried open to the real world, there is no reason that war need break out.

In fact, worries of a different sort have already begun to preoccupy everyone with an interest in Northeast Asian stability. South Korea is wondering how, without going bankrupt in the process, it can engineer a controlled and lengthy decompression of the bottled-up North and its integration into the South's modern society and economy. The United States, China and Japan (perhaps to be joined one day by a revived Russia) are all fumbling to try to understand the new geopolitical equations that would result from a unified Korean peninsula. That prospect may be ten years or more away, but it would pose the biggest challenge for all these powers since the Korean war itself half a century ago.

SUBCONTINENTAL FOLLIES

In 1998 India and Pakistan, the two big subcontinental powers, went openly nuclear. Both tested several bombs, and a year later they almost went to war over a Pakistan-orchestrated guerrilla campaign in Indian Kashmir, a Muslim region that has been in frequently violent dispute between the two neighbors—India with a Hindu majority and Muslim Pakistan—since the partition of British India in 1947. The two countries have already fought three wars since independence, and in recent years things seem to have become more rather than less unstable between them. Just before his visit to the subcontinent in March 2000 Bill Clinton, the first American president to come calling in 22 years, famously said this was "the most dangerous place in the world right now." The cocktail of nuclear weapons and medieval animosity is certainly unsettling. Perhaps the biggest source of imbalance is that, whereas India has long had a stable democratic government under civilian control and in recent years has begun reaching out in economic and business terms to the modern world, Pakistan has been bedeviled by an increasingly bankrupt system that can only be described as feudal, with politicians of every party as grasping and repulsive as any on earth and an army that stages coups as if it were still the 1950s. Moreover, the general who mounted the latest coup, in October 1999, is thought to have been the mastermind behind Pakistan's armed effort to destabilize Indian Kashmir (there's a Pakistani one too) in 1999. President Clinton, who on his visit spent five days in India and four hours in Pakistan, made no bones about where he thought the fault lay for the increased tension over Kashmir, but outsiders have little influence on this internecine quarrel and, with Pakistan more and more of a basket case and increasingly under the sway of "patriots" rather than statesmen, any nightmare is possible.

Especially with the nukes. Bill Perry explains:

India and Pakistan have underway programs to adapt their nuclear capability to delivery systems, including ballistic missiles, and to produce these weapons in some quantity. I believe it is only a matter of time before they deploy nuclear-tipped ballistic missiles. I've discussed this at some length with friends and colleagues in India and Pakistan. And they asked me, "Why are you so concerned?" After all, they say, the United States and the Soviet Union managed a nuclear confrontation during the Cold War and none were ever fired in anger. Unfortunately, I tell them, there is a real danger that some of the Indian-Pakistani weapons will be fired in anger.

These two countries have had three wars since separation. And one of the flashpoints that led to these wars, Kashmir, is still very much a problem. If there were a fourth war, who can say that the loser in that war would not use nuclear weapons in a desperate attempt to head off defeat? Moreover, I believe there is a real danger that their nuclear weapons could be used inadvertently through imperfect command and control. For decades the Unites States and the Soviet Union lived with that problem and managed it through the Cold War without an accidental launch, mostly by good management but partly by good luck. But I can tell you that there were some close calls; during the Cuban missile crisis when nuclear weapons could have been deliberately launched for the wrong reason, and during calmer periods when our missile control system had a number of false alarms, some of which I personally lived through. And I can tell you that they are indelibly embedded in my memory. India and Pakistan will now relive those experiences without the benefit of the hard earned experience achieved by American and Soviet leaders. I can only hope they will be as lucky as we were.

The only reason not to put this conflict at the top of the list of geopolitical dangers facing Asia is that, however awful another subcontinental war would be for the parties involved, its impact on others would be fairly minor. That cannot be said for the third item on this fret list.

ONE CHINA, TWO DOGMAS

If the half-century-old dispute between the antagonists that are still formally called the People's Republic of China and the Republic of China ever got out of hand and became a shooting war, the casualties would include not just a lot of Chinese people—and perhaps American servicemen too—but the whole framework of security in East and Southeast Asia. It would be a heavy blow to China's opening up and modernization, costing it years or even a decade or more of much-needed economic development, it could set off a regional arms race of huge proportions, and it would poison relations between America and China to the point that a second long Cold War, this one focused on East Asia, would be likelier than not. The really worrying thing is that as the years go by, the conflict between China and Taiwan only grows harder to manage.

You would think it should be the opposite. When, in the early 1980s, Taiwan was still run by a strongman, contacts across the Strait with the mainland were forbidden and both places were continually on military alert. By the end of the 1990s Taiwan had as much as $40 billion invested in China through the 40,000 Taiwanese businesses that operated there; 200,000 Taiwanese lived in China itself and Taiwanese paid two million visits a year to the mainland. It looks like direct trade links may be established soon (in another Cold War relic, Taiwan's government has insisted that its people's commercial and other contacts have had to be routed through neutral places like Hong Kong), and although the two governments make official contact only sporadically there is no shortage of private dialogue. But the trouble is not economic or commercial: remember the pre-1914 predictions that Europe would never again go to war because the continent had been so woven together by trade and investment. The problem is that a vast cultural and institutional gap between the two sides has opened and is widening, to a degree that even the cleverest geopolitical engineers are going to have trouble throwing a bridge across it.

Anybody who visits both China and Taiwan knows how different attitudes are in the two places. Taiwan is probably the freest-spirited spot in Asia, with little of the rigid social hierarchy of Japan or Korea, the government-imposed orderliness of Singapore, or the commercial single-mindedness of Hong Kong. In a remarkably short period, say 20 years, it was turned with surprising smoothness from a tough dictatorship into what even in the West would be recognized as a free society. There is liberty in China too, but almost entirely of the commercial kind, and it smacks too much of the "freedom" of anarchy bewilderingly and unpredictably mixed with repression. People can make money in China, but there are just an awful lot of things they have to be careful about, such as what they say and how publicly and to whom and which arbitrary official they think they can cross. And public discourse in China—just listen to the antique Communist and nationalist phraseology—is comical in its crude toadying to the party line and shunning of the real world. If you want to see what political correctness finally leads to, go to Beijing. Shi Chung-yu, a popular Taiwanese writer, summed it up well when she told an American journalist, "This is the problem. Even though we have the same language, history, culture, it's like they've been living as aliens for the past 50 years. They're a foreign country." She went on to add how much she resents the threats from Beijing: "If you want to marry someone, you don't come over to their house with a shotgun and threaten to shoot them, do you? That's what they're doing. They want to have a shotgun wedding."

Unfortunately, she's right. If it's a choice between no wedding and a shotgun one, one of the surest bets in world politics today is that however mad this seems China's leaders will pick up the gun and cock it. This is because institutional divergence is adding so much to cultural incomprehension in widening the divide between the two sides. China has not, in fact, had much of a history as an expansionist power, but it is extremely sensitive to the importance of preserving the integrity of its borders—and it thinks Taiwan, even more than Hong Kong or Macau (both of which it has physically reclaimed), is squarely within them. Add to that a personalized (and still personally dangerous) political system where different points of view are brooked, if at all, only in private and never on an issue of national pride, and you have as uncompromising a political principle as you can get.

Taiwan, by contrast, has been moving the other way—toward an open and democratic society where appeals to cultural or nationalistic Chineseness seem more and more archaic: Taiwan today has a lot more affinity with Silicon Valley than it does with Zhongnanhai, where China's rulers live their cloistered lives. The brutal logic of Taiwan's fast democratization combined with China's (one hopes temporary) political immobility is that China insists ever more stridently on the recognition of its sovereignty over Taiwan, while no Taiwanese under the age of 50 and of sound mind would dream of wanting the Beijing government to control anything in Taiwan.

So things get more and more tense. The stakes kept getting raised as Taiwan's then President Lee Teng-hui made a visit to America in 1995 that enraged the Chinese and then, during a Taiwanese presidential election in 1996, China started test-firing missiles across the Strait in a misguided effort to turn the vote against Lee, who won handsomely. Although Lee, like all his predecessors, was a member of the Nationalist Party, he was also a native-born Taiwanese rather than a descendant of the mainlanders who crossed over with Chiang Kai-shek's soldiers after Mao Zedong had defeated them in 1949. The native Taiwanese, who make up some 85 percent of the population, have always had a cooler attitude toward the mainland than the migrants, and Lee's own view was cooler still since he had been brought up in Taiwan during the Japanese occupation, had been taught in Japanese and probably shared in private the general Japanese mistrust of China. Lastly, Lee is a stubborn man not given to the sort of ambiguity that might have given more room for maneuver in dealing with China. Another Lee, Singapore's Kuan Yew, thought his Taiwanese namesake so stubbornly anti-China that for years he gave up any go-between role until President Lee should leave power.

China's patience began snapping in 1999 after Lee Teng-hui declared that relations between China and Taiwan must henceforth be carried out on "a special state-to-state basis" rather than on the assumption of "one China" that had gone before. The theology of this is incomprehensible to anyone who has not spent a lifetime studying it, but the Chinese clearly thought Lee's shift of stance amounted to a step toward formal independence, something it had always said would provoke it to attack. As the presidential election of March 2000 approached, China listed a new *causus belli:* it said that if Taiwan delayed talks indefinitely based on the "one-China" principle, it would eventually attack.

The real shock came in the election, which was narrowly won by Chen Shui-bian, the candidate of the once-banned opposition Democratic Progressive Party, which had been founded for the very purpose of advocating independence. Chen himself had backed away from his own earlier espousal of independence and spent the few weeks between his election and his inauguration in late May trying to soothe the stunned Chinese, who had thought it impossible the DPP would ever win power. Chen moved deftly enough, but he is surrounded by party hotheads with no experience of the responsibility of government, including a harridan of a vice president who thinks as self-righteously and unimaginatively as the Harvard-trained lawyer she is. Meanwhile in Beijing anger was rising. After a visit to China in April 2000 Goh Chok Tong, Singapore's prime minister, said that China had moved beyond accepting the status quo and was insisting on forward movement with talks based on the precondition of "one China" (something Chen had already ruled out, though he said "one China" could be discussed after talks started). Goh added that anyone talking to China's leaders "in private could sense their seriousness."

Ever since China's intimidatory missile launches in 1996, experts have fruitlessly debated whether China has the military wherewithal to invade Taiwan. On paper it looks unlikely because the Chinese apparently lack either the air cover or the amphibious fleet to carry it out (e.g., say the doubters, look at the amazing effort the Allies had to mount to launch the D-Day invasion in 1944, and they had much more of an upper hand than China's forces do now over Taiwan). Yet all this speculation misses the points, which are that Taiwan's forces are no great shakes either, wars are one of the most unpredictable of human activities, the military balance between China and Taiwan will be shifting a lot over the next five to ten years in unknown ways and, most important of all, there are things short of invasion—like missile launches or a blockade—that could wreck East Asian security almost as much.

Whether anything can be done to stop the slow-motion march to some sort of disaster across the Taiwan Strait is anyone's guess. By early autumn of 2000, tempers in Beijing seemed to have cooled and Taiwan's President Chen, who appeared to be a lot more subtle character than his China-bashing predecessor, was looking for ways to restart talks with the mainland. The advantage of the status quo—no independence for Taiwan, no military action by China—is that it would allow time and growing wealth in China to start healing some of history's wounds. Bill Perry thinks that, if a confrontation can be staved off for ten or twenty years then technology and business will have done enough to bring China and Taiwan closer together that a war will no longer be an option. But, he adds, "It is unclear whether China will be patient enough for this." Lee Kuan Yew, who visited

Taiwan on a highly public "secret" mission—presumably mediatory—in the fall of 2000, reckons a very Chinese solution (and maybe this is what Chen is aiming for) could do the trick: "If they would just start talking, they can drag it on and on."

For no outsider is this situation as agonizing as it is for the United States. It involves almost every angle of American public policy, from the most basic local political and electoral calculations to the tussle for power over foreign policy between Congress and the executive branch, to free trade and the considerable commercial interests of American firms abroad, to the perennial struggle in America between idealism and American values in foreign policy and their interaction with America's national interests, and finally up to the questions of the strategic balance in a region that has always been vital to the United States and perhaps of whether American forces will be committed to a battle in which—unlike the wars of the 1990s—a lot of them would be likely to be killed. One sign of how weighty the China–Taiwan issue can be is that America felt compelled to send two carrier battle groups into the area when China started firing missiles in Taiwan's vicinity in 1996. As Perry points out, "This is not two ships, they [the carrier groups] have more power than most navies of the world." On one hand, says Perry, by 2000 American and Chinese relations were in pretty good shape despite sporadic squabbles over missile technology, supposed Chinese theft of American nuclear secrets, the American bombing of the Chinese embassy in Belgrade during the Kosovo War in 1999, and the cliffhanging fight to get China into the WTO in 1999–2000. But purely because of the Taiwan question, Perry admitted, "I am more pessimistic about U.S.-China relations than for several decades." Whoever the Americans elect president in 2000 will follow the broad outlines of America's established policy toward China—as every single president has since Nixon went there in 1972—but because of Taiwan he is going to have his work cut out for him more than any of his predecessors did. And not just on that.

THE HYPERPOWER

Since this book began with America, it seems appropriate to end it there too. But the America of the next ten years is going to be a different place from the America that was about to create so much success for the world as the 1990s opened. For all the good it is doing, globalization is creating serious strains everywhere. The worry is that America understands little about its proper role in relieving these strains, and will understand even less if (as is likely) it underperforms other regions in the next decade. For one thing, the United States has little conception of the resentment it is beginning to arouse. Late in the 1990s a French foreign minister echoed this widespread hostility when he said it was incorrect to think of America as "the only superpower" but rather as a "hyperpower" that dominated virtually every aspect of global public life. Well, the French will be French, but Asians are disquieted too.

What worries many Asians is how much they depend on the United States. It is not that Europe is absent from Asia: in a commercial sense it is very much present. European firms invest heavily in Asia and in many lines of business collectively have a bigger presence than their American competitors; during the financial crisis of 1997–98 they also often moved faster than the Americans in expanding their reach. Tommy Koh, a Singaporean ex-diplomat who runs the Singapore-based Asia-Europe Foundation, has pointed out that the European Union has a bigger share of world output than the United States (29 percent versus 25 percent) and that it contributed more to the IMF's Asian rescue packages in 1997 than America did. In 1996, before things got distorted by the upheavals, Europe even traded more with Asia than America did, by a score of $308 billion to $295 billion.

Not a bad start. The trouble is, that was about it. The euro, the EU's fledgling common currency, weakened steadily against the dollar almost from its inception at the beginning of 1999 to the fall of 2000. At some point, that will surely be reversed but it soon became clear that, despite the occasional vote of confidence in the euro such as Hong Kong's decision in 1999 to shift several billions of its foreign-exchange reserves from dollars into euros, it would be years if not a decade or more before the European Central Bank, and indeed the economic basis itself of the euro, inspired enough confidence to make the currency a serious alternative to the dollar as a world reserve currency.

One reason is that it is still highly doubtful whether Europe can match the massive restructuring and raising of economic potential that America has achieved by its embrace of the methods of the new economy. The problem is not at the corporate level: European companies have drawn the lessons of America's 1990s. But, as one piece of analysis puts it, "the cyber-economy dictates that the state must shrink and pursue pro-business tax policies"; and, despite some reductions in income-tax rates and improvements in government budgets, as late as 2000 real government spending in Western Europe was still rising (though least in Britain), the government workforce remained 50 percent higher than it had been in 1970 and France, for one, was backtracking fast on proposals to cut public employment and reform state pensions. This political issue will interfere with the ability of Europe's firms to keep up with their American competitors, an interference that will become more harrying if growth slows in Europe and the state protects its role through higher taxes. A second and closely related reason is that it remains untested whether the euro would even survive the strain of a severe downturn because the continent's highly inflexible wages and mostly immobile workforces could, through sharp rises in already high unemployment, make the process of adjustment politically too painful to bear. The odds are that, if Europe remains determined to protect its big governments and social-welfare systems despite the imperatives of globalization and technology, it is strong and wealthy enough to do so. The odds are also that, if this is the path Europe chooses, its economies will grow more slowly than they could and it will fall further behind America in the race for the future.

Most significant of all for the comparative tenuousness of Europe's relations with Asia is that they are one-dimensional—that dimension being commerce—to the point of being superficial. The contrast with America is striking. It is hard to think of any dimension—whether business, finance, culture, language, even the personal—where America is not deeply (and for an outside power dominantly) involved with Asia. Two of these connections are of overwhelming importance, though only the second is talked about much.

The first is that the next generation of Asia's elites, especially the business ones, are increasingly being schooled in the United States and getting their first on-the-job training there. Washington SyCip, whose quote opened this chapter, is an internationally well-connected businessman who set up one of the first big modern financial groups in the Philippines. He told me in 1999 that for every five Asian students in America there is only one in Europe (and most of those are in Britain because the British are lucky enough to speak the same language as the Americans). This is true of Asia across the board. Even despite India's historical affinity for Britain, ever since the 1980s no forward-looking Indian parents who could afford foreign university schooling for their children have wanted them to go anywhere but America. The preference is at least as pronounced in China. It is hard to think of any member of China's Politburo for, say, the past 15 years whose children did not go to an American university; many stayed, along with practically every Tiananmen Square activist who escaped or was thrown out after 1989. In the spring of 2000 Zhu Rongji, China's prime minister, told the visiting Singaporean Goh Chok Tong that 70 percent to 80 percent of China's best university graduates were living and working in America.

For SyCip the implications of this are clear. Already, he says, almost every significant Asian family company has a son or daughter with an MBA or other advanced degree from America. He thinks the next-generation leadership of practically all of Asia (save only Japan) will have been educated in America and have imbibed American values and methods. Astonishingly, what this will mean for how Asia is led and will think in 2020 seems to have crossed few European minds. Recall from Chapter 11 how much of Silicon Valley's success has been powered by Chinese and Indian immigrants. In early 2000 the German government proposed a modest "fast-track" immigration quota to give 20,000 information-technology specialists from India and Eastern Europe residency rights and work permits (while a similar quota in America was about to be raised from 115,000 to 200,000 a year). The proposal created a parliamentary storm, with one conservative populist rallying opposition with the pretty openly racist slogan *Kinder statt Inder* ("children [meaning more training for Germans] not Indians"). Not that the Indians cared about what the Germans were up to. The head of one big Indian software company said, "They'll probably get the people who can't get into the U.S. and other places." Added another, "Maybe they'll attract a few desperadoes."

The second unique connection between America and Asia is the political and military one. The Europeans have no military ties with Asia, except as eager suppliers of arms, and (bar some trivial colonial holdover cases like Portugal's concern with East Timor, newly independent from Indonesia) no political ones except in service of commerce. In 2000 I asked an EU diplomat, on hand in an Asian capital for a worldwide conference of his country's foreign-service officers, why they were bothering with such an event since the country had no political connections with Asia that I could see. The response was roughly, "we get a lot of questions in parliament about human rights in Asia, so we need to know how to respond so that X's sales here won't be jeopardized." Special interests, meet special interests.

The stark discrepancy between this sort of thing and America's role worries a lot of Asians. The most striking worrier is Lee Kuan Yew, not least because for more than 30 years he has been the most outspokenly pro-American leader in Asia. When I suggested to him that it was America's greatly improved economic efficiency that allowed it to set the global rules in the 1990s, he responded:

> I agree with that. But I must add that you succeeded not only because you were efficient. You had military muscle to back you. You set the rules. You decide whether China gets into WTO or not. It's not the Europeans. You told the Japanese, "If you don't do this, I'm going to do this to you and that will hurt you." So they opened up their markets. You forced us [in Singapore] to up-value our currency or else. So, we up-valued.
>
> So what does it mean? It means that is your seignorage [a technical term describing the benefit to a government from having the monopoly power to issue a currency]. Suppose you are not the superpower and have to play by rules settled by consensus. That's a different game altogether, on a truly level playing field. At present you can say, "This is my playing field. It's level, you play on it." That's the position. You've got to consider whether the countries you are inviting to join are capable of playing under those rules without doing themselves harm. Not everybody can go into that playing field and hold their own. It's not possible. You settled the rules and talked them into it. They joined, not knowing the hazards.

Q: How do you compare American power now with American power in the 1950s?

> In the 1950s you did not have the overpowering self-confidence that nobody can stop you. You had to get other players on your side. Otherwise they would have joined the Soviet side. During the Cold War there was real fear and anxiety that the other side could win. That mitigated unilateralism. Now there's no alternative. It's the U.S. side or nothing. Everybody plays by American rules.
>
> America's reach, from military to economic supremacy, is total. Your lead in IT and computers is overwhelming. But others will catch up. It's like your lead at the end of the war with petrochemicals, synthetic fibers and so on. After a while the Japanese and the Germans caught up, then everybody caught up. Your lead in IT cannot last forever.

Q: Do you think a world playing by American rules will have good or bad results?

> Let me put it this way: if any single country is going to set the rules, I would rather have America because from my previous experience America

had a more charitable and sharing approach. The British kept their position as the leading imperial power by holding back the industrial capability to make good woolen fabrics from New Zealand and Australian wool for decades. When I was in New Zealand in the early 1960s they proudly presented me with a rug which they'd manufactured themselves. During the previous 100 years, they'd been sending wool to Britain to be spun and woven. Thus Britain kept its imperial position from being challenged. When the Americans took over—partly because of the Cold War—they allowed the Germans and Japanese the use of patents that enabled them to catch up in petrochemicals, ships, steel, radios, transistors, television and so on. Now the technology has spread around the world. So if there's going to be one rule-maker, maybe this isn't too bad.

In about fifty years the Europeans could develop into a cohesive economic group and offer an alternative, a challenge. If the euro succeeds and they do become one common market, they will have a larger base than the U.S. That will give more of a choice for the Chinese. In 50–70 years, the Japanese and the Chinese could be big players. Economically, it could be a more multipolar world.

Even in military terms, you cannot assume that the Europeans are going to be always inferior. Today in Bosnia or in Kosovo they have subsidiary roles. That's because they wanted the peace dividend, they had not spent on R&D to produce the guided-weapons technology, but they can if they have to.

But look at those time frames! The implication is that at least the first half of the twenty-first century is going to have America's name as deeply stamped on it as the whole of the twentieth century did. Among other things, this means that because there is not going to be much in the way of an external counterbalance to American preeminence, the United States will need a good internal gyroscope to keep both itself and the global system on a true course. Whether a reliable one now exists is highly doubtful. It may be true, as Israel's Yitzhak Rabin once remarked, that no great power has ever used its power in so unimperial a way, but generosity and good intentions on America's part are not enough. The trouble, as Bill Perry has pointed out (and maybe the reason for the generosity), is that America never sought its dominant leadership role, and therefore it "has been oscillating between not using it at all and using it arrogantly." More consistency and steadiness would help, of course, but so would some clear thinking and straight talking about just what brought America to its pinnacle of the

1990s and the world to its potential for much greater wealth and human welfare over the next generation. These good things include the freest possible movement of goods, capital, technology and people across borders—globalization—and, in political and military terms, a sort of leadership that enlists support instead of giving into shoulder-shrugging over whether it exists. This means not only standing up to know-nothing sentiment in Congress but also telling the truth to, instead of buttering up, the growing unholy alliance of special-interest groups whose protectionist ideas, if carried out, would impoverish more people and create more disorder worldwide than anything since the Great Depression and the Second World War.

All of this matters more for Asia, and for America's relations with Asia, than for any other parts of the world. After all, it has been the formerly poor and still poor of Asia who have benefited more, faster and in greater numbers from an open trading system and a stable international order than anyone in history. Whatever path America takes, the huge majority of Asia's 3.5 billion people are going to continue to rise in wealth and sophistication over the next two generations. Because of its close links with Asia—economic, political and personal—America has a unique chance, as the current ruling power, of deeply influencing the shape and nature of the rising power. It would be not just a pity, and a folly for America's own interests, to squander that chance. It would be a tragedy.

ACKNOWLEDGMENTS

The best opening to a book acknowledgments section that I've ever seen was in *The Red Queen* by Matt Ridley, an ex-*Economist* colleague of mine, and in the spirit of it I'll just repeat it: "This book is crammed with original ideas, very few of them my own."

Journalists are almost never creative thinkers (I've known only one who was). This isn't surprising. Their profession is voyeurism, sometimes of a very high order. That doesn't earn them many friends, but it does give them a precious privilege: access, of the sort that only the wealthiest or most famous otherwise enjoy, to the thinking and occasionally the personalities of people who have created things—whether countries, companies, technologies or even economic theories—that have changed the world.

Much of the access I have enjoyed in preparing for this book was a result of work I did between 1997 and 2000 for *Fortune* magazine, first in writing about the Asian financial crisis and, as it faded, about how Asia's basic institutional structures were (or were not) being reshaped by the currents of globalization and technological change that were coursing ever more strongly around the world. I am grateful to *Fortune* for the interest it showed in such a topic despite the temptation—in the rather self-absorbed and self-satisfied United States of the late 1990s—of writing about America alone. I am particularly grateful to Rik Kirkland, the magazine's deputy managing editor, who hired me and has backed me ever since.

It will be obvious from the people I've quoted in the book where I got a lot of my ideas, but over the past few years I have been repeatedly influenced in my thinking about Asia (and other things) by a handful of diverse people who have been generous with their thoughts and time and to whom I owe a big intellectual debt. They include:

In Hong Kong, Toby Brown, Gary Coull, Marc Faber, Stuart Gulliver, Simon Ogus, David Roche, Margie Yang.

In Beijing and Shanghai, Bob Ching, David Mahon, Jim McGregor, Wang Daohan, Wu Jinglian.

In Tokyo, Akio Mikuni, Tadashi Nakamae.

385

In Seoul, Hwang Young Key.
In Jakarta, Chris Wood.
In Bangkok, Supavud Saicheua.
In Singapore, Koh Boon Hwee, Philip Yeo.
In India, Mohan Guruswamy.
In Europe, John Greenwood, Gordon Redding, George Robinson.
In North America, Paul Romer, Vaclav Smil.

I didn't torture too many people to read parts of the manuscript, but Chris Wood and Margie Yang in particular gamely put up with it. Clara Loon of Hong Kong helped with the research and Alice Fung, my long-time assistant and canny Cantonese muse, expertly took care of all the details that would have driven me mad.

JIM ROHWER

Hong Kong
November 2000

NOTES

PROLOGUE

Page x   So there were a . . . The best book on ants is Bert Hoelldobler and Edward O. Wilson, *The Ants*, Belknap Press, 1991.

CHAPTER 1

Page 4   If term mismatches . . . Bing Shen, Toby Brown, conversations in Hong Kong, 1998.

Page 5   Between 1950 and 1973 . . . Angus Maddison, "Poor Until 1820," *Asian Wall Street Journal,* January 19, 1999.

Page 5   Inflation in 1950–73 . . . Maddison, *Phases of Capitalist Development* (Oxford,1982); *The World Economy in the Twentieth Century* (Organization for Economic Cooperation and Development, 1989).

Page 5   By the end of . . . Norman Macrae, "The Neurotic Trillionaire; survey of Mr. Nixon's America," *The Economist,* 1972.

Page 6   It was not coping . . . Joseph Nocera, *A Piece of the Action* (Simon and Schuster, 1994).

Page 8   Arthur Burns, the Fed's . . . Thomas Meyer, *Monetary Policy and the Great Inflation in the United States* (Edward Elgar, 1999); William Greider, *Secrets of the Temple* (Simon & Schuster, 1987) gives a detailed account of the Volcker years.

Page 8   And interest rates . . . Robert Sobel, *Dangerous Dreamers* (John Wiley, 1993).

Page 9   By the last year . . . Peter Peterson, "The Morning After," *Atlantic Monthly,* October 1987.

Page 10   Under this new standard . . . Speech to the Fortune Financial Services Technology Forum, March 4, 1999.

Page 10   But isolation is less . . . Wriston, "Bits, Bytes and Diplomacy," *Foreign Affairs,* September/October 1997.

Page 10   Turner's ambitions were immodest . . . Hank Whittemore, *CNN: The Inside Story* (Little, Brown, 1990).

Page 11   But whether it's good . . . Don Flournoy and Robert Stewart, *CNN: Making News in the Global Market* (University of Luton Press, 1997).

Page 13   Judge Greene died . . . Fred Henck and Bernard Strassburg, *A Slippery Slope* (Greenwood Press, 1988).

Page 14   Being first in . . . *Communications Outlook 1999* (Organization for Economic Cooperation and Development).

Page 14   But whatever you . . . For hostile accounts of Milken and the junk-bond revolution, see James B. Stewart, *Den of Thieves*, and Connie Bruck, *The Predator's Ball* (Simon & Schuster, 1988). For a favorable account see Daniel Fischel, *Payback* (HarperCollins, 1995).

Page 15   Debt issued by . . . Glenn Yago, *Junk Bonds* (Oxford, 1991).

Page 15   The junk-bond market . . . Robert Sobel, *Dangerous Dreamers* (John Wiley, 1993).

Page 15   As Milken explained . . . Interview, Santa Monica, California, March 1998.

Page 17   As a reminder . . . Sobel, *Dangerous Dreamers*.

Page 17   By one calculation . . . Yago, *Junk Bonds*.

Page 18   When he took office . . . Bob Woodward, *The Agenda* (Simon & Schuster, 1994).

Page 23   American business and technological . . . Amartya Sen, "Beyond the Crisis," Institute of Southeast Asia Studies, 1999.

CHAPTER 2

Page 24   Massive and rapid growth . . . *Financial Times,* May 19, 1997.

Page 25   Amid this avalanche . . . The investment banker was Ben Weston of CS First Boston.

Page 25   Such achievements were . . . Paul Krugman "The myth of Asia's miracle," *Foreign Affairs,* November 1994.

Page 25   And growth benefited . . . David Dollar and Aart Kraay, "Growth *is* good for the poor," World Bank, March 2000.

Page 25   There is no parallel . . . Rohwer, *Asia Rising* (Simon & Schuster, 1995).

Page 26   The most perceptive . . . conversation in Hong Kong, July 20, 1999.

Page 28   At their peaks . . . *The BCA China Analyst*, December 1997.

Page 29   In America bank credit . . . World Economic Forum, *The Asia Competitiveness Report,* 1999.

Page 29   As Philippe Delhaise . . . Philippe Delhaise, *Asia in Crisis* (John Wiley, 1998).

Page 30   He went on . . . David Atkinson, "Does Japan Need only 2–4 Major Banks?" Goldman Sachs, October 13, 1998.

Page 31   By 1996 the ratio . . . *Asia Competitiveness Report,* 1999.

Page 32   By 1997 the capacity . . . Gerard Caprio, "Banking on Crises" World Bank, June 1998.

Page 34   The then head . . . Russell Kopp of Dresdner Kleinwort Benson, conversation in Bangkok, June 5, 1998.

Page 34   India, proud of . . . "The Role of Law and Legal Institutions," *The Asia Competitiveness Report,* 1999.

Page 37   David Herbert Donald's . . . David Herbert Donald, *Lincoln,* p. 51 (Simon & Schuster, 1995).

Page 37   On a far grander . . . Brad De Long, "Asia's Flu: A History Lesson," (http://econ161.berkeley.edu).

Page 37   If this was not . . . Edward Chancellor, *Devil Take the Hindmost* (Farrar, Strauss & Giroux, 1999).

Page 38   In any event . . . Edmund Gomez and Jomo K.S., *Malaysia's Political Economy* (Cambridge, 1997); Victor Mallet, *The Trouble with Tigers* (HarperCollins, 1999); Michael Backman, *Asian Eclipse* (John Wiley, 1999).

Page 39   Everywhere else, though . . . "The cost of crony capitalism," *Asia Competitiveness Report,* 1999.

Page 39   A recent book . . . Pasuk Phongpaichat et al., *Guns, Girls, Gambling, Ganja* (Silkworm Books, 1998).

Page 39   But expert studies . . . Summarized in "The Cost of Crony Capitalism," *Asia Competitiveness Report,* 1999.

Page 39   Lee immediately set . . . Lee Kuan Yew, *The Singapore Story* (Prentice Hall, 1998).

Page 40   The redeeming factor . . . Interview in Singapore, April 26, 1999.

Page 41   [In China] the actual . . . Interview in Singapore, August 13, 1992.

Page 41   The tigers—South Korea, . . . *The BCA China Analyst,* December 1997.

Page 41   Between 1990 and . . . Morris Goldstein, *The Asian Financial Crisis* (Institute for International Economics, 1998).

Page 41   In 1989–92 foreign capital . . . "Restructuring Asia's financial system," *Asia Competitiveness Report,* 1999.

Page 44   A crucial element . . . Ronald I. McKinnon, *The Order of Economic Liberalization,* Johns Hopkins, 1991.

Page 45   In 1995 bank loans . . . *Asia Competitiveness Report,* 1999.

Page 45   Unsurprisingly, foreign borrowings . . . *Asia Competitiveness Report,* 1999; *The BCA China Analyst,* December 1997.

Page 46   In the second half . . . *Bank for International Settlements Annual Report,* June 1998, p. 133.

Page 47   In January 1998 . . . Malcolm Surry, "One Crash Too Many," March 1, 1998 (http://web3.asia1.com.sg/timesnet/data/ab/docs/ab1533.html).

Page 47   Between 1990 and 1996 . . . "Exports and Asia's Recovery," *Asia Competitiveness Report,* 1999.

CHAPTER 3

Page 49   In fact, the very . . . By Charles Mackay, reprinted by Crown Trade Paperbacks (New York, 1980).

Page 51   There was less . . . Global Development Finance (Washington, 1998).

Page 53   Of course, if you . . . Bryan, Lyons and Rosenthal, "The Market Capitalization Imperative," *The McKinsey Quarterly,* 1998, No. 3.

Page 53   Any excessive valuation . . . *The BCA China Analyst,* December 1997.

Page 55   Among all the listed . . . Dresdner Kleinwort Benson, *Asian Weekly Outlook,* May 29, 1997.

Page 55   A year later . . . "Japan à la Mode," *Greed & Fear* (ABN Amro, August 26, 1999).

Page 56   A year later . . . Rohwer, "Here's the Cure for What Ails Japan," *Fortune,* December 29, 1997.

Page 56   "Bankruptcy is like . . . Stanford, March 24, 1998.

Page 57   It should be kept . . . For an extended reflection on the two moralities, that of commerce and the other of society, see Jane Jacobs, *Systems of Survival* (Vintage Books, 1994).

Page 57   This meant that . . . "Competitiveness in Asian Manufacturing," *Asia Competitiveness Report,* 1999.

Page 59   Asian conglomerates on . . . McKinsey & Co, "Emerging Market Conglomerates" (Discussion document, February 1999).

Page 62   By the mid-1980s . . . Interview in Seoul, April 8, 1998.

Page 63   It was a disastrous . . . Two good consultancy studies about Korea came out as the crisis broke: Booz-Allen & Hamilton, *Revitalizing the Korean Economy Toward the 21st Century* (October 1997) and McKinsey Global Institute, *Productivity-Led Growth for Korea* (March 1998).

Page 63   Since, over time . . . Rhee Namuh, "The Application of EVA in Korea" (Dongbang Peregrine Country Update, June 10, 1997).

Page 65   Even if the restructuring . . . Details on Ssangyong from Michael Schuman, "Family Values," *Asian Wall Street Journal,* December 9, 1998.

CHAPTER 4

Page 69   Sakakibara, who ironically . . . "The Japanese Model of Mixed Economy: The Anatomy of a 'Non-capitalistic' Market Economy," manuscript, 1990.

Page 69   At the absurd end . . . Told to Christopher Wood, Tokyo, 1989.

Page 71   Japan's resistance to change . . . Christopher Wood, *The Bubble Economy* (Atlantic Monthly Press, 1992) and *The End of Japan Inc.* (Simon & Schuster, 1994).

Page 72   The Bubble Economy . . . A good detailed summary of the Bubble Economy is Kunio Okina et al., "The Asset Price Bubble and Monetary Policy," IMES Discussion Paper No. 2000-E-12, Bank of Japan (2000).

Page 73   But in what Greenwood . . . Interview in Hong Kong, February 10, 1999.

Page 75   After all, it was . . . Hong Kong, March 27, 1999.
Page 76   Meanwhile, Japan was . . . Ronald McKinnon and Kenichi Ohno, *Dollar and Yen* (MIT Press, 1997); McKinnon, "Wading in the Yen Trap," *The Economist,* July 24, 1999.
Page 77   The best-known example . . . David Friedman, *The Misunderstood Miracle* (Cornell, 1988); Yoshiro Miwa, "'Market' and 'Marketization': From the Japanese Experience," University of Tokyo, CIRJE-F-1 (May 1998).
Page 78   In other words . . . Porter and Takeuchi, "Fixing What Really Ails Japan," *Foreign Affairs,* May/June 1999.
Page 78   On company balance . . . Conversation with Jesper Koll, economist, Tokyo, March 1999.
Page 79   The result was that . . . Jesper Koll, "Japan Economic Outlook 1999," presentation, February 28, 1999.
Page 80   This is why Japanese . . . Tokyo, January 26, 1999; Nicholas Benes, "A Day in the Life of Japan Inc.," *Asian Wall Street Journal,* January 21, 1999.
Page 80   In the survey . . . Interview with Shintaro Ueyama, McKinsey & Co., Tokyo, October 7, 1998.
Page 81   He foresaw no real . . . Interview, Tokyo, January 27, 1999.
Page 81   What a lot of . . . Interview, Tokyo, January 29, 1999; NIER, "Japan's Harsh New World," August 1998.

CHAPTER 5

Page 85   If you strip . . . David Asher and Andrew Smithers, "Japan's Key Challenges for the 21st Century," SAIS Policy Forum Series, March 1998.
Page 85   In 1998 Kathy Matsui . . . "Tsunami Alert: The Y80 Trillion Pension Funding Wave," Goldman Sachs research, October 16, 1998.
Page 89   Take, for example . . . Asher & Smithers; "Junk Bonds in Drag," Independent Strategy (London), June 17, 1998.
Page 90   In 1998 David Roche . . . David Asher, "Epilogue to Japanese Version," manuscript, December 10, 1998; David Asher and Robert Dugger, "Could Japan's Financial Mount Fuji Blow Its Top?" MIT Japan Program, 2000; "Junk Bonds in Drag."
Page 91   But just as America . . . See Diana Helweg, "Japan: A Rising Sun?" *Foreign Affairs,* July/August 2000.
Page 91   In the first half . . . See Diana Helweg, "Japan: A Rising Sun?" *Foreign Affairs,* July/August 2000.
Page 91   In 1994–95 Japanese . . . Jesper Koll, "The End of Japan's Financial Socialism," *Asian Wall Street Journal,* August 27, 1999.

Page 91   Indeed, in 1999 . . . Akio Mikuni interview, Tokyo, December 13, 1999.

Page 91   Although up-to-date . . . "Japanese Firms Step up Sales," *Asian Wall Street Journal,* March 7, 2000.

Page 93   A couple of simple . . . Tokyo, February 9, 1998.

Page 94   The rest will go . . . Koll, "The End of Japan's Financial Socialism."

Page 95   By MITI's own calculation . . . Nakamae, Tokyo, January 1999; Brian Walker, "Japan's New Dual Economy," *Asian Wall Street Journal,* July 13, 1999; Jesper Koll, "Japan Economic Outlook 1999."

Page 97   Hoya was globalizing . . . Tokyo, February 13, 1998.

Page 98   A year earlier . . . "Putting the Bounce Back in Matsushita," *The Economist,* May 22, 1999.

Page 98   The new CEO . . . "Jack Welch Lite," *Forbes,* June 14, 1999.

Page 102   "The establishment never . . . Gillian Tett, "Profit without Honour in Japan," *Financial Times,* January 14, 1999.

Page 104   It is another echo . . . Neel Chowdhury, "Mr Japan.com," *Fortune,* August 16, 1999; "Softbank Makes Hard Drive," *Asian Wall Street Journal,* June 22, 1999; "Japan's Softbank," *Asian Wall Street Journal,* June 25, 1999.

CHAPTER 6

Page 110   When I flew into . . . *New Sunday Times,* October 19, 1997.

Page 112   But it did . . . "Asia's Economic Meltdown," manuscript, December 1997.

Page 113   This circularity, in turn . . . "What Happened to Asia?" http://web.mit.edu/krugman/www/DISINTER.html.

Page 119   But after a year's . . . "Malaysia: Mirage or Miracle?" *Fortune,* May 24, 1999.

Page 120   It is no wonder . . . Bhagwati, "The Capital Myth," *Foreign Affairs,* May–June 1998; IMF, World Economic Outlook, September 1999.

Page 120   He did not necessarily . . . Conversation in Manila, February 17, 1999.

Page 122   And Indonesia might . . . Singapore, April 24–25, 1999.

Page 123   The point here . . . Taipei, June 3, 1999.

Page 125   Steven Radelet and . . . "The Onset of the East Asian Financial Crisis," Harvard Institute for International Development, March 30, 1998.

Page 125   In early 1998 . . . "Who Needs the IMF?" *The Wall Street Journal,* February 3, 1998.

Page 127   You're right, the IMF . . . Hong Kong, March 27, 1999.

Page 128   The IMF should stick . . . "Refocusing the IMF," *Foreign Affairs,* March/April 1998.

Page 129   Thailand and Korea . . . Singapore, April 26, 1999.

CHAPTER 7

Page 131   When told by the . . . "TPI Shows Problems of Foreclosure after Default," *Asian Wall Street Journal,* December 3, 1998.

Page 133   Just as important . . . For more on the history of Asia's export orientation see Rohwer, *Asia Rising,* Chapter 5.

Page 133   A year later . . . "Asia's Export Engine Is Already Firing," *Fortune,* July 20, 1998.

Page 134   On top of this . . . IMF, World Economic Outlook, September 1999; Martin Wolf, "The Tigers Turn," *Financial Times,* July 28, 1999.

Page 134   Moreover, contrary to . . . Warburg Dillon Read, *Asian Economic and Strategy Perspectives,* July 1999.

Page 135   The meltdown of . . . ABN-Amro, Asia Maxima, October–December 1999.

Page 137   The country's great . . . "Slump Is Paradise for Parking Lots," *Financial Times,* May 12, 1999.

Page 138   Almost alone among . . . Heinecke, Hong Kong, November 11, 1999; Uwe Parpart, "Restructuring East Asia," *The Milken Institute Review,* Third Quarter 1999.

Page 139   How can you have . . . Quoted in Warburg Dillon Read, *Asian Economic and Strategy Perspectives,* September 1999.

Page 141   How effectively IBRA . . . IMF, World Economic Outlook, September 1999; "IBRA Shakes up Indonesian Business," *Asian Wall Street Journal,* July 29, 1999.

Page 141   One skeptic was . . . Delhaise MS, 1999.

Page 142   In fact, I would . . . "Is the Recovery in Asia for Real?" *The Gloom, Boom & Doom Report,* September 13, 1999.

Page 142   He also thought . . . Hong Kong, May 26, 1999.

Page 143   But in addition . . . Jakarta, September 14, 1998.

Page 144   The TPI deal may . . . "TPI Nears Landmark Debt Restructuring," *Asian Wall Street Journal,* October 12, 1999; "TPI, Creditors File Plan," *Asian Wall Street Journal,* January 18, 2000.

CHAPTER 8

Page 146   It is a 'socialist . . . the latest official phrase for moving-to-market, Shanghai, September 29, 1999.

Page 148   A devaluation could . . . "Asia's Meltdown: The Risks Are Rising," *Fortune,* February 16, 1998; "Asia's Meltdown: It Ain't Over Yet," *Fortune,* July 20, 1998; "China: The Real Economic Wild Card," *Fortune,* September 28, 1998.

Page 149   One study of private . . . "China's Private Surprise," *The Economist,* June 19, 1999.

Page 150   In northern China . . . "The Next Shoe to Drop," *The Gloom, Boom & Doom Report,* September 2, 1998.

Page 151   Lardy's estimate was . . . Nicholas Lardy, *China's Unfinished Economic Revolution,* Brookings Institution Press, 1998.

Page 152   Despite the fierce . . . "Cleaning Up the Chinese State," *The Economist,* November 14, 1992.

Page 155   The secret seemed . . . "The Haier Group," Harvard Business School Case Study N9-398-101 (November 13, 1998); interview Shanghai, September 28, 1999.

Page 156   Around the same time . . . CMG Mahon, *China Watch,* July 1999.

Page 156   Likewise, in 1998–99 . . . "Beijing Moves to Cut Steel Sector Output," *Financial Times,* November 15, 1999.

Page 157   With a clean balance . . . Beijing, September 1, 1999.

Page 157   Wu Jinglian, probably . . . Shanghai, September 29, 1999.

Page 158   It has the option . . . "Asset Transfers Offer Lifeline," *Financial Times* October 28, 1999.

Page 159   China would risk . . . Wu Jinglian, Beijing, April 15, 1999.

Page 159   Whether all this . . . Beijing, August 31, 1999.

Page 160   It is likely that . . . ABN-Amro, *Greed & Fear,* October 28, 1999.

Page 163   By mid-2000 . . . *China Business Weekly,* August 29–September 4, 1999; ABN Amro, *Greed & Fear,* September 7, 2000.

Page 164   Housing privatization can . . . CMG Mahon, *China Watch,* July 1999; "A Nation of Ward Cleavers," *Fortune,* May 25, 1998.

Page 165   These government ventures . . . Hong Kong, March 27, 1999.

Page 166   Without Deng, China . . . *Financial Times,* May 19, 1999; Singapore, April 26, 1999.

CHAPTER 9

Page 167   Indeed, in 1998 . . . *The Economist,* October 30, 1999.

Page 167   Begin with South Korea . . . Greenwood, Hong Kong, May 19, 1999.

Page 169   And Korea Asset . . . "Korea's Bad-Loan Agency Thinks Big," *Asian Wall Street Journal,* November 3, 1999.

Page 170   The sum total . . . "Restructuring South Korea's *Chaebol,*" *The McKinsey Quarterly,* 1998 Number 4.

Page 172   That space would . . . "He's What Korea Needs," *Fortune,* December 29, 1997.

Page 172   As noted many . . . "Just When You Thought It Was Safe to Go Back in the Water," *Fortune,* January 11, 1999; "Death, Where Is Thy Sting?" *The Economist,* July 17, 1999.

Page 173   Uninterested in "meaningless" . . . Seoul, April 8, 1998.

Page 174   Lee's view was . . . Seoul, April 7, 1998.

Page 174   And as late as . . . You Jong Keun, Seoul, November 11, 1998.

Page 175   Both groups, still . . . "Hyundai Still Doesn't Get It," *Fortune,* July 19, 1999.

Page 176   The only thing . . . Seoul, November 11, 1998; "The Big Squeeze," *Asiaweek,* November 12, 1999.

Page 177   It may not have . . . "South Korea Eager to Shed Its Old Ways," *Asian Wall Street Journal,* August 17, 1999; "The Death of Daewoo," *The Economist,* August 21, 1999; "Battle of Wills," *Far Eastern Economic Review,* August 26, 1999; Warburg Dillon Read, *Asian Economic and Strategic Planning,* September 1999; "Controlled Implosion," *Financial Times,* November 5, 1999; "Daewoo's Debt Buyout Plan Is Accepted," *Asian Wall Street Journal,* July 25, 2000.

Page 178   Then came the crisis . . . Hong Kong, July 22, 1999.

Page 180   The crisis will . . . Singapore, April 26, 1999.

Page 181   Lastly, the Singapore . . . Singapore, March 12, 1998; "Remaking Singapore Inc.," *Business Week,* April 5, 1999.

Page 182   Bonuses were even . . . "Asia's Economy: A Precarious Balancing Act," *Fortune,* June 26, 2000.

Page 183   Fund managers, take note . . . Singapore, April 26–27, 1999.

Page 184   And it had more . . . Andrew Sheng, June 1999.

Page 184   Singapore, by contrast . . . See Lee Kuan Yew, *From Third World To First* (Times media, 2000).

Page 185   Hong Kong's own . . . Hong Kong Trade Development Council, "The Rise in Offshore Trade and Offshore Investment," September 1998.

Page 185   It may not . . . Salomon Smith Barney, *Hong Kong Perspective,* August 1999.

Page 185   With China and America . . . Hong Kong, May 31, 1999.

Page 186   Richard Li, the head . . . Hong Kong, September 10, 1999.

Page 188   A year or so . . . Hong Kong, November 29, 1999.

Page 190   Such a structural revolution . . . "Can Hong Kong Stay Great?" *Fortune,* June 21, 1999; ABN-Amro, *Greed & Fear,* October 14, 1999.

Page 193   He has also found . . . David Scott, "What the Thais Did Right," *W.I. Carr Regional Strategy,* September 1997; Heinecke, Hong Kong, November 11, 1999.

Page 194   But this will produce . . . "Why Racial Harmony Matters," *Fortune,* February 1, 1999.

Page 197   The attitude in Asia . . . A.T. Kearney, "Kowloon-Canton Railway Corporation, Discussion Draft," June 4, 1996; "Train Spotting in Asia," *Asian Wall Street Journal,* July 17, 1996.

Page 198   David Bloom and . . . "Demographic Transitions and Economic Miracles in Emerging Asia," National Bureau of Economic Research Working Paper 6268, November 1997.

Page 198   As a rough guide . . . "Why Asia Will Keep Growing," *Fortune,* July 19, 1999.

CHAPTER 10

Page 205   A study by . . . OECD, "Technology and Industrial Performance," 1997.

Page 206   Thus, the surest . . . Rohwer, *Asia Rising,* Simon & Schuster, 1995.

Page 206   And, in addition . . . Romer interview, Singapore, August 26, 1999.

Page 208   In Asia the personal . . . Hong Kong, February 22, 1998.

Page 208   The question is how . . . Hong Kong, November 16, 1999.

Page 209   That's the great hope . . . Hong Kong, February 22, 1998.

Page 209   That is where . . . Taipei, June 3, 1999.

Page 210   If true, this is . . . "Manufacturing May Be a Downhill Venture," *Los Angeles Times,* December 5, 1999.

Page 211   If the Philippines . . . "Stealth Technology," *Far Eastern Economic Review,* July 15, 1999.

Page 211   One high-level . . . Hwang Young Key, Seoul, November 11, 1998.

Page 212   The turnaround of . . . "Samsung," *Business Week,* December 20, 1999.

Page 212   Taiwan also dominates . . . Market Intelligence Center, Institute for Information Industry, "Taiwan's IT Industry in 1999," Taipei, November 1999.

Page 213   Taiwan is the world's . . . Marc Faber, "Is the Recovery in Asia for Real?" *The Gloom, Boom and Doom Report,* September 13, 1999.

Page 213   If the danger . . . Hong Kong, May 27, 1999.

Page 214   In the decade . . . Taipei, June 3, 1999.

Page 214   With some 60 percent . . . Market Intelligence Center, November 1999.

Page 215   This is computer . . . Yang, Taipei, June 3, 1999.

Page 216   In these circumstances . . . AnnaLee Saxenian, "Silicon Valley's New Immigrant Entrepreneurs," Public Policy Institute of California, 1999.

Page 218   Before 2000, there . . . Jardine Fleming, "Datawave Breaks Over Asia," October 1999; Morgan Stanley Dean Witter, "Global Telecommunications Primer," June 1999.

Page 219   In the 18 months . . . McKinsey & Co, "Asia Pacific Telecom," January 1999.

Page 219   Using a new technology . . . Jardine Fleming, "Datawave Breaks Over Asia."

Page 220   Sony is setting up . . . "Who Needs NTT?" *The Economist,* December 18, 1999.

Page 220   At that rate . . . "Talking Cheap," *The Asian Wall Street Journal,* September 27, 1999; Jardine Fleming, "Datawave."

Page 222   Started only in . . . "Today Tokyo, Tomorrow the World," *Fortune,* September 18, 2000.

CHAPTER 11

Page 224   In 1999 Asian . . . ABN-Amro, "Interactive Animal Spirit," *Greed & Fear,* November 25, 1999.

Page 225   The products or services . . . "Mr Buffett on the Stock Market," *Fortune,* November 22, 1999.

Page 226   His thoughts were . . . Shanghai, September 25–28, 1999.

Page 230   I now think . . . E-mail, August 30, 1999.

Page 232   Information is both . . . CLSA Global Emerging Markets, "Companies That Have 'Got It'," January 2000.

Page 233   Conversely, whereas in . . . Merrill Lynch, "The Internet Tsunami," September 1999; Eric Ritter, "Asia's Time Lag," *The International Economy,* November/December 1999.

Page 234   Already in Korea . . . ABN-Amro, "Kosdaq Konvulsion," *Greed & Fear,* December 9, 1999.

Page 237   Taiwan's Hambrecht & Quist . . . Paul Slawson, Tokyo, December 14, 1999.

Page 238   The sharp reduction . . . Interview with Michihiro Sujino, Sakura Bank, Tokyo, December 6, 1999.

Page 238   The biggest gains . . . Interview with Shinichi Yokohama, McKinsey, Tokyo, December 7, 1999.

Page 239   But, like America's . . . Interview in Tokyo, December 9, 1999.

Page 240   It seems to be . . . Interview in Tokyo, December 10, 1999.

Page 241   Recruit is assembling . . . Interview with Yasuo Usuba of Recruit, Tokyo, December 8, 1999.

Page 241   His NetFront software . . . Interview in Tokyo, December 8, 1999.

Page 243   By 2000 Japan's . . . "Upwardy Mobile," *Forbes,* February 7, 2000.

Page 245   He says that . . . Interview in Tokyo, December 10, 1999.

Page 248   By the end . . . Hiren Ved, "Indian Software Industry," *The Gloom, Boom and Doom Report,* October 15, 1999; "India Information Technology," *Financial Times,* December 1, 1999.

Page 250   A former head . . . "India's Time?" *Finance Asia,* December 1999.

Page 251   Already, four Indian . . . Hiren Ved, "Indian Software Industry," *The Gloom, Boom and Doom Report,* October 15, 1999.

Page 252   When Clark raided . . . Michael Lewis, *The New New Thing,* (W.W. Norton, 2000).

Page 252   The goal of the . . . "A Typhoon of Venture Capital?" *Business Week,* January 31, 2000.

Page 252   That gave it . . . "The Top Entrepreneurs," *Business Week,* January 10, 2000.

Page 253   One of the main . . . "India's Mr TV," *Asiaweek,* January 21, 2000.

Page 254   Between 1995 and 1998 . . . *The Economist,* July 24, 1999.

Page 254   When the central . . . "The IT Raj," *Asian Wall Street Journal,* January 18, 2000.

Page 255   It is the most . . . "India's Youth," *Business Week,* October 11, 1999.

CHAPTER 12

Page 258   And IT's share . . . David Hale, "Rebuilt by Wall Street," *Financial Times,* January 25, 2000.

Page 260   McKinsey has estimated . . . Dominic Casserley and Greg Gibb, *Banking in Asia* (John Wiley, 1999).

Page 261   Lastly, in the poorest . . . Interview, Toby Brown, Hong Kong, March 26, 1999.

Page 263   Until a partly . . . "Where Does China Get Its Money?" *Fortune,* July 5, 1999.

Page 264   It will be a . . . "Bank M&A," *McKinsey Quarterly,* 1999 Number 2.

Page 266   Even a dollop . . . Bangkok, November 12, 1998; "An Old Dutch Firm Learns New Tricks," *Fortune,* December 20, 1999.

Page 266   There is an obvious . . . "Pressures for Change Building," *Financial Times,* December 17, 1999.

Page 267   That points the way . . . Interview in Tokyo, December 8, 1999.

Page 268   Meanwhile, issues of . . . "Asia Is Banking on the Capital Markets," *Asian Wall Street Journal,* December 30, 1999.

Page 268   At the outset . . . "New Building Blocks," *Far Eastern Economic Review,* February 3, 2000.

Page 269   In just three . . . "Korean Housewives Are Heading to the Market," *Financial Times,* June 8, 1999.

Page 269   Even more Japanese . . . "Mrs Watanabe Learns to Invest," *The Economist,* December 18, 1999.

Page 270   Similarly, in Thailand . . . "Asia Firms Are Indebted to New Financing," *Asian Wall Street Journal,* February 3, 2000.

Page 270   There remains a crying . . . "Here's the Cure for What Ails Japan," *Fortune,* December 29, 1997.

Page 271   Refreshingly, he said . . . "Thai Steel Mill Finds Way to Revive," *Asian Wall Street Journal,* August 26, 1998.

Page 271   Asia shows no sign . . . Interview in Hong Kong, December 14, 1999.

Page 273   Yet, Hsu notes . . . Interview in Hong Kong, May 21, 1999.

page 274 What is going . . . Thomson Financial Securities Data, Press Releases, December 22, 1999.

CHAPTER 13

Page 276 We have never . . . Quoted in Jonathan Spence, "The Search for Modern China" (Hutchinson, 1990).

Page 278 Car-makers, for instance . . . "Ford to Challenge GM for Daewoo Motor," *Asian Wall Street Journal,* February 14, 2000.

Page 279 Cemex nonetheless started . . . Cancun, October 7, 1996.

Page 280 Far more important . . . "Bagged Cement," *The Economist,* June 19, 1999.

Page 280 Now all are reacting . . . BCG, "Western Multinationals in Asia: Keeping Options Open," World Economic Forum, *The Asia Competitiveness Report,* 1999.

Page 282 Also by 2000 NI's . . . Harvard Business School Case Study, 1998; Interview in Jakarta, February 23, 2000.

Page 284 The opportunities kept . . . "Going Cheap," *The Economist,* August 15, 1998; "Carrefour Adds Japan to Global Expansion," *Asian Wall Street Journal,* June 15, 1999; "Indonesian Middle Class Saves Western Retailers," *International Herald Tribune,* November 19, 1999.

Page 285 The Asian theme . . . "The Man Who Vows to Change Japan Inc.," *Fortune,* December 20, 1999.

Page 286 Having seen the books . . . "Shifting Gears," *Business Week,* February 17, 2000; "Kicking Tires in Seoul," *Business Week,* January 24, 2000.

Page 286 Likewise, Volvo's acquisition . . . Seoul, April 8, 1998; November 9, 1998.

Page 288 Koh Boon Hwee . . . Interview in Singapore, March 13, 1998.

Page 290 It is a process . . . Interview in Hong Kong, May 31, 1999.

Page 290 Trevor MacMurray, who . . . Interview in Singapore, April 21, 1998.

Page 291 Otherwise, technology sharing . . . Interview in Taipei, January 16, 1999.

Page 293 Another 14 would . . . "The World (Trade Organization) Is Not Enough," January 24, 2000.

Page 294 Cineplexes in Xian . . . Interview in Beijing, September 1, 1999.

Page 296 Perhaps predictably for . . . "China's Terrifying Private Firms," *Asian Wall Street Journal,* May 13, 1999.

CHAPTER 14

Page 311 At the end . . . Singapore, April 27, 1999.

Page 312 He thinks that . . . Interview in Paris, May 3, 1999.

Page 312   My own guess . . . A good overview of how, in nuts-and-bolts terms, this is coming about is Michael Hamlin, *The New Asian Corporation* (Jossey-Bass Publishers, 2000).

Page 314   "Contract substitution" takes . . . *Journal of Law and Economics,* April 1983.

Page 316   That increases both . . . "Cyber," *Independent Strategy,* February 24, 2000.

Page 318   The younger ones . . . Stan Shih, Hong Kong, July 13, 2000.

Page 320   Ditto for Henderson Land . . . "Pulling Away," *Far Eastern Economic Review,* February 10, 2000.

Page 321   And of course . . . Interview in Hong Kong, August 17, 2000.

Page 321   But, despite the power . . . Interview in Hong Kong, May 21, 1999.

Page 321   Banthoon of Thai Farmers . . . "Re-engineering in Thailand," *The Economist,* October 11, 1997.

Page 322   Phil Elvis, a Hong . . . Interview in Hong Kong, August 3, 1999.

Page 323   Because of the temporarily . . . "Son Shines," *Financial Times,* August 18, 2000.

Page 325   Malaysia's Sime UEP . . . "Some Asian Managers Reap Rewards," *Asian Wall Street Journal,* June 22, 1999.

Page 325   Unsurprisingly, the truly . . . "Small Niche Firms Lead," *Asian Wall Street Journal,* December 15, 1999.

Page 325   In South Korea . . . Interview in Seoul, February 23, 2000.

Page 326   Not a bad response . . . "A Crony Capitalist Bounces Back," *Fortune,* May 10, 1999; Cesar Delacruz, Jakarta, April 9, 1999.

Page 328   More Asian companies . . . Manila, June 2, 1999; "Blue-Chip Ambitions," *Far Eastern Economic Review,* December 17, 1998; "What Have We Done?" *Forbes Global,* February 21, 2000.

Page 329   No wonder the . . . "Taiwan's 'Black Gold' Politics," *Asian Wall Street Journal,* March 17, 2000; "Goodbye, KMT Inc.," *Economist,* March 11, 2000.

Page 331   The firm has . . . Interview in Hong Kong, July 14, 1999.

Page 333   Yet when the . . . Hong Kong, March 26, 1999.

Page 333   From the mid-1970s . . . Interview in Hong Kong, June 16, 1999.

Page 333   In Hong Kong . . . Interview in Hong Kong, September 10, 1999.

Page 335   Only with much better . . . Los Angeles, October 2, 1996.

Page 335   Three Hong Kong firms . . . "The Internet vs. Overseas Chinese Networks," *Asian Wall Street Journal,* October 6, 1999.

Page 337   The program has . . . Hong Kong, May 24, 1999.

Page 338   So much for . . . Interviews in Hong Kong, March 31, 1999, and August 17, 2000.

Page 341   The devotion to . . . Interview in Hong Kong, May 31, 1999.

CHAPTER 15

Page 346   Chris Baker, an economist . . . Interview in Bangkok, March 20, 2000; "How Much Did Thailand Suffer?" *The Economist,* January 22, 2000.

Page 346   What, if anything, . . . "Elite Ranks Grew," *Asian Wall Street Journal,* October 21, 1999; "Indonesian Middle Class," *International Herald Tribune,* November 19, 1999.

Page 347   Yet there is plenty . . . Kishore Mahbubani, *Can Asians Think?* Times Books International (Singapore, 1998).

Page 348   If you want your . . . Singapore, April 27, 1999.

Page 348   As long as he's . . . Hong Kong, February 1998.

Page 350   In this way . . . Interview, *Asian Wall Street Journal,* January 3, 2000.

Page 350   Lee Hsien Loong . . . "The Next CEO of Singapore Inc.," *Fortune,* April 3, 2000.

Page 352   The culture has got . . . Interview in Singapore, April 27, 1999. For an extended version of Lee Kuan Yew's views on how Singapore's political and social system will change, see the second volume of his memoirs, *From Third World to First,* Times Media, 2000.

Page 353   Again, I am sure . . . Berkeley, March 26, 1998; see also Lucian Pye, "Asian Power and Politics" (Harvard University Press, 1985).

Page 355   He adds separately . . . Mahbubani, pp. 49 and 78.

Page 357   But he still thought . . . Mancur Olson, *Power and Prosperity* (Basic Books, 2000).

Page 360   Not surprisingly, democracy . . . Amartya Sen, "Beyond the Crisis: Development Strategies in Asia," Institute of Southeast Asian Studies, 1999.

Page 361   As Scalapino points out . . . Robert Scalapino, "Will China Democratize?" *Journal of Democracy,* January 1998.

Page 361   Indeed, an argument . . . Hong Kong, March 26, 1999.

Page 362   Unless the system . . . Shanghai, September 29, 1999.

Page 363   Savings and investment . . . *Asia Rising,* 1995.

Page 365   WE WERE THE . . . E-mail from Medan, May 11, 1998.

Page 365   As pointed out . . . For details on Lee's views, see his *From Third World to First,* Chapter 17.

Page 367   Under Wahid's prodding . . . ABN-AMRO, "Nouvelle nonsense," April–June 2000.

CHAPTER 16

Page 369   A couple of these . . . Hong Kong, April 11, 2000.

Page 369   The most important . . . "Seven paradoxes on Asia-Pacific security," *Can Asians Think?* (Times Books International, 1998).

Page 373   I can only hope . . . Asia Society Speech, Hong Kong, March 22, 1999.

Page 374   They want to have . . . "Taiwan and China Further Apart Than Ever," *International Herald Tribune,* March 7, 2000.

Page 376   Goh added that . . . Asia Society Speech, Hong Kong, April 18, 2000.

Page 376   Lee Kuan Yew . . . Perry speech in Hong Kong, April 11, 2000; Lee interview in Singapore, April 27, 1999.

Page 378   In 1996, before . . . "Europe and East Asia Need to Get Acquainted," *International Herald Tribune,* April 14, 2000.

Page 378   But, as one piece . . . "The Not-So-Shrinking State," *Independent Strategy,* London, March 24, 2000.

Page 380   In the spring of . . . SyCip interview, Manila, February 17, 1999; Goh Asia Society Speech, Hong Kong, April 18, 2000.

Page 380   The head of one . . . "Indian IT Specialists Lukewarm," *Financial Times,* April 19, 2000.

Page 382   That's because they . . . Singapore, April 27, 1999.

INDEX

ABN-Amro (Holland), 266
Acer Group, 215, 316
Agnäs B., 99
AIG, 294, 296
Aikawa, Kentaro, 55, 56, 103
Aiwa, 96
Alphatec Electronics, 143
Amaret Sila-On, 140, 142, 143
America, 3–23, 127, 128, 129, 256, 317, 377–83
America Online (AOL), 230, 242, 323
Anwar Ibraham, 110, 117, 353
Arakawa, Toru, 241
Argentina, 114, 126, 264
Asean Regional Forum (ARF), 368
Asher, David, 85, 90
Asia/Asian:
    America's role, 3–23
    bankruptcy laws, 35–36
    bond markets, 47, 269
    change drivers, 132–34
    corporate governance (pre-crisis), 34–35
    cronyism/corruption, 33, 37–41
    demographic shifts, 197–99
    economy (1955–1995), 25
    exchange rates (1997/1998), 108
    exports, 132–33
    crisis, 24–48, 49–66
    financial ratios, regional (1990–97), 52
    financial sector, 256–75, 330–32
    foreign capital, 41–46, 276–308
    GDP and fixed investment, 50
    geopolitical issues, 368–83
    globalization, 309–41
    government/politics, 328–30, 345–67
    institutional deficits, 32–37
    institutional ratings, 35
    Internet, 223–55
    lessons of, 25–26
    optimistic trends (three), 195–99
    output gap, 233
    pressures on, leading to crisis, 24–48
    recovery, 130–44, 309–41
    regional defense organization (ARF), 368
    social/cultural issues, 345–67
    stock markets (1993–1998), 109
    strengths, 22, 195–99
    structures/cycles, 167–99
    technology, 203–22, 223–55
    tiger economies, 41
    transitions (four) shaping firms in, 318–24
    value deterioration (financial crisis), 49–66
    values, 347–52

Asia Inc., 35
Astra International, 367
Atkinson, David, 30
AT&T breakup, 7, 11–14
Australia, 10, 126, 257, 274, 325, 382
Avon, 283

Baker, Chris, 346
Baldwin, Rone, 304
Banco Bilbao Vizcaya, 4
Bangkok International Banking Facility (BIBF),
    44–45
bank(s)/banking, 28–32, 33–34, 83, 111,
    138–41, 158, 259, 261, 263–72
    consolidation, 265
    loans, 266–68
    shrinking, 263–64
Bank Central Asia (BCA), 326
Bank of England, 30
Bank of Japan, 71, 74, 75
bankruptcy laws, 35–37, 56–57, 130, 172, 261
Banthoon Lamsam, 319–20, 321
BASF, 173, 286, 288
Baxter, William, 12
BCA, 326
Beijing Cement Factory, 158
Benes, Nicholas, 79
Bhagwati, Jagdish, 119, 120
Bhasin, Pramod, 303
Bhatia, Sabeer, 252
Bloom, David, 197
Boehringer Ingelheim, 270
Boston Consulting Group (BCG) studies/
    taxonomy, 57, 60, 280–87, 324
    crises, 280
    merger, 281–82
Bowers, Tab, 80
Bretton Woods agreement, 6, 20, 119–20
Brown, Stephen, 189, 190
Brown, Toby, 20, 259, 260, 332–33, 361
bubble economy, 71–73
Buddhism, 194
Buffett, Warren, 54, 224, 338
Burns, Arthur, 8
Bush, George, 11
Business Roundtable, 17

Cable News Network (CNN), 10–11
Camdessus, Michel, 125, 128
Canon, 59
capital controls, 121–22, 124
Carrefour, 191, 284, 287

403

Carter, Jimmy, 6, 9
cement, 57, 143, 158, 192, 278, 279, 328
Cemex, 279
chaebol, 31, 58, 61–66, 168, 169, 170, 171, 174, 318
Chan, Ronnie, 334, 335
Chandra, Subhash, 253
Chandrasekhar, K. B., 252
Chang, Morris, 213, 214
Chang, Nelson, 291
Chang Dae Whan, 62
Chatumongol Sonakul, 138–39
Chen Chih, 306
Chen Shui-bian, 375, 376, 377
Cherry Lane Music, 294
Cheung, Steven, 313, 314
Cheung Kong Holdings, 322, 323
Chiang Kai-shek, 375
China, 145–66, 261–63, 292–97, 301, 332–35, 373–77
    car exports, 292
    entertainment business, 293–94
    insurers, 294
    World Trade Organization (WTO), 292, 295–96
Chuan Leekpai, 194
Chung Yu Jung, 175
Ciba-Geigy, 281
Cinda Asset Management, 158
Cirrus Logic, 252
Citibank, 10, 30, 65, 100, 287, 288
Citigroup, 265, 266, 268
City Telecom, 219
Clark, Jim, 252, 309–10
Clinton, Bill, 18, 177, 292, 368, 371, 372
CNBC, 306
CNN, 7, 10–11
Coase, Ronald, 313
Coke, 283, 289, 322
Cole, Carson, 271
Compaq, 296
conglomerate index, 58–59
contracts, 313–14
convoy system, 77–78, 83–86
Coorey, Michael, 295–96
corporate diversification, 58–59
credit clubs, 259
cronyism, 33, 37–41, 49, 311, 327, 328

Daesang, 173, 286
Daewoo, 62, 170, 174, 175, 176–77, 178, 234, 285–86, 287, 289, 319
DaimlerChrysler, 285, 286, 295
Dai Xianglong, 159
DBS Bank, Singapore, 30
DebTraders, 271
Delhaise, Philippe, 29, 141
Dell Computer, 213, 316, 339
Deng Xiaoping, 106, 148, 166, 255, 292
deregulation, 9, 93, 94, 103

Development Bank of Singapore (DBS), 181
Disneyland in Hong Kong, 188
diversification (conglomerate index), 59
DoCoMo, 221, 222, 236, 242, 243, 245
dollarization, 18–23
Donald, David Herbert, 37
Drexel Burnham Lambert, 14, 17, 271
Drucker, Peter, 229

Eagleburger, Lawrence, 11
Eckert-Maudsley, 229
Economic Value Added (EVA), 63
Edelheit, Lewis, 308
Ellison, Larry, 241
Elvis, Phil, 322
Emerson, 59
Enoki, Keiichi, 242
Enright, Michael, 178
Eriksson, Jan, 281, 282
Esquel Group, 320, 337–38
euro, 378
Europe,-368–83
Evergreen Marine, 231–32
Exodus Communications, 252
Exxon, 293

Faber, Marc, 141–42
family firms, 58, 64, 137–38, 288, 289, 290, 318
Fang Xinghai, 159
Federal Reserve, 6, 8, 18, 110
Feldstein, Martin, 128
FILP (Fiscal Investment and Loan Programme), 86–89
First Bangkok City Bank (FBC), 288
First Pacific, 326–27
Fischer, Stan, 127
Ford, 285, 286
Fox Television, 16
Friedman, Milton, 8, 73–74, 89, 115, 125, 128, 165
Fuji Heavy Industries, 285
Fujimori, Yoshiaki, 305
Fujitsu, 97, 213, 237
Fung, Victor, 339
Fung, William, 185, 339, 340, 341

Gaeta, Gordian, 208
Gates, Bill, 7, 42, 230, 241
General Electric, 42, 53, 58, 59, 60, 70, 98, 100, 210, 231, 250, 283, 291, 297–308, 312
    buying spree, 297–98
    consumer finance, 304
    e-business, 307
    GE Edison Life, 303–4
    Japan, 302–5
    medical business, 305–6
General Motors, 285–86, 289, 294
General Oriental Investments, 20, 332
Ghosn, Carlos, 284
Gillette, 283, 320, 338

Giordano, 207, 336
Giuliani, Rudolph, 14
Goh Chok Tong, 180, 376, 380
Goldsmith, Sir James, 20
Gorbachev, 166
government/politics, 7, 9, 31, 316, 328–30,
    345–67
  democracy, 357–60
  Malaysia, 353–55
  social indicators, 345–46
  values, 347–52
Greene, Harold, 7, 11–13
Greenspan, Alan, 37, 43
Greenwood, John, 73, 114, 127, 167, 191
Grove, Andy, 7, 323
Gulf War, 10

Habibie, B. J., 365, 366
Hagemayer, 327
Haier, 153–55, 161, 296
Hale, David, 257
Hamada, Takeo, 98
Hanbo Iron & Steel, 172
Hang Seng index, 188
Hanwha, 288
Hashimoto, Ryutaro, 92
Healtheon, 252
Heinecke, Bill, 135–36, 139, 193, 194
Henderson Land, 320
Hewlett-Packard, 250
Hikari Tsushin, 235, 236, 237, 242, 244, 245,
    267, 334
Hindustan Lever, 250
Hitachi, 97
Hokkaido Takushoku, 265
Holderbank, Switzerland, 279
Honda, 236, 285
Hong Kong, 178–90, 336–41
  problems, 186–87
  shift in economic structure, 185–86
  vs. Singapore, 178–83
  swimming with sharks, 182
Hong Kong Monetary Authority, 43
Hong Kong Telecom (NKT), 219, 235, 323
Hoya, 97
HSBC, 266
Hsu Ta-lin, 273
Huang, Frank, 209, 216
Huang, J. P., 156, 157, 158
Hughes, Michael, 203
hui, 259, 262
Hutchison Whampoa, 321, 322
Hwang Young Key, 175
Hyosung, 289
Hyundai, 62, 170, 174, 175, 319

ICIL, 251
Immelt, Jeff, 305
Inchcape, 340
India, 245–55, 371–73

Indonesia, 362–67
Indonesian Bank Restructuring Agency (IBRA),
    141
information providers (Turner/Greene), 10–14
Information Standard, 7, 10
Infosys Technologies, 252
institutional deficits, 32–37
Intel, 13
International Monetary Fund (IMF), 3, 4, 22, 110,
    120, 125–29, 136, 142, 190, 246, 367, 378
Internet, 21, 103, 204, 205, 206, 222, 223–55,
    310, 314, 317, 323
  banking, 237–38
  changes for Asia, 233–35
  delivery methods, 241
  high-tech companies, 224–25
  PCs, 241
  Yahoo, 226, 239
investment trust companies (ITCs), 234
Ito-Yokado, 237, 267

"Jack & Bill" index, 42, 70
Japan, 26–28, 69–81, 82–105, 235–45, 301
  banking, 237
  Internet, 235–37
Japan Net Bank, 237
Japan Transaction Partners, 79
Japan Travel Bureau, 241
Jardine Fleming, 221
Jasdaq, 240
J. H. Whitney & Co., 237
Jiang Zemin, 40
Johnson, Lyndon, 6
Johnson Electric, 331
Jollibee, 135, 136
junk bonds, 14–18, 19, 91, 270, 271, 272

Kaplan, Robert, 345
Kaye, Bill, 125, 136–37
Keating, Charles, 37
Kia Motors, 175
Kim, Milton, 64, 65
Kim Dae Jung, 168, 174, 177, 354, 356, 370
Kim Suk Won, 65
Kim Woo Choong, 176
Kim Young Sam, 168, 354
Kissinger, Henry, 145
Kitao, Yoshitaka, 103
Ko, Anthony, 333
Ko Doo Moo, 173
Koh, Tommy, 378
Koh Beng Seng, 180
Koh Boon Hwee, 288
Kolon, 173
Koo, Jeffrey, Jr., 320
Koo family, 291, 320
Korea, 41, 61–66, 167–78, 369–71
Korea Asset Management Corporation (KAMCO),
    169
Korea First Bank, 141, 169, 172, 266

Kosdaq, 224, 234, 268
Kowloon-Canton Railway Corporation (KCRC), 196, 197
Krugman, Paul, 112
Kuok, Robert, 320, 322

Lai, Jimmy, 206, 208–9, 336, 347–48
Lall, Rajiv, 290
Lapin, Jay, 304
Lardy, Nicholas, 150
Lasserre, Philippe, 291, 293, 296
Latin America, 28, 47, 198, 328
Lau, Peter, 336
Lee, Andre, 46
Lee Hsien Loong, 180–81, 350
Lee Kuan Yew, 3, 5, 27, 39, 40, 41, 116–17, 120, 129, 145, 166, 179–80, 183, 188–89, 310, 320, 347, 350, 352, 362, 365, 376, 380
Lee Kun Hee, 175
Lee Kuo-ting, 214
Lee Teng-hui, 375
Lee Woong Yeul, 173–74
Legend Holdings, 296
Leung, Francis, 46
Lewis, Michael, 309
LG Group, 62, 170, 171, 175
Li, Richard, 95, 186, 223, 226, 235, 237, 322, 323, 334
Li, Victor, 322, 323
Liem Sioe Liong, 325
Li & Fung, 185, 339–40, 341
Li Ka-shing, 320, 322, 323, 333
Lion Group, 328
Li Peng, 40, 207
Liu Benren, 150, 155, 156
Long Term Capital Management (LTCM), 110

MacMurray, Trevor, 290, 291
Macrae, Norman, 228
Mahathir Mohamad, 4, 24, 28, 38, 110, 116–22, 188, 276, 330, 353, 367
Mahbubani Kishore, 355
Malaysia, 116–22
Malone, John, 16
Mao Zedong, 295, 359, 375
Marcos, Ferdinand, 38, 367
mass-transit railways (MTRs), 196
Matsui, Kathy, 85–86
Matsushita, 236
McCaw, Craig, 16
McGowan, William, 12, 16
MCI, 12, 16
McKinnon, Ron, 75, 76
Mead, Walter Russell, 210
mergers and acquisitions (M&A), 272–75, 278
Metro, 284
Mexico, 28–29, 111, 126, 127, 133, 257, 263, 279
Microsoft, 42, 53, 59, 70, 219, 241, 250, 252, 317

Mikitani, Hiroshi, 240
Mikuni, Akio, 80, 92
Mikuni & Co., 81
Milken, Michael, 7, 14–18, 271, 274
Mitsubishi Heavy Industries, 55, 56, 103, 104
Mitsubishi Motors, 285
Mitsui, 101, 220, 237, 238, 241
Mitsuyoshi, Okano, 267
Morita, Akio, 97
Mothers (Market of the High Growth and Emerging Stocks), 237
Motorola, 251
MSCI Hong Kong *vs.* MSCI Singapore market performance, 179
Murdoch, Rupert, 16, 323
Murray, Simon, 321, 322
Mussa, Mike, 127

Nakamae, Tadashi, 81, 83–84, 90, 95
Nakornthai Strip Mill (NSM), 271
Nasdaq, 224, 237, 252
Nayden, Denis, 303
NEC, 241
Nestle, 283
New Zealand, 126, 325, 382
Nifty, 237
Nike, 286
Nintendo, 98
Nippon Life, 237
Nissan, 284, 285
Nissen, Dave, 304
Nixon, Richard, 6, 377
Nomura Securities, 80–81, 96, 103, 181
nonperforming loans (NPLs), 113–14, 118, 140, 144, 264
Norbom, Mark, 299
Novartis Indonesia (NI), 281–82
Novell, 250, 252
NTT (Nippon Telegraph and Telephone), 219, 220, 222, 236, 242, 243

Ogus, Simon, 29, 112
Okada, Kazuo, 98
Olds, John, 181
Olson, Mancur, 357, 358
OPEC, 6
Oracle, 250
Orix, 96, 100, 103, 267, 270
O'Rourke, P. J., 246
Oshima, Kenshin, 101, 102

Pacific Century CyberWorks (PCCW), 186, 224, 235, 237, 323
Pakistan, 245, 371, 372
Pangilinan, Manual, 326–27, 328
panic *vs.* crisis, 111–12
Park Chung Hee, 61–62
Park Kyung Hong, 170–72
Pasuk Phongpaichit, 346
Patil, Suhas, 252

Peregrine Investment Holdings, 46–47
Perry, Bill, 368, 370, 372, 376, 377, 382
Petronas, 38
Peyman, Hugh, 54–55
Philippine Long Distance Telephone (PLDT), 327
Plaza Accord, 42, 47, 71, 76, 96
Poon, Dickson, 321
Porter, Michael, 78
Portland cement, 192
Prachai Leophariatana, 130, 131, 143
Primont, Michael, 293
private-equity firms, 272, 273
privatization, 229
Procter & Gamble, 65, 289
Promodâs, 284
PT Telekom, 218

Qianlong, 276, 295

Rabin, Yitzhak, 382
Radelet, Steven, 125
Rakuten, 240
Ramos, Fidel, 106
Reagan, Ronald, 7, 8–9, 19
Recruit, 240–41
Redding, Gordon, 311–12
Redstone, Sumner, 16
Reebok, 286
Rekhi, Kanwal, 252
Renault, 284, 285
return on equity, 51, 55
Rhee Namuh, 63, 325
rice-in-famine theory, 111–16
Roche, David, 90, 314, 315
Rogers, Gary, 306
Romer, Paul, 56, 205–6, 228
Roubini, Nouriel, 24
Royal Dutch Shell, 150
Russia, 191

Sachs, Jeffrey, 125, 129, 229
Safire, William, 347
Sail-Star Commercial Machinery, 152
Saito, Hitori, 98
Sakakibara, Eisuke, 69
Sakura Bank, 237, 243
Salim, Anthony, 326
Salim Group, 325, 326
Samkoo, 171
Samsung, 62, 63, 170, 175, 176, 177, 285
Samsung Electronics, 211–12
Samsung Heavy Industries, 286
Samsung Life Insurance, 175
Samsung Motors, 285
Samsung Securities, 325
Sandoz, 281
Sanwa Bank, 97
Satyam Computers, 251, 252
Satyam Infoway, 252
Saxenian, AnnaLee, 216, 251, 252

Sazaby, 99–100
Scalapino, Robert, 353, 354, 356, 361, 367
Schneider, Steve, 306, 307
Scoble, Ian, 92, 93
Scott, David, 191, 192
Sega, 241
Sembawang Group, 181
SembCorp, 181, 182
Sen, Amartya, 23, 358–61, 364
SeoulBank, 172
service sector, 232–33, 293
7dream.com, 241
Seven-Eleven, 100, 237, 241
Shanghai, 159–62
Shanghai Sail-Star, 152
Sheng, Andrew, 26, 27, 28, 71
Sheng Huaren, 145–46, 157
Shi Chung-yu, 374
Shigeta, Yasumitsu, 243, 244
Shih, Stan, 215, 316–17, 318
Shoei, 270
Shohkoh Fund, 101
Shultz, George, 125
Siam Cement, 143, 279, 328
Sigler, Andrew, 17
Silicon Graphics, 252
Silicon Valley, 216, 247, 251–52, 309
Simon, William, 125
Singapore, 178–83
Singapore Technologies, 181
Singapore Telecom, 219, 235
Singha, 191
SK, 62, 170, 175, 319
Smithers, Andrew, 85
Social Security, 85
Soewandi, Rini, 142–43
Softbank, 102, 103, 104, 219, 235, 236, 237, 239, 267, 334
Son, Masayoshi, 102–3, 104
Sondhi Limthongkul, 35
Sony, 96, 97, 213, 220, 237, 241, 267
Soros, George, 107, 110, 119, 166
Soviet Union, 106, 166
Spanish banks, 264
SpeedNet, 219
Ssangyong Investment & Securities, 64, 65
Ssangyong Motors, 177
Starbucks Coffee, 99
Steady Safe, 46–47
Suharto, 47, 110, 115, 116, 128, 138, 325, 362–67
  democracy ideas, 364
  economic development, 363
  resignation, 365–66
Sukarno, 362
Sukarnoputri, Megawati, 362, 366
Sumitomo Bank, 237
Sun Hung Kai Properties, 320
Surathip Group, 191
Suruga Bank, 267

Suzuki, Rikuko, 99
Suzuki, Tetsuo, 97
SyCip, Washington, 120, 368, 379, 380

Taiwan, 122–25, 212–17, 373–77
 attitudes, 374
 military, 376
 presidential election, 375–76
Taiwan Semiconductor Manufacturing
 Corporation (TSMC), 213, 214
Takashimaya, 100
Takefuji, 101–2
Takei, Yasuo, 101
Takeuchi, Hirotaka, 78
Tanamur factor, 287
TCI, 16
technology, 7, 13, 203–22
 electronics, 211–14
 Internet, 204–6
 manufacturing, 210–11
 Silicon Valley, 215–17
telecommunications services, 217–22
Temasek Holdings, 181
Tepco, 237
Texas Instruments, 250
Thai Farmers Bank, 319, 321
Thailand, 190–95
 baht devaluation, 43, 107, 303
Thailand Financial Restructuring Authority (FRA),
 140, 142
Thai Petrochemical Industry (TPI), 130, 131, 143,
 144, 319
Thaksin Shinawatra, 138
39 Home Shopping Television, 170–72
Thurow, Lester, 112
tiger economies, 41
Time-Warner, 230
Toho Mutual, 304
Tokyo Electric Power (Tepco), 219
Tokyo-Mitsubishi (Bank), 30
Tokyo Stock Exchange (TSE), 236, 237, 270
Tose, Philip, 46
Toshiba, 96, 97, 213, 305, 316
Toyoda, Shoichiro, 98
Toyota, 96, 98, 285
Trans Cosmos, 235, 237
Tsang, Donald, 188
Tung Chee-hwa, 183, 187, 188, 190
Turner, Ted, 7, 10, 16

Ueyama, Shinichi, 96
Ujie, Junichi, 96
Umax, 216
Unilever, 283
United States, 3–23, 256, 317, 377–83
 Asian eduction, 379–80
 communication, 10–14

globalization, 377
government influence, 8–9
junk bonds, 14–18
political/military influence, 380–82
United States Treasury, 127, 128, 129

valuation, 289
values, 347–52
Varitronix, 331
venture capital, 272–73
Viacom, 16
Vietnam, 35, 193, 218, 284
Vodafone AirTouch, 274
Volcker, Paul, 7, 8–9, 19
von Neumann, John, 229
VTech, 331, 335

Wahid, Abdurrahman, 363, 366, 367
Wal-Mart, 283–84
Wang, David, 306, 307
Wansley, Mike, 130, 131, 132
Warburg Pincus, 290
Welch, Jack, 42, 63, 210, 297, 298–301, 305,
 306, 307, 308, 338
Western Electric, 12
wideband CDMA (WCDMA), 221, 243
Williamson, Jeffrey, 198
WIPRO, 251
Wolf, Martin, 134
Wong, Alan, 331
Wong, K. S., 181, 182
Wood, Chris, 42, 70, 134
World Bank, 125, 137
World Trade Organization (WTO), 159–60, 233,
 292, 293, 294, 295, 297, 298
Wriston, Walter, 10, 11, 117, 125
Wuhan Group, 150, 155, 156, 161
Wu Jinglian, 157, 160
Wuthelam Holdings, 288

Yahoo, 102, 226, 230, 236, 239, 240, 317, 323
Yamaichi Securities, 100
Yamakawa, Tak, 304
Yang, Jerry, 226, 227, 230, 231, 234, 317, 323
Yang, Margie, 320, 321, 323, 337
Yang, Raymond, 307
Yang Shih-Chien, 123, 214, 216
Yeo, George, 349, 350
Yun Jong Yong, 211

zaitech, 330
Zambrano, Lorenzo, 279
Zee Telefilms, 253
Zhang Ruimin, 153–55
Zhu Rongji, 40, 148, 160, 162, 183, 380
Zhuzhou Gear Works, 156
Ziff-Davis, 102, 103

ABOUT THE AUTHOR

Jim Rohwer, who has lived in Hong Kong since 1991, is a senior contributing editor at *Fortune* magazine and a private consultant. Previously he was the editor and publisher of Asia, Inc., a director and emerging market strategist for CS First Boston, and the executive editor of The Economist. He has a J.D. from Harvard Law School and an M.A. in economics from the University of California, Berkeley.